A GLOBAL GUIDE TO

INTERFAITH

A GLOBAL GUIDE TO
INTERFAITH

Reflections from around the world

Sandy & Jael Bharat

BOOKS

Winchester, UK
Washington, USA

A GLOBAL GUIDE TO INTERFAITH—Reflections from around the world
Sandy and Jael Bharat

First published by O Books, 2007
O Books is an imprint of John Hunt Publishing Ltd., The Bothy, Deershot Lodge,
Park Lane, Ropley, Hants, SO24 0BE, UK
office1@o-books.net
www.o-books.net

Distribution in:
    UK and Europe
    Orca Book Services
    orders@orcabookservices.co.uk
    Tel: 01202 665432 Fax: 01202 666219 Int. code (44)

    USA and Canada
    NBN
    custserv@nbnbooks.com
    Tel: 1 800 462 6420 Fax: 1 800 338 4550

    Australia and New Zealand
    Brumby Books
    sales@brumbybooks.com.au
    Tel: 61 3 9761 5535 Fax: 61 3 9761 7095

    Far East (offices in Singapore, Thailand, Hong Kong, Taiwan)
    Pansing Distribution Pte Ltd
    kemal@pansing.com
    Tel: 65 6319 9939 Fax: 65 6462 5761

    South Africa
    Alternative Books
    altbook@peterhyde.co.za
    Tel: 021 447 5300 Fax: 021 447 1430

Text copyright Sandy and Jael Bharat 2007

Design: Sandy and Jael Bharat

ISBN-13: 9781905047970
ISBN-10: 1 905047 97 5

All rights reserved. Except for brief quotations in critical articles or reviews, no part of this book may be reproduced in any manner without prior written permission from the publishers.

The rights of Sandy and Jael Bharat as author have been asserted in accordance with the Copyright, Designs and Patents Act 1988.

A CIP catalogue record for this book is available from the British Library.

Printed by Maple Leaf Press

If you contact God within yourself,
You will know that He is in everyone,
That He has become the children of all races.
Then you cannot be an enemy to anyone.
If the whole world could love with that universal love,
There would be no need for men to arm themselves against one another.
By our own Christlike example we must bring unity
Among all religions, all nations, all races.
— *Paramahansa Yogananda*

Royalties from this book go to UNICEF
Working for the world's disadvantaged children

CONTENTS

PREFACE · i

FOREWORD BY MARCUS BRAYBROOKE · iii

PART I. INTRODUCTION TO INTERFAITH · 1
Introduction

1. INTERFAITH ORIGINS · 3
Imagining the Beginning 3 Ammachi 3 Kofi Annan 4
What is Interfaith Exactly? 4 The Interfaith Movement 4
Swami Vivekananda 5 Mary Braybrooke 6 Marcus Braybrooke 7
Network of International Interfaith Organisations 8
Alison Van Dyk 9 Seshagiri Rao 10 Ways to Dialogue 10
Alan Race 11 John Hick 11 Marcus Braybrooke 12
Paramahansa Yogananda 12
Mussie Hailu: Religion and Diversity in Ethiopia 13

From Faith to Interfaith: Introduction 14 · 14
Anantanand Rambachan: Hinduism and Religious Diversity 15
Swami Satchidananda 16 Navnit Dholakia: Hinduism in the UK 17
Minakshi Yogi: A Highland Lass 18
Paul Trafford: Buddhism and Religious Diversity 20
Tsubaki Grand Shrine and Shumei Taiko: Shinto: Spirit and Sound 22
Karoki Lewis and Jayni Gudka: Jains: Devotion and Diversity 24
Parvine Foroughi: The Baha'i Faith and Religious Pluralism 25
Vernon Marshall: The Unitarian Approach to the Interfaith Reality 26
Shahin Bekhradnia: Zoroastrianism and Religious Diversity 28
Jackie Tabick: Judaism and Religious Diversity 30
Mohammad Talib: Islam and its attitude to Interfaith 32
Mussarrat Bashir Youssuf 34

2. INTERFAITH RATIONALE · 37
Introduction 37 Rationale 37
Community Bridge Building 37 Combining Resources 37
David Craig 38 Jael Bharat 38 Eva Tucker 39
Joint Action on Local or Global Issues 40 Wendy Tyndale 40
Travis Rejman 41 Religious and Theological Exchange 42
John Hick 42 Anant Rambachan 43 Richard Thompson 43
Inner Transformation 43 John Hick 44 Peter Bowe 44
Mohamed Mosaad 44 Creating a New World Religion 46

Mark Gifford 47   Nelson Mandela 48   Dialogue Partners 49
Harriet Crabtree 50   Peter Bowe 51   Dag Hammerskjöld 52
Summary 52   Maureen Goodman 52

3. INTERFAITH EXPERIENCING   53
Introduction 53   Huston Smith 54   John Hick 54
Peter Bowe 56   Joan Miller 57   Anuradha Devidasi 57
Albert Nambiaparambil 58   Marcus Braybrooke 59
Hans Ucko 60   Peter Riddell 61   Experiencing Interfaith Through
Art 62   Ashmolean Inter-Faith Exhibitions Service 62
Anas Al-Abbadi 62   David Partridge 64   Isobel Smyth 65
David Clark 66   Experiencing a Parliament of World Religions 68
Eileen Fry 69   Richard Boeke 70   Norbert Klaes 72
Sevan Ross 73   Visiting Faith Communities 74   Syed Hussaini 74
Gracie Riddell 75   Bede Gerrard 75   Gill Sanders 75
Paddy Meskin 76   WCRP South Africa 78   Summary 81
Our Interfaith Office Experience 82

4. INTERFAITH ORGANISING   83
Introduction 83   Getting Started 83   Building Good Relations with
People of Different Faiths and Beliefs 84   Fundraising 87
Implementing the Great Idea 89   Location, location, location 89
Choosing the Right Day and Time for Your Event 90
Middle East Report 90   The Speakers 91
Preparing Your Participants 92   Preparing the Room 93
Greeting the People Attending Your Event 93
Starting and Ending a Meeting 94   Catering 95
Prayer or Reflection Times 97
Making the most of your corridors 98   Final Statements 99
Postscript 99   Summary 99   Ramola Sundram 100
Celia Storey: Sarva Dharma Sammelana 102
Religion, Community and Conflict Conference 104
Maurice Ryan 105   Desmond Cahill: An Australian Multifaith
Response to S11 106   Charles Carroll Bonney 108

PART II. INTERFAITH ISSUES   109
Introduction

5. RELIGIOUS DIVERSITY   111
Introduction 111   Yehuda Stolov 112   Deepak Naik 112
Seeing Beyond Appearances 114   Jehangir Sarosh 115
Albert Nambiaparambil 116   Mahatma Gandhi 118
Yasutomo Sawahata 118   Reinhard Kirste 120
John D'Arcy May 122   Lao Tzu 123   Andrew Stallybrass 124
Jay Lakhani 126   Review 127   Paramahansa Yogananda 128

6. RELIGIOUS FREEDOM   129
Introduction 129   Conversion: Assessing the Reality 130
Arvind Sharma 132   Report on Religious Freedom 132
Universal Declaration of Human Rights 132
International Association for Religious Freedom 132   Karel Blei 133
Harriet Crabtree 133   Pope John Paul II 133
Mahatma Gandhi and Rajmohan Gandhi 135
Voluntary Code of Conduct 136
Religious Freedom Young Adult Network 137
Scenario on Religious Freedom 139   Shlomo Alon 140
Pamela Wilson 141   Punjab 142   Tibet 142
Britt Strandlie Thoresen 143   Center for Studies of Holocaust and
Religious Minorities in Europe 145
Oslo Coalition on Freedom of Religion or Belief 145
The Oslo Declaration on Freedom of Religion or Belief 146
Real Freedom 148   Summary 148

7. PEACE   149
The Golden Rule 149   Introduction 150
Simon Keyes 151   Marcus Braybrooke 152   Xinzhong Yao 154
Upanishads 156   Thomas Matthew 156
Brian Walker and Religions for Peace UK 158
Yehuda Stolov 160   Monica Willard 161
Inner Peace Dalai Lama 163   Karan Singh 163   Stephen Fulder 164
Maureen Goodman 165   Penny Faust 167
Paolo Dall' Iglio 168   Jael Bharat 169
Summary 170   Sandy Bharat 170

8. LIVING TOGETHER
Introduction 171   Heather al-Yusuf 172   Ibn' Arabi 172   171
Paul Knitter 173   Mary Pat Fisher 175   Guru Nanak 175
Ruwan Palapathwala 176   Living Together in Harmony 177
Yvonne Gunayat Pangsiw 178   Elizabeth J Harris 180
John Taylor 181   Rachel Montagu 182   Angie Grapa 183
Andreas D'Souza 184   Hamid Al-Rifaie 186
Summary 188   Elizabeth Amoah 188

PART III. THE FUTURE OF INTERFAITH
Challenges.   189

9. INTERFAITH YOUTH
Introduction 190   Ebrahim Patel 190   190
Joanna Jeczalik 190   Eboo Patel and Patrice Brodeur 191
Interfaith Youth Corps 193   Dan Steinhelper 193
Molly Hoisington 194   Usra Ghazi 195   Anas Al-Abbadi 196
Satyata Shreshta 197   Jagannath Kandel 197   Chicago Story 198

Youth Around the World
Philip Rizk 201   Tricia Deering 202   Woodrow Maquiling 203
Hakuin 205
Youth in the UK
Rebecca Hatch 206   Jayni Gudka 207   Louise Mitchell 208
Maimonides Foundation 210   Simon Cohen 210
International Interfaith Centre
Through Another's Eyes (Gracie and Ellie) 212
Interfaith in Action in a Global Age (Bill Swing and Paul Trafford) 213
Budapest Lecture and Workshops (Morse Flores) 215
Coventry 2000 (Sandy Bharat) 216
From Conflict to Trust (Ines Babic, Vladimir Mandic, Dotan Arad, Ghada Issa, Peter Brinkman) 218
Summary 221   Faith in the younger generation 222

10. THE ROLE OF RELIGIONS   223
Questions 223   Swami Vivekananda 223   Dalai Lama 224
Marcus Braybrooke 225   Tao 226   Wendy Tyndale 226
Robert Traer 227   Andrew Clark 228   Swami Agnivesh 229
Farid Esack 230   Andrew White 231   Ravi Ravindra 233
Fergus Capie 233   Michael Barnes 234   Sidney Shipton 235
Dena Merriam 237   Paramahansa Yogananda 238
Matt Weiner 238   Meru Devidasi 240   Don Cupitt 241
Summary 241   Kabir 242

11. ENGAGING CIVIL SOCIETY   243
Introduction 243   Zoroastrian Tradition 244   Paul Knitter 244
Brian Pearce 245   Global Responsibilities 247
Poverty and Development 247   Wendy Tyndale 247
Economics 249   Kamran Mofid 249   Kishore Shah 250
Education 252   Samuel Wintrip 252   From the Global Ethic 254
Ian Markham 254   Ranvir Singh 255   Howard Shippin 257
The Environment 258   Seyyed Hossein Nasr 258   Seshagiri Rao 258
Globalisation 259   Mehboob Sada 259   Jonathan Sacks 261
Josef Boehle 261   André Porto 262
Travis Rejman: The Goldin Institute 263
Spirituality and Religion at the United Nations
Bawa Jain 264   Gerardo Gonzalez 266
An Integrated Approach 268   Vinya Ariyaratne 268   Barney Leith 270
Summary 271   Rajmohan Gandhi 272

12. INTERFAITH FOR THE FUTURE   273
Interfaith for the Future 273   Chandra Muzaffar 273
Wendy Tyndale 274   Sioux Story 275
Critical Moments in Interreligious Dialogue 276
Chidi Denis Isizoh 277   Ehud Bandel 277   Anant Rambachan 277

Tarik Ramadan 277   Swami Satchidanand 277   Asaf Hussain 278
Adrian Mitchell 279   Diane Williams 280   Mussie Hailu 282
Meister Eckhart 283   Rowan Williams 284   Shahzad Syed 284
Paramahansa Yogananda 286
The Special Role of Women 286   Julia Ward Howe 286
Global Peace Initiative of Women 287   Harriet Crabtree 288
Dalai Lama 289   HRH Prince Hassan 290   Eric Gladwin 292

NOTES	293
IMAGE ACKNOWLEDGEMENTS	300
CONTRIBUTORS	303
INTERFAITH GALLERY	318
RESOURCES	320

REMEMBER THAT YOU ARE SPECIAL
AND THAT THE RIPPLES OF YOUR LIFE
AFFECTS OTHERS TOO

PREFACE

Sandy & Jael Bharat

This book aims to give readers both an introduction to interfaith and an insider's view of it. Interfaith activists and academics from around the world have contributed to this and their messages, insights and experiences fill the pages. Information about the contributors can be found in the Contributors section and contact information about the interfaith organisations mentioned can be found in Resources. As there is always a time gap between writing and publishing, check with the organisations that interest you for updates on their work.

Our sincere thanks to everyone who has helped make this a collective initiative, especially those who sent their stories and photographs, Madeleine Harman for proof-reading and helpful suggestions, and Marcus Braybrooke for his Foreword. Our gratitude includes our publisher, John Hunt, for his commitment to this project.

As we spent most of our interfaith years deeply immersed in the International Interfaith Centre (IIC) in Oxford, so most of our memories and experiences, peppered through the text with many of our photographs, come from this time. Some, in one form or another, have appeared in IIC newsletters or on the e-learning website Sandy began to develop before leaving the IIC. We are grateful to the IIC trustees for enabling our access to IIC archives from the years we worked there and we dedicate our work on this book to all those individuals, at the International Interfaith Centre and other interfaith organisations, who shared their interfaith journeys with us and made our interfaith years so special, such a privilege.

You might wonder about the logic we used to decide in which section each reflection should be placed. It was not exactly the equivalent of rocket science. So many of the reflections could have fitted in several of the categories. There is a lot of interconnection and overlapping. Just as it should be! So, here and there you will find, for example, contributions from young people that are not in the Youth chapter. Hopefully you will not be diverted by your own superior arranging skills and will be content with everything just as it is!

The interfaith movement is awash with acronyms so it might help to familiarize yourself here and now with a few examples, some of those that crop up often in this book. There are many more waiting out there!

- IIC – International Interfaith Centre, based in Oxford, where we spent most of our interfaith incarnations.

- WCRP – World Conference on Religions for Peace, also known as Religions for Peace, a major global interfaith player with headquarters in New York.
- IARF – International Association for Religious Freedom, founded in 1900, first off the block after the 1893 Parliament of World Religions. Based in Oxford with individual and organization members around the world.
- CPWR – Council for a Parliament of the World's Religions, the organization, based in Chicago, which now organizes regular Parliaments.
- IFYC – Interfaith Youth Core – major centre for youth activity, based in Chicago with international outreach.
- URI – United Religions Initiative – fast growing and significant interfaith organization, with headquarters in San Francisco and locally rooted, globally connected cooperation circles around the world.

Because this book has become possible only through the dedication and friendship of so many interfaith people around the world it seemed only right to commit any royalties the book might earn to charity. UNICEF is working internationally to help and protect the world's most vulnerable children. Buy copies for your friends and help the fund!

We hope you will find reflections inside these pages that resonate with your own thoughts and feelings and propel your own faith and interfaith journeys. May we together, in our different but connected ways, build bridges of harmony and peace that end forever artificial separation and divisions.

FOREWORD

For those who are new to interfaith this amazing book will give a wonderful picture of the variety and excitement of this journey of discovery. It tells us something about the world religions, about interfaith history and organisations, how to plan an interfaith meeting and much more – mostly through the words of practitioners. Those already involved in interfaith activity often feel quite isolated as they work with a small group in a hostile environment. Now they will suddenly become aware that they are part of a spiritual fellowship which can transform society.

The interfaith story is told by individuals, from every faith and every continent, whose lives have been changed by a friendly encounter with people of another faith. Indeed in several traditions there is a sense that God resides in the image of the other person, who therefore becomes a 'sacred Other.'

The Hindu poet Tulsidas wrote:
> Treat all people well
> Perhaps to your surprise,
> The one whom you are meeting
> Is God in some disguise.[1]

The Bible says:
> Remember always to welcome strangers, for by doing this,
> some people have entertained angels without knowing it.[2]

[1] The translation is by Fr. Roger Lesser.
[2] Hebrews 13, 2.

Once strangers, now friends: Marcus Braybrooke and Laxmi Saha of ISKCON, together at the First Congress on Prayer in Hamburg, June 2005.

Sandy and Jael Bharat played a major role in establishing and developing the International Interfaith Centre in Oxford and in creating the International Interfaith Organizations Network. They draw on these contacts, but the book shows that their network of friends is indeed global and that through them many people have been put in contact with each other. We are grateful for their work and dedication and the patience and skill shown in the production of this book.

There is a Chinese saying, 'Change the world and begin with me.' This book is encouraging evidence that many people have been changed and spiritually enriched by sharing with people of other faiths. May their discovery help to change the world so that war, poverty and pollution become a long forgotten chapter of a by-gone age.

MARCUS BRAYBROOKE
President of the World Congress of Faiths
Patron of the International Interfaith Centre

Oxford 2006

Two people who help change the world: HH Dalai Lama and Marcus

PART ONE INTRO

What is it all about?

PART I.
INTRODUCTION TO INTERFAITH

What is interfaith? When did it begin? Why is it important? Who are the interfaith activists? What are they doing, and how? Where is it all happening? What organisations have evolved to take interfaith forward? Are there special challenges and concerns? What is the future of interfaith? Can we be part of it? Will it change me? Will it threaten my faith? What actually happens? These are some of the questions this book will address.

They will be illustrated with reflections and profiles from people at the interface of interfaith around the world. Through their stories and experiences you will understand more of the reality facing people of faith in our world today as they try to build bridges across religious divides and between religious and secular peoples and establishments. You will see how interfaith activists are working together for peace and for enhanced communication and co-operation at individual, community, local, national, regional and global levels, everywhere where religious consciousness impedes on human co-existence and community cohesion.

Before you start you might like to think about your own understanding of interfaith. What does the term mean to you? Perhaps writing down your thoughts and returning to them at the end of the book might be interesting. Have they changed at all? Were your worst fears confirmed or your greatest

Christian-Muslim Meeting Point: Jill Gant and Ibrahim Mogra explore understanding at an International Interfaith Centre Seminar on Karma.

dreams realised? Has it become clearer what your contribution might be to interfaith relations? A list of organisational contacts and resources will be provided to expedite your journey if you want to travel further on the interfaith road.

> *We must be the change we wish to see in the world.*
>
> Mahatma Gandhi

IN THE FIRST PART OF THIS BOOK we begin the exploration of how interfaith began, why it matters, and what we need to think about if we plan interfaith action. Our text is interspersed with reflections by interfaith activists, profiles of interfaith people and organisations, encouraging quotes from famous figures of the modern world, and relevant thoughts from humanity's saints and sages.

This interfaith journey is not one that everyone undertakes easily. For some it may be difficult to step out of comfortable and known religious surroundings to investigate and come face to face with other religious identities. Almost everyone who does so will be changed. How we are changed is for each one of us to determine. The impact may change over time as we ourselves change and grow and understand more. Interfaith is not an end in itself. We do not usually become 'interfaith' though some of us will become ardent and dedicated promoters of interfaith engagement. For others it may lead to the end of religion in the realization that humanity and a universal spirituality are our most fundamental shared realities.

In a world so troubled and divided as our own, we cannot stay inside our insular boxes. There is no safety there. Others will enter. Let us come out willingly, joyfully, and meet one another. Let us feel the freedom that comes when we know Truth is already there in all others we meet. The Real embraces us all according to our capacity to receive and we have much to learn from one another. There is much we can do together. We can travel together for at least part of our journey of learning, grateful for the good and challenging company!

Good company: Dialogue group at IIC conference: Eileen Barker, Meru Devidasi, Josef Boehle, and Brian Pearce.

When did it all begin?

Chapter I

INTERFAITH ORIGINS

IMAGINING THE BEGINNING

Shadows flickered on damp cave walls. Paintings etched in amber shimmered in the dance. Flames red with danger, golden with warmth, rose enigmatically into the darkness. People gathered round the fire, gazed into its mystery, and wondered.

Legs, lifted in rhythmic undulations, returned to earth, a sacred dance. O Mother Earth, provider, sustainer, most beloved, we tread upon you lightly and reverently. We are new to you and are nourished by you. The people watched the rise and fall of the dance and wept with joy.

Along the river's banks, children played. The waters had their own life current, sometimes angry, often gentle. Many voices murmured from the flowing depths, ancient voices, powerful with unheard time. The people watched the light shining on the surface and bowed their heads.

To the North, high on the hills touching heaven, the people looked upwards and outwards. Unending, undivided vistas filled their eyes, filled them with vision. O, the heights to reach, the openness to receive. They stretched their arms, lay back their heads, and roared into the sky.

The search for food, the quest for adventure, the need for community brought these peoples onto each other's trails. They met and tried to communicate: to sing songs, to share stories. Their songs and stories told of their religious imaginings, nurtured by the fire, the water, the earth, the heavens. The stories intermingled and became changed. They developed in new directions, vibrant with invigorated meaning amidst old understandings. Some people tried to hold onto the old and fight the new. Others merged both into something entirely different. Some learnt from the new and adapted the old. So the songs and stories walked on through time, constantly interconnecting, dividing, reforming,

> Only when we work together as a global family, instead of concentrating on belonging to a particular race, religion or nation, will peace and happiness prevail on this earth. [1]
>
> Sri Mata Amritanandamayi Devi, World Renowned Hindu Preceptor

> Men and women of faith are a strong influence on group and individual conduct. As teachers and guides, you can be powerful agents for change. You can inspire people to new levels of commitment and public service. You can help bridge the chasms of ignorance, fear and misunderstanding. You can set an example of interfaith dialogue and co-operation.[2]
>
> Kofi Annan,
> Secretary General,
> United Nations

refreshing, pulled by two primary forces - inner, individual, understanding and outer, community, action - into evolving synthesis.

WHAT IS INTERFAITH EXACTLY?

Some people get confused about the nature of interfaith. Celia Storey tells how she had to educate friends when she and her husband, David, began interfaith activities. Friends asked, 'You mean you are working with Methodists and Baptists?' Celia's response was 'Well no, not actually; interfaith means working with people with different religious beliefs such as Buddhists and Muslims. Methodists and Baptists are all the same faith, Christian.' So, interfaith does not mean intrafaith (dialogue within a tradition), although it is often on 'home' territory that interfaith activists have to work the hardest to demonstrate and inculcate the importance and relevance of interreligious engagement. Even intrafaith encounter is difficult for some!

What then is interfaith? Interfaith is the encounter of one person of faith with a person of another faith with all the changes this can engender. This process can be multiplied at organised interfaith events. The fruits of interfaith can bring an improvement in human lives, upliftment of human societies, and greater realisation of the spiritual inter-connectedness of all beings.

THE INTERFAITH MOVEMENT

Interfaith began when people did, when imagination, creatively responding to environment, became religious, a mystical mix of awe and appreciation. The interfaith movement can be seen as a conscious expansion of that evolution, a realisation and acceptance that knowing you, your faith, will enhance my life and my faith. There is gratitude for religious diversity, dawned down the ages. It is challenging but not threatening. It brings spiritual growth. It keeps us humble.

The interfaith movement began when this natural phenomenon blossomed into organised activity. The inspiration for this is generally understood to have been the moment Swami Vivekananda addressed his 'Sisters and Brothers of America' at the first Parliament of World Religions in Chicago in 1893. His Vedic quote set the tone: 'As the different streams having their sources in different places all mingle their water in the sea, so, O Lord, the different paths which men take through different tendencies, various though they appear, crooked or straight, all lead to Thee.'[3]

THE PLATFORM OF THE PARLIAMENT ON THE MORNING OF SEPTEMBER 11.

Can you imagine what it felt like at that innovative event in Chicago more than one hundred years ago? Now we are used to multi-cultural diversity in our cities but then it was a most exotic and hope inducing spectacle. Using imagination and original sources, Marcus Braybrooke sets the scene:

When the parliament opened on 11 September 1893, more than four thousand people crowded into the hall of Columbus. At ten o'clock, representatives of a dozen faiths marched down the aisle, arm in arm. On the platform the central position was taken by Cardinal Gibbons, 'clad in scarlet robes.' Henry Barrows describes those seated next to the Cardinal. 'On either side of him were grouped the Oriental delegates, whose many coloured raiments vied with his own in brilliancy. Conspicuous among these followers of Brahma and Buddha and Mohammed was the eloquent monk Vivekananda of Bombay, clad in gorgeous red apparel, his bronze face surmounted with a huge turban of yellow. Beside him, in orange and white, sat B B Nagarkar of the Brahmo Samaj and Dharmapala from Ceylon.'

One can sense the organisers' excitement…that, after all the time and correspondence, people from around the world had assembled in Chicago. Names on papers had begun to become friends. As Barrows said in his opening address, 'When, a few days ago, I met for the first time the delegates who have come to us from Japan, and shortly after the delegates who have come

> THE PARLIAMENT OF RELIGIONS HAS PROVED TO THE WORLD THAT HOLINESS, PURITY AND CHARITY ARE NOT THE EXCLUSIVE POSSESSIONS OF ANY CHURCH IN THE WORLD, AND THAT EVERY SYSTEM HAS PRODUCED MEN AND WOMEN OF THE MOST EXALTED CHARACTER. MY THANKS TO THOSE NOBLE SOULS WHOSE LARGE HEARTS AND LOVE OF TRUTH FIRST DREAMED THIS WONDERFUL DREAM, AND THEN REALIZED IT.
>
> SWAMI VIVEKANANDA

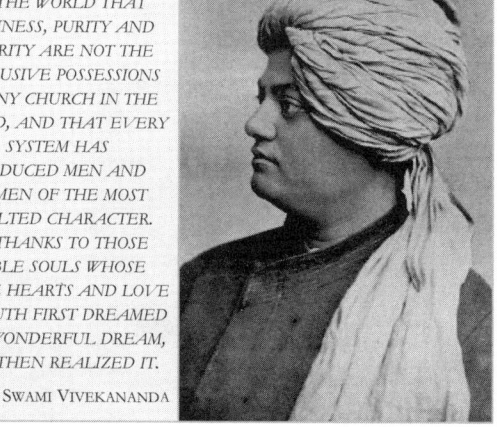

MARY BRAYBROOKE describes an interfaith moment in her life:

For me meeting with people of other faiths and sharing personal stories has always been of the uttermost importance – more than learning what they believe intellectually, even spiritually. If we can have fellowship and see beyond the label to the person behind it, and the human being with the same joys, sorrows and needs as ourselves, then this surely is true dialogue.

One story illustrates what I am trying to say. It was 1993 and we were in South India at a preparatory conference before the special Bangalore celebrations, Sarva Dharma Sammelana, to remember the 1893 World Parliament of Religions.

We were staying in a modest Indian hostel in Kanya Kumari. We decided to go to Vivekananda's rock. It was where Swami Vivekananda dedicated himself to the service of the poor before setting out to travel to Chicago for the Parliament. The only way to get to the rock was by boat. The rock was crowded and it was very hot. Suddenly I felt faint and nearly passed out, possibly due to dehydration. People gathered round concerned to help and our son, a junior doctor at the time, had to keep them at bay. As I recovered it was necessary to get me to the boat as soon as possible in spite of the large number of people queuing up for it.

A member of the Baha'i faith escorted me, a Christian, through the crowds to the boat. A Muslim gentleman then drove me back to the hostel, which was run by Hindus. An hour later, there was a knock on the door. A Zoroastrian lady stood there holding a large envelope. 'I think you left this on Vivekananda's rock', she said. 'Perhaps it might be important.' It was! Inside the envelope were our passports and air tickets back to Great Britain!

What a wonderful group of neighbours we met that afternoon.

Two Peace Workers:
Mary Braybrooke (right) with Mairead Maguire

to us from India, I felt that the arms of human brotherhood had reached almost around the globe.'⁴

> *The sacred heritage of the great faiths is a rich resource for all people in the search for a more fair and harmonious world.*
>
> Marcus Braybrooke

Not long after the Parliament of World Religions, in 1900, the organisation that has come to be known as the International Association for Religious Freedom was born. It started a stream of interfaith activity that has become a mighty river with many, many rivulets, some straight, some crooked, some heading to the sea, some flowing inland! The great interfaith historian, archivist and activist, Marcus Braybrooke, has charted these waters in many interfaith books, most prominently in *Pilgrimage of Hope: One Hundred Years of Global Interfaith Dialogue*, quoted above.

In this book and in the years since it was published we can see the genesis of interfaith dialogue and action as immensely diverse, earnest and energetic, alert to changing times and circumstances, though sometimes too competitive. It is still primarily a child of the western and northern worlds. Here most resources and retinues are still to be found. It is early days and interfaith people are increasingly aware and hungry for more integrated, truly global engagement. There is an increasing eagerness too for greater gender balance and youth involvement in the interfaith movement.

There are many interfaith organisations operating locally, nationally, regionally, and internationally, addressing a host of concerns and agendas: community initiatives, religious freedom, peace and conflict transformation, poverty and development, medical research, animal theology, global theology, comparative studies, economics, issues of particular interest to women and youth, dialogues between specific religious groups, the United Nations, spirituality, inter-monastic dialogue, global ethics, religious Parliaments, solidarity, intergovernmental projects, religious terrorism, ethnic and cultural alienation, debt relief, religious and spiritual education, interfaith studies, architecture, hospice and hospital care, organ transplantation, multi-faith

Women make a vital contribution to interfaith.

Anuradha Devidasi, Vivienne Cato and Mehri Niknam dialogue together at an International Interfaith Centre seminar on Karma that we initiated.

chapels at airports and other public buildings, immigration and race relations, art and literary matters. There are not many areas left where the combined or collective interests of faith communities are not addressed as part of the search for community cohesion and consensus.

One example of changes unforeseen a few years ago is the recent partnership between the faith communities belonging to the Inter Faith Network for the UK and the Commission for Racial Equality, the Association of Chief Police Officers, and the Chief Fire Officer's Association to 'assist in responding together as communities to increase our safety and security.' A leaflet was produced by the Network called *Looking after one another*.[5] It gives advice on how to respond jointly in times of tension by building on existing good inter-community relations and by remaining calm - 'an attack on one is an attack on all.'

Today governments, councils, NGO's, most organisations and institutions are aware not only of the need for community cohesion but also of the role that religions still play or increasingly play in that, despite secular developments. Most are willing to encourage, support and participate in consultations and engagement with the faith communities that can help facilitate good inter-community relationships. Even multi-national bodies like the United Nations are increasingly becoming conscious that religions are not extinct dinosaurs but active volcanoes and must be taken into account in negotiations and plans that affect the world's populations.

An initiative that we helped facilitate is the NETWORK OF INTERNATIONAL INTERFAITH ORGANISATIONS.[6] During our IIC symposium, *Interfaith in a Global Age*, at the 1999 Parliament of World Religions in Cape Town, we suggested that maybe international interfaith organisations could dedicate a person who could work together with others for the common good. Back in Oxford we began to develop this idea and eventually invited representatives from fourteen organisations to meet in Oxford in March 2001. Every organisation responded positively and although it was a tough meeting in some ways it was also the beginning of this tentative network with the aim of enhancing

Farid Esack at the 1999 Parliament of World Religions: addressing community issues that affect millions.

Some of the Network participants at the Oxford 2003 meeting.

communication and cooperation between participating members. The International Interfaith Centre has the responsibility and privilege of coordinating the network and arranging an annual meeting. At the time of writing five such gatherings have taken place - four in Oxford and one in Budapest. An informal meeting was also organised at the Parliament of World Religions in Barcelona in 2004.

ALISON VAN DYK of the Temple of Understanding, a founding member of the Network for International Interfaith Organisations, shares this reflection of a friendship that initiated her interfaith life:

My first experience with the idea of interfaith was when I was 15 and had been invited with my mother by Juliet Hollister to lunch at her home on Steamboat Road in Connecticut, USA. Her home was magical and everything about Juliet was exciting. Juliet told us that she had had a vision about bringing the religious leaders of the world together to stop war and bring peace to planet earth while having a peanut butter sandwich with a friend. I am not sure why I was tagging along on this particular occasion but as a young person it was almost as if I was part of the visionary experience that Juliet had. I was wildly excited by this wonderful new idea.

Meeting Juliet that day had a profound impact on me and our continued friendship has influenced the course of my life in more ways than I would ever have guessed. My mother tried to help Juliet and joined the early Board of the Temple of Understanding, Juliet's name for her work which came from an Indian friend who said that this is sacred work, sacred space and a

2005: Alison with Fr Thomas Keating at the 45th anniversary of the Temple of Understanding.

temple is a sacred name. However pressure from my step-father ended that. The friend who ate the peanut butter sandwich had the same problem, I guess. It is hard today to imagine that Juliet was ostracized by many of her friends and her community for believing that religions had common values and that leaders of different faiths should talk to each other and work together.

When I was 18 I was asked to be the Youth Representative for the TOU. I was thrilled as it meant that I was on the Board. I travelled to Washington DC monthly, organized meetings at Sarah Lawrence College where I was a student and did what I could. This was the time when the eastern religions and their representatives were arriving in the US. The TOU offered them a platform at Summit conferences which were held at Harvard Divinity School, Cornell and Yale to name a few. As a young person I felt so blessed to be able to attend these conferences and to personally meet some of the great religious leaders of our time.

Four years ago I took over as the Chair and Executive Director of the TOU. I have been a clinical psychologist with children for the past 23 years so this was a major career change for me. One of the main reasons for my decision is that I believe that a spiritual perspective is critical for young people today. My friendship with Juliet was really a mentorship. She taught me a great deal about the importance of interfaith work which has guided my interest in interfaith education. To teach young people to look at the world through tolerance, justice and a determination to make a difference is crucial if we are really going to achieve the UN's Millennium Development Goals.

> Prof Seshagiri Rao
>
> *The essential aspiration of religions is for reconciliation, human fellowship and peace. By awakening the spiritual consciousness of humanity, we can establish moral order in human society. Spiritual traditions of the world should, therefore, stand together and work for the greater glory of God and the greater happiness of humankind.* [7]

WAYS TO DIALOGUE

Just as when the earliest peoples came together, a common language is needed. If we cannot communicate, we cannot co-operate. One Buddhist monk told how he went to live in the Tamil Hindu part of Sri Lanka, then divided by a war that separated Hindus and Buddhists. He was met with great suspicion. He just smiled. There was no common language so he smiled. Soon, smiles began to return to him and, after one year, he was invited to stay with a Hindu family. By this time he had begun to learn the language of his hosts so could greet them with both smiles and speaking. The story of interfaith so far is still about finding the common language. There is still too much speaking of our own language at interfaith events, not yet enough authentic listening and learning. There is still much trust building needed, too, to move beyond the similarities between us and address with confidence the differences that divide us.

Some of the contemporary themes and challenges of interfaith - the common language - were generated at that first significant, symbolic Parliament of World Religions in 1893, over one hundred years ago. In his book, *Interfaith Encounter,* Rev Dr ALAN RACE (pictured right) summarised these as:

- The struggle of 'interreligion' against the 'absence of religion' in modern secularism;
- The need to overcome the historic connection between religious disagreement and violence;
- Religion as a liberating and motivating force for good in the world;
- The significance of the Golden Rule ('Do to others what you would have done to yourself') as a potential focus for developing shared values between traditions;
- The problematics of absolutism in commitment to a particular religious path versus the relativism of granting parity of value to all;
- The possibility of a mystical unity of the religions.[8]

When we interviewed Prof JOHN HICK some years ago, he identified these three main types of interfaith activity or ways of 'talking' together.

One is 'highly intellectual, a matter of trying to understand one another's belief systems and discussing them – not trying to persuade each other that the other was wrong but in actual fact learning from the others.' His own experience of Christian response to participation in Buddhist-Christian dialogues was that 'it changed our ideas and ways of thinking a lot more than the other way round.'

A second type of interfaith activity is more grassroots, community oriented, leading to a better understanding of our neighbours. In California, he found that 'quite ordinary people, not religious leaders, not the rabbis and ministers and so on, but ordinary people, got together in one another's houses and they were interested to find out about daily life, what you do in family life, how you deal with children's problems, what you eat and what you don't eat

Participants from South Africa, Northern Ireland, Philippines, Canada and the UK discussing common areas of concern at an International Interfaith Centre conference.

and all that sort of thing, and this was enormously creative of interfaith friendships, genuine friendships.'

The third type of activity Prof Hick identified was that which deals specifically with concrete local problems that people of different faiths, together, can help solve. This is possibly one of the best first entry places for people to engage with interfaith issues. Broader concerns of mutual interest are also productive ways to get involved. '[The] problems of the environment, of peace, of poverty, the problems of the world, because they are common to all human beings, and you find that different ideas spring up from different sources, (are) quite possibly the most valuable thing at the moment.'[9]

MARCUS BRAYBROOKE reminds us of how we need to stay alert when entering the interfaith arena. We can presuppose nothing. We must be aware of our own vulnerability. We must take it seriously.

'There are various levels of dialogue and it is a process of growth. An initial requirement is an openness to and acceptance of the other. It takes time to build trust and to deepen relationships. This is why some continuity in a dialogue group is helpful and why patience and time are necessary – all of which are particularly difficult to ensure at an international level. Too easily, we find ourselves imposing our presuppositions on the conversation. Christians, for example, often assume that Muslims really adopt a critical attitude to the Qur'an similar to that common amongst Christians in their reading of the Bible. We have to learn to enter another world that may seem alien and which has different presuppositions. We have to allow our deepest convictions to be questioned. Some Buddhists, for example, will question deeply held Christian assumptions about God and the self. It is important for those venturing into dialogue to be secure in their own faith. They need to beware of becoming marginalised in or alienated from their own religious tradition.'

THE MELODY OF HUMAN BROTHERHOOD

Heavenly Spirit, we are traveling by many right roads to Thine abode of light.
Guide us onto the highway of Self-knowledge, to which all paths
of true religious beliefs eventually lead.

The diverse religions are branches of Thy one immeasurable tree of truth.
May we enjoy the luscious fruits of soul realization that hang
from the boughs of scriptures of every clime and time.

Teach us to chant in harmony the countless expressions of our
supreme devotion. In Thy temple of the earth, in a chorus of
many-accented voices, we are singing only to Thee.

O Divine Mother, lift us on Thy lap of universal love.
Break Thy vow of silence and sing to us
the heart-melting melody of human brotherhood. [10]

Paramahansa Yogananda

RELIGION AND DIVERSITY IN ETHIOPIA

Ethiopia is my home country and it is a beautiful mosaic of cultures, faiths, and lifestyles. It is a land of plenty with a long and noble history giving rise to ethnic, linguistic and cultural diversity. It is the home of Christians, Muslims and Jews, as well as those with various traditional beliefs.

Ethiopian civilization represents the longest unbroken chain of cultural continuity in the history of the world. The rift valley is the home of Denkinesh who is known to the world as 'Lucy' - the earliest humanoid. Thus, Ethiopia is the cradle from where human society first emerged. It is also a country that is the custodian of the Ark of the Covenant. The worldwide Christian community considers Ethiopia an illustrious realm. It is mentioned in the Bible more than forty times.

Ethiopia is a predominantly Christian country and the majority of Christians belong to the Ethiopian Orthodox Tewahedo Church. Islam was introduced to Ethiopia in 615 AD when the followers of the prophet Mohammed, including his wife, sought refuge in the northern part of Ethiopia known as Aksum. The king of Aksum welcomed them, respected their religion and offered them protection. They later settled in Negash, in the region of Tigray, which became the foundation and one of the most important places for the Islamic faith in Ethiopia. The Prophet Mohammad called Ethiopia 'the land of righteousness' and ordered his followers never to provoke Ethiopia.

The introduction of Judaism to Ethiopia is recorded in the Kebre Negest (The Glory of Kings) book. This book focuses on two historical events: The birth of Menilek, Son of Solomon, the king of Israel, and the Queen of Sheba of Ethiopia (970-33 B.C) and The Ark of the Covenant, which was brought to Axum from Jerusalem by the Levites.

With all of these marvellous traits and traditions, one can easily see why Ethiopian civilization is considered a world treasure of great importance. It is the root of Judeo-Christian civilization as well as the fabric of Muslim society. This is why I consider Ethiopia 'a land of interfaith.'

By Mussie Hailu

What does my faith say about itself and other religious paths?

FROM FAITH TO INTERFAITH

It might be helpful at this point to introduce some of the faiths from which interfaith emerges. As this is not a book on comparative religions, the introductions here are naturally very concise and the authors of them have done a marvellous precision job! Also, as there are so many faiths and spiritualities, not every one can be described in this book. Here are introductions to just a few traditions that include some old, some newer, some from the Middle East, some from South East Asia, some which have evolved with new vision from older traditions, some which stand alone. Knowing something about them, if you do not already, could help create a context for understanding both the impetus to interfaith and resistance to it. It may also help you reflect on the way other religious and spiritual traditions respond to the interfaith imperative. Reflections throughout the book will show you how individuals and organisations from many belief positions are engaged in interfaith activities.

Interfaith people come from a broad range of religious and spiritual perspectives, most though not all associated with the mainstream historical traditions - each of these, of course, is incredibly diverse even if we are used to thinking of them with one label eg. Christianity or Judaism. Some interfaith activists are humanist or pagan, people who respond to the Divine as imminent or indwelling in the world. Some belong to ancient traditions like Shinto with its potent world-view of reverence and respect for all and the innate harmony of all. Others have their own explanations and motivations. André Porto from Brazil, whom you will meet later in the book, once described his religion to us as 'service.' For some people of faith, practice is more important than belief. For others, the reverse is true. In interfaith activities people learn how their practices and beliefs relate to those of others and what can be done together.

Interfaith is natural to some religions, especially those that have always been a collection of different traditions and those that have long developed in religiously plural environments. The Sikh holy scripture, the Guru Granth Sahib, includes writings from many spiritual sources. The most ancient, earth religions like Shinto and the many pagan traditions, generally have no exclusivist aspects, despite their own particularities. Where religions claim exclusive authority then problems arise. Missionaries do not generally find interfaith activities either attractive or legitimate. Even so, especially in recent times, human conditions and shared global concerns have encouraged broader perspectives, if only as a kind of collective security.

The first introduction is to one of the most ancient, enduring and richly pluralistic of the great world religions.

HINDUISM AND RELIGIOUS DIVERSITY
Anantanand Rambachan, Professor of Religion,
Saint Olaf College, USA

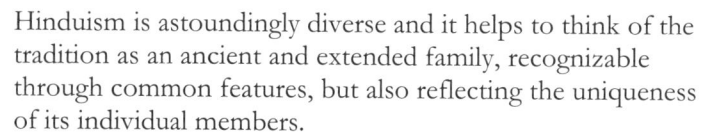

Hinduism is astoundingly diverse and it helps to think of the tradition as an ancient and extended family, recognizable through common features, but also reflecting the uniqueness of its individual members.

Many of the common features of the Hindu tradition are derived from the scriptures known as the Vedas. Orthodox Hindus consider the four Vedas as revelation. Particular Hindu groups regard many other texts as revelation, but the Vedas enjoy an almost unanimous recognition as revealed knowledge.

Contrary to popular stereotypes, the Hindu tradition is neither life denying nor otherworldly. Wealth (artha) and pleasure (kama) are among the four legitimate goals of life.

Vyasa, also known as Veda Vyasa or 'Splitter of the Vedas,' who made the one Veda into four parts so its Knowledge could be accessed by everyone.

Deepak Naik telling interfaith guests about the shrine room of a Hindu mandir or temple in Coventry, UK

Wealth and pleasure must be sought by being responsive to the demands of the third goal, referred to as dharma. Dharma is violated when we obsessively pursue private desires that destroy the harmony of the community on which our lives depend. Non-injury (ahimsa) is the best expression of dharma. Hinduism's highest goal is liberation (moksha). It is a common view in the Hindu tradition that ignorance of the true nature of the human self (atman) and God (brahman) is the fundamental human problem and the underlying cause of suffering. Liberation cannot be obtained without right knowledge of reality.

The great theologians and traditions of Hinduism teach that the self cannot be equated with the time-bound physical body or the ever-changing mind. In its essential nature, the self is eternal. Consciousness and bliss constitute its essence. Ignorant of the true nature of the self, one wrongly identifies it with the body and mind and becomes subject to greed and want. Desire-prompted actions generate results (karma) that lead to subsequent rebirths (samsara). Moksha is consequent upon the right understanding of the nature of the self. It implies the recognition of the self to be different from the psychophysical apparatus and to be immortal. Such an understanding of the self's essential nature brings an end to the cycle of death, birth and rebirth.

> *This world is going to be filled with people who love each other, care for each other, and together build peace through better understanding.*[11]
>
> Swami Satchidananada

For all traditions of Hinduism, moksha implies the cultivation of compassion for all beings and freedom from hate and greed.

Hindu sacred texts and traditions remind us constantly that, in relation to God, our language is always limited and inadequate. God is always more than we can define, describe or understand with our finite minds and fragmented language. A God whose nature and essence could be entirely captured in our words or who could be contained within the boundaries of the human mind would not be the absolute proclaimed in Hinduism. No representation of the divine in image or words can ever be final or complete.

As it is impossible to capture the limitless within the boundaries of our religion or to define it comprehensively through the limited language of our theology, Hinduism teaches that we must be open to meaningful insights from others that may open our understanding to the inexhaustible nature of the divine. The limits of human understanding and language provide a powerful justification for a pluralistic outlook and for meeting one another in a spirit of humility and reverence. We can learn from and be enriched by the ways in which others have experienced God. Religious arrogance is the consequence of thinking that one has a privileged relationship with and understanding of God. It is a consequence of falsely limiting God to one's own community, the pages of one's sacred text, or the walls of one's place of worship. Hinduism is not challenged by the fact of other traditions claiming revelation from, encounters with and knowledge of God.

HINDUISM IN THE UK

The Lord Dholakia of Waltham Brooks OBE DL

The vast Hindu community in Britain has observed at first hand life in a predominantly Christian country. Isn't it remarkable that there has been no conflict in the way we have developed our economic and social life here?

All religions have similar basic values at their core – truth, respect, empathy, compassion, tolerance and love amongst others. The values we often subscribe to our own beliefs are also reflected in Christianity. No longer are we seen as a misunderstood religion worshipping deities. What are often talked about are the values we represent.

Immigration to this country since the early fifties has stood the test of time. it has also proved that the affinity between different religions is based on values we attach to our own beliefs and the values others attach to those ideals. It is by recognising and understanding this commonality that people of all religions can live together in harmony.

It is an approach that contributes immeasurably to integration, peace and individual enrichment. [12]

A HIGHLAND LASS by MINAKSHI YOGI,
Member of the Youth Society for Peace, Nepal.

A few years ago, a beautiful highland lass, Shruti, aged 18, lived in a village in the western part of Nepal. She and her only brother lived with their caring parents in a small thatched roof house with only two rooms. Their house was on the bank of a holy river and she was lucky to feel the lovely breeze blowing from the river. The family was poor but everyone in the family valued duty and responsibility. Shruti used to wake up at 4:30 in the morning every day and fetch water for the family, cut grass for the animals, wash dishes, and perform all other household works. She was bubbly and cheerful. Along with her parents she worshipped every evening to develop her inner capacity to realize the presence of the Almighty within herself. Regardless of all these daily household schedules, everyone in her family used to remain happy and smiling. Above all, Shruti had wonderful smiles on her face and a profound faith in God.

She was so inspired by the discourses of the people during *Pooja* (worship) that she wanted to read some books on spirituality and eastern philosophy. At first people thought she was crazy. None of the girls in that village were allowed to touch spiritual books. Shruti became more determined to read such books, to quench her thirst for learning about her own religion. Therefore, during the nights, she secretly read the Upanishads. Having read them, she realized what one has to do and feel in life. And realizing, practicing and maintaining the following formulas in life is true religion: *Dhriti* (Patience), *Kshama* (Forgiveness), *Dama* (Self-control), *Asteya* (Non stealing), *Saucha* (Purity), *Indriyanigraha* (Control of Senses), *Dhi* (Insight), *Vidya* (Wisdom), *Sattya* (Truth) and *Akrodha* (Not getting angry).

She shared her feelings with everyone in the family on what she understood about true religion. Everyone was so impressed with her. She then lived her life with the motto - 'work without any selfish motive is worship' - and truly practiced this maxim as her life's ideal.

Shruti became very relaxed, peaceful and happy. In spite of being a girl of a poor family, she always kept her spirits up. She was loved by everyone at her school. Her honesty and sincerity were beyond words. Her way of thinking about religion and culture made people around her aware of how they had to live in their society. She not only taught other people the scientific importance and social value of our culture but also succeeded in making people aware of utilizing religion for the sake of humanity.

She became an ideal woman for everyone in her village.

The sacred temple of Pashupati Nath, full of devotees.

BUDDHISM AND RELIGIOUS DIVERSITY
Dr Paul Trafford, Oxford University

Buddhist practice may be summed up in three Pali words: *dana, sila* and *samadhi*, which can be translated as generosity, virtue (or ethical conduct) and meditation. As Buddhists, we train ourselves to know how our intentional actions are linked to particular results or outcomes, trying to cultivate purity of mind for:

1. Mind precedes all mental states. Mind is their chief; they are all mind-made. If with an impure mind a person speaks or acts suffering follows him like the wheel that follows the foot of the ox.
2. Mind precedes all mental states. Mind is their chief; they are all mind-made. If with a pure mind a person speaks or acts happiness follows him like his never-departing shadow. [Dhammapada, Canto 1 verses 1, 2]

We tread this path until it leads to the supremely happy and peaceful state in which there is permanent release from the spectres of birth, old age, sickness and death. By practising diligently, we may gradually see three characteristics about our normal existence: it is inherently unsatisfactory, is ever-changing and what we thought of as 'self' is not what it seemed. So we strive for transcendence. This is a universal path open to all 'sentient beings,' but is exceedingly subtle in nature, so hard to find and difficult to tread because we have three exceedingly deep-rooted fires to overcome: greed, hatred and delusion.

We know about this through the Lord Buddha, a Fully Enlightened One, who followed the path to supreme realisation and further was able to transmit the path to others so that they too might become Enlightened and continue the transmission. Those who follow his path are called 'Buddhist' and today Buddhists live predominantly in Asia - the 'Northern Schools' that range from Nepal and Tibet to Japan, and the 'Southern Schools' that range from Sri Lanka through to Thailand and Cambodia. However, there are Buddhists in almost every country of the world.

Accordingly, Buddhists constantly recollect and pay homage to the 'Triple Gem,'

Zen monks on Mt Hiei, Japan

Thra Pathom Chedi Thai Wat.

namely: the Buddha, born some 2500 years ago in India as Siddharta Gotama, and all the Buddhas since time immemorial; the Dhamma (both his teachings and supramundane reality); and the Sangha (both the monastic community who practice and continue the transmission and the noble followers who tread the path beyond our place and time).

For Buddhists real peace is peace of mind and hence the motto, 'world peace through inner peace,' but it is increasingly recognised that our actions and those of our neighbours are strongly interdependent, affecting the conditions of practice at many levels. So Buddhists need to seek and offer wisdom and compassion that elevate humanity, individually and collectively, through ever-widening spheres radiating outwards. We can learn from anyone with noble qualities such as patience, truthfulness and loving kindness, and we find them especially in people of faith. Hence we engage in interfaith so as to help each other in the steps towards lasting peace, to the end of suffering.

Shortly after the tsunami struck on 26 December, 2004CE, Buddhists were working around the clock to mobilise relief operations, sending supplies to worst affected regions. They also organised ceremonies for those affected, involving thousands of people, ordained and lay, not only Buddhist, but also members of other faiths, supporting each other to offer tranquillity and light in dark times, expressing how far spirituality goes beyond the material, and thus showing the value of interfaith.

SHINTO

THE SPIRIT OF SHINTO

The picture (top) is if the late Rev Yukitama Yamamoto, the inspiration at the Tsubaki Grand Shrine, Japan, and (below) the picture illustrates 'the *Gishiki* ceremony for the Great Spring Ceremony at the Tsubaki Grand Shrine of America. This is the most sacred Ceremony when the Shinto Priest prays for everyone's health, happiness, safety and mutual prosperity.

Shinto is optimistic and bright. Human life is part of nature and the manifestation of the generative vital forces (*musubi*). Human life is essentially good and a gift from the divine world - obstructing energies exist but through the purifying (*harae*), straightening (*naobi*), and invigorating (*kiyome*) action of Shinto we can return to harmony with life giving creative power (*Kami*).

Shinto is based on *Kyoson Kyoei* (mutual co-existence and co-prosperity) so it is a form of spirituality that can embrace other religions very easily.'

Tsubaki Grand Shrine of America

Shumei Taiko Ensemble

The Sound of Shinto

A most powerful and uplifting experience at the last two Parliaments of World Religions was the Shumei Taiko Ensemble drumming events. Here is Shumei's explanation of why it is so moving:

> In ancient Japan, the beat of a drum or *taiko*
> accompanied petitions to God.
> Today, the ceremony lives on and is called *Mikotonori*,
> in which the sound of drumming bridges the divide
> between the human and the divine.
> The thunder of taiko is pure.
> It cleanses both the senses and the surroundings of those who pray.
> Mikotonori is a prayer in which the hopes and thankfulness
> of those participating rise straight to God.
> Such occasions of transcendence are known as *kanno doko*,
> moments in which the spiritual and physical worlds speak
> to each other and are entwined with divine light.
> It was at such a moment that Shumei Taiko Ensemble was born

JAINS: DEVOTION AND DIVERSITY

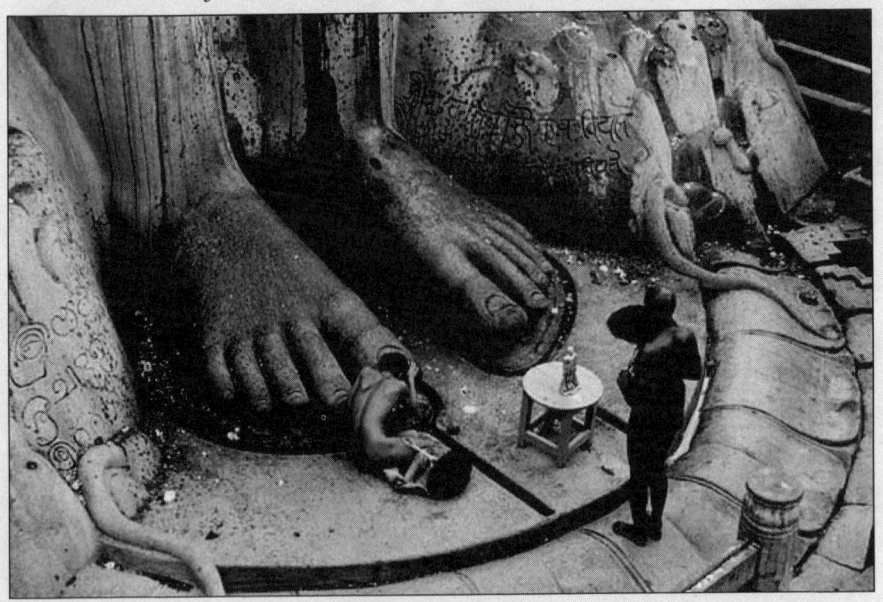

Naked Jain Munis (monks) pray before the 58.8 feet high statue of Bahubali, the revered 2nd Jain Tirthankar (teacher) during the Mahamastakabhisheka (great head anointing) in 2006. Believers of Ahimsa (non violence to any living form), Jain monks and nuns are strict vegetarians. They also never use public transport, but walk everywhere barefoot.

KAROKI LEWIS, an award winning photographer who captured the image above, writes this about the munis: My brief encounter with the ascetic munis during the Mahamastakabhisheka celebrations left an indelible impression on me. I was very impressed by their incredibly strict discipline - eating and drinking only once a day, some walking thousands of miles over several years to arrive in Shravanabelagola, their giving up of all worldly possessions and even their family lives. But, what touched me most was their impassioned plea to people to live in peace and to respect life.

JAYNI GUDKA, one of our young contributors, introduces us to another aspect of the Jain tradition, one that calls us all to the interreligious arena: An important Jain principle called Anenkadvada tells us that there are no absolute theories that can describe reality in absolute terms. Rather, the belief of Anenkadvada tells us that we do not know the complete truth. We can learn from others as well. A famous Jain saying is 'Let truth prevail.' Truth in its final analysis is wholesome and one which leads us to love and understanding. And that is the very essence of all religions, religious tolerance and understanding, making multi-faith work important for Jains and humankind in general.

THE BAHÁ'Í FAITH AND RELIGIOUS PLURALISM
Parvine Foroughi, International Baha'i Centre, Israel

The central figures of the Bahá'í Faith are the Báb (1819-1850), Bahá'u'lláh (1817-1892), 'Abdu'l-Bahá (1844-1921), and Shoghi Effendi (1896-1957). Since 1963 the Bahá'í community has been led by the Universal House of Justice, an institution ordained by Bahá'u'lláh, and elected internationally and democratically once every five years.

The Báb and Bahá'u'lláh and their followers faced the most severe persecutions, tortures and killings at the hands of the fanatical clergy and the tyrannous rulers of the 19th Century Iran. A series of imprisonments and banishments took Bahá'u'lláh and His family to Akka, Palestine (now Israel), and today Akka and Haifa together are the spiritual and administrative centres of the Bahá'í world community.

While covering spiritual issues such as God and creation, Prophets (or Manifestations of God) and their relation to God, to each other, and to humankind, purpose of life, life after death, worship, good and bad, and all that leads to personal spiritual salvation, the Bahá'í Faith also includes social teachings which lead to the prosperity and happiness of the society as a whole. Teachings that fall in the second category are blueprints for the realization of unity of humankind and world peace. They include elimination of all prejudices, independent investigation of truth, equality of men and women, education for all, abolition of extremes of poverty and wealth, an international tribunal or world court, unity of science and religion, a universal auxiliary language, and many more.

Abdu'l-Baha in Paris in 1912.

The Bahá'í Faith's attitude towards 'Interfaith dialogue' is based on the following beliefs:

Bahá'ís believe that despite different understandings of God, in essence God is unknowable, therefore all approaches to Him are acceptable provided that it is understood that God's reality transcends man's limited apprehension. This paves the way for dialogue with different faiths with a genuine desire to search for truth with humility and free from condemnation of other faiths.

Bahá'ís also believe in the unity of all Faiths. It does not mean that all Faiths are similar in their views, but that they are all based on divine inspiration and provide different approaches to the same Reality. All religions have provided divine guidance, but societies evolve and need further dynamic and progressive guidance. Therefore, all faiths complement, rather than contradict, each other.

Another principle concerns the unity of humankind. Bahá'ís reject any discrimination based on race, colour, faith, gender, or nationality. Bahá'í teachings go beyond tolerating other cultures and races and stress on mutual respect and a desire to learn from one another. Their aim is to establish universal peace based on the equality of people and the oneness of Truth.

International House of Justice, Haifa, Israel

The Bahá'í Faith is forward-looking instead of dwelling in the past. It calls on all faiths to unite and create a better future for all, rather than being exclusivist and enmeshed in past differences. It believes that man's search for religious truth, similar to his search for scientific knowledge, must go on, and that religious communities should be prepared to move with the times and embrace new understandings of divine realities.

The Bahá'í Faith is action-oriented, rather than concerned only with pure theoretical speculation. It does not mean that the Bahá'í do not value debates about God and spiritual issues. They believe, however, that the well being of humankind also depends on united, vibrant and progressive action, rather than on endless abstruse speculation and debate.

THE UNITARIAN APPROACH TO THE INTERFAITH REALITY
Rev Dr Vernon Marshall

British Unitarians have always taken an interest in the beliefs and practices of other major religions. Throughout history Unitarians have been amongst the first scholars to study in detail the teachings of the world's religions. These have included Sir William Jones (1746-1794), the first Unitarian to have a detailed knowledge of one of the great Eastern religions. Joseph Estlin Carpenter (1844-1927) was a Unitarian scholar who produced no less than 37 articles, essays or books on various aspects of World Religions. Will Hayes (1890-1959) was a Unitarian Minister who set up an organisation called the Order of the Great Companions, identifying all the great religious leaders of the world's different traditions as equally valid.

Contact with members of other religions has been a feature of Unitarian life for a very long time. It was a Welsh Unitarian, Jenkin Lloyd Jones (1843-1918), who was one of the organisers of the Parliament of World Religions in Chicago in 1893, the first event that sought to bring the different religions together. This inspired the founding, in 1900, of the International Association for Religious Freedom, the world's first inter-faith organisation. There are now many local inter-faith organisations on which many Unitarian ministers and lay people are represented. Unitarians see it as their duty to be involved in this way. Unitarians also often devise All-Faith services and there are worship resources now being created specifically for use at all-faith events. British Unitarians often see themselves as tools for the creation of worshipping initiatives, bringing together adherents from different faith traditions. Prayers, hymns and meditations are being composed that use material from non-Christian sources and appeal to an inter-faith worshipping community.

In the last seventy years, the use of the resources of other religions in Sunday worship has become more apparent. It is very common for services to include material from the sacred literature of other world religions. Also new material is being composed that draws on non-Christian traditions. Hymns are also being written that reflect the interest in world religion themes and that celebrate the great festivals of the world's religions. Occasional services too use much non-Christian material. In *Celebrating Life* (1993), the funeral service alone managed to include material from Jewish, Hindu, Buddhist, Zoroastrian, and Native American sources. The Marriage Service has provision for the drinking from a wine cup inspired by the Jewish tradition. The service for the Scattering of Ashes includes an invocation of the elements of the departed, using words drawn from a Brahmin burial service. A service to celebrate the birth of a child introduces the idea of the invocation of the spirits of the natural world upon the child, something from the Native American Omaha tradition.

The knowledge of the faith and practices of the world's religions is an integral part of the Unitarian consciousness. Respect and integrity are the two words that most aptly define the Unitarian approach to the religions of the world.

Olivia Holmes of the Unitarian Universalists and Megumi Hirota of Rissho Kosei-Kai enjoying a break from the IARF programmes at the Sikh Langar provided for the 2004 Parliament of World Religions in Barcelona.

ZOROASTRIANISM AND RELIGIOUS DIVERSITY
Shahin Bekhradnia, Oxford UK

The religion taught by its originator, Zoroaster, (the name coined by the Greeks and derived from the Old Persian name of Zarathustra) is one based on freedom of choice and personal responsibility. The message attributed to the founder of this religion is found in the Gathas, at the core of the Zoroastrian religious texts that are collectively known as the Avesta. Zoroaster is believed to have originated on the Eastern side of the Iranian plateau, perhaps in modern-day Afghanistan or Tajikistan, and the dating of his existence to around 1500 BC relies on linguistic analysis of the Gathas along with other historical references. The accuracy of the dates is a matter of on-going academic disagreement.

While adherents of the religion are clear that theirs is a monotheistic belief, the religious message has been described by some as an ethical dualism. The creative energy that has given existence to everything within nature is referred to as Ahura Mazda, the wise Lord. Within the creation brought about by this conceptual entity is the ability of the human to understand that two powerful forces may control our minds; one such force persuades us to increase the happiness of life on earth by choosing the path of Asha which equates to purity, kindness, and truth. However we must also be vigilant against a negative force that may easily take control over our thinking and sully our minds, thus propelling us towards bad deeds.

Because the fundamental ethic is to increase the stock of positive energy in the world, the religious calendar is full of festivals which celebrate the bounty of nature: the first day of spring is the most important ceremony of the year, and there are others such as festivals of water, fire, harvest etc. An extension of such thinking leads to cultural developments allowing the community

Jashan ceremony - a flower ceremony or a ceremony of communal celebration or of communal blessings. Fire is present and prominent—as it is in almost all Zoroastrian ceremonies.

occasions to give thanks through rituals and to share happiness together: singing and dancing, drinking alcohol and laughing, wearing brightly coloured clothes and feasting communally.

> *Turn yourself not away from three best things: Good Thought, Good Word and Good Deed.*
> Zoroaster

As the teaching is based on clear minded thinking, it is necessarily a tolerant faith that has at its core an equality of respect towards women and men. The Gathas show that Zoroaster wished to share his message with as many men and women who would listen to him and join him in increasing the store of goodness that abounds on the earth resulting through humans consciously developing good thinking. From this it is clear that any decent human, regardless of faith, may be respected for his/her humanity.

The Zoroastrian ethics of Cyrus the Great, renowned for having liberated and helped the Jews when he conquered Babylon and found them imprisoned there, is publicised in the British Museum's Cyrus Cylinder known as the first charter of human rights. While it is clear that religion was not forced upon their subject peoples, the vast Persian Empire did see forms of Zoroastrianism fused with local practices throughout an enormous expanse of territory. Because of the antiquity of the faith additional texts and legends consequently developed reflecting this fusion of cultures and beliefs.

Another branch of the community, known as Parsees from India, originally left Iran in the 10th century CE because of the persecution of Zoroastrians after the conquest of Islam on the Iranian plateau. At the time of this migration it was a capital crime to try and help someone convert out of Islam back into Zoroastrianism. This led to a prohibition on conversion. Those who derive from this Indian branch are anxious to maintain some of the 10th century cultural and social norms including the prohibition on conversion; this is to some extent helped by aspects of Hindu culture such as the caste system. Most Iranian adherents have maintained a different tradition with its reference point derived from the Gatha that permits conversion into the religious community.

Today there are many individuals and groups outside Iran and India which have adopted the religion of Zoroaster (pictured right) and who call themselves Zoroastrians. Such movements on the one hand are welcomed by the 'progressive' Zoroastrians as an endorsement of their forward thinking faith, but also suspected by some of having ulterior motives.

It is commonly accepted by scholars that Zoroastrian ideas have strongly influenced later religions such as Judaism and Christianity in areas such as the concepts of heaven and hell, angels, the coming of a messiah and the general values they embrace. Some concepts have also been borrowed by Islam, such as the importance of the colour green and the number of daily prayers, but there are fewer common values.

INTERFAITH

JUDAISM AND RELIGIOUS DIVERSITY
Rabbi Jackie Tabick, Chair, World Congress of Faiths

Jewish tradition teaches, 'How great is the Sovereign and Creator of the Universe. When a ruler of flesh and blood, an ordinary king, makes coins and moulds them all bearing his likeness, all the faces are exactly the same, but the great sovereign of the universe creates each and every individual in the Divine image, and yet no two are exactly alike.'

It is a teaching that infuses Jewish teaching and one that is vital to the Jewish understanding of other religious traditions. We believe firmly in One God who created the universe. And if there is just one God, then it follows that it must be the same God, however differently perceived or worshipped, who created us all and conversely, that we are all created in the image of that one God. That belief has consequences for our beliefs and our actions. For many Jews it implies that we must honour the likeness of God in all people - however difficult that may sometimes be! - and not only celebrate the differences between us, but acknowledge the right and the duty to be different.

Within classical Jewish texts it is taught that provided people obey a basic moral code, not killing, not stealing, nor committing incest or adultery and establishing a system of justice for all, then all peoples have a place in the World to Come. Being Jewish is not the only route to Heaven. Indeed, some commentators say it is harder for Jews to get to heaven as we have so many other ritual laws to obey! And therefore, apart from a few minor and disastrous escapades around 2000 years ago, Judaism has never been a proselytising faith.

Penny Faust showing the Torah scrolls to an interfaith group at the Oxford Jewish Centre.

All coins but no two alike. Difference is the essence, the core of our humanity. Then, how we, I, treat the other is a key test of our faith.

> *You must accept the truth from whatever source it comes.*
> Maimonides

Judaism has a Messianic goal, to make the world into the sort of place we feel God had in mind when the Divine creative act took place. Just thinking about God has little or no effect on our world. We have many rituals and detailed laws that help us remember this task. We are great believers in the idea that having beautiful ideas and thoughts is not enough, these must be backed up by specific actions that we are obligated to carry out as part of our covenant with God. It is only if we act, if we try to carry out what God wants of us, that the existence of God has meaning and reality.

We are taught that the Torah is a tree of life. The teachings contained in our tradition challenge us to carry out our responsibility to God by accepting our Messianic obligations. That is what we mean by calling ourselves the Chosen People. We believe we have been chosen to carry out a specific task. At the same time we understand that God is beyond our meagre minds, we cannot fully understand the Divine. But if we play our part fully, then we can be true partners with God in the work of creation and hopefully help bring about a world of justice, truth and peace and along the way find purpose, meaning and joy in our Jewishness.

The Wailing Wall, Jerusalem

ISLAM AND ITS ATTITUDE TO INTERFAITH
Prof Mohammad Talib, Oxford Centre for Islamic Studies

Religious traditions that have survived the test of time have plenty of spiritual resources to view the matters of earth, the heavens, and the fellow human beings both within and outside the specific faith in a single harmony. Clearly determinants outside faith sometime evoke a discordant note. Let such a note not bother us for the duration of the present thought.

The thought for the moment is Islam and its attitude to interfaith. Islam views the beginning of humanity on earth as one religious community (*ummatan wahida*) who lived in active 'submission to the Will of God' (literally Islam). The German poet Goethe captured the spirit:

> If Islam means 'surrender into God's will,' it is in Islam that we all live and die.

Subsequently, diversity set in, and a chain of Prophets brought the word of God for guidance and caution. The Quran recognizes the long chain of prophets that form part of other revealed books such as Torah and Bible. This affinity of Islam and its Prophet with other revealed traditions finds a confirmation in the following:

> O People of the book! You have no ground to stand upon unless you stand by the Torah, The Gospel and all the revelation that has come to you from Your Lord. (Surah. 5 A 68)

A Quranic vision of human diversity holds that Allah made peoples (nations) and tribes that we may come to know one another. This reflects how Islamic civilization learnt from the cultures that preceded it.

Oxford imams from the Madina Mosque, one of four mosques in Oxford, during a visit from an interfaith group.

Such learning is facilitated in the recognition that 'to every people has been sent a messenger.' (S 10:47 and 16:36) The foundation of cultural diversity and religious co-existence draws upon the following:

> To each among you have we prescribed a law and an open way. He would have made you a single People, but (His plan is) to test you in what He hath given you; so strive as in a race in all virtues. (Surah 5:48)

The religious diversity is part of a divine plan so that humans can get to know one another and they compete in doing good works. Similarly, guidance is not the function of communities but of God and virtuous people, and no community can boast of being uniquely guided and elected. No ground for complacence and arrogance in matters of faith.

A true believer never scores an extra point in piety for s/he knows that practices of faith may just be the outer husks needing extra effort to get to the inner grain. This needs knowledge of the right practice and belief involving continuous interpretation and clarification. The holy Prophet gave special value to sacred learning: 'The ink of the learned will be weighed against the blood of the martyrs on the resurrection day,' or a learned man is superior to a worshipper, even to a martyr.

The believer in Islam is reminded that remembrance of God is better than spending gold and silver and better than facing enemy in a battle. A valid practice of faith, like the fragrance of the musk, is evident to the believers as well as any human soul around.

Clearly, the Islamic recognition of diversity is supportive of self-identity coupled with a sense of responsibility toward others. One is not merely different but the presence of others is a normal source of continuous enrichment.

Prayers in Morocco.

INTERFAITH

SUFISM is the mystical path of Islam. MUSSARRAT BASHIR YOUSSUF from Pakistan tells us about the inspiration she has found in its teachings and her special teacher.

With shining eyes and compassionate smile, Dr Mohammad Youssuf Shaheen, (pictured left), lovingly known by his disciples as Baba Jaan Jee recited:

Masjid dha de, mandir dha de, dha de jo kujh dhenda; par kissay da dil nah dhaain, Rabb dilaan vich rehnda.
(Raze the mosque, the temple and whatever else that you can; but never break anyone's heart, as that is the true abode of the Divine).

Through this couplet of a Punjabi Sufi poet, he was stressing what all the great Sufi Masters have accentuated for centuries.*

Sufism is the way of my Baba Jaan Jee to lead seekers of the Truth to the light of Mohammad (Sal-Allah-o-Alaih-i-Wa-Sallam). The term 'Sufism' is the anglicized version of the Arabic word *'Tasawwuf'* to describe the spiritual realm of Islam. It entails the mystic and esoteric trends and practices and the quest for spiritual development in the Islamic world. Thus it pertains to the inner, deeper, subtler, yet strongest currents of the spiritual ocean of Islam. It is not a cult but is the universal way of thinking, which he believes to be the true essence of Islam.

Looking at his glowing face, one can neither notice nor stop love tiptoeing into the deepest niche of one's heart, until the life-changing impact starts showing gradually. Being a doctor by profession, he works full time in his clinic at the age of 68 years. But, it is not only the bodies that he cures of ailments. The soul also convalesces and finds its true potential under his care. He has journeyed deeply into and accomplished the highest levels of spiritual teachings of various Sufi orders of Islam. He is one of those rare Sufis in today's times who takes pains to explore spiritual teachings of various religions and was trained in Hindu and Christian spiritual traditions as well. However, his most favourite way to train seekers of the Truth is through the Qadiri-Qalandri order, with a focus on *Tauheed* (Oneness/Unity), *Noor-i-Mohammad* (Light of Mohammad Sal-Allah-o-Alaih-i-Wa-Sallam), *Ishq* (Eternal Love) and *Ham-aahangee* (Harmony) with the universe.

---

* In Islam, a seeker of the Divine Truth is generally known as a Sufi but there are also titles such as wali, dervish, faqeer, majzub and others depending upon the specific teachings received and intensity of one's personal quest.

My Baba is the University of Tasawwuf where one gains both knowledge and practice of Eternal Love.

Baba Jaan Jee's *Murshad-i-Paak* (Spiritual Guide), Baba Jee Fazl-ur-Rahman, was directly educated in the secrets of Tasawwuf by the Great Sufi Master Hazrat Ghaus Ali Shah Qadir Qalandar, who was born in a Sayyed family (descendents of the Holy Prophet Mohammad, Sal-Allah-o-Alaih-i-Wa-Sallam). His grandfather accepted the wife of a Hindu Pandit to be his foster mother. He deeply loved his foster parents. Along with the highest levels of Islamic teachings received from his family and various Sufi Masters, he also learned Hindu spiritual teachings from his foster father and other Hindu mystics. While being a practicing Muslim and a great Sufi Master, he went to Hardawar to perform the Hindu pilgrimage for the sake of his foster parents.

Continuing the tradition of his spiritual ancestors, Baba Jaan Jee opens the doors to the realm of inner reality of the universe beyond legalistic and ritualistic explanations of faith. He says that Sufism does not advise to nullify or disgrace faith.* On the contrary, it helps to understand the true reality of any faith. The Sufis find unity among diversity, as the message of *Wahdat-al-Wajood* (Oneness of Existence) guides them to focus on the inner reality of things, which is unchanged and prevails in every atom of the universe. This helps them reach out beyond the differences of caste, creed, colour, status and gender: all distinctions created through intellectual or dogmatic understanding. When the so-called religious scholars try to differentiate one faith from the other, the good from the bad and the righteous from the sinners, the Sufis tie everyone together with the bond of the Divine Mercy and Eternal Love that Mohammad (Sal Allah-o-Alaih-i-Wa-Sallam) brought to the whole universe.

He believes that without acquiring some spiritual understanding of the mundane, people would always fall prey to anxiety, fear and hatred. To reach that stage where perception transforms, indefatigable efforts are required to negate and purify common thinking under the guidance of an illumined teacher. Some use ascetic practices to conquer the ego, but my Baba's route is Ishq.** He says that Eternal Love is the panacea that can cure people from the sense of 'otherness' that results into mistrust, conflict and violence.

In Baba Jaan Jee's words: A Sufi resides at the station of harmony with his/her own inner reality and the world around; hence the whole universe becomes a friend. Inter-faith respect can only exist after people achieve inter-heart harmony; which is a gift that can only be granted by the true spiritual teachings of any faith.

---

* Sufis help the seekers of the Truth journey through teachings of faith via four stations ie. *Shriat* (the law), *Tareeqat* (the Way), *Haqeeqat* (the Reality) and *Maarifat* (the Gnosis). At every station the meaning and impact of teachings on one's being widens and deepens to different levels.
** Ishq unfortunately does not have a synonym in English. It can best be translated as purest and deepest love entering into the Divine circle of Eternity. However, it contains all forms of love and yet attains what any other emotion or passion can not.

> Everything else can wait, but our search for God cannot wait.
> — Paramahansa Yogananda

Chapter II

INTERFAITH RATIONALE

INTRODUCTION

Can interfaith really make a difference? Don't religions cause the problems in the first place? What is the point of interfaith? Why should we be interested in it? Here are two good reasons from people who know in South Africa.

NELSON MANDELA, Former President of South Africa said: 'The strength of interreligious solidarity in action against apartheid, rather than mere harmony or coexistence, was crucial in bringing that evil system to an end.'

YASMIN SOOKA, a human rights lawyer and former Truth and Reconciliation Commissioner in South Africa said: 'We need to pursue peace even when we are grossly provoked; in the end people die, not Catholics or Hindus or Muslims.'

In this chapter we explore some of the reasons why people may engage in interfaith activities. They are quite diverse, ranging from community cohesion to scholarly exchange to inner transformation. Reflections on some of these themes can be found throughout this book. The issue of who is invited to the dialogue table is also broached.

Our first rationale keeps many people active.

COMMUNITY BRIDGE BUILDING

There are often tensions between different religious communities sharing close or contested space. The situations in Israel and Palestine, in Kashmir and Sri Lanka illustrate this point vividly.

Is it really reasonable?

COMBINING RESOURCES

Every individual effort for peace and harmony is important and relevant but working together with others, creating the solidarity Nelson Mandela praises (opposite), acting together for common concerns and from a common humanity, may prove even more effective as illustrated by this story from SRILA PRABHUPADA, founder of the International Society for Krishna Consciousness:

A man found a gourd lying on the road and picked it up and then found a stick and a wire and picked them up. In themselves, the three parts were useless. But by putting the gourd, the stick and the wire together, the man made a vina and began to play beautiful music.[1]

Making beautiful music with a vina

Levent Altinay, George Diakos and Deepak Naik

There are many options people can explore to reduce those tensions – political, economic, cultural. Where the tensions involve religious dimensions then there is a responsibility for religious people to address the problems religiously. Quite often the adherents of one religious group know nothing beyond the usual stereotypes about the other religious group. They have never met someone from that religion. They are the 'enemy' only.

A clear example of this came at one of the International Interfaith Centre conferences, 'Facing the Past, Freeing the Future.' This is what DAVID CRAIG wrote about two young men meeting there from opposite religious and national divides:

George Diakos, a theological student at Athens University and an orthodox Christian from Cyprus, sat next to Levent Altinay, a Muslim Turkish Cypriot reading for a PhD at Brookes University in Oxford. Both came from the same island but an island separated and divided. History, ideology and political analysis were clear to each and clearly expressed: the two articulate young men were a paradigm of what it really meant to face the past so that the future might be freed. There was a tangible tension in the room but when Deepak Naik asked what each was going to do when he got back to his community, common ground had been found: each would tell the young people in his island group that the other side wanted peace, and co existence and an end to division. The applause was loud and prolonged and one felt that in that Oxford room, some small step had been taken on either side and that indeed there was a sign that the future would be faced.[2]

> *A Muslim student from N-Cyprus and a Greek-Orthodox Christian student from S-Cyprus, resisting to be brought together at an interfaith conference in Oxford, and leaving as friends.*
>
> *This is what interfaith is about: meeting one's neighbours and enemies as equals.*
>
> Jael Bharat

Interfaith can help bring about positive change by introducing one person or group to another on safe ground. The understanding this produces can even lead to friendship. We have seen it. How beautiful and inspiring it is. Building community bridges includes building personal bridges.

EVA TUCKER of Hampstead Interfaith Group reflects on why she thinks interfaith engagement is important, helping to make a 'kin of all the world.'

About twenty five years ago, soon after I became a member of the Religious Society of Friends (Quakers), I met Margot Tennyson (d.1999). Like me, she had been a refugee from Nazi Germany but unlike me she had long been involved in interfaith activities, had spent time in an ashram in India where she had met Gandhi. Inspired by her, I took on the running of Hampstead Interfaith Group which for ten years from 1995-2004 met monthly in my home and now continues at Hampstead Friend's Meeting House three or four times a year.

I have approached people from different backgrounds - Bahais, Buddhists, Christians, Hindus, Humanists, Jains, Jews, Muslims, Sikhs, Zoroastrians - convinced that in the human condition bounded by birth and death more unites us than divides us. A crucial aspect of Interfaith work has begun as soon as people who might never have met come together in the same room. A seminal moment for me was when, at the last meeting of speakers and members of the group in my home in May 2004, I introduced a humanist professor of biology to a Hindu swami, both of whom had addressed the group on different occasions.

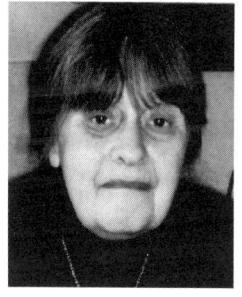

Eva Tucker

I see the different faiths as ladders towards the unknown, perhaps reaching towards a place, if words like 'place' retain their relevance, where the absolute engages in a breath-less dance with the infinite. In the meantime, before that kind of vertical take-off can be achieved, our feet are on the ground. Different religions lay down different directions for those feet to follow. That is where the difficulties begin. The directions are intended not to cage people, rather to set them free to get a more vibrant sense of life, to see the whole of life as a holy experiment.

However, diversity of geographical and cultural background, as well as a sense of being at different points in time, frequently gives rise to misunderstanding, sometimes wilful misinterpretation. The first time I got this sense of time warp was in the 1980s in Nigeria. Ten minutes drive from the university campus in Lagos one was in a village where ways of living had not changed for centuries. But when we in Britain were at that stage there were no jet planes flying overhead. The sense of disorientation is enormous. Political, territorial, consumer oriented motives fan flames of animosity, give rise to conflicts in the name of religion which have little or nothing to do with religion. As when the deity is invoked to aid the killing of individuals, obliteration of groups, the wiping out of whole nations. Where ethnic groups have been uprooted and find themselves in close proximity with others who have previously been at a geographical distance angry confrontations based on trivial incidents can flare up.

For effective engagement in conflict resolution faith and reason, myth and reality, need to interact. It is to try to break down barriers of ignorance and prejudice, very much including my own, that I join in Interfaith activities. Dialogue is as much listening as talking. I try to school myself out of thinking: How can you believe that? into This is how it is for you, to encourage a mutual loosening up of attitudes so that cultural mindsets can begin to be transformed. This does not mean jettisoning one's own beliefs but a realisation of them in a wider context. The words may sound glib, anodyne: it is trying to put them into practice that throws up the rocks of hatred which have to be broken up.

Three hundred years ago William Penn, one of the founding fathers of the religious Society of Friends, said: 'Devout souls are everywhere of one religion, and when death takes off the mask they will know one another.' In the 21st century, with means of communication Penn could not even have dreamt of, we can surely hope to know one another while we are still alive. That hope includes people who may not consider themselves devout souls. I go on trying to modify the way I live, to meet people as individuals without attaching preconceived labels to them, trusting that they, like me, are looking for ways of living which make the need for violence fall away. As a writer, I am in thrall to the power of words as a means towards achieving that end, as a Quaker I experience the power of corporate silence.

JOINT ACTION ON LOCAL OR GLOBAL ISSUES

When we were planning an interfaith event in Germany, we had discussions with many people. One woman we met in Berlin was working with Balkans refugees, people who had been traumatized by the recent wars there. She had found that talking about religion was impossible. Religions were too deeply implicated in what had happened. People's faith had been too radically challenged. Gradually, by focusing on cultural similarities and by bringing people together for social and educational purposes, trust began to grow and eventually the vexed issues of religion could be discussed again. This was needed for the healing process to be developed. Religion was part of the problem so had to be part of the solution.

The raison d'être of many interfaith organizations today shows in their concentration on global, regional, national or local issues affecting many people. There are organizations addressing most issues of mutual concern, including poverty and development, conflict transformation, and solidarity with peoples in distress. Interfaith inclusion has also extended to governments,

> *If we return to a more spiritually-filled life, we shall be able more fully to grasp the need for our commitment to contribute to building a fairer and less destructive society, by working alongside the poor in our own communities, by adopting simpler life-styles, by cutting down on the resources we are wasting, by causing less pollution and by working for more justice in our own countries as well as globally.*[3]
>
> Wendy Tyndale

multi-national organizations like the World Bank, indeed to almost every corner of administrative affairs and ambitions. This is quite new still, a development primarily of this millennium, and the implications of 'official' participation in interfaith agendas will need to be analysed.

Have you noticed it making a difference where you live? If so, how? If you have studied this at all or have any personal experience then you might like to share it with your local interfaith group. To find out where they are, see the Resources section of this book. Get involved. You are needed.

TRAVIS REJMAN, Director of the Goldin Institute, was reminded (not that he ever forgets it!) of the importance of interfaith during a visit to the religiously troubled Philippines:

> As I was getting ready to pack my suitcase and catch my 7 am ride to the airport, a frantic man begins beating on my door. 'House Keeping! Open the door!' House keeping at 6:30 am? What about house keeping is so urgent? But urgency was indeed in his voice.
>
> I had heard many times to be quite wary and to protect myself in this region of the Philippines. That in mind, I opened the door cautiously and thick acrid smoke billowed in from the hall. Having been through the trauma of a fire before, I was surprised at how calm I was as I threw my belongings into my suitcase and made my way out the door.
>
> It was nearly impossible to breathe, and sight was not much easier. I followed the sound of frantic calls, although through the smoke it was impossible to tell if they were near or far - even the sounds seemed to get trapped in the smoke. Outside, I gathered with all the others looking sleepy and confused and we waited as the firemen arrived and worked to contain the fire. Having awoken and dressed to catch an early morning flight I looked oddly prepared for the fire - I think I was the only one with shoes tied and luggage in tow.
>
> My pre-arranged shuttle to the airport was waiting for me as the firemen rushed in, and the desk manager of the hotel approached me to finalize my bill. Following the firemen through the front door, I waited nervously at the desk while he printed my bill and asked me to check it for accuracy. I handed him my credit card watching firemen race up the stairs behind me. He told me that yes; everyone was out safely, and then apologized for the inconvenience.
>
> We walked back outside; I got inside the shuttle, and watched the smoke rise out of the top of the building as we pulled away towards the airport.
>
> I have great respect for the men and women fire fighters who enter these bleak situations and fight the blaze. I was equally amazed by the willingness of the staff of the hotel to go into such a dangerous situation and continue to work:

Travis Rejman

continue to try to make things function in an extremely adverse situation.

I left Manila with the same great admiration for the grassroots religious and spiritual organizers and leaders who are similarly working for peace amidst a painful and difficult - often dangerous - conflict. The current situation is characterized by ignorance, fear, misunderstanding, hatred, violence, and discrimination. Far from a luxury to be conducted in remote academic or civic locales, these courageous leaders are leading a vital movement for interreligious dialogue, understanding, harmony and cooperation. Against this backdrop, many courageous leaders from the Christian, Muslim and indigenous communities are expanding movements for peace.

Reflecting on the experience of the fire the morning I left, I had and have great appreciation for these grassroots leaders who are willing to fight through the choking smoke of a smouldering history of mistrust and discrimination. I am amazed at their courageousness and vision. It is not easy or popular to mobilize towards a vision of a community that respects all the religions and ethnicities when violence and tension mar relationships. Given the region's history, it is a miracle that they can still see diversity not as a problem to be solved, but as a resource.

I am proud to stand shoulder to shoulder with the organizations, communities and courageous individuals profiled in this book as we strive to promote understanding and cooperation in a world in need.

RELIGIOUS AND THEOLOGICAL EXCHANGE

After horrors like the attack on the World Trade Center, bombings in European cities, the invasions of Afghanistan and Iraq, and communal violence in India and Africa, the confidence of particular religious or ethnic groups may be especially vulnerable. Following such occurrences, the ignorant may herd whole groups of people together and brand them 'enemy.' People from some religious groups, particularly where they are minorities, may feel marginalized, misunderstood, misrepresented. Interfaith dialogue can provide a forum where the unheard can be heard, where stereotypes can be dissolved, where the alienated can become integrated. The existence of such a forum can be a real resource when something happens to disrupt relations beyond the norm.

Theologians too find such forums relevant in their explorations of religions. What is different, what is shared in world religions? Are there mutual influences? Are there universal teachings? Do our sacred texts promote division and violence or lead us to peace and unity? Can there be such a thing as a global theology?

JOHN HICK, the great pluralist theologian and philosopher wrote: 'Between ourselves and God, as God is in God's ultimate transcendent being, there is a screen of varied and changing human images of God - not graven images but mental images, or pictures, or concepts of God. And our awareness of God is always through and in terms of these human images. We worship God through our own images of God, to which our human ideas and cultural assumptions have inevitably contributed. These mental images not only differ considerably between religions, but also within a given religion. In fact if we could see into one another's minds now I believe we would find a great range of images or concepts of God.'[4]

Can a theological exploration together - Hindus, Muslims, Christians, Jews etc - help us understand the Divine better, fill in the gaps as it were?

ANANT RAMBACHAN, Professor of Religion at St Olaf College, thinks we must do this. He said at a World Council of Churches meeting: I seek insights within my tradition, knowing that the questions which are asked in other traditions and the wisdom which they embody, could be profoundly instructive. For if God is the one God which my tradition proclaims God to be, then, surely, what my fellow human beings are saying about God is relevant and challenging to me and requires explanation and understanding on my part. My Christian and Muslim brother or sister may be speaking differently, but they are speaking about that which is dearest to me and which is also the goal of my own existence. This is a truth of tremendous significance which unifies me with the worshipper in every tradition, in whose prayer I hear the longings of my own heart.[5]

> *We were delighted to be told a parable of an 'Inter-Number Conference.'*
>
> The numbers present were far too polite to argue but each of them nonetheless considered themselves as superior to the others. Each was closer to Infinity than the others. No.1 thought he was naturally first. No.2 felt that a lot of the others were decidedly odd. He was the top of the evens! Everyone knows that 3 is the most mystical of numbers. Zero maintained that none of the other numbers could reach infinity without him.
> The parable does not warn us away from reaching out to the Infinite, but reminds us not to be judgmental.[6]
>
> Richard Thompson
> Oxford Society of Friends

INNER TRANSFORMATION

It might be possible that meeting a person of another faith, participating in an interfaith event or practicing the meditation or prayer style of another tradition, may not only change our outer life or enhance our thinking but also lead to deeper inner transformation.

There are many people in the world today who can no longer say they are exclusively of this or that faith but define themselves by two faiths, for example, Hindu Jain or Buddhist Christian. Many others, while still identifying their allegiance to one particular faith, yet turn to another for additional sustenance. Books abound of Christians practicing Zen Buddhist meditation or incorporating Hindu rituals into their devotions. Many Hindus revere the saints and sages of other traditions and place pictures of them on their altars. The holy book, Guru Granth Sahib, of the Sikhs, contains inspiration from beyond the Sikh Gurus. Interfaith worship provides opportunities to explore the mystic and ritual heart of faiths different to our own.

Here are two examples of the impact of entering a tradition different from our own. The first comes from John Hick, Christian philosopher and theologian, and the second from Dom Peter Bowe, a Benedictine monk who participates in inter-monastic dialogue.

JOHN HICK: I have been practising meditation, in a faltering sort of way, for some years, using the mindfulness method that I learned from the Sri Lankan Buddhist monk Nyanaponika Mahathera....The one moment of breakthrough that I have experienced so far was only a few months ago. In normal consciousness I am here and the world is there, apart from me, surrounding me and so to speak hemming me in, and arousing all sorts of hopes and fears. But as I opened my eyes after perhaps ten minutes of meditating I was suddenly vividly aware of being an integral part of the world, not separate from it, and that that of which I am part is a friendly universe, so that there could not possibly be anything to fear or worry about. It was the same world, and yet totally transformed, and for a short time - only one or two minutes - I was completely free and completely happy. I was by myself at the time; but if this new consciousness had continued into daily life I believe that my attitude to others would have been a liberation from self-concern making possible love and compassion for everyone I had to do with.[7]

PETER BOWE: I recall an interfaith retreat for monks and nuns of all faiths held about ten years ago at Amaravati, the Theravada monastery in Hertfordshire. At the early morning meditation we were all seated together before a large, golden image of the Buddha. For myself I was seated before Christ, and yet for a moment I had the clear intuition that the figure of the Buddha and the figure of the Christ were overlapping. Do the Enlightened One, the Purusha and the Cosmic Christ in some indefinable way overlap? I do not know, but I hope that they do. And I do not know if the various faiths can ever agree that this, unknowingly, is what they seek? But I do hope it can be so.[8]

As we have read, interfaith dialogue brings challenges but also the possibility for inner transformation, for the awakening of real faith, resilient and not afraid.

MOHAMED MOSAAD of the United Religions Initiative in Egypt shares his thoughts with us about this process in 'Dialogue: The Need to Distance.'

Quietness, tranquillity, serenity and confidence are good characters, which are usually attributed to someone having faith. They reflect how this faith is deep, solid and firmly established in the heart of believer. That is certainly right, but if this is the quality of faith you want for yourself then you may want to think carefully before joining interfaith dialogue. I do not mean interfaith dialogue made me have no faith. I think I have; and I think it is not less strong.

My faith, however, has become anything but quiet; it is turbulent, wild, rampant and unruly. Now, I hardly enjoy coming back home after attending night prayers in the mosque to peacefully sleep in bed. Questions, ideas and possibilities keep popping up in my head, banging and nagging, sometimes so persistently that they became normal and expected companions.

Learning about Buddhism makes me rethink Islamic Sufism; reading Judaism I find myself making analogies with Islamic Law; listening to a lecture about Christianity I instantly revisit all that I have known about revelation in Islam; and

Mohamed (right) next to Swami Agnivesh at an interfaith dialogue meeting.

making acquaintance with Hinduism I startle from the flow of questions, which could never come to my mind earlier. You keep thinking, reading, asking, reflecting and rethinking; and you keep doing this forever. The quietness is over, but what remains is even more desirable. What remains is a vivid and living, active and throbbing form of faith, which I call the positive faith. You do not believe; you are believing. You stop resisting the flow of questions, for you now enjoy them. You enjoy the answering, that ongoing process that never ends. You keep knowing God and you thrill with the experience of this most of your time. You welcome what others dismiss as doubt because it has became the source of your joy and ecstasy.

Faith as an ongoing process of questioning and answering, or self dialogue, is impossible without a necessary distance between the believer and the beliefs; and it is interfaith dialogue that can create this distance. It creates the necessary distance for the faith journey. It is not haphazard, I guess, that all the Prophets in the Quran had travelled it in one way or the other. Moreover, it is an explicit

Buddhist, Muslim, Jew worship together in the Holy Land.

Inner Transformation: Meeting the Mystical.

Quranic commandment to 'travel through the earth.' We need to travel, to quit what we are used to so that we know the yet unknown and reflect on what we thought we knew. We need the feeling and the look of the stranger to continue our faith journey.

Interestingly a reader of Hadith, the sayings of Prophet Muhammad, comes quite often to this introduction: 'A Bedouin came to the Prophet and asked him about such and such.' One of the Prophet's companions once marvelled at the size of knowledge that had come through the answering of those 'questions of Bedouins,' the people who live a large distance away from the Prophet. They are questions that had not come, in fact that would not have come, to the minds of those who lived with the Prophet.

Serenity is neither an abandoned hope nor a desperate dream. It is a promised end we hopefully find at the end of our life journey. It is only there where we meet the truth!

CREATING A NEW WORLD RELIGION

This has not happened yet but may well be an agenda for some people. Those with a universalist approach may feel that a new world religion, combining the best of all traditions and abandoning the worst, will enhance peace and harmony in a world too troubled and bruised by religious differences. There are organizations that train people to be interfaith ministers.[9] Organizations that claim to be spiritual not religious, so welcoming all.[10] Religious syncretism in its many varied forms is increasingly popular, especially with young people. At certain stages in life many of us may feel we want to be free to explore our spirituality and not have it confined to narrow dogmatic tunnels.

Some people feel threatened by interfaith for this reason. They do not want their faith subsumed in a 'soup.' Others value the rich diversity of different religions and what can be learnt from them about Ultimate Reality. They see religious difference as a blessing, given by God.

Many interfaith organizations, working with established religious traditions, prefer to maintain religious boundaries and not engage with religious syncretism. This is partly because those from the established religious traditions themselves do not want to be too closely associated with religious groups that may have sharply different world-views or methodologies from their own or which may even be perceived as heretical or unbalanced. There is in many interfaith organisations a cautiously conservative approach to who is invited into the dialogue and some 'new' religious traditions or organisations are seen as troublesome. Difficult questions might need to be asked to unravel all the motives for this.

MARK GIFFORD, Interfaith Director with Minorities of Europe, tells us about his interfaith journey and his freedom from specific religious labels:

I am from a mixed faith background. My family, who brought me up with values and love, never directed me towards a particular spiritual path and I have never been initiated into any religion.

Mark Gifford

I've always found the question 'what faith are you?' a bit difficult to answer. My mother is a Zoroastrian, my father is a Christian, I have a Hindu guru and I strongly suspect that I'm a reincarnated Muslim! So you could say that the idea of 'interfaith' has a particular resonance for me! Despite this diversity however, my spirituality is not an area of confusion. I feel spiritually grounded by my connection with my guru and I am inspired by and seek to recognise the beauty and wisdom in all spiritual paths. For me, this approach is deeply nourishing. The only difficulty I have is classifying my 'faith' according to notions of religious affiliation.

I do remember on one occasion being asked the question and remembering, as part explanation, Guru Naanakji's famous words, spoken after his divine vision in the River Bein: 'There is no Hindu, there is no Muslim. So whose path shall I follow? I will follow God's path for God is neither Hindu nor Muslim and the path I follow is God's.'

What does Naanakji mean? Certainly not that God is a Sikh! Perhaps he means that God, the single, supreme source of all existence, actually transcends religious boundaries. That, as human beings, our relationship to this Ultimate Reality is not, in the end, mediated through anything other than our own inner qualities. I believe these words of Guru Naanak are of particular relevance to us now, as more and more people in our increasingly diverse, multi-faith societies find themselves, either by birth or conviction, in a similar position to my own, finding it difficult, misleading or unnecessary to define their religious

NELSON MANDELA, when he became President of South Africa, created a deliberate inclusion policy for all the faiths represented in his country. He felt that 'the strength of interreligious solidarity in action against apartheid, rather than mere harmony or coexistence, was crucial in bringing that evil system to an end.'

Receiving the Juliet Hollister Award at the Parliament of World Religions in Cape Town, 1999, he spoke of the influence of religion and religious people on his life. When Mandela was growing up in the apartheid regime, no one was interested in educating black youth. In South Africa at that time 'it was religious institutions whether Christian, Moslem, Hindu or Jewish…who bought land, who built schools, who equipped them, who employed teachers and paid them. Without the church, without religious institutions, I would never have been here today.'

Also, when he was imprisoned and subject to human cruelty in many forms, it was religious people who helped him and the other prisoners. Again, it was 'religious institutions, Hindus, Moslems, leaders of the Jewish faith, Christians… who gave us the hope that one day we would come out…. And in prisons, the religious institutions raised funds for our children who were arrested in thousands and thrown into jail.' Because of this support from religious institutions, many black South Africans became educated and open to new opportunities. 'That is why we so respect religious institutions and we try as much as we can to read the literature which outlines the fundamental principals of human behavior like the Bhagavad-Gita, Koran, the Bible and other important religious documents.'

Religion was one of the motivating factors of the first post-apartheid government. The President stated: 'In our own South African society, we have identified as a crucial need…an RDP of the soul - a moral Reconstruction and Development Program.'

Mandela's message for the whole world is not different. 'In drawing upon its spiritual and communal resources, religion can be a powerful partner in such causes as meeting the challenges of poverty, alienation and the abuse of women and children and the destructive disregard for our natural environment.'[11]

affiliation in a straight forward manner.

It is often pointed out, quite rightly, that the goal of the interfaith movement is not the creation of a single Super Religion; and that the special integrity of each faith should be recognised and celebrated. Each faith is certainly unique, but just like St. Anthony, who sought to embody admirable qualities that he observed in other people, we can also learn from and savour so much in other faiths. In so doing we move towards a richer experience of life; perhaps finding our own tradition illumined, or the opportunity found to heal aspects of ourselves that have lain dormant or been denied. This movement in turn leads towards unity with others. Knowledge, sympathy and love come to characterise our relationship with other faiths, also thereby assisting them to express the best of themselves.

This healing of division and journey towards unity within ourselves and with others is, I think, the true significance of 'Interfaith.' Guru Naanak's words point us beyond sectarian preoccupation and the importance of self definition. They focus us on the truth of our strivings and our primary identity as followers of God.

Naanak says it is so!

DIALOGUE PARTNERS

This issue of inclusion and exclusion is increasingly part of arranging interfaith events. Organisers worry that if such-and-such a group turn up in numbers, others will stay away and credibility will be lost. When in Germany, we heard a story about a conference in Berlin that was going really well until someone stood up and said 'I'm a Scientologist.' This was enough to collapse the whole event. Surely this has to change? People of faith can surely show some of it on such occasions?

Sandy Bharat: One of my earliest interfaith experiences of this kind of anxiety was as a member of the coordinating committee for the launch event of the 1993 Year of Interreligious Understanding and Cooperation. We were seated around a table discussing whether or not pagans should be invited to contribute to this event. The Hindu swami sitting next to me asked me quietly, 'What are pagans?' I whispered to him, 'Swamiji, that is what Christians used to call us!' In the same year, at the 1993 Parliament of World Religions in Chicago, the inclusion of Pagans there caused the initial walk-out of some Christian participants. One day a Pagan walked into the offices of the International Association for Religious Freedom where I then worked and told how she was being discriminated against at her work-place - a hospital - and asked for support as an issue of religious freedom.

We hear politicians tell us that they won't talk to such and such a group until they have reformed their ways whilst they continue to make their own plans for war and invasion of another country. Why are we so afraid of who joins the dialogue? If we do not fear a new world religion do we fear the breakdown of the old familiar religious worlds?

Sandy: The first meeting of the Exeter University Interfaith Group, initiated by Helen Fry and myself, was with Marcus Braybrooke. He choose as the title of his talk, 'Dialogue or Die.' It is that important. I remember though, going with Helen to a local shop keeper, a Sikh, with the hope of enticing him and other members of his community to this opening event of our new group. He took one look at the title and became very anxious - who was going to die if he did not join the dialogue? Alas, we never did see him at our meetings!

In a lecture given at the Congress of the International Association for Religious Freedom in Budapest, 2002, DR HARRIET CRABTREE (left), Deputy Director of the Inter Faith Network of the UK, addressed this topic of 'Who comes to the table of dialogue?'

[A] particularly thorny question, in contexts where inter faith initiatives are set up to be 'representative,' is the question 'who comes to the table of dialogue?'

Some may think that 'who comes to the dialogue table' is a non question. Indeed it is one that people can get quite angry about and think should not be asked. 'Why,' they may say, 'Surely anyone who wants should be allowed to be involved?' All very well on the face of it but a statement that an event is to be utterly inclusive is likely to ensure heavy participation from universalist inclusivists but almost to guarantee the non participation of the more conservative strands of the historic faiths. Similarly, some of the older religions, for example, rarely agree to be part of a process where the really new religious movements such as Scientology are at the table. And the prospect of Pagans at the dialogue table can lead some Christian Churches, Muslim organisations and others to stay away.

Each situation is, of course, different. An informal organisation set up to explore spirituality in different traditions may flourish with a completely open door policy because it is about spiritual quest rather than representative 'religious politics.' But by contrast, organisers setting up a national interfaith organisation with a public role in a multi faith country, may want to involve first and foremost the largest faith communities and organisers and be willing to leave out small controversial groups whose presence could drive the main faiths away.

This is because unless the main faiths are actively involved, there is little chance of this kind of organisation flourishing in its intended role. So, decisions about the pattern of involvement usually have to be taken or they often take themselves by default with some faiths opting out or fading quietly out of the picture because others have been allowed in. We have to recognise reality and decide how to deal with it if we are to achieve our particular goal. There is no right or wrong answer but each answer inevitably has its consequences. I should add, though, that flourishing inter faith initiatives around the globe prove that we are all finding ways to surmount the challenges on this front![12]

Dom PETER BOWE shares with us his reflection on the challenges and rewards of dining at the dialogue table!

Perhaps I may start on a personal note with a question I constantly face: How can I, a Christian, approach people of other faiths with a completely open mind, giving full weight to their beliefs, while at the same time holding fast to my Christian faith? And another question: in my desire to build bridges, so urgently needed in our society, by interfaith dialogue am I in danger of surrendering the ground of my faith? How can I be both practically committed to my own faith - faithful to my practice - and at the same time open to the new?

I have been a Christian monk for some forty years now, committed to the search for God, as St Benedict puts it. But in the latter years I have discovered the riches of other faith traditions, and have come to recognize the parallels, the contradictions and the challenges of these ways of faith. We can say that we are all seeking God, seeking the Divine, the Other, the Absolute, the Tao, or the Great Void. Do I seek only in terms of my own faith as I have always done, or am I now somehow seeking in a new and wider context of inter-religious consciousness?

For me as for many my Lord is Christ, himself icon of the ineffable God. For many more their Lord is the Buddha or the Dharma, or Krishna, Shiva or Brahma, Yahweh or the Torah, the All-Merciful One or his Word in the Qur'an, or the Tao and so on. But being faithful to my faith and practice does not mean that I just meet with others and listen to them politely, sharing with them what I believe and no more. I learn from them, am inspired by them, from them find new insights into my faith and inspiration for my practice, even hear God speaking through them to me. Yet I remain ready too to confess to them who is my Lord.

In the end there is for us in this interfaith journey nothing more to be done than to delve deeper into our own roots of faith. If I am truly and deeply rooted here, in my place, then I am already there, in the other place, the place of the other faith. Consciously or intentionally to go there may paradoxically distract and deflect me from my own search for the

Peter (r) at Nalanda, a Tibetan Buddhist Centre in Southern France.

Divine, for my going there is liable to be less personal, to be more intellectual or emotional and therefore somewhat superficial. For each of us our own place is the best place, the right place, our source. And our task is to know and to own this place more fully.

None of us can discard our preference for our own way. A Christian cannot discard the Trinity or Christ's incarnation, and no Muslim would think of abandoning the way of the Prophet, no Buddhist the Middle Way of the Enlightened One.

In the final analysis, my own experience is that the more I have entered with integrity into an inter-religious context and awareness the more I feel I have grown in my own faith commitment.

SUMMARY

Interfaith activity can help us learn more about others, their beliefs and values. It can help eliminate ignorance, stereotyping and prejudice. It can help lay firm foundations to overcome and appreciate differences, address perceived injustices, provide a forum to meet common goals, and facilitate dialogue and deep listening by linking people and organisations for the common good. It can help us learn a lot about ourselves too.

All together there seems to be quite a strong rationale for developing interfaith relationships!

> *Community is actually a loaded word; who is within or without of our community?*
>
> *At what point do I exclude someone from entering the community?*
> *I think it is important to ask oneself, each day, why am I a member of my community?*
> *What is my purpose of being here?*
> *Whatever faith I belong to, these questions never cease to be relevant.* [13]
>
> Sr Maureen,
> Brahma Kumaris

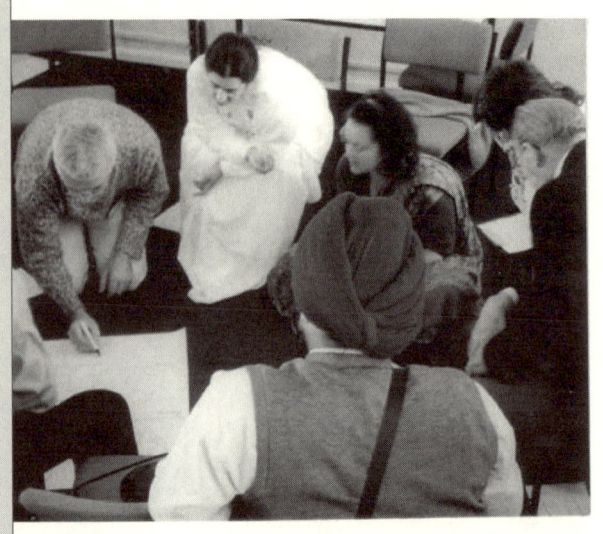

Maureen (in white) with interfaith group at an IIC conference.

This interfaith is great!

Chapter III

EXPERIENCING INTERFAITH

INTRODUCTION

What happens when people try out interfaith activities? Is the experience positive or negative, mystifying or mystical? Of course, everyone will have a different memory of or motivation for interfaith actions in which they have engaged. Sadly, the majority of religious people never get to experience interfaith at all. Some of them choose not to do so, others have never heard of its possibilities. One of the great challenges for the interfaith movement is to make itself known and relevant to more of humanity. Recent events labelled 'religious terrorism' are beginning to awaken the world to the value of interfaith while at the same time denting many people's perceptions of the value of religions. An interesting paradox!

Sandy: My own first interfaith event was a World Congress of Faiths (WCF) conference. Coming from a Hindu world-view, religious pluralism was natural for me so I had no problems with meeting in a mixed religious context. Soon after this, with a friend and fellow student, Helen Fry, we started the Exeter University Interfaith Group. At our stall on Freshers evening we enjoyed the company of several Christians who felt the need to warn us of the perilous journey we had begun! One regular attender at the group was a Muslim student who sat quietly attentive through meetings but raced to the door at the end in readiness to hand out his rather exclusivist leaflets!

Some of the Exeter Interfaith Group at the last meeting before Sandy left for Oxford.

> **Professor Huston Smith:**
>
> *At every stage in my religious life I was perfectly happy with what I had -- until along came a tidal wave that crashed over me.*
> *For example, I was perfectly content with Christianity until Vedanta -- the philosophical version of Hinduism -- came along. When I read the Upanishads, which are part of Vedanta, I found a profundity of worldview that made my Christianity seem like third grade.*
> *Later, I found out that the same truths were there in Christianity -- in Meister Eckhart, St. Augustine, and others. But nobody had told me, not even my professors in graduate school. So, for 10 years, though I still kept up my perfunctory attendance at my Methodist church -- a certain kind of grounding, I think, is useful -- my spiritual center was in the Vedanta Society, whose discussion groups and lectures fed my soul.*
> *Then Buddhism came along, and another tidal wave broke over me. In none of these moves did I have any sense that I was saying goodbye to anything.*
> *I was just moving into a new idiom for expressing the same basic truths.* [1]

More significantly, I met many people from different faiths in those early interfaith days who have become and remained close to my heart and from whom I have learnt much. From one, Tom Gulliver, a Quaker, former WCF Secretary and founder of a Buddhist-Christian dialogue group, I even learnt important social skills such as the necessity of deciding at tea ceremonies whether you are a pre or post-lactationist!

On reflection I don't think that what I learnt about the religion of these friends has had much impact on my life but what I experienced from them as people of faith certainly went deep. Indeed Jael and I met at an interfaith event. Quite an experience!

Tom Gulliver

JOHN HICK, the eminent and ground-breaking philosopher and theologian, who has spent a lifetime advancing intellectual and spiritual insights into religious pluralism, wrote this reflection on the significance of experience:

> By religious pluralism I mean the view that all the world faiths are authentic and, so far as we can tell, equally effective contexts of salvation/liberation. In my own case, the move to this from my Law student evangelical-fundamentalism (verbal inspiration of the Bible etc) was a slow evolution, not a sudden jump. Having already moved well away from that earlier theology, the critical change came when I moved to the multi-faith city of Birmingham to teach the philosophy of religion at the university. I soon became involved in

'community relations.' This included the religious communities, and I visited mosques, synagogues, Sikh gurudwaras, Hindu temples, as well as Christian churches. It became apparent to me that, beneath all the differences of architecture, decoration, atmosphere, languages, belief-systems, essentially the same thing was going on in all of them – namely, human beings coming together, under the auspices of an ancient tradition, to open their minds and spirits 'upwards' to a higher reality which makes a claim on the living of their lives. And the basic principle of this claim is the same, a regard for others as fellow children of God, although of course the detailed applications differ. (My encounter with Buddhism, which does not think in terms of a God, was to come later).

This decisive step for me in Birmingham was not caused so much by thinking as by the new experience of meeting people of other faiths. And the most effective contribution of the interfaith movement to a more global religious outlook is, I think, to enable and bring about that experience as widely as possible. I myself continued it in several visits, usually of about four months, to different parts of India, one to Sri Lanka, two shorter visits to Japan, and a short visit earlier this year (2005) to Iran. All this, together with the annual meetings in the U.S.A. of an International Jewish-Christian-Muslim group and also of a Buddhist-Christian group, has led to a profound respect for these other faiths. But without having to roam the world there is plenty of opportunity for inter-faith meeting and dialogue, both organised and between individuals, in this country.

However in the course of that roaming I have had the very good luck to encounter several 'saints,' in the sense of people much more open to the Transcendent than I am, people in whose presence one cannot but believe in the higher reality which inspires their lives, and which they speak of as God, Allah, the Holy Trinity, Brahman, the Tao, Nirvana or the universal Buddha nature.

One, who died a few years ago, Kushdeva Singh, was a doctor and religious activist at Patiala in the Punjab, inspired by Mahatma Gandhi; one was the Buddhist monk Nyanaponika who also died a few years ago and who lived in a forest hermitage near Kandy in Sri Lanka, a profoundly impressive spirit who was also a considerable scholar; one is an Anglican archbishop

John in dialogue with Sandy and Jael Bharat.

whom I knew in South Africa during the apartheid years and have kept in touch with ever since, another religious activist; and one a Catholic priest in Birmingham who died a few years ago, yet another religious activist.

None of them of course thought, or think, of themselves as saints. But such people – and there are innumerable others, in many degrees and many spheres of life, not at all well known – by the spirit that shines through them and the example of their lives help the rest of us to persevere on our own path.

The overall lesson, to me, is that an ounce of experience is worth any amount of theorising.

Experiencing interfaith can have many impacts on us, not all positive. Meeting others at an interfaith event is like meeting people anywhere. Some you will feel drawn towards immediately as friends, some will touch you in a way that changes some aspect of your own faith life forever, still others will need some serious attention before either their message or they themselves appeal to you! At interfaith events people bring their faith with them, out in the open as it were, so this can also be both enchanting and disconcerting. Proselytizing can be in the air and is usually most unwelcome.

Sandy: I recall an event where a Muslim member of the group began to explain how Islam had come to India to dislodge the weeds and plant fresh and beautiful flowers. Not everyone at first realized the implicit message in this. However I felt incensed and told him this was not the way to speak of the religion of some other members of the group (including my own of course!) He just shrugged and said, 'Well, it's the truth.' Of course, becoming angry about such matters does not show much spiritual development on my part!

> **DOM PETER BOWE:**
>
> *At the end of a day in which we had entered into four quite different religious traditions, I found myself reflecting that the Sikhs seemed to me to demonstrate the best of what I am more familiar with in the Protestant tradition, and the Jains, with their attention to detail, to purity and to non-violent living, to mirror the tradition of some committed religious confraternities and orders.*
> *But it was the Hindus, with their powerful symbolism and lively popular participation, whom I most warmed to as closest to the sacramental tradition of my Catholic faith. I reflected that, were I not already Catholic, I might well find it most natural to turn to the throbbing human symbolism - even sacramentalism - of South Indian Hindu faith to express my human longing for the divine!*
> *The stunning ancient Tamil temples, awesome in their architectural grandeur and powerful symbolism, are deeply spiritual places and have quite captivated me.*
> *But however that might be, I am at least clear that the rich treasuries of faiths other than mine not only expand my horizons and open up converse with other men and women, but more importantly also water the deep wells of my own spirit searching for God in and through Christ.[2]*

Japan Dialogue Tour

JOAN MILLER describes a day in a Dialogue Tour of Japan that she joined, organised by the International Interfaith Centre and hosted by Rissho Kosei-kai. The tour introduced us to various kinds of Buddhist and Shinto practices which we experienced against a backdrop of cherry blossom.

Despite the strong Christian connotations of this particular day it turned out even more an interfaith experience than expected! Joan wrote about it this way:

Joan and John Miller

'We celebrated Easter by a short service in the Great Hall, Kyoto with a Buddhist lighting the candle, a Hindu playing the organ and the element consisting of bread and sake. It was indeed different, and a significant experience for many of us.'[3]

It was Joan's husband John who initiated and led this celebration and the participants included Bahai's and a Unitarian as well as Buddhists, Hindus and Christians.

ANURADHA DEVI DASI (right) explains how an interfaith music gala, organised by the International Interfaith Centre, affected her and enhanced her own spiritual experience. Anu wrote:

Some had written their own songs, or composed their own music while others chose more traditional expressions. It was clear that all were offerings of the heart.

The first Jewish song took me by surprise. It was an experience of Judaism I had never before encountered in interfaith gatherings and set the mood for what was to follow. I felt engaged in interfaith at a level beyond verbal presentation or dogmatic overviews. This sharing of intimate devotional practice was an awakening for me. It was an engagement not just of the mind but of the heart and although the styles and melodies varied greatly, the underlying mood and intent was re-echoed in each contribution.

Navleen Kaur (right) with Sikh musicians from UK, Punjab and Afghanistan at the Interfaith Music Gala

> The whole event stimulated this understanding:
> Despite all cultural or philosophical differences, this was a unified
> out-pouring of devotion through music and song.
> Different styles and different beats but the same yearning, the same
> reaching out beyond and, deep within, to the Self.[4]

In his biography, Fr ALBERT NAMBIAPARAMBIL of the World Fellowship of Interreligious Councils in India tells this story of a transformation brought about by a person of one faith experiencing a realization about the experience of a person of a different faith and how he moved others by sharing his story. Albert writes about a participant at a three-day interfaith gathering in Kerala in 1974:

> There was one known Gandhian among the participants. He was all silence on the very first day. On the second day he came out with this sharing: he went home all pensive as to what his religion – as a Hindu – was to him. He had till then never asked this question to himself. Casually, he took a weekly, the Illustrated Weekly of India. His eyes fell on the cover page of the journal with the picture of Mother Teresa holding an emaciated black child in her hand, with a crucifix as the background.
>
> He turned the page, started reading her story: that every morning she took part in the Holy Eucharist, in the celebration of the Mystery: This is My Body. Later on, going out into the street, she felt her life as the continuation of this, 'This is My Body;' that for her the abandoned, the dying, and everyone is Jesus. At this moment, he told us, he began to cry like a child. He added that he understood, then, what his religious experience is for him.
>
> There was a deep silence in all the partners of that deep communion, an experience of growing by sharing.[5]

MARCUS BRAYBROOKE has been involved, on a voluntary basis, in interfaith work for over forty years, initiating and supporting innumerable interfaith organisations. He has found a way to embrace God in all people and faiths he meets. He is not afraid for his own faith but has found it deepens through his interfaith interaction.

Not everyone is able to realise this. They wonder if their faith will be compromised by contact with others or if they have to promote their own religion at interfaith events. Marcus shows us that the best promotion of any faith is through the person you are, the example you give.

All who know Marcus know how caring he is, not only of people of his own faith. We have experienced this personally. He is also an excellent educator. Wherever in the world he speaks about interfaith he always inspires. Also he is someone willing to encourage and support as well as inform at every level, in every place, from the personal to the communal, from local to international.

My vision is of a world with a Heart; a world in which we live out the teachings of non-violence, love, compassion and reverence which are to be found in all the great faiths. The vision will not come true without our co-operation. It will be realised as we allow the Divine to touch us and to transform our hearts.[6]

Marcus Braybrooke

HANS UCKO of the World Council of Churches tells us how a special woman inspired him and contributed to his interfaith experiencing:

Let me pay tribute to a Zanj. Thawra is an Iraqi woman of African descent and belongs to a community in Basra, whose existence is the legacy of slavery throughout the Middle East, one thousand years old. Arab traders brought Africans across the Indian Ocean from present-day Kenya, Tanzania, Sudan, Ethiopia and elsewhere in East Africa to Iraq, Iran, Kuwait, Turkey and other parts of the Middle East. Though centuries have passed since the first Africans, called Zanj, arrived in Iraq, African traditions still persist among the Zanj. Thawra is a doctoral candidate in theatre and acting at Baghdad University's College of Fine Arts and is now writing her dissertation about healing ceremonies through dramatic performances in her community.

The Office on Interreligious Relations and Dialogue of the World Council of Churches and the Vatican Pontifical Council for Interreligious Dialogue invited her and some 40 Africans from Africa as well as from the African Diaspora to a conference in Addis in 2004. We wanted to provide an interreligious space enabling Muslims, Christians, people following African traditional religions, Candomblé, Santeria, as well as African-American Christians, to explore the contribution of Africa to religious and spiritual life in the world. Thawra, a devout Muslim woman, could hardly believe her ears that a Christian organisation had invited her to 'come home' to Africa. She said she would do anything to participate. She did. She tried to go from Basra to Kuwait and from there on a flight to Addis but was refused entry. She went the dangerous way to the Jordanian border and was turned back by the Jordanian border control. In an email she told me that she would try via Damascus. Finally her persistence paid off.

As she opened the door and entered the room and the conference, one after the other rose and applauded her. She had made a long journey, Thawra from Basra in Iraq. Now she was finally at home. Africa welcomed her back home. Her presence, her stories about the Zanj (the name echoes the origin in Zanzibar) in Iraq, how they sang and lived their daily trials, surviving through thinking of Africa, came to incarnate the very meaning of the conference: Africa as the continent bringing together its children from all over the world, people, who have never forgotten Africa, who have always longed to go back, people who now together could celebrate being together. This togetherness gave this interreligious conference a powerful spiritual community dimension.

Prof. John Mbiti, Thawra, and Maria Lourdes de Siguiera, a mother in the Afro-Brazilian religion Candomblé.

The other day she sent me an email about her life right now: 'Many times I think about ...that the summit, to which you invited me, changed my life. Now I'm working with civil society and putting myself up as a candidate for election to the parliament. The situation in my city (Basra) is not good. As you know there are many Islamic parties and people seeking a secular government.'

Thawra, a pillar of strength: a Muslim woman, a Zanj in Iraq today. Praise be to God for such people.

PETER RIDDELL (pictured below) from Initiatives for Change offers this reflection on how interfaith encounter can help us deepen our own faith: 'Everyone has a next step.'

When I started work in London in the mid-1970s with a programme to foster trust between Britain and the Arab world on the basis of common moral and spiritual values, I got to know a leader of the Arab students in Britain. I used to visit him from time to time, and he seemed to value the chance to talk. He was Muslim by culture, but he inhabited a cynical world in which members of his committee were agents for different embassies, and where nothing in the Middle East was as it seemed. As I didn't have much to say on these subjects, I mostly listened, though I used to tell him something about my own work and, when asked, about my (Christian) faith.

Then one day, he had something new to tell me. He had encountered financial difficulties, and in desperation had resorted to prayer. The next day, out of the blue, a relative had phoned and offered him exactly the sum that he needed. He felt it was an answer to prayer. It was a turning point in his life, and a new spiritual dimension began to make itself felt. He began to pray the Muslim five daily prayers. He told me that previously, if he was attacked verbally in a meeting, he used to set out to 'kill' (metaphorically!) his opponent. But now, he said, he had stopped responding in that way: what the other person said or did was between him and God, and God would treat him appropriately. I recognised a similar phrase from my own scriptures.

He later told someone, in my presence, that his rediscovery of his faith owed something to our conversations. I did not know what part I played, or what to make of a Muslim rediscovering his own faith in part thanks to a Christian. But the fact that he was taking steps towards what I understood as holiness gave me confidence.

It is a precious gift to be an instrument in the process by which another person finds the next step in his/her spiritual development. I can similarly identify important moments in my life when I have been helped by people of other faiths. I believe this is the noblest relationship that people of different faiths - or of the same faith, for that matter - can have with each other. In that spirit, people deeply rooted in their own faith traditions can live in close communion with each other, and work together on matters of common concern.

EXPERIENCING INTERFAITH THROUGH ART

The Ashmolean Inter-Faith Exhibitions Service (AIFES) is a new initiative which aims to bring people of different faiths together through works of art. AIFES is directed by Professor James Allan, a specialist on the art and architecture of the Islamic world. The aim is to put on exhibitions on religious themes, using works of art representative of the different faith communities represented in the UK. The first exhibition was entitled 'Pilgrimage - The Sacred Space' and was held at the Ashmolean Museum in Oxford in January 2006. The Heritage Lottery Fund provided financial support for an Education Outreach Officer to work with the exhibition and local faith communities. The exhibition was accompanied by a book of the same title. AIFES is encouraging other museums in the UK to share similar experiences, and to borrow this, or other similar exhibitions, to help bring together people of different faiths within their own communities.

Glass enamelled mosque lamp, early 14th century, Egypt or Syria

ANAS AL-ABBADI, of the Jordan Interfaith Action Cooperation Circle, shares this report of how art was used as a medium to bring together young people for an interfaith experience at the Art and Religion Contact-Making Seminar held in Amman, Jordan:

The theme of the initial contact-making seminar was using art as a tool for dialogue between religions. It was held in Jordan in the spring of 2004, where 29 participants representing 21 organizations coming from 14 different countries (Palestine, Egypt, Israel, Tunisia, Turkey, Portugal, Spain, France, Sweden, the Netherlands, Germany, Greece, Italy, and Jordan) gathered in Amman to come out with projects addressing young people on the theme of art and religion.

The five-day event went through several stages, where participants were introduced to each other. An interesting highlight was when an Egyptian young man for the first time in his life met with a Jew, or even an Israeli. Participants represented the three Abrahamic traditions, Judaism, Christianity, and Islam, and the

The true artist helps the world by revealing mystic truths

By Bruce Nauman from a window or wall sign, 1967

harmony and the relationships that were built between the Palestinian participants and the Israeli participants were good proof that peace is possible in our region. Our organization was claiming - and still does - that religion is not the problem in the Middle East, but for sure it can be the solution.

It was also a great chance for European participants to learn more about the situation in the Middle East, and especially in Jordan. One of the interesting things was said by one of the participants from Europe: 'I really want to apologize to all the Arabs and especially the Jordanians; I was planning to not attend, because I was worried and afraid because of what I see every day in the news. But now since I am here, I can see with my eyes the reality and the great hospitality that you practice here.'

The Jordan Interfaith Action Cooperation Circle is the first of its kind in Jordan, and it aims to build bridges of understanding between Jordanian youth and youth from all around the world, especially in the Middle East region.

Canon DAVID PARTRIDGE, a retired Anglican priest and totally non-retiring peace/interfaith activist, recently wrote about his experiences of regularly joining Muslims for Friday prayers:

There were two main factors behind my decision to join those praying at my local mosque every Friday. First, came the discovery that, suddenly, the make-up of the protest marches expressing concern about the prospect of another war in Iraq had changed beyond all recognition. One of the things that struck me about this newly politicized Islam was its prayer times in Hyde Park and Trafalgar Square. It came home to me that Muslims and Christians were not only protesting together they were also praying (and crying) about the same questions of peace and justice.

The second factor was a reflection on sheer numbers. At a Good Friday service a couple of years ago, organised by six churches and led by our diocesan bishop, the total congregation, including part attenders, came to no more than 60. From that service I went straight on to Friday Prayers at the new but unfinished mosque in the Muslim part of the city. It clearly wasn't a special or 'Good' Friday; just the equivalent of a normal Sunday service, but attended by at least 600 males of all ages.

For me every Friday feels like Good Friday in the intensity of listening to the Punjabi or Urdu prayers whispered by my neighbours. Their never failing acceptance of me as a fellow-pilgrim rather than a semi-detached fly on the wall hints of Easter, especially when their elbow-warmth is accompanied by a correction about some detail of the liturgy I have missed or performed inappropriately.

One of the amazing things about this journey is that my own faith doesn't

A Christian-Muslim-Jewish Walk for Peace in Oxford, 2005 (David is far right in his cassock)

feel in the least threatened. People seem pleased to see me, and accept that becoming a Muslim is not on the agenda. My Christian faith feels challenged and confirmed by meeting with the godliness of others on the road, and on the other side of all the religious barriers of history. I have come to believe passionately in the godly mission of Christians and Muslims in their struggles to understand and trust each other.[7]

Sr ISABEL SMYTH of the Scottish Inter Faith Council tells us about how she became committed to interfaith dialogue and understanding:

I often think I am a very unlikely candidate for inter faith work. I grew up in a Catholic family in the west of Scotland, went to a Catholic primary and secondary school, trained to be a Catholic teacher and then entered a convent and became a Catholic nun. On reflection this was a very closed if secure and happy upbringing for which I am very grateful but it gave very little thought to people of any other faith.

This all changed when I went as a young sister to do religious studies at Lancaster University. Not only was I exposed to the beliefs of others but I met people of faiths other than my own who were obviously committed to and inspired by their faith. It was as though scales were removed from my eyes and my horizons were enlarged so that I could see my view of the world was one perspective among many. This was unsettling as it challenged many of my core beliefs and led me to question many aspects of my own faith but it also led me into the world of others and a vast reservoir of sacred texts and wisdom which have both inspired me at a personal level and helped me come to a new and deeper understanding of my own faith.

Lancaster University was a turning point in my life which, to use Christian terminology, I think of as the most graced moment in my life and which, in spite of the fact that it is a secular space, was for me a sacred place changing my life and leading me to many new experiences and many new friends. One of these friends became very significant in my life and has remained so although she died nearly twenty years ago.

Returning to Glasgow I knew I did not want to get drawn back into a narrow religious community and was surprised to discover a place called the

Christian-Buddhist dialogue: Isabel (left) with Gelongma Ani Lhamo on Holy Island.

International Flat which was home to the first inter faith group in Scotland called the Glasgow Sharing of Faiths. The flat was run by a Church of Scotland deaconess called Stella Reekie, an amazing woman who had been a missionary in Pakistan and now worked tirelessly for inter faith understanding and the integration of people of all faiths into Scottish society. Stella was an inspiration to many and when times are difficult in my inter faith work I imagine her sitting on my right shoulder and whispering in my ear 'don't give up, don't give up.'

Perhaps the sentiments expressed at her funeral sum up the ideal of good inter faith relations. These came from a Sikh friend who said 'Many of you think of Stella as a Christian but she encapsulated the virtues of compassion, love, justice which are important to a Sikh. Just as liquid takes the shape of the vessel into which it is poured so too for me Stella Reekie was a Sikh.'

Rev DAVID CLARK from the Leicester Council of Faiths tells us about the highlights of a pilgrimage he joined, organized by Christians Aware:

Our pilgrimage in October 2004 was to the Holy Sites of Sikhism in the Punjab. We were led by Amarjit Singh Grewal, a young religious leader from Leicester. The climax of the pilgrimage was three days spent in Amritsar in the Golden Temple.

Pilgrimage seems to be a feature of all faiths. It usually involves travelling and putting your body in places which have become holy. Such places are set apart because of their association with people and events which are still significant for the religion in question. In Sikhism it involves visiting beautiful and tranquil gurdwaras (temples), with heads covered, hands and feet washed.

At the beginning of the pilgrimage, I was reminded of one of the Bani (songs) recited every morning by Sikhs, which translates thus:

(Men) may take baths at places of pilgrimage, exercise acts of mercy, control their passions, perform acts of charity, practise continence and perform many more special rituals....Even then all these are worthless and of no account, without meditation upon and Love for God.

The Golden Temple At Amritsar

Pictured is a small group of Christians and Sikhs with the Jathedar of Sri Akal Takhat Sahib (supreme authority of the Sikhs) and some of his officials. (David is far left)

A Sikh Pilgrimage also means empathizing with some of the tragic pages of the faith's history. When we visited the Gurdwara at a place called Pariwar Vichhora Sahib (Family Separation Place) near Roopnagar we learned that this was the place where 10th Guru Gobind Singh's mother and his two young sons were separated from him. They were surrounded and captured by a vast army of Moguls, leading to the deaths of the boys. This was marked by another beautiful gurdwara built on a high raised platform, like a pyramid, with a school at its feet.

The high moment of the pilgrimage is the early morning visit to the Golden Temple. We paddle through a gully of flowing water to wash our feet and enter a gateway into the open space mostly filled by the spacious still water of the sacred Tirath or pool. In the centre, reached by a causeway, rises the breath-taking and perfectly proportioned Golden Temple. Inside, every space in the sanctuary is filled around the musicians and the granthi or reader of the scriptures. All sorts of pilgrims are sitting around reading prayers, contemplating, or listening to the holy songs from the Guru Granth Sahib (Sacred Scriptures of the Sikhs): children, teenagers, old folk and British pilgrims. The sense of goodness and devotion all around is present and almost palpable. I felt my own trust in God strengthened, as I sensed the love of God in these calm respectful crowds.

In the picture (above), we have each received the siroopa. This is an orange length of cloth, which the granthi (temple official) unfolds and ceremonially drapes around your neck with the chanted prayer *Bolé sonehal*, to which all reply *Sat sri akal*. (Whosoever says it is blessed: God is truth). We were honoured in this way in each holy place.

EXPERIENCING A PARLIAMENT OF THE WORLD'S RELIGIONS

The mission of the Council for a Parliament of the World's Religions is to cultivate harmony between the world's religious and spiritual communities and foster their engagement with the world and its other guiding institutions in order to achieve a peaceful, just, and sustainable world.

Barcelona Parliament 2004: Feeding the 8,000! The Sikh community provided a tent where they served langar every day to Parliament participants.

Parliaments are held every five years and attract thousands of participants from around the world, from different countries, faiths and cultures. The last Parliament was held in Barcelona in 2004. Over 8,000 religious leaders and lay people took part in this amazing event. Rev Dr. William Lesher, Chair of the Council for a Parliament of the World's Religions' board, pointed out the immeasurable outcomes of the Parliament. 'Along with the strong commitments made, the mere presence of 8,000 people from so many different religious and spiritual traditions and places in the world is a meaningful outcome in and of itself.'

The Council for a Parliament of the World's Religion's Executive Director, Dirk Ficca, said: 'When people of faith commit to address religious violence and other pressing issues facing the global community they follow through. We make a commitment not only to the world, but out of a deeply rooted religious or spiritual conviction. The Parliament's priorities over the next five years are to assist the world's religions in meeting their commitments. Our organization's work does not start or end here.'

One recent trend is the creation of buildings especially for interfaith. So far the most successful projects of this kind have been linked to religious communities or universities. They have all required immense dedication, patience, and perseverance from the project teams. Fund raising can take years and is not for the faint hearted! In this book we have contributors from two of these special centres in the UK: Fergus Capie from the London Interfaith Centre (see Role of Religions chapter) and EILEEN FRY from the University of Derby. In the profile opposite Eileen tells us all about the wonderful new interfaith centre now in action that she, with many others, has helped nurture into being.

THE MULTI-FAITH CENTRE AT THE UNIVERSITY OF DERBY

The Multi-Faith Centre at the University of Derby is not a place of worship although worship may take place. The Centre has a Board of Trustees, an Executive Committee, a Programme Committee, three paid staff and about twenty volunteers. The project, started in 1992, has been a culmination of seven faith traditions (Bahais, Buddhists, Christians, Hindus, Muslims, Jews and Sikhs) working together with a common aim and purpose to build a Centre of neutral spaces to be used for education, dialogue and discussion.

In 1996 an architect's competition was launched with the brief to produce plans for a building which would be acceptable to all faiths as a 'village of spaces' with rooms for administration; social activities; Ecumenical Chaplaincy of the University; Reading Room; Quiet Space and Meeting Rooms. Backed by the University of Derby a fundraising campaign started and eventually raised £2m with 50% from the Millennium Commission and in June 2001 the Centre became a registered charity. In 2004 a unique building with curved white walls and an impressive wood clad prow like a ship opened with principal rooms of different heights, a minimum of furniture and no religious artefacts or imagery. An outside staircase leads to the roof garden set with low growing mosses and plants for outdoor events or a quiet place just to sit and be. The Centre has been running events since the Autumn 2001. For example:

The 'Big Question' series took a topical or ethical issue with a debate from two or three faith perspectives.

The 'Female in Religion' involved female speakers talking about their roles within their faiths.

Using the Multi-Faith Directory, Religions in the UK, as a basis for a 'World Religions' series we investigated nine faiths over nine weeks culminating in a session on inter-faith.

Two very successful events of Asian Music, when over 200 people came to listen to 'Sarangi' and 'Thoughts and Beats' concerts.

Joint celebration of Divali with the Sikhs and Hindus.

First Annual Lecture: Bishop Kenneth Cragg, 'Seven Decades of Christian Islamic Dialogue: Illusion or Reality; what might genuine Meaning-Meeting require of both?'

University of Derby Multi-Faith Centre

Our website will continue to advertise and promote the work of the Centre as will the twice yearly newsletter distributed across the UK to members and supporters.

All citizens would wish to build a better future for the generations to come, with education about other faiths, looking at similar and differing points of view and working at respect and understanding. To live together in peace and harmony can only work when we know more about each other; understand, respect and value our differences and acknowledge our common humanity.

The Derby Multi-Faith Centre will not shrink away from difficulties but will work with friends and supporters to resolve issues and problems. My wish is that we might be a blue-print for other Multi-Faith Centres to spring up around the UK. However, in all this fluidity one thing is certain it won't be easy and we won't always get it right but at least we can say we tried!

Dr RICHARD BOEKE, a Unitarian minister, centres on thoughts about his interfaith journey and some landmarks along its way:

In our global village, life is not independent, but interdependent. In the words of Martin Luther King, Jr, 'By the time we have eaten breakfast, we have depended upon half the world.'

In 1958, I read Albert Schweitzer's autobiography. I was struck by his words, 'Example is not the main thing in influencing others. It is the only thing.' I realized that to be a more effective human being, I needed to belong to groups that shared my convictions. I became a Unitarian Universalist. From my base as a minister, I began an interfaith journey in the International Association for Religious Freedom (IARF). To me, at heart, the IARF is a religious community that works to create a wider circle of religious trust and friendship.

Later, I met a young Dutch lady named Jopie. She became my partner and wife a year later. After our marriage, we drove south for a summer in Mississippi as part of the civil rights struggle. One week we drove to Selma, Alabama, where Martin Luther King Jr had marched after the murder of Unitarian Minister, James Reeb. Our last night in Mississippi, I was to preach at an old Universalist Church in Ellisville. I asked, 'Where is a good place to spend the night?' A lady whispered to me, 'Get out of town.' After I preached the sermon, we 'got out of town.' That night another Unitarian minister in Mississippi was shot in the back and almost killed.

The 1990 IARF Congress in Hamburg, Germany was a dramatic time! The Berlin Wall had come down. Hope was in the air. Yet Catholic Theologian Hans Kung opened the Congress by saying, 'There will be no peace in the world until there is peace among religions.' As we witness the present wars of religions we see how true this is. Let us take the next step, and fill the world with interfaith friendships. I cherish my friendships with those of other religions.

In 1996, at the Korea Congress, Chief Priest Yukitaka Yamamoto of Tsubaki Shine became IARF President. In World War II he survived in the jungle of New Guinea. On return to Japan, he stood under the purifying waterfall daily for ten years to clear his spirit. There is no suitable waterfall near my home, but several times each week, I take a long walk beneath old trees. I face the sunset and chant a Buddhist Sutra. In the evening I stand in the shower, and repeat the Tsubaki chant: *Harai tamae; kiyoei tamae; rokkonshojo.* Purify me, wash my soul, all six senses.

When my wife Jopie also became a Unitarian minster, we moved to England, where she could have a church of her own. At IARF 2002 in Budapest, she became President of the International Association of Liberal Religious Women and a Trustee of the IARF. She is much in demand to conduct weddings and has co-edited a book of religious poetry.

I became active in the International Council of Unitarians and Universalists (ICUU), and became their 'ambassador' on over a dozen journeys to Eastern Europe, India, and Japan. I have prepared several services on the Unitarian Martyr, Michael Servetus, who was burned at the stake by John Calvin in 1553. Servetus discovered the pulmonary circulation of the blood. He found holiness in the breath. He found rigid creeds divisive. He found the breath of the Holy Spirit, inspiration, in faiths outside Christianity. I find him a spiritual ancestor in our struggle to bring peace between religions.

Richard, Jopie and their 2 daughters in front of Horsham Unitarian Church (founded 1648).

After I arrived in England, Dr Marcus Braybrooke, the President of the World Congress of Faiths, invited me to join. As a trustee of the WCF, I enjoy friends of other faiths. I learned the difference between faith and belief. I organized conferences on 'Faith as Trust—Fideology.' Fideology is a word I coined from the Latin, Fides. Often interfaith dialogue is blocked by talk of theology, a word that leaves out Buddhists, Jains, and Humanists.

FIDEOLOGY, the practice of Trust, is a task for every human being.

We all seek our separate peace, but we have to make peace together.

Prof NORBERT KLAES shares with us an interfaith experience that he has never forgotten:

Together with many friends of Religions for Peace, I have been working, planning, organising, struggling for many years. As an inter-religious organisation we jointly aim at global peace, social justice, the realization of human rights and cultural values and the liberation of people. In trying to achieve a little bit of these demands we often experience a tremendous sense of unity with our fellow workers, with the under-privileged people who suffer, with all those who try to overcome these difficulties, and with the earth to which

Norbert in professorial mode at our home

we belong. In co-operating for the realization of world peace, we are not primarily interested in the religions as such but in the future of this planet. We hope that the religions relativize their absolute claims and devote themselves in full responsibility to the fostering of world peace in dialogue, in agreement and understanding with other religions. They are challenged to draw from the most vivifying of their respective traditions and spiritualities that which best advances justice and peace in the world. In this context, I sometimes unpredictably experience moments of great happiness and envisage the realization of an emerging harmonious community of nations and people.

Though it is not a direct intention of our interfaith movement to cultivate dialogue as a possibility of a deeper mutual inter-religious understanding, or to discover elements of unity in diversity in the religions, nevertheless, the comprehension of the universal demands and beliefs of the various religious persuasions, with profound respect for their differences, and personal relationships and deep friendships of the members of the various religions, are of significant importance for the practice of inter-religious co-operation. This is emphasized in the many, often moving multi-religious services which are held at all the occasions of conferences and assemblies of Religions for Peace.

But personal encounters and conversations are often as important as the common prayers. Still today I am impressed by an intensive discussion which took place some years ago. One evening, in the context of a conference of our interfaith movement, some of us sat together and talked. Two women, an Israeli and an Indian follower of the Hindu non-dualistic school (Advaita), told us about their deep friendship and how they felt united even in their profoundest religious experiences. A Christian from Europe doubted whether such a religious unity could be possible between a Jew who believed in Jahweh and a Hindu who tried to dispel the Illusion by Knowledge of the Ultimate Reality or

Brahman. At first, the women jokingly said that the poor man probably felt a certain uneasiness since he was not included in their friendship. But then we began to seriously and thoughtfully discuss. We told each other about our experiences and meditated together. The later it became, the shorter was the exchange of views, the longer was the time of silence. The night passed by in a flash...We discovered great differences in our convictions of an ultimate reality, and, at the same time, the awareness of a deep belonging together. We understood one another better than ever before. We cautiously interpreted this experience that by trying to comprehend the ultimate source of all beings we were seized by this *in*comprehensible and evading divine reality....

Hopefully, such experiences might lead to a deeper understanding of the *inter-faith* dimension of the common responsibility for world peace.

SENSEI SEVAN ROSS, Chicago Zen Centre.

In my own experience, argument does not bridge the gulf between traditions - only experience does. So I have concluded that we must try another, fairly radical approach to free us from this cycle of entrenched prejudices repeating themselves. I really feel that it is the only way to short-circuit the process. Stated simply, it is this: We should make little, or possibly no attempt at all to exchange information about, nor to try to 'understand,' the various institutions, beliefs, or doctrines of each others' faith traditions or communities; we should instead only seek to exchange practices and throw ourselves into each others' actual practice settings. We need to wear each other's traditions PHYSICALLY for there to be any hope of our finding real, enduring common ground, respect, or understanding. Doctrinal exchanges, discussion of ideas or beliefs or institutions - indeed, even discussions of the physical practices themselves - can be counter-productive, confusing, and are certainly woefully insufficient. We need to 'walk in the shoes of the other' in order to come to know the other as ourselves.

There is a clear reason for this conclusion: Every spiritual tradition requires at some point a suspension of disbelief - a leap of faith, if you will - for that tradition or community to come alive. No religious tradition makes 'sense.' All require us to make two moves beyond where words and reason can go. The two moves are Faith and Experience. And these two are linked. One cannot have faith that passes common intellectual understanding without that faith being informed and invigorated by real tactile, on-the-ground experience. And there will be no experience without that initial faith in the meaning and potential of experience....

(With) faith leading to the willingness to experience the inner truths available in any real faith tradition, and experience leading to yet deeper faith, spiritual traditions can bubble over with deep insight, behavioural change, inner peace, and even some inter-tradition community.[8]

VISITING FAITH COMMUNITIES

Experiencing a visit to another faith community can have quite an impact. Going in a group can be a safe introduction to a different faith world from your own. Not everyone finds the experience positive - sometimes the cultural differences we experience can be challenging or we may find we are not ready to take part in a community's devotional or ritual life if the opportunity is offered - but usually what we discover changes our perceptions and breaks down our prejudices and opens our eyes to new understandings and possibilities.

This is what a young student, SYED HUSSAINI, reflected on and experienced on a visit with our International Interfaith Centre interfaith group to faith communities and centres in Oxford:

'I think that fear of the unknown is one of the causes of hatred. In many instances this has led to deadly conflicts. In our present day world most people don't know enough about the religion of other people or they have twisted knowledge. Throughout history and in the present, this has caused a lot of bloodshed. With this view in mind and my interest in other faiths, I thought that I should find out how much I know about other religions or how much wrong information I have. This would be a good indicator as to how much ordinary people of our planet know.'

After visiting the Oxford Centre for Hindu Studies (OCHS), Syed continued, 'Although I have lived next to India, and have watched a lot of Indian television, I realized that I know nothing about the Hindu religion and most of the things I knew about the religion were false. For example I came to know that one can become Hindu, previously I thought that one could not. I also came to know that this religion is totally non violent, unlike the deeds of some violent factions of Hindus in India…I came to know that different deities represent different aspects of God.'

The result? 'The experiences from this visit, along with my other two visits to the Christian Orthodox Church and the Jewish Centre, strengthened my view that ordinary people know very little about other religions. The IIC is doing an excellent job in providing people with first hand knowledge. I wish we would have more such organizations in all parts of the world. This will make societies more tolerant.'

Bhajans, devotional chanting, at OCHS during our visit

This is how another young participant, GRACIE RIDDELL (r), experienced her visit to the Orthodox Church in Oxford which serves three communities – Greek, Russian and Serbian:

'The Orthodox Chruch was incredibly beautiful – it took my breath away. The scent of flowers mixed with the incense to create an amazing atmosphere. I learnt that icons are important in the Orthodox Church because they are an affirmation of God's incarnation – if he hadn't become human it would be impossible for us to depict him.'

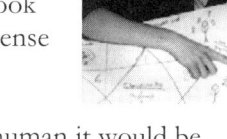

The experience of such a visit does not just belong to the visitor It is a two way process. BEDE GERRARD (left, showing the group round this church), spoke about what he learnt from such a visit: 'As I showed the group round, I needed to consider the idea that there are certain key concepts within faiths which both make one faith different from another and also bring out different elements they have in common. Trying to convey to others the essential concepts of the Orthodox Christian faith helped me to make concrete my own faith. By telling others what I hold pivotal, I was led to examine these central elements and see where they are expressed in my own life.'

GILL SANDERS, then Deputy Lord Mayor of Oxford, spoke of how all her visits to and engagement with other faith communities had impacted on her. 'All of these occasions were incredibly enriching experiences that I will always remember and, on each occasion, I went away with a better understanding of the many religions and cultures that we are surrounded by and also, I have to say, appreciation of the delicious food that accompanies many of these events.'

As Gill said, 'We are living through very difficult times when religion is occasionally being used as a tool to create unrest and distrust between countries and people of different faiths and beliefs.' Visiting others in their centres, finding out who they really are, getting to know them, becoming at the very least better informed, can provide the foundations for an understanding and experience that prevents religion being misused and misrepresented.[9]

Gill (r) viewing IIC's Through Another's Eyes Exhibition

INTERFAITH

> PADDY MESKIN of Religions for Peace shares her moving experience of
> 'Celebrating Difference'

As a young girl growing up in the Apartheid years in South Africa, I was always aware that my parents treated all people with great courtesy and kindness, no matter who they were. Considering that, at the time, the law of the land encouraged the white community to see people of colour as subservient and to treat them with neither respect nor dignity, this could sometimes be surprising.

Strangers often came to our home and were given whatever assistance my parents could give them. A favourite saying of my Mom's was, 'It is better to give than to have to receive, and if you don't have to receive, you must give.' She certainly practiced this maxim.

We had a very mixed religious upbringing (my father's parents were Jewish and Christian and my mother used to describe herself as a 'Bush Baptist' having had a taste of many different religious communities) that is until we started school at the convent, when finally my father decided that we would now be Catholic.

I believe that I was very fortunate to have been exposed to these values at such an early age. They have stayed with me all my life and influenced me in the work with which I have been involved over the past thirty five years, particularly in the interfaith arena.

My experiences were in sharp contrast to some of the tragic stories that I have witnessed during this time. So much of the inhumanity to humankind, the violence and abuse, particularly of women and children, and the destruction of communities is a result of the fear of the different, the lack of understanding of those who do not behave as we do, who eat or talk or dress or believe in an 'other' way.

I want to share a story with you that took place during the Truth and Reconciliation Commission (TRC). It was to make an enormous impact on me then, and continues to do so to this day.

In 1996 I was asked to assist with art therapy for children who would be making their depositions to the TRC over a three day period. I was happy to

Paddy (left) with students from the Youth Peace Forum presenting Peace Quilts on International Peace Day.

Children at Maveli Nursery - an AIDS/HIV project assisted by WCRP

be of assistance, although I knew that the experience would be extremely grueling. I had just finished interviewing some of the Holocaust survivors living in Durban for the Holocaust Survivor's Remembrance programme, initiated by Steven Spielberg, and knew how traumatic that had been.

On the first day, we started the morning playing and singing with the children and keeping the group occupied as each child made his or her deposition. The children ranged in age from about 7 to 17 years. Some were shy, others smiled and even laughed. All were nervous. They had already told their stories to a counsellor and now it was time to tell their story to the Commission.

I had seen Bishop Desmond Tutu, the chairman of the TRC, crying on TV as he listened to some of the stories. The tragic experiences of thousands of men, women and children who had been persecuted, violated and even killed, because they were different. The children's stories that were told over those two days were to make us all weep. It was hard to believe that human beings could behave in this manner.

As the children finished their depositions, we would take them aside and work with them, either on their own, or with a group if they wished. On the second day, I was working with a little boy who was almost nine years old. He wanted to draw and I sat and chatted to him as he completed his picture. The picture is as clear in my mind today as it was that day nearly ten years ago.

A small square house burning; on one side a big tree with a little figure sitting in the tree; in front of the house three figures lay on the ground, one a woman; all three had 'blood' pouring out of them; and in the background, three figures with no faces, but holding guns.

I put my arm around him and asked, 'Mandla' (not his real name), would you like to tell me about your picture?'

'This is my story,' he said in a very quiet voice. 'That day the men came, my Mama told me to run and hide. I was very frightened and didn't know what to do, but I climbed the tree in our garden. The men pulled my Mama and Daddy out of the house and also my brother, and they shot them. Then they ran away.'

He gave a big sniff and continued, 'I waited in the tree because I was so frightened. At last, one of the neighbours came and took me to their house.'

We were both crying and as I hugged him I said, 'Mandla, do you know why those men came and hurt your family? Were they cross? Had your Mama or Daddy done something wrong?'

'No!' he cried. 'My Mama and Daddy were good people. They killed them because we were different.'

'But Mandla,' I said, 'Just because you are different does not mean that you cannot get along and even like or love someone.'

'I don't know,' he said, 'I only know that for us, if you were different you got hurt.'

As I listened to his story, I thought of how, through the centuries, so often war, violence and destruction erupted because two people or two families or two countries were different. My own father-in-law had ended up in Auschwitz because of Hitler's hatred of those who were different. Mandla's story made me realize how vital it is to *celebrate* the differences! To see the joy, the colour, the gifts that are there for us all to enjoy, if we only open our eyes.

I have worked in the Interfaith World for some twenty years now. The more I share and learn from my colleagues in the many faith groups within which we operate, the more I realize how far we have come, but also, how far we still have to go.

When I sit around the Pesach Seder table with my extended family, I see how it is truly possible for people to come together from different walks of life, yet love and care and share with one another. For we are an interfaith family, a family with many different parts. We celebrate those differences. We have learnt that although we believe in One God, there are many paths by which to reach Him.

I conclude with the words of a beautiful song from our Jewish liturgy that says:

> *Hine ma tov umanaim shevet achim gam yachad!*
> How good and pleasant it is for brothers and sisters
> to come together in unity!

Paddy also introduces us to the
WORLD CONFERENCE ON RELIGION AND PEACE - SOUTH AFRICA.

As men and women of religion, we confess in humility and penitence that we have very often betrayed our religious ideals and our commitment to peace. It is not religion that has failed the cause of peace, but religious people. This betrayal of religion can and must be corrected.
(Kyoto Declaration, First World Assembly of WCRP in Kyoto, Japan, 1970)

Working on an international, regional, national and local basis, Religions for Peace creates multi-religious partnerships that mobilize the moral and social resources of religious people to address their shared problems. Religions for Peace is active in more than 50 countries, working with national affiliates and regional organizations to find and implement local solutions to local challenges. In the world's great capitals and in remote rural villages, Religions for Peace affiliates empower religious communities to improve lives and promote peace.

The South African Chapter of WCRP came into being amidst the struggle against the gross injustices and cruelties of apartheid. Established in 1984 upon the initiative of Archbishop Desmond Tutu, it mobilized religious leaders and grassroots members in a unified, prophetic and defiant stance. In response, WCRP-SA became a target for systematic state harassment by the apartheid regime, some of its members being banned, others detained and charged with high treason. Furthermore, many of its gatherings were held under heavy police presence, its first inaugural Desmond Tutu Peace Lecture in 1985 being placed under a Government banning order, and the Johannesburg hall where the fourth lecture was to be held in 1988 being fire-bombed the previous day.

With the political dismantling of apartheid, and the first democratic elections of 1994, came also the tenth anniversary of WCRP-SA. To celebrate this event the Peace Lecture was delivered by Archbishop Desmond Tutu and entitled 'Let us celebrate our Diversity.' President Nelson Mandela in his response highlighted the continued importance of our dialogue for the next decade of our work when he remarked, 'I wish however to emphasize the role of the religious community in reconstruction and development. On the one hand, we view it as only natural that the partnership against apartheid should mature into one for the betterment of the life of all South Africans, especially the poor. On the other hand, your prophetic voice is crucial in reinforcing the moral fibre of the new democratic state - be it in the application of human rights statutes or the integrity of its financial and other practices.'

June 1999 marked South Africa's second democratic election. The general peacefulness of this important event clearly showed the maturing of our young democracy. With the inauguration of a new president however, there also came a new phase in our new nation's history: that of social and economic transformation.

WCRP/Hope for African Children Initiative meeting in Nairobi June 2002

WCRP-SA hereby continues in its partnership for a just and equitable South Africa by:
- Promoting religious tolerance, freedom and dialogue
- Assisting in conflict resolution and peace monitoring
- Working for disarmament and demilitarization
- Developing peace-education programs
- Encouraging equitable and sustainable development
- Furthering human rights, gender equality and racial harmony
- Maintaining the rights of refugees and other displaced persons
- Working for social and economic justice for the poor
- Ensuring environmental justice and awareness.

TWELVE GUIDING PRINCIPLES

The following are the guiding principles to which we as WCRP-SA adhere as an organization:
- We are committed to our respective faiths and at the same time striving for inter-religious understanding and cooperation
- We are concerned over the lack of unity and peace in our land
- We are convinced that each of our different faiths expresses itself clearly in favour of justice and harmony in society
- We recognize our religious differences and respect one another's convictions and hopes
- We regret that religion has in the past been instrumental in separating us from one another
- We refuse to be polarized by suspicion, ignorance and intolerance
- We do not intend to start a new universal religion which replaces all our different faiths
- We do not suggest that the missionary efforts of religions should come to an end
- We do not accept that religious communities should withdraw from the problems and tensions of society
- We want to clarify and stress the role of religion in all concerns involving justice and peace
- We want to promote mutual understanding between religious communities
- We want to foster closer inter-religious co-operation in addressing the ills of our society.

> *Central to interfaith is the question 'who is, where is, your neighbour,' and interfaith dialogue is my answer to this question, reaching out to us wherever we are. There is no substitute for this bridge-building or networking, for the formation of the human chain of friendship cutting across the boundaries of religion.*
> Fr Albert Nambiaparambil[10]

SUMMARY

Maybe reading about some of these experiences that people have had during an interfaith activity or encounter may help persuade you of their potential significance and encourage you to begin your own interfaith journey.

If you are already an interfaith traveller, when reflecting on interfaith experiences you have had, you might like to consider these questions formulated by Scarboro Missions in Canada:

> Has it been enriching?
> difficult?
> positive?
> challenging?
> threatening?
> perplexing?
> What issues have those experiences raised for me?
> Do I have a story I can tell about these experiences?[11]

Experiencing the art of Japanese flower arranging:
An enriching cultural and spiritual experience in Kyoto for participants in the
International Interfaith Centre / Rissho Kosei-kai Dialogue Tour of Japan.
L/r clockwise: Anne McClelland, Kiyo Sawa, Jael and Sandy Bharat.

INTERFAITH

OUR INTERFAITH OFFICE EXPERIENCE 1994-2004

Since 1994, the International Interfaith Centre, International Association for Religious Freedom and Rissho Kosei-kai have shared a small office in the centre of Oxford. Until quite recently the World Congress of Faiths was also based there. As well as working together we also received visitors, ate, laughed, cried and had outings together. We belonged to various faiths, including Christian, Hindu, Buddhist, Bahai, Muslim, Unitarian and Shinto. We were an interfaith family. Here are most of those who shared office space in this period.

From top left clockwise: Robert Traer, Ramola Sundram, Andrew Clark, Helen Wüscher, Robert Papini, Margaret Paton, Klaus Glindemann, Dinah Mayo, Robert Bowler, Yukimasa Hagiwara, Megumi Hirota, Kimie Yamaura, Diana Hamner, Henry Wai, Paul Trafford, Josef Boehle, John Gant, Jonathan Jeczalik, Bryan Roebuck, Madeleine Harman, Sarita Cargas, Samuel Wintrip, Kashif Shahzada, Zarrin Caldwell, Sangho Kim and Neil Farrow (inside).
Group photo under the text, l/r clockwise: David Storey, Shige Wada, David Partridge, Celia Storey, Jill Gant, Jael Bharat, Sandy Bharat, and Joanna Jeczalik.

CHAPTER IV

INTERFAITH ORGANISING

INTRODUCTION

Thinking now about some of the details involved in interfaith activities might be helpful in developing awareness of their different components.

All interfaith activities include an ingredient that promotes inter-religious understanding and co-operation. They are the foundations of the exchange between people of faith and faiths. We only need to look at our troubled world to realise how difficult it is to lay secure foundations.

Take a look, on the next page, at the Inter Faith Network for the UK's guidelines on building good relations with people of other faiths. They are, of course, crucial. If you have not developed such relationships and learnt from them then your event is in jeopardy or may be very superficial.

Keeping this in mind, here are some suggestions for arranging interfaith events, avoiding problems, and making such occasions more welcoming and comfortable. They range from the food to offer to the ways chairs are positioned, from the format of the meeting to the formalities of who to invite. The Golden Rule of ethics can be usefully applied when you are planning an interfaith event. Don't arrange for others what would bore you rigid!

It might also be helpful to keep in mind this old joke. How do you make God laugh? *Tell her your plans!*

GETTING STARTED

Of course, before you can start organising events, you have to organise yourself into the right position to begin interfaith. There are many levels, many models you might adopt. First entry is often through meeting neighbours who are from another culture, another faith, and becoming friends. This is interfaith. It may happen that at some point you decide to address an issue together, something that concerns you both or in which you both have expertise. Maybe a group informally comes together to discuss a situation of mutual interest, to create a forum for discussion or to lobby for a particular outcome. A time may come when you want to formalise this engagement in order to attract others to your cause, to be able to attract funding, to create more of an impact.

BUILDING GOOD RELATIONS WITH PEOPLE OF DIFFERENT FAITHS AND BELIEFS

In Britain today, people of many different faiths and beliefs live side by side. The opportunity lies before us to work together to build a society rooted in the values we treasure. But this society can only be built on a sure foundation of mutual respect, openness and trust. This means finding ways to live our lives of faith with integrity, and allowing others to do so too. Our different religious traditions offer us many resources for this and teach us the importance of good relationships characterised by honesty, compassion and generosity of spirit. The Inter Faith Network offers the following code of conduct for encouraging and strengthening these relationships. As members of the human family, we should show each other respect and courtesy. In our dealings with people of other faiths and beliefs this means exercising good will and:

- Respecting other people's freedom within the law to express their beliefs and convictions
- Learning to understand what others actually believe and value, and letting them express this in their own terms
- Respecting the convictions of others about food, dress and social etiquette and not behaving in ways which cause needless offence
- Recognising that all of us at times fall short of the ideals of our own traditions and never comparing our own ideals with other people's practices
- Working to prevent disagreement from leading to conflict
- Always seeking to avoid violence in our relationships.

When we talk about matters of faith with one another, we need to do so with sensitivity, honesty and straightforwardness. This means:

- Recognising that listening as well as speaking is necessary for a genuine conversation
- Being honest about our beliefs and religious allegiances
- Not misrepresenting or disparaging other people's beliefs and practices
- Correcting misunderstanding or misrepresentations not only of our own but also of other faiths whenever we come across them
- Being straightforward about our intentions
- Accepting that in formal inter faith meetings there is a particular responsibility to ensure that the religious commitment of all those who are present will be respected.

All of us want others to understand and respect our views. Some people will also want to persuade others to join their faith. In a multi faith society where this is permitted, the attempt should always be characterised by self-restraint and a concern for the other's freedom and dignity. This means:

- Respecting another person's expressed wish to be left alone
- Avoiding imposing ourselves and our views on individuals or communities who are in vulnerable situations in ways which exploit these
- Being sensitive and courteous
- Avoiding violent action or language, threats, manipulation, improper inducements, or the misuse of any kind of power
- Respecting the right of others to disagree with us.

Living and working together is not always easy. Religion harnesses deep emotions which can sometimes take destructive forms. Where this happens, we must draw on our faith to bring about reconciliation and understanding. The truest fruits of religion are healing and positive. We have a great deal to learn from one another which can enrich us without undermining our own identities. Together, listening and responding with openness and respect, we can move forward to work in ways that acknowledge genuine differences but build on shared hopes and values.[1]

Deep dialogue: Religion, Community and Conflict conference participants Hari Vaudrey and Sr Anna getting to know each other

Most local interfaith groups use a volunteer model. Shown here in dialogue are Paul Trafford, Penny Faust, Mohammad Talib and Meru Devidasi from the Oxford Round Table of Religions.

It may be that you want to form an organisation, charity or focus group recognised as a legal entity. When you reach this point you will usually need at least two members of your group who are willing to work in official capacities, as Secretary and Treasurer. Of course, if it is an interfaith group, you will want to involve others in decision making roles. Do make every effort to be gender and age inclusive and broad in religious participation.

Will you want to do all the work of your organisation yourselves as volunteers or will you want paid staff as well as volunteers to manage the day to day functions of your organisation, prepare the events etc? The latter will require ongoing fundraising to pay salaries, office costs and all the other essentials of salaried positions. The former may mean that your members are more motivated to engage themselves actively with event organising and all that goes with that. The World Congress of Faiths is one interfaith organisation that runs on this model of an active and engaged board of trustees. If you use this same approach, try to ensure that board members have varied skills. Almost every organisation longs for people involved to have accounting and fund raising skills. It's a rare success story!

Having had experience of paid and volunteer organisations, we would vote for the latter overall as the most effective way to utilise the enthusiasm and experience of the foundational team without the endless hassle of raising funds to pay staff costs in order that they can then raise funds to pay for programming. It's a bit like an argument for vegetarianism – if you plant the fields directly with food stuff then this is more effective than using the fields to feed cattle in order that they might then feed people.

If you go for the salaried staff option it is quite likely that you will also need to attract volunteers as the number of staff you can afford to pay may be limited. Interfaith funding is not always easy and core funding for items like salaries and office rents is always difficult! Major interfaith organisations like WCRP and IARF do have salaried staff and also rely on others in various parts of the world who work out of their passion and commitment to the cause rather than for any financial reward. Several organisations have key players who remain unsalaried yet who give their utmost to support and develop the organisation's activities. Naturally, these are usually older people who have the financial security to make this possible. Younger people do not so often have that option. All organisations with paid staff have to work very, very hard to raise the funds needed and often they will hit difficult times when the funding does not seem enough. Most of those very few who succeed are blessed by significant and well endowed supporting communities. Such blessings may sometimes have a downside too if those funders feel their money buys them undue influence in the organisation's affairs.

The United Religions Initiative (URI) has an interesting model of local and regional initiatives being linked to the global coordinating body. This is mutually beneficial, creating a powerful international resource and an effective springboard for multi-dimensional activities around the world. Bishop Bill Swing, the founder of the URI, may have been one of the most significant interfaith fundraisers so far as he has helped, with other dedicated members, build up the URI from his original vision to the international reality it is today.

In many countries/continents you may find that your organisation can link to a network in a similar way, providing you with support, experience and a wider family of people who understand your motives and aspirations. For example, in the UK there is the Inter Faith Network; for the USA and Canada, there is the North American Interfaith Network.

Some organisations stay rooted in local agendas; some embrace many continents; some have national status; some work with the United Nations; some function as meeting places for people of different faiths without any additional focus; some focus totally on universal concerns like poverty or the environment.

When you reach a point where you feel only an organisation can match your calling, do take some time out to study what already exists. Don't try to reinvent the wheel. If someone has already set up something that addresses your concerns, get connected. Don't become competitive. Too many of us think that only we can deliver the dream that has entered our consciousness. It's not true. We will need others and they might need us. Get together. Be willing to be a worker and not just a boss. Set new examples of cooperation that will make others think again and perhaps even try your way. As Gandhiji said, be the change you wish to see.

Your organisation is up and running. You feel wonderful. You are going to change the world! But first, before planning your events you will have to engage with the vexed area of fundraising.

INTERFAITH FUNDRAISING

This aspect can't be avoided. Don't join the interfaith movement if you want to get rich! You may get many rewards from your interfaith work but an overflowing bank account is not usually included.

The situation for interfaith funding is rapidly changing. As all areas of civil society wake up to the power of religion in a secular world, funding can come from a variety of sources, some unknown ten or so years ago.

If you are a small local organisation one of the best ways to get your agendas off the ground is to build up relationships with other local organisations. Maybe one of you has a useful venue, another good local government or business contacts, a third has computer and internet facilities. Share, cooperate, liaise. This saves everyone money and allows for competent skill sharing. The same applies if you are running a programme at a major international event, like a Parliament of the World's Religions. The people who have already decided to attend will prove a valuable and free resource for your work. Find out who are the experts in your field that will be at the event. Ask them if they will take part in your programme. This is usually affirmative if you have planned your event well. Not only will you be able to include these interesting people in your event, there will be no cost, they will learn about your work, and you will provide them with new networking opportunities. The host organisation will have increasingly powerful programmes to offer and everyone will benefit from the cooperation you have engendered.

The European Union, governments, trusts, foundations, philanthropists are all useful sources of income for your projects. Nobody gives money away so you will have to create effective projects that make sense to others too. This will take time and a dedicated team. Individuals may find it hard to attract funding, however innovative their ideas, unless they are connected to an organisation that can be held accountable for any funding received.

You may be surprised to know, that with some significant exceptions, faith communities may not be the most substantive funders of your work. Generally members of faith communities like first of all to support those communities – with new temples, church restoration, help for those most intimately connected to each community etc. If you are running a network, of course, your members, which may be different faith groups, will pay you a subscription, but generally speaking you may not be first on their list for donor purposes. If you find you do attract a faith community's funding, you may at the same moment find it is because that community needs the platform you can provide for increased awareness of its own identity, for increased power for its own aspirations, to bring it into mainstream discussions in a way that might not otherwise be possible. Maybe this will not worry you but be alert to all agendas that may not be as pure as your own. At the same time, be realistic that everyone engaged with your cause may have their own perspective on it and even disagreements about that may be productive, broadening the outlook and inclusivity of all involved. Like religions, maybe you only saw part of the outcome when you were converted to your cause, and working together with others who see things differently but share your enthusiasm may be a good learning curve for you.

Until recently at least, most of the funding for international programmes came from the north and west. Participants at events from the east and south have been sponsored. There has been, in the past an expectation that the west equals wealth and the east equals poverty. There is wealth and poverty everywhere. Wherever possible, sponsorship should diminish and participants take the responsibility to be independent, self-funding. This promotes dignity and equality at events; reduces 'circuit' speakers; and brings expectations into a more responsible focus. Circuit speakers evolve when people get used to thinking of one or two people only as representatives of a particular faith, culture, or genre. They get invited over and over again to events and so must gradually lose touch with their roots. This will end up in their being less and less representative of any particular interest group. It is the responsibility of circuit speakers to train others from their milieu and encourage them to accept any invitations to events. This enlarges and freshens the speaker pool, allows people to remain more closely connected and in touch with their area of specialisms, and creates a stronger mass of experience to share both locally and internationally. Don't hog the headlines. Bring others in. Help the movement grow.

You have filled in endless forms, sent hundreds of letters, communicated with everyone you can think of in your field. You have the funding. You are so happy! You are ready to begin planning your event.

IMPLEMENTING THE GREAT IDEA

Interfaith means thinking co-operatively. When you've woken up with a great idea, think about what other person or organisation could help make it a reality. Working together brings all the challenges that interfaith embodies so it's good for you as well as for those you hope to attract to your meeting. And, if you know someone else is working out a similar idea, it does not show much spirit of interfaith cooperation and understanding if you still try to go it alone. Combining creativity, energy and databases will prove the best idea of all for everyone involved.

LOCATION, LOCATION, LOCATION

If it is your own event then getting the location right can get your event off to a good start. Generally, a religiously neutral or 'safe' environment works well – somewhere that presents no faith specific challenges to any of your participants – for example, no icons or images that might be offensive or challenging to some, even if welcomed by others. Of course, if a particular faith community is hosting your event, then this is totally different. In this case, ensure you visit the site prior to your event and find out the exact protocol so that you can advise your participants in good time and avoid anyone being embarrassed on arrival by turning up in inappropriate clothing or without the usual gift, donation etc.

It is also important to publicise your event well so share databases where possible, get posters out, prepare a mailing to all your supporters, advertise on your website, hire the town crier if you have one and let everyone know when and where your event happens!

If your programme is an international one that will be delivered in a different country from your own then it is also a good idea, if at all feasible, for someone from your organisation to reconnoitre the distant location, determine the particular aspects relevant to it, and become familiar with answers to all the questions your participants might want to ask you. Visas, accommodations, local weather, time differences, contact phone numbers, internet facilities, food, places of worship near event location, travel information, health risks, special insurance needs and a host of other imagined and unimaginable enquiries may come your way so be well prepared to give the information and assurances needed.

Similarly, if your event is an international one in your own country, guests arriving from elsewhere will be asking you for comparable details. It can be very helpful to have a collection of airport coach and train timetables in your office ready to mail out with registration forms etc. People may need to know not only how to get to your event location but what local currency they may immediately need available to buy their travel tickets.

CHOOSING THE RIGHT DAY AND TIME FOR YOUR EVENT

Many faiths have special days for worship or obligations which might make it difficult for them to attend meetings. For example, events scheduled for Shabbat (Friday evening to Saturday evening) will certainly exclude much Jewish participation (though some liberal Jews might be willing to attend in a passive capacity). Sunday mornings are difficult for many Christians, especially ministers who may have

---

> In the Middle East some years ago, we were invited to a conference on conflict resolution in Tiberias. En route we had an unplanned adventure. A bomb scare at a coach station placed us on the wrong bus with an inexperienced driver who spoke no English. Hours later, the only passengers remaining, we drove through the desolation of the Golan Heights. The driver got lost and had to turn the bus in a narrow road with mines either side. Finally he insisted we get off, finding enough English as the coach doors closed behind us to say 'sorry'. Russian émigrés helped us find our way to a coach that returned us to Tiberias.
> Very late we arrived at the event venue and found participants enjoying the terrace of a luxury hotel beside the lake, mounds of food everywhere, an ensemble playing classical western music. Conflict was on the lips but not in the context.
> Point: If you're discussing conflict in a conflict zone, chose a location that fits such a serious agenda.

to take services at their churches. Fridays are days when Muslims make particular effort to attend community prayer at mosques. Of course, having this cluster of days to avoid creates its own difficulties. Weekends are the one time many working people can get to interfaith gatherings. It is also often the time when your venue is most likely to be available if it is used during the week by its own affiliates.

There is no complete solution to this. Where you have to hold your event at a weekend, consult with your local Jewish and Christian colleagues so they at least know you are aware that they may not be able to participate fully and that you have tried to make alternative arrangements. Try to engage them in thinking about the event so that it is as inclusive as possible. Offer a separate space for Muslim participants so they can pray at the allotted times (five times daily).

Before you finalise the preparations of your event, check interfaith calendars to ensure no major religious festivals fall at the same time.² Such collisions will affect participation. If your event is international, you will need to check with your overseas guests to see how such clashes will affect them. If your event is planned for another country the same research is needed. This might help you avoid everyone disappearing for some days to celebrate special holy days!

THE SPEAKERS

If you have speakers there are some important considerations to make. Don't ever let them read from the beginning of a paper to the end. Provide copies of the paper if necessary and request the speaker to tell it her own way at the conference, make it personal, relate to her audience, get them involved. There is nothing worse than arriving at an event and seeing up on a platform, way out of reach, a whole line of people nervously fingering their lengthy papers, ready to read them in full. Hours pass by and the listeners pass out! Nothing is learnt except the vow never to come again to such an event!

When you think about whom to invite, you will naturally consider speakers from a diversity of faiths. Far too often you will come up with a list of men only. There are many reasons for this but one of them is the intrinsically patriarchal stance of religions even today. Work hard to include women and youth in your speaker list. They bring quite different tones and energies to events. You need them all to be truly dialogical and inclusive. Try to reach out beyond the established circuit speakers and broaden opportunities, look for new experts. This will benefit everyone.

When you prepare your invitation to a speaker, be sure she understands that you are not inviting her to represent a religious tradition. You are inviting her, with her particular experience, understanding, commitment and concerns, to share what she has learnt or tell what she is doing to further inter-religious relations. No one can represent a religion. There are as many versions of it as there are people adhering to it. When people try to speak for 'the' religion it rarely works well. Usually, their honesty is impaired. They only want you to know the best of their religion. They give you information you could read in a book. It is very boring and sometimes worse. It can even be offensive because many participants may have broad interfaith experience and know more than the speaker about the diversity of her faith and how that can be expressed in different parts of the world, under different conditions. Your speaker is not a missionary for her faith, she is a person who has brought her faith into a wider world and has been changed or enhanced or challenged by that.

Another, rather modern, caution is to take care you do not place your speakers on unassailable pedestals because of recent historical events. For example, in Canada we saw several examples at interfaith gatherings where First Nations speakers were allowed to say anything they wanted. No one challenged them. Too many present felt guilty, too closely associated with all that had happened to the indigenous peoples of Canada: the theft of their lands; the destruction of their cultures; the abuse of their children. We have noticed the same tendency at UK interfaith events after the 2002 New York Trade Center atrocity and the 2005 transport bombings in London. People would arrive in the IIC office after such events with one objective: to meet a Muslim, be kind to a Muslim, take tea with a Muslim! Most wanted to show their solidarity with a religious group likely to receive retaliatory responses. There was a kind of guilt by association again. In our view, translating this to speaker idolatry is not honest and helps no one, especially the speakers and, by association, their communities. Such superficial respect will not be able to withstand the challenges of serious dialogue and will not give birth to the genuine love needed to change our world. The incentive can be a start and meeting a Muslim (for example) can begin to change our lives but at meetings there must be the freedom to ask more.

PREPARING YOUR PARTICIPANTS

Before they arrive, advise your participants about the clothing to wear or bring with them that will not cause offence. Let them know if all the food is vegetarian and why so they understand your motives. Explain that interfaith worship, if it is participatory rather than observational, is optional, they are under no compulsion to attend. Try to anticipate any serious questions or challenges that might arise and let people know how you are dealing with these.

If your programme includes a visit to a place of worship, a mosque or gurdwara, for example, check first to see what dress code will be expected of visitors there and pass that information on to those attending your event so they come prepared. Advise people that slip on shoes could be very handy as there can be a lot of taking shoes on and off when you visit Hindu, Buddhist, Sikh or Jain temples. Women need head covering at many places of worship. Men also need to cover their heads at gurdwaras. Men and women will not be able to sit together at some worship centres so your participants should be prepared for this. Sitting in certain ways, with your feet towards the deities is often considered offensive. Many religious groups like arms and legs to be covered when people enter their holy places. There is much to learn and appreciate in your visits and good preparation can greatly enhance the experience.

PREPARING THE ROOM

Whatever kind of event you are planning try to be inclusive, to bring into the event, in an including way, as many of the participants as possible. Arranging the chairs in a circular or horseshoe way usually works well. Your speaker is then part of the group, communicating with them and not at them. This may also help her to feel more relaxed, connected, willing to open up more.

In the centre of the circle or circles it is uplifting to place a candle and some flowers or a plant. This creates a spiritual ambience and also draws people close, allowing for more intimacy in the exchange. Even a formal lecture can be enhanced by such preparations. Try to keep the entrance to the room at the back of the circles so that people arriving later or having to leave early cause the minimum distraction.

Check the acoustics of your room in advance. Will everyone be able to hear your speaker? A microphone, while intrusive in some ways and best avoided, can improve the listening experience in a room with fuzzy sound quality, especially if the group is large and the speaker's voice soft. It can also help when your speaker is communicating in a language not as familiar to her as her own.

Having a tape recorder on a table near the speaker is a simple way of recording your event for later transliteration to a publication or for your organisation's archives. If it is good quality, you may even be able to raise some funds for your cause through sales of recorded talks, especially when they are by experts on particular themes that may not be readily available elsewhere.

GREETING THE PEOPLE ATTENDING YOUR EVENT

Be aware that people attending your events may come from different cultures. For some, any touching, including hand shaking, may not be possible or acceptable. It is a difficult moment when you extend your hand to someone and he ignores it. The one who ignores the gesture is not always mature or articulate enough to explain his actions so the tension remains unresolved and

INTERFAITH

grows as your ego thinks it has been slighted or you are regretful that you seem to have unwittingly done something to upset another. Remember this cultural difference when you plan parts of your programme that involve a sign of peace that includes touching. What is natural and beautiful to you may be unnatural and threatening to another. Placing the palms together in front of the body and bowing slightly is a form of greeting familiar to most of your participants from South Asia and the Far East. It is becoming increasingly used at interfaith gatherings too.

STARTING AND ENDING A MEETING

Welcoming people with refreshments is a good way to start your meeting. Right away people are engaged in dialogue, feel their participation is valued, and can relax after tiring journeys. They do not have to rush straight into a listening experience but can unwind first.

Closing a meeting with refreshments provides a similar process: an opportunity for de-briefing, sharing thoughts about the event with others (maybe there is no-one at home interested in interfaith who wants to hear this); time for dialogue with new friends, ensuring you know how to contact each other again; a feeling that you are valued for yourself and not just as an audience for someone else; and a period of preparation for return journeys.

Just as important is the beginning and closing of the actual programme you have prepared. Ideally, start and end with periods of shared silence. Usually just a few minutes are long enough for a large, inexperienced group. Not everyone will feel comfortable with this but it will be the making of your event. It is a time for excitement to fade, anxieties to be put aside, calmness to enter in.

It is a time for people to remember why they have come, what they can contribute, what they can learn. It is a time of faith. If there is no time for faith in interfaith meetings, what is the point?

In all our years of interfaith experience there was only one event where sharing silence together was impossible. This was in 1998 when the

Tea at Thrangu House Buddhist Centre, Oxford during an interfaith group visit

94

International Interfaith Centre (IIC) in association with the Northern Ireland Interfaith Forum, the World Conference on Religion and Peace (WCRP), and Action for Peoples in Conflict prepared 'Religion, Community and Conflict,' the first ever interfaith conference in Northern Ireland. Our IIC team had the most challenging meeting we had yet experienced when we went to meet potential Northern Ireland colleagues for the event. Suspicions and anxieties dominated the (oblong) table discussions. The room was divided between those affirming the event and those to be convinced. As Celia Storey explains, 'The atmosphere was red hot and not helped by someone letting off some fire crackers in the street outside. Quite rightly they were extremely concerned that either we could be bringing a group of people to come as voyeurs of their situation or, alternately, we were coming to tell them what they should be doing to solve their situation.'

Happily, problems gradually resolved. It was not easy but every difficulty was worth the effort it took to break through and the conference proved the precursor of other interfaith events in Northern Ireland. Speakers came to Armagh from South Africa, Israel, Palestine and Sri Lanka. They joined those from Northern Ireland, many of whom had never entered an inter-religious arena before. It was even risky, threatening, for them if misunderstood by their compatriots.

One knotty issue though was never resolved. At IIC we were used to always starting events with silence. This was never accepted for the Armagh event. It was just too theologically difficult in the tense circumstances then prevailing. Religious divisions were just too entrenched. Who might be prayed to in that silence? What devils might be invoked to attack the faith of participants? There was the feeling though that, by the end of the three days together, that maybe enough trust had built up to make shared silence possible. We will never know.

CATERING

If your event is for a whole day or more than one day, then catering will be a primary concern. What do people of different faiths eat? What is *halal* (acceptable) and what is *haram* (forbidden)? A vegetarian menu is without doubt the safest option. It is kosher, so Jewish friends will be able to share the feast. Most Sikhs, Hindus, Jains and some Buddhists are vegetarian by faith as well as inclination. Meats that are unacceptable to Jews and Muslims can be avoided. Special vegetarian diets may be needed for some Jains, Hindus and Sikhs who are unable to eat foods like onion and garlic that might normally be considered vegetarian. Products with egg content can also be a problem for some religious people.

One interfaith horror story comes from an interfaith event in Bangladesh. The Muslim hosts, with all good intentions, served up lunchtime beef sandwiches to their Hindu dialogue guests. There was outrage and uproar. The

INTERFAITH

Devotees from the International Society for Krishna Consciousness provided the tasty vegetarian food during the Religion, Community and Conflict conference in Northern Ireland.

cow, of course, is sacred to Hindus so there could not have been a more provocative choice! The Hindus felt they had been deliberately insulted. This was not the case, their hosts just did not know enough to have avoided this problem, and after some mediation and management, peace was restored and an alternative lunch provided. A vegetarian event is a safer event – though you may well get a few moans from inveterate meat eaters that their needs are never acknowledged and met by interfaith people. Better this than the air filled with flying missiles as *haram* foods are thrown back at their providers!

Another aspect of catering preparation is the need to educate your caterers if you are not doing the food yourself. Quite often, even today, preparing vegetarian food (as opposed to a normal meal without the meat), will be quite new to them. They will usually welcome your advice. If you decide not to go totally vegetarian they will also need you to let them know that meat and vegetarian meals should not be prepared and presented together.

At another event in Vancouver we witnessed the vulnerability of catering staff facing the distress of a Jain whose vegetarian choice was served from the same utensils as the meat dishes. No one had advised them how offensive this can be. 'Ahimsa,' harmlessness, is a vital component of Jain faith, not just a fussy preference for uncontaminated goods.

Avoid serving alcohol. It is forbidden to many people of faith. Offer herb or fruit teas with your refreshments for people unable to partake of caffeine or other stimulants.

PRAYER OR REFLECTION TIMES

How to pray together at interfaith events? Is it even possible? If it is, what formats could it take? There are several options, ranging from observing the tradition of another and mixing traditions in different ways.³ All can be interesting, moving or deadly dull, depending on the thought that goes into it.

Probably the least adventurous and therefore the safest, but also the dullest, option is to ask participants of different traditions to offer a prayer or a text during a period allocated for collective worship. People will hear what other faiths have to say about the Ultimate and the world and this can be an enlightening and non-threatening introduction for people new to interfaith.

More experienced activists will want to go deeper, either by exploring and entering into another tradition or by bringing several of them together in new and creative ways. The first experience can be offered though a participant from a particular religion (for example, a Buddhist or Quaker) preparing a meditation period or service exactly as they would do for people of their own faith. There is no dumbing down, no adaptations for 'outsiders.' You might find yourself doing Zen *zazen* or sitting in silence for an hour in the Quaker way; you may chant the Hare Krishna *mahamantra* or swirl around the room in Sufi style. There should be no compulsion of course and everyone should know this in advance. People at your event should choose to expose themselves in this way to the spirit and practice of another tradition. It can be a very special experience if you are ready for it, transcending the cerebral, merging in the mystical.

Interfaith worship as participation in multiple traditions during the same session is perhaps best left to experts.

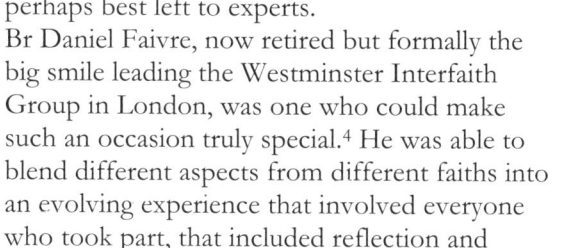

Brother Daniel

Br Daniel Faivre, now retired but formally the big smile leading the Westminster Interfaith Group in London, was one who could make such an occasion truly special.⁴ He was able to blend different aspects from different faiths into an evolving experience that involved everyone who took part, that included reflection and action, embraced the body, mind, heart and spirit. The floor was prepared by covering it with a white cloth; lamps would be lit and fruits placed around them to be offered as *prasad* later; stones or earth would be represented; personal contributions and scriptural readings would be offered; a thread would weave around everyone to form a chain; this thread would then be broken and everyone would wind a piece around their wrist. Cerebral, emotional, spiritual, ritual

Prasad being offered to an interfaith group by Hindu students in Oxford

and symbolic components combined to create a rich interfaith celebration.

When you prepare for collective reflection at your event, consider carefully the inclinations and experience of your participants so that you know what may or may not be appropriate for that particular occasion.

Sandy: One of the most impressive interfaith worship sessions I ever attended, from my perspective, was at the 1992 Modern Churchpeoples Union (MCU) conference. The MCU is a progressive Anglican organisation that seeks to provide a relevant and inclusive Church. Many of its members are Anglican ministers. Participants that year explored Hinduism, Buddhism and Sikkhism. Derek Barnes, an Anglican priest married to a Hindu, organised the worship sessions. On the final day it was an all out Hindu event! A Vaishnava, Ranchor Prime, chanted the Hare Krishna mantra beside an altar where Lord Krishna resided. I took the arti lamp around to everyone present. All but one person took the light from the lamp. Everyone seemed to be chanting Hare Krishna. It was deeply moving. It took real faith. The organisers had got it right because they knew their audience, knew that MCU people wanted to explore to the full the 'other,' and trusted God enough to do that. They had taken time during the conference to build up the bonding and trust that also helped make it possible. In different circumstances, such a daring experiment could have been disastrous.

MAKING THE MOST OF YOUR CORRIDORS

Many people who attend your event will be eagerly anticipating the network opportunities it presents to them, opportunities to make contact with others in their field and to recruit them for their own activities! Your speakers will hope to sell some of their books or distribute some publicity about their organisations. Let them know in advance they can bring their material. Prepare yours too. It could mean an extra printing job which takes time. Your corridors or the areas where people meet over tea to browse and chat, during breaks and before/after meals, are an integral and important part of your planning. Make them as accessible and attractive as possible.

In the corridor at an IIC conference

FINAL STATEMENTS

Some organisers allow themselves to come under pressure to produce an agreed statement by the end of the event. Sponsors naturally see this as a fruitful 'result,' a proof of money well donated. However, the truth is often flying in the opposite direction. Organisers that know, before they start, that they have to come up with some kind of consensus declaration 'saving the world,' are already compromised. Plans have to be integrated to push the programme in this direction, instead of allowing it some freedom of movement, allowing participants to move towards a commitment they really can make – and keep. Also, for all the fine and sincerely meant pledges made at conferences, few are followed through for development and few are individually fulfilled. The process may make a few people feel more content and self-achieving for a short while but the reality check soon follows and lasts much longer! Personally we think it is better to be honest and to aim personally and collectively for the best but not to confess this in some kind of artificial acclamation.

POSTSCRIPT

After your event, write or e-mail your speakers, your helpers, venue hosts etc to thank them for their participation. Contact your participants too and ensure they feel valued. Have they got useful feedback for you? Would they like to know about your future events? Might they be interested in becoming a Friend of your organisation and support it on a regular basis? Keep in touch. Build relationships. This is what interfaith is all about.

SUMMARY

Although there is much to consider when planning an interfaith event or a multi-faith visit to a place of worship, many of the aspects are more cultural than religious and the primary focus is on making everyone feel informed and comfortable to enjoy the programme you have planned without any distracting surprises. This is not something you can necessarily hope for yourself as organiser but you can anticipate and prepare for most eventualities and so have time for the unexpected ones!

The chapter concludes with some tips about planning young adult projects and some descriptions of international events by those who helped organise them.

Organising our interfaith workshops in Budapest: consultation on site with some of the facilitators

RAMOLA SUNDRAM, Programme Coordinator for the International Association for Religious Freedom (IARF), shares her insights into the methodologies of interfaith organising with a particular focus on young adults:

Since 1999, I have had the good fortune to be able to help bring to fruition interfaith projects involving young adults in various countries, particularly in India and the Philippines.

Projects need to be enjoyable but not superficial. Getting the balance right is not easy, and the length of time that people can spend together is a crucial factor. Right from the start, be realistic and practical. No hidden agendas!

Have you made a project design plan? Where are you going to get your funding? What preparation will participants have prior to the event? Who will be the key people in your planning team? An ideal core team will include people from different faith traditions who have complementary skills.

An essential component of any project is team building. Don't assume that people from the same faith tradition, living in the same area, need less building up of trust. Personalities are a factor not to be forgotten! Ground rules, including respectful language, are a must. One effective way of giving back to communities and having fun whilst team building is doing 'shramadan' or the 'gift of labour.' Ideally, work is carried out in at least two different sites, for example, sweeping part of a mosque and painting part of a Hindu temple.

Deepening understanding of each other's belief traditions requires an honest sharing face-to-face. Spending time visiting each other's spiritual sites can be helpful. Taking part in a spiritual ceremony can be very meaningful and have a strong impact on the group. Allow sufficient time for discussion of relevant issues. Sometimes, a programme can be overly crammed; it is often during the more informal times that friendships are fostered. Try also to encourage a creative approach for certain tasks, variety keeps the project vibrant.

Encouraging leadership is important. In many countries, not only is the hierarchy often much older people but also male dominated. Getting a good gender balance is not easy but should be the ideal. If elders are to trust their young people to take on more important roles, skills-based learning is necessary; in the Philippines, our young adults have termed this 'empowerment training.' Learning the process of designing and setting up projects, evaluation, effective communication etc is really helpful.

Hard at work in the temple, India.

Intergenerational work is needed. Elders should support their youth and the latter have much to learn from their seniors. Young adults need opportunities to help with and sometimes take the lead in event preparation. Tokenism is not acceptable – adults like to have young adults at their meetings, without necessarily being prepared to listen to their valuable experiences.

Gaining the respect and trust of elders can be crucial for breaking down barriers. In India, the head of a madrassa agreed to allow his pupils and our interfaith group of young adults (including women) to spend time in small groups sharing relevant issues. It was a very significant moment for our participants, and for the Muslim young men who rarely left their school. Also, a Hindu teacher told me she had a really life-changing experience when our interfaith team entered a Muslim village, close to her town, and helped to sweep part of the mosque. She could not previously have imagined doing something like this, seemingly a small and simple gesture, yet for many, including the Imam himself, ground breaking. He had trusted the sincerity of my colleagues, who, prior to this, had built up good relations with him.

An interfaith project can spark off the wish of a participant to gain a deeper understanding of her/his own spirituality. An example of this is when several young indigenous Filipinos arranged their own project in conjunction with their elders, who were delighted. In the past, the youth had not been keen to attend when the elders had tried to initiate something, but this time the impetus had come from the young people. Together they structured the project in which they celebrated their spiritual traditions and got a chance to truly share with and learn from each other. The young adults were able to form a strong core team, which was very valuable when they next took part in an interfaith event.

To sum up, young adult interfaith projects are essential if we are to engender good relations among people of different faiths and beliefs. Have a vision of what you want to achieve, some risks may have to be taken, but always ensure there is adequate planning. Young adults have much to offer, not just because of their enthusiasm and energy. Many elders talk of them being 'our future' but I believe we need to make the most of their ideas and experiences right now.

Having thought about how to organise an interfaith event or a young adult project, here follow three descriptions of special interfaith gatherings where the organisers learnt a lot. The first details a major gathering in India. The second refers to a conference already mentioned in this chapter - the first ever international interfaith event in Northern Ireland. The third describes an Australian response to the shattering events in the USA on 11 September 2001.

Some Sarva Dharma Sammelana participants.

CELIA STOREY of the International Interfaith Centre writes about 'Religious People Coming Together *(Sarva-Dharma-Sammelana)*,' an international interfaith event that took place in Bangalore, preceding the second Parliament of the World's Religions in 1993:

It was a joint event between the four major international interfaith groups of that time. At a gathering at Ammerdown conference centre near Bath, UK, in April 1988, members of the International Association for Religious Freedom (IARF), the Temple of Understanding (ToU), World Congress of Faiths (WCF) and World Conference on Religion and Peace (WCRP) adopted a statement that they would 'stimulate and initiate participation in the planning process for the global celebration of the 1993 centenary of the 1893 World Parliament of Religions, held in Chicago.' This group subsequently became know as the International Interfaith Organisations Coordinating Committee for 1993 (IIOCC) with Revd Marcus Braybrooke (WCF) as its chair.

Representatives of these four organisations used to meet at each other's major conferences or other allied events. The following year they were in Melbourne, Australia for the World Council of Churches General Assembly. Subsequently they met at offices in Frankfurt and New York, and our home in Chichester, UK among others. It became evident that there were no plans at this stage for a centenary event to be arranged in Chicago. Over time it was agreed, by way of contrast, to host an event in India, and Bangalore became the chosen venue.

The International Association for Religious Freedom decided to hold their tri-annual conference in Bangalore just prior to the centenary event that became known as Sarva-Dharma-Sammelana (SDS). The IARF would act as a platform from which SDS could perform; though it would be clear the two were separate events. This proved a substantial advantage as the IARF secretariat, at that time situated in Frankfurt, Germany, could carry out much of the necessary prior arrangements. Also, most of the delegates to the IARF Congress would also attend SDS and substantially swell the numbers. All four organisations were to encourage their membership to attend and the event was widely advertised throughout the different religious communities.

My husband David and I were appointed coordinating secretaries for SDS and had four increasingly busy years helping with the arrangements with some overseas tours. We made two visits to Bangalore and, on the first, were able to establish an essential local representative, a Jain silk merchant, Ramesh Vardya, who gave us invaluable help with local knowledge of where to get things done, hire a computer, and so on. The venue was the Ashoka Hotel, a controversially western style location but considered necessary for the large number of Americans, Europeans and Japanese who might find simpler living a trifle uncomfortable.

The IARF Congress began; IIOCC moved into its own office in the Ashoka Hotel; assistance walked in through the door in the form of non-IARF participants who had arrived early and offered help. There was something for everyone to do including one octogenarian who sat the door diverting people from the busy office within. Local dignitaries and religious leaders were invited to grace us with their presence at our opening ceremony. Ramesh had an inspiring idea for the backdrop of our stage which was totally covered in orange marigolds and red roses spelling out 'Welcome to Sarva-Dharma-Sammelana 1993.' The poles of the

Christian-Sikh sharing at SDS

awning were draped in garlands of sweet smelling jasmine and frangipani. There was no doubt that this was a different event from the normal religious congress.

Seven hundred people attended SDS. They were divided by choice into three groups: the first group, *Our Visions for the Next Century,* shared their hopes, before considering what might hinder progress; the second and most popular choice was *Prayer and Meditation: Experiencing Indian Spirituality* with visits to different centres and ashrams where teaching was given by the leaders; the third group was entitled *Voices from Different Religions* with presentations by a panel of religious leaders and scholars with perspectives on their traditions and interreligious cooperation. The programmes were interspersed by various social events such as afternoon tea in the lovely gardens of Raj Bhavan, the residence of the Governor of Karnataka, Khursheed Alam Khan, and an evening at Taralabalu Kendra where we were richly entertained with dance, music, speeches and a feast. Twice daily there were prayers and meditation giving a flavour of all the different faith communities.

Those who attended Sarva-Dharma-Sammelana have a lasting memory of something very special among the list of interfaith conferences that preceded and succeeded it. It was intimate and spiritual and marked a new awareness in people's minds of the possibility of an interfaith future. Chicago did celebrate the centenary of the first Parliament of the Worlds Religions. They had a majestic event in Chicago where seven thousand people attended. Some of us went there from Bangalore and witnessed a more masculine or Western style conference whereas Bangalore had been more feminine or Eastern in its style. There is need for both. Subsequent years have witnessed a burgeoning of interfaith activity, where hopes have been raised and set back, for better understanding and cooperation between people of all faiths.

RELIGION, COMMUNITY AND CONFLICT

In 1998, several organisations, including the Northern Ireland Interfaith Forum, International Interfaith Centre, World Conference on Religions for Peace, and Action for Peoples in Conflict, cooperated to organise 'Religion, Community and Conflict,' the first ever interfaith conference in Northern Ireland.

It proved a significant step forward for the Northern Ireland Interfaith Forum (NIIF) which has gone on to organize many other projects, including a major travelling exhibition of religious life in Northern Ireland, an annual multi-faith calendar, and the establishment and maintenance of a Quiet Room for reflection at Belfast International Airport. It also now has its own training department, Diversiton, working in cooperation with other Northern Ireland organizations.[5]

NIIF gives this message: 'All are welcome to join the Northern Ireland Interfaith Forum. Northern Ireland is still a religious society and we can only be enriched by learning about each other's traditions.'

MAURICE RYAN, founder of the Northern Ireland Interfaith Forum, wrote this about the conference, which was held in Armagh:

The conference was a groundbreaking opportunity to examine the role of religion in community conflict situations, from the widest possible perspective, with Hindu, Buddhist, Muslim, Jewish and Christian presenters from South Africa, Sri Lanka, Israel, Canada, England and Ireland, as well as Roman Catholic and Protestant representatives and members of the ethnic/religious minority communities from within Northern Ireland itself.

One of the most helpful features of this conference was the sense of realism and concern, which pervaded the two days of reflection and debate, to face squarely the paradoxes and contradictions endemic within cultural and religious conflict situations. Eminent speakers and widely representative delegates were concerned to 'tell it how it is,' refusing to blur distinctions or gloss over differences, while at the same time strenuously seeking positive pathways to reconciliation. And there was clear and unequivocal recognition that religion can have both positive and negative influences as far as communities in conflict are concerned - we have 'the good' but also sometimes 'the bad and the ugly' in our religious affairs and affiliations.

One of the most salutary comments of the day came from Yasmin Sooka, chairing the conference as Commissioner of the Truth and Reconciliation Commission of South Africa, when she said that, 'We need to pursue peace even when we are grossly provoked; in the end, people die, not Catholics or Protestants or Hindus or Muslims!'[6]

Celia Storey found 'the atmosphere was riveting. Everyone in the audience found something with which they could relate.'

Dr Robert Traer, then General Secretary of IARF, reflected that in this event, 'there was more truth, and thus more about healing, than in any other interfaith conference I've attended.'

Yasmin Sooka at the RCC conference

He continued: In greeting the visitors to his divided city the mayor of Armagh noted that 'People, who proclaim their faith on a Sunday, throw a bomb on a Monday.' The archbishop of the Church of Ireland suggested that the troubles in Northern Ireland might be understood in the same way that his small son had explained why he had fallen out of bed: 'I think I stayed too near to where I got in.'[7]

Sometimes world events engender special responses and special organising. Prof DESMOND CAHILL describes how events across the ocean changed the nature of interfaith events in Australia: Triggering Event…Triggering response: An Australian Multifaith Response to S11:

On September 11th, 2001, religion was placed at world centre stage by the terrorist attacks on New York and Washington. Never again could we look at skyscrapers in quite the same way. The impact upon Australia was immediate and profound, especially because of the audacity of the attacks and the depth of the relationship between the two countries. Subsequently, there has been triggered a continuing series of interfaith initiatives beginning with a multifaith service. It was held a week later in Melbourne Park, better known to the world as the place where the Australian Tennis Championship, one of the four Grand Slam titles, is held each January. It was a most moving experience, unlike any previously conducted in Australia.

Political and religious leaders, together with police and fire fighting contingents in memory of the USA service workers who died in the two towers at Ground Zero, gathered before the assembled 10,000 people. The following is a resume of each tradition's contribution to the multi-faith service, drawing upon their spiritual heritages to reflect on the evil of the terrorist attacks:

- The Buddhist community, to the deep-throated gong of a bell sounding the passing of life, asked those present to close their eyes and become bodies of light, praying for this disaster not to worsen; it also asked for all to be enlightened that the enemy and those who harm can often be our best teachers and that everyone consider the Karmic causes and origins of the hatred that drove the terrorists.
- To the sound of the ram's horn, the oldest known musical instrument, in the year 5762 of its calendar, the Jewish community asked all to reflect on the Talmudic saying, 'Those who share in the grief of the community will share in its redemption;' they invited everyone present to respond with 'Amen.'
- The Hindus focussed on the aphorism that 'experience is not what happens to you; it is what you do with what happens to you,' lighting the candle of love for peace and prosperity for the world and for the departed souls, and praying 'may there be peace in the heavenly regions' in line with the great Hindu principle of *ahimsa* or non-injury that 'it is the principle of the pure of heart never to injure others, even when they themselves have been fatefully injured' and with the advice that 'an eye

for an eye and soon everyone will be blind.'
- The Sikhs were consumed by the horror of it all, and in despair they cried out, 'O God, the world is going up in flames; save it; by whatever means, deliver it. O God, who can save it?'
- The Muslim imam, focussing on 'the convulsion of the days,' in sending his condolences to the people of the USA, prayed for peace and harmony in the whole world and reminded us, 'O all mankind, fear your Lord.'
- The Bahais prayed, 'O my God, O my God, unite the hearts of Thy servants; help them to serve Thee; leave them not to themselves,' enjoining all that 'the thought of hatred must be destroyed by the more powerful thought of love.'
- And lastly the Christian singer sang of 'beautiful brokenness,' the beautiful brokenness of the cross to be followed by the resurrectional transformation. And the reader recited the Beatitudes, 'Blessed are they who mourn – they shall be comforted; blessed are the merciful – they shall have mercy shown them,' imploring through the voice of the carpenter, 'we want justice, not vengeance.'

A month later, exactly forty days after S11, I was in New York representing Australia at the emergency assembly of the World Conference of Religions for Peace. At the conclusion, I gathered with other leaders from across the world for another multi-faith service at St. Peter's Church within fifty metres of Ground Zero. In the darkness of the night to the background din of the huge machines and trucks clearing away the debris, we prayed together in this church which had been used as a medical staging post for those injured in the attack. The New York Philharmonic Choir provided the necessary solemnity and peacefulness so near to where so many had died so horribly.

From Melbourne to New York, the local had become the global.
And the commitment to the inter-faith agenda by religiously inspired people to bring the faith communities together in this time of unpredictability and provocation must be both local and global.

September 11, 2003: Annual Interfaith Service of Commitment to the Work of the United Nations

1893: Parliament of World Religions, Chicago

> What men deemed impossible, God has finally wrought. The religions of the world have actually met in a great and imposing assembly; they have conferred together on the vital questions of life and immortality in a frank and friendly spirit, and now they part in peace, with many warm expressions of mutual affection and respect.
>
> Hon. Charles Caroll Bonney.[8]

2000: Millennium Peace Summit of Religious and Spiritual Leaders, New York

Some of the two thousand participants at the historic Summit held at the United Nations and the Waldorf Astoria Hotel.

These events took a lot of organising!

Does interfaith address my concerns?

PART II. INTERFAITH ISSUES

INTRODUCTION

Interfaith people and organisations, like everyone else, have many concerns to address today, including conflict transformation and peace building, religious freedom, religious pluralism and how to live together in harmony.

This chapter will introduce some of the ways interfaith people and agencies are addressing some of these themes, the challenges they face, the projects they create, the experiences they have.

As mentioned in an earlier chapter, the Network of International Interfaith Organisation was formed in Oxford in 2001 by fourteen organisations to help enhance interfaith co-operation, communication and co-ordination.[1] Network members (*pictured below at first meeting*) meet annually and share ideas and issues between meetings through an e-group.

A Joint Statement was issued following the 11th September 2001 tragedy at the Trade Center in New York:

> In response to recent tragic events in the United States of America and ongoing conflicts with religious dimensions around the world, our international interfaith organisations offer our inter-religious dialogue expertise and resources to address the current crisis and promote peace building initiatives. We have direct experience of bringing into peaceful and constructive dialogue the mainstream and marginalised, moderate and militant religious voices of our world. Working with the world's

Jim Kenney addressing participants at the Parliament of the World's Religions, Cape Town, 1999

faith communities, we have found that inter-religious dialogue can help heal wounds caused by feelings of injustice, isolation, and inequality. Our international interfaith organisations with their global outreach and networks offer peaceful alternatives to war.[1]

Cooperation between people and organisations is what interfaith is all about; our combined voices and action will be more effective, our agendas will be more inclusive, and our resources will go further. If we - those who share the same cause - can't work together, how can we claim to be reconcilers to a wider world? Peace begins at home. As Mother Theresa said, it's no good being street angels and house devils!

Our contributors enable us to explore some of the ways in which interfaith people and organisations are addressing the global issues of our time, starting with some people who feel strongly about the positive values of religious diversity. Without multiple religious traditions there would be no need for interfaith. As there are and always have been varied religious outlooks and communities this might suggest an inherent human circumstance that has to be calculated into any global concern.

Celebrating diversity at the 1999 Parliament of the World's Religions

> *Hold on! We'll reach the top together.*

Chapter V
RELIGIOUS DIVERSITY

INTRODUCTION

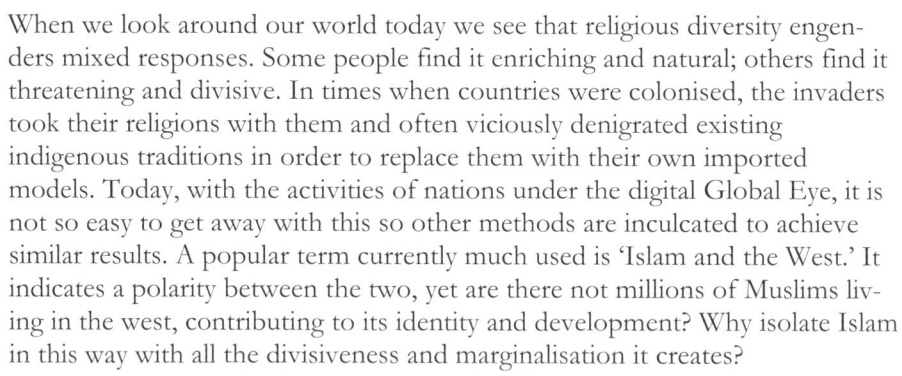

When we look around our world today we see that religious diversity engenders mixed responses. Some people find it enriching and natural; others find it threatening and divisive. In times when countries were colonised, the invaders took their religions with them and often viciously denigrated existing indigenous traditions in order to replace them with their own imported models. Today, with the activities of nations under the digital Global Eye, it is not so easy to get away with this so other methods are inculcated to achieve similar results. A popular term currently much used is 'Islam and the West.' It indicates a polarity between the two, yet are there not millions of Muslims living in the west, contributing to its identity and development? Why isolate Islam in this way with all the divisiveness and marginalisation it creates?

One reason may be the rapid rise of the Christian evangelical agenda in the USA. Religions often seem to be implicated in, contributors to, the world's conflicts even if they are not the sole factors. Too often too, lurking behind fear or intolerance of religious diversity, there is racism. After atrocities like the attack on the Trade Center in New York or the London transport bombings, Asians of any faith are subjected to revenge assaults. Muslims are not discriminated from Sikhs or Hindus. All are plunged into one corporate 'alien' identity. Then it is clearly revealed that, for all our smug multi-cultural self-congratulation, the 'other' still powerfully exists as 'other'. Of course, this is

Unexpected dialogue at the International Interfaith Centre in Oxford as Buddhist monks from Thailand pop in and engage with guests Ibrahim Abuelhawa and Eliyahu McClean from Palestine and Israel.

not one-sided. Atrocities such as those perpetuated against Afghanistan and Iraq can lead some to identify all 'westerners' as enemies.

One of the great benefits of interfaith activity is that it helps break down the 'otherness' of 'others.' At interfaith gatherings, sooner or later, you are bound to meet, in a personal way, someone who significantly and movingly impacts on your consciousness. Your stereotypes will be blown away; your hidden prejudices will have to be faced; new friendships renew your own life; and love will change everything.

YEHUDA STOLOV, Director of the Interfaith Encounter Association in Israel gives an example of this. When we video interviewed him, Yehuda told us about some of the difficulties he had encountered with people who did not, at first, recognise their dialogue partners as legitimate. After one meeting between Jews and Arabs the Jewish participants told him off for not bringing 'real' Arabs to the meeting. They had found the Arab participants to be too like themselves and not at all the alien creatures they had anticipated! Yehuda told us how such meetings, with the dissolution of stereotyping they allow, are essential in any reconciliation process – even when they may also bring disappointment, as you will read:

I think the biggest problem in Israel is that the Jews and non Jews don't meet; with non-Jews I mean mainly the Arabs. They have to interact, but don't really meet; there is no real deep encounter between the two. A friend of mine from Egypt always says 'you think you have a full picture of the other and what you don't have as real information you complete with prejudices!' I think this is the main source for many problems in the Middle East. And once you really do meet the other and know the real truth about the other, whether you agree with it or not, at least you get the real picture about the other. And this meeting of the real other makes him human to you. So I think bringing Jews and Arabs together is the real way to bring peace; it works. When people meet for the first time, you see the transformation of people who had many prejudices, and suddenly are even disappointed and say 'they are human; they are very similar to us; you said you would us bring Arabs, but these are like us; bring us the real Arabs!'[1]

The following four reflections on religious diversity, its impact and potential, come from different perspectives and from experienced interfaith activists – Hindu, Zoroastrian, Christian and Buddhist.

DEEPAK NAIK is one of the founders and Director of Minorities of Europe. He was born in Uganda of Gujarati Indian parents, moving to England at the age of five years. His mother, an active advocate of religious and cultural diversity, was an early influence and Deepak considers himself African, Indian, Hindu, British, European and a world citizen. He has been very active in the arenas of equality, citizenship, youth and interfaith and his work has been recognised by the British Government with an MBE. Deepak writes:

For me Inter-faith is a state of mind, it is my way of understanding the world and living comfortably in society. As a Hindu I feel that God makes decisions and if God wants to have more than one religion then who am I to disagree. I feel that my path to God is called Sanatan Dharma, 'Hinduism.' For other people the path may be different and they may not choose to recognise that they have a path – this is the beauty and gift of God.

Some people need more assurance and a sense of guarantee, 'uniqueness,' that their path is above other paths like Sanatan Dharma. I can live with their need as long as they do not use violence to persuade to me to convert, that when 'missionaries' come to share their beliefs with me they are upfront with their agenda to convert me to their religion.

The above state of mind brought me to enter the family of inter-faith activists, it works for me, for others in the family it may be different. Together with others from the spectrum of religions, traditions and value systems, I believe that we have a mission to claw back God from other individuals whose reason for using God is to gain power – political, economical, religious. To me God is sacred and not the religion, and I cannot understand how people who believe stand to one side when 'leaders' of their religions use their scriptures or other holy books to discriminate against others of another faith, or no faith. Injustice, hatred, violence need to be eradicated by all for all.

For me the beauty of the world is diversity of people – some black, others white, diversity of cultures, diversity within nature, etc. This is a gift and when God made the world it was with diversity. God made man and woman, each one unique, each one different and equal, each one totally dependent on and independent from the other.

For me this diversity has two purposes, first to be celebrated, second to learn from. Celebration means to me there are points within life when I can come together with others to experience joy and happiness. Celebrations provide a framework of living, with births, festivals and anniversaries that take me from birth to death smoothly. Through diversity I learn. I have learnt more

Deepak leading an international interfaith workshop in Budapest

about my religion from people who are from a different religion. They ask questions and naturally I need to reflect or read, ask advice from others in my religion, or seek spiritual guidance. To me this learning is so beautiful and so pure.

A friend and trainer once said to me that it is only when you take fish out of water that the fish knows that its lives in water. Similarly, I think we should help each other to create safe, secure, non-judgemental conditions where we can ask each other questions, place our fears on the table, say 'I am not sure.' My passion is to create these kinds of conditions, especially for young people. As a founding member of Minorities of Europe I feel that, at this stage of life, this is my Dharma. To me young people are not the future but the present – they just have more potential for changing society. So, influencing young people to be active, positive and passionate members of society is a must. I think that at the core humanity is good, we just need to open the tap and let it flow. This to me is love, is God.

SEEING BEYOND APPEARANCES:

Two traveling angels stopped to spend the night in the home of a wealthy family. The family was rude and refused to let the angels stay in the mansion's guest room. Instead the angels were given a small space in the cold basement. As they made their bed on the hard floor, the older angel saw a hole in the wall and repaired it. When the younger angel asked why, the older angel replied, 'Things aren't always what they seem.'

The next night the pair came to rest at the house of a very poor, but very hospitable farmer and his wife. After sharing what little food they had the couple let the angels sleep in their bed where they could have a good night's rest. When the sun came up the next morning the angels found the farmer and his wife in tears. Their only cow, whose milk had been their sole income, lay dead in the field.

The younger angel was infuriated and asked the older angel, 'How could you have let this happen? The first man had everything, yet you helped him,' she accused. 'The second family had little but was willing to share everything and you let the cow die.'

'Things aren't always what they seem,' the older angel replied. 'When we stayed in the basement of the mansion, I noticed there was gold stored in that hole in the wall. Since the owner was so obsessed with greed and unwilling to share his good fortune, I sealed the wall so he wouldn't find it. Then last night as we slept in the farmers' bed, the angel of death came for his wife. I gave him the cow instead. Things aren't always what they seem.'[2]

JEHANGIR SAROSH is a Zoroastrian and President of Religions for Peace Europe. He is also a businessman, founder and executive member of the European Religious Leaders Forum and active in many other interfaith arenas. His reflection blends the relevance of interfaith with the richness of religious diversity:

Jehangir hard at work under his interfaith umbrella!

There are as many different understanding of the word 'Interfaith' as there are different understandings of the word 'religion.' Just as many find a need for religion for their personal philosophical and ethical code, many find a need for Interfaith for communal philosophical and ethical codes.

This simply means that there is no one understanding of Interfaith: the diversity and maturity of a community decides its particular appreciation. A community with a monolithic faith tradition sees no need for interfaith dialogue or multi-faith co-operation, whereas a multi-cultural society realises the need for dialogue and co-operation to avoid potential conflict. Far too often, the need is seen as a conflict resolution method rather then a preventative requirement with a natural organic growth of the interfaith movement.

It is a movement, and yet too often groups turn it into an organisation or institution. It is a movement to change the mindset of all who are bound by the limitations of their own culture, creed, ethnicity and all the other cocoons that have given them a sense of security. It does not generate insecurity, it offers freedom in security, freedom to know and love the 'other' and thereby understand and love oneself, thus offering the possibility to 'love thy neighbour as thy self.'

Interfaith is an ever-changing fine phenomenon better described by what it is not rather than defining it with a definition and thereby limiting it. It does not demand uniformity to be imposed; instead it allows diversity to be celebrated. It does not fail to differentiate between faiths and thereby does not attempt to synchronise them. Any suggestion of syncretism will ensure the

Jehangir (standing) with youth at a Coventry 2000 Interfaith Workshop.

death of the movement or the group that attempts it.

Interfaith dialogue and co-operation broadens the outlook enabling a faith community to seek the common good rather than fight for their own corner. The movement generally begins with dialogue, dialogue enables understanding, understanding brings forth respect, and respect for the 'other' opens the door to co-operative action for the common good, bringing forth cohesive communities. This offers the potential for what we all seek - happiness.

As Asho Zarathushtra, the prophet of Zoroastrianism, stated, 'Happiness to him who gives happiness.' Be happy, stay happy, share happiness. Happiness is one entity that the more you give the more you have. The Interfaith movement facilitates that.

FR ALBERT NAMBIAPARAMBIL CMI is General Secretary of the World Fellowship of Inter-Religious Councils based in India. He has been a Catholic priest in Southern India for over fifty years and has broad international interfaith experience. In this reflection Albert shares his responses as 'A Christian Partner in a Hindu-Muslim Dialogue:'

As one involved in the organization of multilateral interfaith dialogue, I was happy to take part as a Christian in a Hindu-Muslim Dialogue that was organized in the Hindu Shri Udasin Karshni Ashram in Mathrua from September 30 to 2 October 2005. The majority of the participants were Hindus and Muslims. This encounter was preceded by another interfaith meeting, in April 2005, organized by this Ashram in collaboration with the Banaras Hindu University. It was great that both initiatives, in two sensitive areas with memories of communal tension, came from a Hindu Swami.

I went into this Hindu-Muslim meeting with my own fears that this one may rekindle wounding memories from the past history of conflicts. This did not happen. From the very beginning to the very end a cordial, warm atmosphere of love and appreciation prevailed. Swami Gurusaranandaji deserves all gratitude and appreciation for the great generosity and hospitality we all experienced.

The focus of almost all the presentations, especially from the Muslim side, was to shed light on the meeting points in the encounter between the two religions, Islam and Hinduism. Muslim presentations repeatedly affirmed that they accept all the prophets of all religions; that they are against all wars in the name of religions; that true 'Jihad' has nothing to do with interfaith conflicts or wars; that Islam is a religion of peace; that they do not accept the theory of 'clash of civilizations;' that true Islam stands for the rights of women; that they are against a 'uniform civil code' if this means the imposition of the civil code of the majority religion

Fr Albert in Oxford.

Albert (right) with some of the other participants.

on a minority. Speakers from both sides pointed to the painful situation of the politicization of religion as the real cause of conflicts between the two communities.

In the search for meeting points, a good many presentations, especially from the Islamic side, dwelt at length on Sufi mystics. The sayings and poems of the mystic saints of Islam were cited, mostly in Urdu. An experiential touch was brought in by these citations! Bringing in a rare note, I requested the participants to pick up the differences between the two great traditions. These differences are also to be appreciated and accepted, and to be given due emphasis in interfaith meets. But - I am afraid - this plea did not receive much attention and consideration, even though one great difference between Islam and Hinduism had to be addressed – the use of 'idols' for worship.

Islam, as a religion, insists on the Transcendence of God or Allah and some Hindus like to evoke the presence of God through murtis or images of the divine. Pressed by a question from the Hindu Swami, participants searched to find an acceptable form for the Formless Absolute for those who needed it. It was a rich moment in this encounter when a speaker pointed out that some interpretations of the Hindu tradition also leave room for the formless! Will this be acceptable to the majority of the ordinary members of the Islamic community? Will the majority Hindu community understand the sensibilities of the Islamic community in accepting or rejecting idols as expressions of religiosity?

Personally, I felt a missing note - that of interfaith prayer - in this Hindu-Muslim dialogue. I understand this is not that easy between these two traditions. Perhaps we have to be on the look out for creative interfaith vibrations, in moments spent in meditative songs and reflections. But, the very fact that such an encounter, with the collaboration of the Banaras Hindu University, Aligarh Muslim University, and Jamia Millia, took place is a gift to us involved in interfaith dialogue.

Let me end with a note from Rabindranath Tagore:
There are numerous strings in your lute;
let me add my own among them.

> *Like the bee gathering honey from the different flowers,*
> *the wise person accepts the essence of the different scriptures and sees only the good in all religions.*
>
> Mahatma Gandhi

REV YASUTOMO SAWAHATA is a minister of Rissho Kosei-kai, a lay Buddhist organisation, at their Geneva branch. He writes his reflection on interfaith dialogue and religious diversity from this particular Buddhist perspective:

Rissho Kosei-kai (RKK), a lay engaged Buddhist organization in Japan, has devoted itself to interfaith dialogue, based upon the modern interpretation of the Lotus Sutra by the late Rev Nikkyo Niwano, Founder of RKK: Truth is universal and all religions are manifestations of that truth; all life springs from the same source and thus all people are interdependent and belong to the global family. Rev Nichiko Niwano, President of RKK, has acceded to this idea and paraphrased it: each one of us is a 'child of life' who is supported in being alive at this moment in this place by a single great life force.

The declaration of Nostra Aetate at the Second Vatican Council and the private audience between Pope Paul VI and Founder Niwano also encouraged and even reaffirmed RKK's commitment to interfaith dialogue. Since then, RKK has been engaged in many interfaith works and is one of the leading members of Religions for Peace (WCRP), the International Association for Religious Freedom (IARF), the Federation of New Religious Organizations in Japan, and the China-South Korea-Japan Buddhist Friendly Interaction Conference.

Interfaith dialogue has become, in some ways, a kind of a trend and widely accepted since people have inevitably realized the reality of religious pluralism. I believe, however, continuous efforts have to be made for soliciting ordinary believers and religionists who are not interested in dialogue. Organizing a special prayer event for sharing common concerns exemplifies one concrete way to do this. For instance, The World Day of Peace in Assisi, in 2002, was organized by the Vatican in order to pray together and to reflect on the role of religions in public. It really impressed me that so many ordinary believers, though mainly Catholics, actively participated in that. In my local setting, interfaith prayers for victims of the Tsunami were held at Saint Pierre Cathedral in Geneva in January 2005. More than one thousand people, mainly ordinary believers and public citizens as far as I saw, attended that.

Needless to say, people of faith must not wait for some tragic incident that might sadly occur in the world to engage in interfaith dialogue and prayer. Rather, dialogue should be a significant component of our daily lives, one that sheds light on co-existence and pluralistic society. Dialogue should not function just as a forum in which participants discuss religious differences. There has been much of this in the past and it hardly bears fruit at present.

Two types of dialogue should be explored. First, dialogue has to be a means of fostering mutual respect and trust that lead to common actions. Many local religious associations in Japan have been established for this. Their purposes are not only to develop mutual understanding and trust by means of prayer and reciprocal visits but also to commit to social issues such as environment and youth education that can be attractive to the general public.

The second type is to implement some common actions and concrete projects for wider humanity. The tremendous endeavors to form inter-religious councils for tackling issues such as HIV and poverty eradication are good illustrations. Already fifty-seven of these have been established by Religions for Peace (WCRP).

Furthermore, as far as Buddhism is concerned, intra-religious dialogue is of great importance. RKK has joined with other Japanese Buddhists to form the China-South Korea-Japan Buddhist Friendly Interaction Conference, an organisation that consists of Buddhists and many senior leaders from the Mahayana tradition. One of the actual outcomes is a compilation of 'Fundamental Buddhist Sutras' that can be utilized at intra-Buddhist ceremonies. This dialogue could be extended to other Asian countries where Theravada Buddhism is the mainstream. Prayer is a foundation for interfaith dialogue. It manifests and motivates our religious spirituality, mutual understanding and trust, and common actions. I would also like to emphasize the necessity of collaborative efforts by international interfaith organizations. Competing against each other, either directly or indirectly, proves ineffective. It is time to collaborate for true dialogue.

Yasutomo leading a World Council of Churches workshop about Hoza, circle of compassion, as a means of reconciliation.

REINHARD KIRSTE & INSTITUTE OF INTERRELIGIOUS STUDIES

I was born in 1942 in Berlin, a city that had not forgotten its multicultural character. I learnt already as a young boy to accept the other in his or her otherness. That did not mean that I had contact with people of other faiths, it was more an inner feeling. When I studied Protestant theology I had good teachers but I had no glimpse of the importance of encountering people of other religions.

When ordained as a Lutheran priest, my first parish was near Hildesheim, where 'my' church had been the pilgrimage chapel of an ancient Cistercian monastery. There I learnt the importance of meditation that transcends the frontiers of my own confession. Travels in North Africa and Asia widened my horizon in other cultures.

At the end of 1975 I began work as a Religious Education schools advisor and I strengthened my engagement in Christian-Muslim-Jewish dialogue. Since summer 2006 I lecture regularly at the University of Dortmund in the Evangelical Theology Unit of the Department of Human Sciences. My emphasis is on religion, interfaith dialogue and spirituality.

John Hick, the English philosopher and theologian, played a crucial role in my theological and interfaith development. His book, *God Has Many Names,* made a big impression when I bought a copy while on holiday in Malta. The author was new to me then. While reading it during the flight home and becoming more and more inspired by discussing it with my wife, we decided to translate it into German, because Hick's theories on religious pluralism were not yet known in Germany. So the first German translation came out in 1985 and found enthusiastic agreement. Because it was published in a very limited edition we planned a revised edition. It was extremely difficult to bring out the book again and we did not succeed until 2001!

In 1989 some colleagues and I founded the 'Interreligiöse Arbeitsstelle (INTR°A or Institute of Interreligious Studies) because one of my main objectives in working with teachers was to address the problems of interreligious and intercultural learning experienced by the high percentage of migrant children in our schools.

As part of our research into religions we have also built up a special library for inter-religious studies and research. This library is virtually connected with Dortmund University Library. With the help of the Apfelbaum (Apple Tree) Foundation we offer the annual INTR°A Project Award for the Complementation of Religions. As our world as one world is challenged by various mortal threats, we need dialogue-orientated contributions in order to perceive the future more authentically than before.

In 2004, as a consequence of my work at INTR°A, my wife and I founded 'Omnis Religio,' a foundation with the aim of dedicating our work to peoples of different religious traditions and to support projects and initiatives of interfaith quality. From the beginning we have organized many conferences and encounters with people of other faiths. We have published many books and articles (often together with teacher groups and INTR°A), including 8 volumes of *Religionen im Gespräch* (Religions in Dialogue) and *Interfaith Reading of the Bible* (2005).

To conclude – INTR°A and I aspire to the following foundations for interreligious encounter:

- Dialogue can only happen in a meaningful way between equal partners.
- Absolute claims of single religions can only refer to the binding force of individual faith.
- Inclusive thinking, no matter how well hidden, that may label different religious traditions as being inferior, is not permitted, nor are inclusive claims (e.g. 'anonymous' Christians, Buddhists, Muslims, etc.)
- The understanding of mission must therefore be interpreted in the sense of personal testimony and engagement without trying to convert the other to one's own expression of faith.
- The different religions do not express the ultimate truth. They are linguistic, ritual, and spiritual approaches to the transcendental. Their message is temporary, and they require revisions. Religions form part of various cultures and different ways of thinking. Therefore they have to be understood as varying ways to salvation.

Interfaith meeting at the mosque (Hagen-Hohenlimburg)

JOHN D'ARCY MAY of the Irish School of Ecumenics shares his insights into what it means to become truly catholic:

During the 1960s two defining events of the twentieth century had a decisive influence on me: the Vatican Council and the Vietnam War. I spent those years in Roman Catholic seminaries in Canberra and Melbourne. I was studying with a missionary order, which meant a certain familiarity with Aboriginal people and Pacific Islanders, Filipinos and Japanese. But these two events opened up new theological horizons, the Council by endorsing the idea that 'non-Christian religions,' as we called them then, were somehow included in God's plan of salvation by virtue of what they already are, and the war by focusing attention on the Asian Buddhists who were trying to define a 'third way' between their Communist oppressors and their American invaders. Who were 'Buddhists'? What gave them this aura of calm commitment which led some monks and nuns to bear witness to the transcendent reality that inspired them by immolating themselves in public?

The questions never left me as I pursued theological qualifications in Rome and Münster, and as soon as I was free to chart my own scholarly course I started learning Sanskrit and Pali, eventually holding Buddhist-Christian seminars with an Indologist colleague for both his students and mine. A visit to Sri Lanka in 1979 as the guest of Aloysius Pieris SJ in his Tulana Centre for Study and Dialogue confronted me with the realities of a rapidly developing, conflict-ridden, multi-religious society, and Aloy's tireless enthusiasm and theological creativity encouraged me to start teaching and writing about Buddhist-Christian relations.

Since coming to Dublin to teach at the Irish School of Ecumenics I have had the opportunity to introduce ecumenically-minded Christians to Buddhism and 'primal' religious traditions in a context marked by the memory of oppression, rebellion and civil war and by the sectarianism and violence of the Northern Ireland conflict. There has also been the satisfaction of working together with Jews and more recently with Muslims to build mutual understanding and prepare for the challenges which Ireland's newly multi-cultural society is bound to bring.

At times I wonder, however, whether we are seeing a new Eurocentrism which restricts 'interfaith' to Jewish-Christian-Muslim relations,

John (right, back) with colleagues from the European Network of Buddhist-Christian Studies in Chiang Mai during an interfaith conference in 2003

John (2nd from right) with Rissho Kosei-kai Buddhists in Japan

arising out of a 'Mediterranean' agenda dictated by the Middle East conflict and Muslim immigration. This is perfectly legitimate as a response to Europe's new role, but I try to keep alive an 'Asia-Pacific' perspective in order to complement the 'Atlantic' context of so much mainline scholarship with a 'Pacific' one, an awareness of the contributions that can and must be made by the religious traditions of indigenous peoples and the great universal religions that take their rise in India and China.

Fundamentalism, though an ever-present temptation, is not the answer because it distorts truth and incites to violence; what we need is something more like an 'ecumenical cosmopolitanism,' though in theological terms one could also call it 'realised catholicity.' It demands the discipline of dialogue as we learn from one another's spiritual practices and ethical ideals. This is not easy to argue for in a world gripped by the power politics of economic globalisation, but it is no soft option for dreamy idealists. Interfaith dialogue, understood in this sense and in this context, is a hard path to follow, but I am convinced that it is the only way ahead if the human family is to learn to live in both ecological and political security. And over and above this goal of mere survival there are the intellectual and spiritual discoveries to be made as the world's religious traditions grow together.

> The supreme good is like water,
> which benefits all of creation
> without trying to compete with it.
> It gathers in unpopular places.
> Thus it is like the Tao.
>
> Only when there is no competition
> will we all live in peace.
>
> Lao-Tzu, Tao Te Ching [3]

ANDREW STALLYBRASS ponders on 'An elephant on the road to Emmaus: The other religions, group or culture - A threat or an enrichment?'

You may know the story of the group of blind people meeting an elephant for the first time. One touches the tusks and notes that they are smooth and hard and cold; another touches the trunk and says, 'No, it's soft and a bit wet, like a large hose pipe.' A third touches the side of the elephant and disagrees: it's flat and rough and rather hairy. The elephant is a little like the religious phenomenon. We are all the partially sighted or the blind, in the presence of a great mystery, an elephant that goes beyond our limited Understanding

Never before in human history have there been so many daily touches between the different faiths and their believers, so much mixing and meeting. So how do we relate to the other, who isn't like us, who doesn't believe like us, who doesn't share our history and traditions? I cannot start by denying what the other faith traditions, the other nations and races have brought to humanity. The truth with a capital T does not belong to me. At an inter-faith event organised by Initiatives of Change and the Geneva Interreligious Platform, Tariq Ramadan said, 'What divides us is simplification. When we acknowledge the complexity of the other's situation, we find humility without judgement.' So we must work on ourselves, start with the beginning, with the person we have most hope of changing! To open up to the other, we need to know who we are, what we believe, to deepen our own faith and its roots. To open to the other, we need to be at home with ourselves.

PLATE-FORME INTERRELIGIEUSE
GENEVE

The Geneva Interreligious Platform, of which I am the Vice-President, includes Christians, Muslims, Jews, Buddhists, Hindus and Ba'hais. We believe that such a group of believers is needed, because the future of a cosmopolitan society like ours is constantly in construction through relationships with each other. We meet regularly to prepare events, meetings, annual inter-faith days aimed at a wider audience, we produce an inter-faith calendar that is widely used in schools, and organise visits between communities. We helped set up an inter-faith 'chapel' at Geneva airport. When there was a world AIDS congress in Geneva, we helped organise an inter-faith celebration in the cathedral for the participants. When a Swissair plane crashed in the Atlantic off Halifax, we helped create an inter-faith service, which was televised.

In the charter, we tried to put into words what we share from different traditions. We really had to listen to each other. It took months. In it, we say:

'We believe that the true inter-faith encounter implies each one giving freely and sincerely to others the experience of his or her faith and our lives, and that we equally welcome the sharing of others. We are certain that the encounter between what each of us believes to be true and what others believe leads us to a deeper understanding of the Truth - and that this does not imply any syncretism. It is as we start a dialogue about our convictions and concerns that we measure the gap between our lives and our ideals. We are ready for an apprenticeship of the road, a journeying together. We hope that our encounter will further a dynamic of communication between our communities. We know that daily we must start afresh, to live together, and so modestly make a contribution to repairing the long centuries of ignorance, hostility and intolerance between our faiths.'

There is a challenge to people of faith, to move beyond dialogue to discerning the common tasks. The needs of our societies, of the world, are so gigantic that we need each other. We can only tackle these common tasks together. Are we pilgrims, on the road, on the move, who discover other brothers and sisters on the journey, searching like ourselves for a greater understanding of Truth? Or are we defenders of a besieged fortress? They are two powerful, but conflicting images of the believer and of faith.

One of my very favourite stories in the Bible is of Jesus, after the Crucifixion and the Resurrection, walking with the two disciples on the road to Emmaus. The other disciples were shut up in the upper room, besieged in their fortress, but these two disciples were pilgrims. Christ walked with them, talked with them, and they didn't recognise the man that they'd spent so much time with in the previous months. They can teach us humility - we should be cautious in trying to decide where Jesus is and where He isn't, whom He is with and whom He is against. I believe that Jesus walks, recognised or unseen, with all those who are on the road in search for meaning.

A few years ago, I had to hurry to Britain. I'd already spent a week with my mother, but she was getting over a major operation and I went home. Then she took a turn for the worse, and my brother rang to say he needed me, even if she felt that she'd said her farewells to me. For another week, day and night, we took turns beside her hospital bed. The night before her death, my brother arrived to spend the night with her bringing the family Bible. For twenty minutes, he read his favourite passages to us, and we all wept. But I should tell you that my brother calls himself an agnostic. After the church service, which he largely planned and organised, I felt able to tell him that I had seen in him, the agnostic, something of the Christ I try to love and serve. The mystery of the elephant, and the mystery of the pilgrim road.

The Role of Religious Pluralism for a Pluralist Society

Extracts from a lecture given by JAY LAKHANI, Director of Education for the Hindu Council UK, at the conference on 'Leadership in a Pluralist Society' at the East London Mosque.

Some theologians object to the idea of religious pluralism as they equate it to relativism suggesting that this concept dilutes their religion. Pluralism is certainly not relativism, which suggests that there is no absolute hence anything goes! Suppose we are all standing in a circle and we all want to reach the centre. We all point to the centre as the direction we have to take. Every one of us will be pointing in a different direction; if we compared our prescription to go to the centre, we will not come to any agreement. It may appear that there is no agreement as to which direction is right and the whole thing is pure relativism, yet we know that not to be the case. Even though we are all pointing in different directions, the direction we have to follow is binding.

Each prescription, though different, is binding as it allows us to make spiritual progress taking into account our different starting points. The binding nature of our prescription translates into practice in insisting that even though there are many different pathways (religions), we have to stick to the one that suits our needs and relates to our starting points. There is no need to shift or water down our faiths just because others are using different methods.

One interesting bonus is that, provided we use our own methods to progress spiritually, as we move towards the centre we begin to feel greater affinity with people of other faiths who are also making progress towards the centre.

Pluralism does not expect us to be Hindus in the morning, Christians in the afternoon and Buddhists in the evening. That is not what pluralism means. It simply affirms that there are many ways of making spiritual progress. The path that suits our requirements is the best for us. We do not have to discard our pathways when we give educated acceptance to other pathways. Why should our pathways become any less potent when we discover that there are other pathways?

REVIEW:

You have just read some very positive responses to religious diversity.

Take a look at this picture of some participants at an interfaith conference in Northern Ireland.

In this small space there are two Hindus, a Sikh, a Buddhist, a Christian, a Muslim and a Zoroastrian!
They are happily talking with each other.
They meet as humans interested in each other.
They are meeting together in a country once notorious for its religious divides.

Interfaith still hardly touches those with negative approaches. Somehow they must become included if the richness of religious diversity is to make a real difference to our societies. How can we do this?

Reflect for a moment on the situation where you live.

> Are there inter religious tensions? Why?
> Are they based on theology, economics, fear, something else, something particular to your region?
> Are there local intra-religious challenges that fuel these poor relationships?
> Are there already people working to bring reconciliation within and between faith communities? Who are they? Have remedies been tried? What were they? How did they fare?
> What suggestions could you offer that could make a difference?

O Spirit, I worship Thee in all shrines

Into the temple of peace
come Thou, O Lord of Joy!
Enter my shrine of meditation, O Bliss God!
Sanctify me with Thy presence.

Eternal Allah, hover over the lone minaret
of my holy aspiration.
The mosque of my mind exudes
a frankincense of stillness.

On the altar of my inner vihara
I place flowers of desirelessness.
Their chaste beauty is Thine, O Spirit!

In a tabernacle not made with hands,
I bow before the sacred ark
and vow to keep Thy commandments.

Heavenly Father, in an invisible church
built of devotion granite,
receive Thou my humble heart offerings,
daily renewed by prayer.

PARAMAHANSA YOGANANDA [4]

Self-Realization Fellowship Lake Shrine and Mahatma Gandhi World Peace Memorial

Free at last!

CHAPTER VI

RELIGIOUS FREEDOM

INTRODUCTION

Issues of religious freedom abound in our world today. They are often complex. For example, in India, there is huge controversy over Christian Mission there. Do Christians have the right to preach freely or are they exploiting the religious tolerance of Hindus? There are no easy answers but a clear incentive, in the light of religious violence from all sides, is to meet, to dialogue, to come to an understanding that all can accept.

In August 2000, we attended the Millennium World Peace Summit of Religious and Spiritual Leaders held at the United Nations and the Waldorf-Astoria Hotel in New York. During one of the workshops the opportunity was taken by some Hindu Swamis and their disciples to forcefully bring to the agenda their views on Christian mission in India. One important instant result of this was a statement signed by some of the Hindus and Christians present that altruism should never be connected to conversion and aid should not be corrupted by mission. They said, 'We prefer to stay poor and keep our dignity!' Behind-the-scenes meetings, partly mediated by Dutch rabbi Abraham Soetendorp, led to a statement, 'Informal Working Understanding: Freedom from Coercion in Religion.' It contained the following points:

Rabbi Soetendorp

- We agree that the free and generous preaching of the Christian Gospel is welcome in India.
- We condemn the use of coercion and religious proselytism; we particularly reject the exploitation of the issue of poverty in religious outreach and missionary work.
- We agree that the giving of aid to those in need is a primary commandment of all our religious and spiritual traditions; we are resolved that this act of justice should never be tied to compulsory conversion.
- We commit ourselves to a continuing dialogue in the spirit of interreligious harmony, mutual respect, and the cooperative common effort to build a better world.

CONVERSION: ASSESSING THE REALITY

Addressing this issue, here are some extracts from the Report of an inter-religious consultation organised by the Pontifical Council for Interreligious Dialogue, Vatican City, and the Office on Interreligious Relations and Dialogue of the World Council of Churches, Geneva:

Two of the participants from India: Dr Renu Rita Silvano and Sr Nirmala Mary Joshi

We, the participants in the inter-faith reflection on 'Conversion: Assessing the Reality,' met at Lariano (Italy) on May 12-16, 2006. We, 27 of us, belong to Buddhism, Christianity, Hinduism, Islam, Judaism and Yoruba religion. We shared our views and experiences on this important subject over five days of co-living in the peaceful, idyllic and spiritually vibrant surroundings of Villa Mater Dei – a kind of inter-faith pilgrimage, brief but fulfilling. Our deliberations were intense, and took place in an atmosphere of cordiality, mutual respect and commitment to learn from one another's spiritual heritage, which together constitute the common inheritance of the entire humankind.

We affirm our commitment to the process of inter-religious dialogue. Its necessity and usefulness have increased exponentially in our times for promoting peace, harmony and conflict-transformation - within and among nations in our speedily globalizing world - especially since religion has often been used, rather misused, to shed blood, spread bigotry and defend divisive and discriminatory socio-political practices.

We hold that inter-religious dialogue, to be meaningful, should not exclude any topic, however controversial or sensitive, if that topic is a matter of concern for humankind as a whole or for any section/s thereof.

It is our conviction that honest and candid dialogue can enlighten and deepen our understanding even on the most contentious of issues. The clarification and, hopefully, resultant reduction in the areas of disagreement and ignorance can help communities to expand the possibilities for reconciliation and living together in peace, love and amity, according to our respective religious precepts.

Many differences and disagreements among the participants remained at the end of the consultation. Indeed, there was no unanimity even on the meaning of 'conversion.' Nevertheless, we wish to record that our deliberations helped us develop a convergent understanding of the several aspects of the issue of religious conversion, making us more sensitive to each other's concerns, and thus strengthening our understanding that such concerns need to be addressed through appropriate action locally, nationally and internationally.

A summary of reflections and recommendations

Freedom of religion is a fundamental, inviolable and non-negotiable right of every human being in every country in the world. Freedom of religion connotes the freedom, without any obstruction, to practice one's own faith, freedom to propagate the teachings of one's faith to people of one's own and other faiths, and also the freedom to embrace another faith out of one's own free choice.

We affirm that while everyone has a right to invite others to an understanding of their faith, it should not be exercised by violating other's rights and religious sensibilities. At the same time, all should heal themselves from the obsession of converting others.

Freedom of religion enjoins upon all of us the equally non-negotiable responsibility to respect faiths other than our own, and never to denigrate, vilify or misrepresent them for the purpose of affirming superiority of our faith.

We acknowledge that errors have been perpetrated and injustice committed by the adherents of every faith. Therefore, it is incumbent on every community to conduct honest self-critical examination of its historical conduct as well as its doctrinal/theological precepts. Such self-criticism and repentance should lead to necessary reforms inter alia on the issue of conversion.

A particular reform that we would commend to practitioners and establishments of all faiths is to ensure that conversion by 'unethical' means are discouraged and rejected by one and all. There should be transparency in the practice of inviting others to one's faith.

While deeply appreciating humanitarian work by faith communities, we feel that it should be conducted without any ulterior motives. In the area of humanitarian service in times of need, what we can do together, we should not do separately.

No faith organization should take advantage of vulnerable sections of society, such as children and the disabled.

We see the need for and usefulness of a continuing exercise to collectively evolve a 'code of conduct' on conversion, which all faiths should follow. We therefore feel that inter-religious dialogues on the issue of conversion should continue at various levels.[1]

*Participants
Venerable Bhiksunji
Chuemen Shih of Tiawan with
Rev Yoshiharu Tomatsu from
Japan*

Professor ARVIND SHARMA responded to these kind of religious freedom issues from a specifically Hindu perspective when he addressed the United States Commission on International Religious Freedom in 2000 CE. He identified two principal Hindu responses to the threat of conversion in recent times: firstly, conversion makes no sense when all religious paths are accepted by Hindus and, secondly, while conversion generally is undesirable, re-conversion to Hinduism 'is now valid, as it represents the righting of a historical wrong' following forced conversions by Muslim and Christian colonialists. Sharma also quotes Mahatama Gandhi who was once asked: 'What if a Hindu comes to feel that he can only be saved by Jesus Christ?' Gandhi replied that was fine but why should such a person change religion? Sharma concludes: 'In the Eastern cultural context, freedom of religion means that the person is left free to explore his or her religious life without being challenged to change his or her religion. Such exploration need not be confined to any one religion, and may freely embrace the entire religious and philosophical heritage of humanity.'[2]

Religious freedom and religious persecution can affect all religious groups, in different ways, in different countries. Freedom House's 'Religious Freedom in the World: A global report on freedom and persecution,' gave some examples:

A variety of groups – Christians and Animists in Sudan, Bahá'ís in Iran, Ahmadiyas in Pakistan, Buddhists in Tibet, and Falun Gong in China – are perhaps the most intensely persecuted, while Christians are the most widely persecuted group. ... Religions, whether large, such as Christianity, Islam, Hinduism, or Buddhism, or small, such as Bahá'í, Jehovah's Witness, or Judaism, all suffer to some degree. In many cases, these restrictions come from people who are members of the same general religious group but who are part of a different subgroup. Thus, non-Orthodox Christians in Russia, Greece, and Armenia suffer discrimination from the Orthodox, while Shiite Muslims in Pakistan and Afghanistan suffer persecution and even death from some of the dominant Sunni groups.[3]

The INTERNATIONAL ASSOCIATION FOR RELIGIOUS FREEDOM (IARF), in its earliest incarnation, was the first interfaith organisation to be founded after the 1893 Parliament of the World's Religions in Chicago. Initiated principally by liberal Unitarians it now has 90 affiliated member groups in approximately 25 countries, from a wide range of faiths. Every five years or so it convenes an annual Congress where members and guests gather to discuss issues of

---

UNIVERSAL DECLARATION OF HUMAN RIGHTS　　　　　　　　　　　　　　　　*Article 18.*

Everyone has the right to freedom of thought, conscience and religion; this right includes freedom to change his religion or belief, and freedom, either alone or in community with others and in public or private, to manifest his religion or belief in teaching, practice, worship and observance.

> DR HARRIET CRABTREE:
> Religious freedom and positive inter faith relations are two intertwined goals. In countries where the rights of some faith communities and their members are truncated there will be a sense of discrimination and this is almost guaranteed to undercut positive inter faith relations. But similarly, there is little point in working for the religious freedom of people of all faiths if this process is not accompanied by a process of education which enables those of different faiths to understand and respect each other and to live in peace and with a sense of contributing to a society rooted in shared values.[4]

interfaith relations and religious freedom. At the Congress in Budapest in 2002, DR KAREL BLEI, former general secretary of the Netherlands Reformed Church and Central Committee member of the World Council of Churches, made these remarks about 'Religious freedom: the basis of all freedom:'

How can the dream of religious freedom become true? What kind of State and State policy would be needed for that?

Religious freedom cannot survive or exist in a society where one religion is oppressively dominant. Religious freedom for all means that religious dissidents, religious minorities, have the same rights as the majority religion. It is the duty of the State authorities to take care that these rights are for all. In that sense, Western Europe could learn something from its own history. The French Revolution was a major break-through in the struggle for freedom against an old and oppressive Christian regime. Its triumphant proclamation of freedom included the proclamation of religious freedom. As it was stated in the Declaration of Human Rights, issued in August 1789 by the new National Assembly, 'No person should be troubled for his opinions, even religious ones.'

However, history shows also how easily the ideal of personal freedom can be absolutized resulting in its contrast: new terror, new oppression. That happened in France, soon after the revolution of 1789. The revolutionaries mistrusted each other and fell victim to each other's violence, until the 'strong leader' (Napoleon) seized power and the young French republic changed into a dictatorship, an 'empire.' Some fifteen years later, the emperor was defeated and the ancient order (in France and everywhere) was restored.

In the European Convention on Human Rights, it is stated that 'everyone has the right to freedom of religion,' which right includes, it is added, everyone's right 'to manifest his religion or belief.' An additional part of the article, however, deals with 'limitations' of this right that

> *No peace without justice, no justice without forgiveness. To pray for peace is to pray for justice, for a right-ordering of relations within and among nations and peoples. It is to pray for freedom, especially for the religious freedom that is a basic human and civil right of every individual. To pray for peace is to seek God's forgiveness, and to implore the courage to forgive those who have trespassed against us.*
>
> POPE JOHN PAUL II

'are prescribed by law and are necessary in a democratic society in the interests of public safety, for the protection of public order, health or morals, or for the protection of the rights and freedoms of others.' Where exactly does what is called a 'restriction' of that right in fact begin to be a violation of it? It is difficult to answer this question in practice. That, in turn, gives the authorities the opportunity of interfering in religious matters whenever they think that is needed.

I am not pleading in favour of a return to a closed, Christian monoculture like in Western Europe in the Middle Ages. I am pleading in favour of a State community in which the power centre will be kept ideologically empty, i.e. kept free from any tendency of totalitarianism. Politicians, political leaders, are often inclined to overestimate the importance of politics. It is not up to the State to authoritatively determine what is to be considered (ideologically) true or morally good, either in a Christian sense or in any other religious or non-religious sense. Rather, the State has the modest task 'to provide for justice and peace' so that human life can be lived in an imperfect world. As such, however, it has to be aware of the other, essential dimensions in life, to be taken seriously and to be discussed openly and freely. That such discussions really take place is in the interest of the State itself, of society at large. The State should encourage these discussions and facilitate them.

That is why religious freedom is so important, really indispensable, the basis of all freedom. It has to be defended and guaranteed, not out of indifference but out of an understanding of what really matters in society. There are many religions and beliefs represented in society today. Via their representatives, all are possible partners in the social discussion. Churches and other religious groups themselves have every reason to participate, as well as to promote that it takes place indeed, instead of being blocked by economic or bureaucratic forces (as it is so easily the case). Nothing less than the quality of democracy is at stake here. That should be a matter of major concern, also for

Some of the participants at the 2002 IARF Budapest Congress

MAHATMA GANDHI: DEFENDER OF RELIGIOUS FREEDOM

Mohandas K Gandhi was a great defender of human and religious rights. He set an interfaith precedent that includes ahimsa, non-violence. When in Delhi, Gandhiji would hold daily prayer meetings on the lawn of the residence where he stayed, Birla House. These occasions consisted of readings and prayers and songs from different faith traditions. Sometimes people in the audience protested about including prayers from the Qur'an due to the religious tensions of that period.

Rajmohan Gandhi, a grandson of the Mahatma, writes: 'My grandfather would listen patiently to the protesters, praise them if they presented their case soberly, praise others if they were courteous toward objectors, and then ask the audience if they agreed with the objection. The audience would always say they did not agree, whereupon he asked the protesters to withdraw their objection. Sometimes it was withdrawn; at other times it was not. If it was not, Gandhi would say that if the Muslim prayer was to go, he would also eliminate the rest... So the prayer ground became also a class in tolerance and in tactics.'[5] It was while walking to this prayer session on 30 January 1948 that Gandhiji was killed; assassinated by a Hindu who could not understand his support for Muslims.

The Mahatma said: I believe in the fundamental truth of all religions of the world. I believe that they are all God-given, and I believe that they were necessary for the people to whom these religions were revealed. And I believe that, if only we could all of us read the scriptures of the different faiths from the standpoint of the followers of those faiths, we should find that they were at the bottom all one and were all helpful to one another.

He also said: True religion is not a narrow dogma. It is not external observance. It is faith in God and living in the presence of God. It means faith in a future life, in truth and Ahimsa.

Rajmohan Gandhi beside his grandfather's statue in Hull.

those who represent religious views.

Yes, it should be. But what if it is not? What if a certain religious group would try to impose its views upon society in a totalitarian way, thus aiming at occupying the power centre for itself? We cannot close our eyes for that dark possibility (a possibility that so often was a reality in a 'theocratic' past). I think, in such a situation a firm conclusion would be necessary. The State would have the right and the vocation to intervene in favour of democracy, in order to keep the power centre ideologically empty. Such a State intervention, that would block specific antidemocratic actions of a specific religious group, would then not be a restriction of the right to religious freedom; it would rather be a step in defense of real religious freedom.

Of course, this is tricky. A State action against a specific religious group can easily be out of place, based upon a misjudgment or a prejudice. The State authorities should be aware of the danger and act very carefully. Churches and other religious groups could and should be helpful in giving their advice, using their right to religious freedom and speaking out in public.[6]

The relationship between states and religions is a pivotal contemporary concern. It is so multi-layered and the freedoms involved so inter-mixed that clarity is for the truly wise alone! For example, what is most important - freedom of press or respect for fundamental and sacred religious beliefs? Who decides? States, societies, religious communities are split in all directions. Sub agendas are rampant. Where does freedom really lie? The debate – internal and external, intra and inter – continues! Much greater understanding – and perhaps remembering – is required. There is much at stake.

Of course, the right to religious freedom involves the obligations of religious responsibility. With the help of a grant from the Rockefeller Foundation, IARF began to work on CREATING A VOLUNTARY CODE OF CONDUCT FOR ALL RELIGIOUS (OR BELIEF) COMMUNITIES. The draft states:

Why is this work so important? While governments are expected to adhere to standards of international law related to freedom of religion and belief, situations do exist where the religious or belief communities themselves are not accountable or are not ensuring that their own practices uphold the fundamental dignity and human rights of their members and others. These practices include, for example, lack of financial accountability, problems with health practices, and failures to protect minors. Indeed, recent incidences of such abuses by religious groups have led, and may continue to lead, to a backlash by governments in which freedom of religion and belief will be curtailed beyond reason. Hence, legislation has been introduced in some countries that is misconceived or repressive. Regional institutions such as the Organisation for Security and Co-operation in Europe (OSCE) have been examining these topics.

Initially, IARF will be working with selected experts in the field to develop voluntary guidelines to encourage responsible religious practices. The members of a small drafting committee came together in mid-March 2002 for an initial meeting in England. They represented a variety of backgrounds, including Shinto, Hindu, Christian, Muslim, and indigenous traditions. Dr Eileen Barker, Director of the Information Network Focus on Religious Movements (INFORM) at the London School of Economics, took a leading role in the project. Following its work in March, the drafting committee brought an initial text to the IARF Congress in Budapest in July 2002 for further discussion by member groups.

Ultimately, developing a Voluntary Code of Conduct for all Religious (or Belief) Communities is meant to establish that there should be a standard of conduct against which religious and belief communities should be ready to explain their practices. The process of formulating such a document may itself affect the behaviour of religious groups in a positive direction. In the longer term, it is hoped that this initiative will serve to improve the tolerance between the followers of different religions and beliefs, as well as between such groups and state authorities.[7]

One of IARF's current developments is the RELIGIOUS FREEDOM YOUNG ADULT NETWORK (RFYN), initiated and co-ordinated by Ramola Sundram (left). The objectives of RFYN are: To gain a deeper knowledge of religious freedom issues locally, nationally and globally; To become familiar with the concepts underlying article 18 of the *Universal Declaration of Human Rights* and its application to IARF's Statement of Purpose; To learn through action by creating small and large scale projects that enable interfaith encounter to take place, especially in areas where religious intolerance threatens religious freedom.

Projects have so far taken place in Hungary, Philippines, India, Japan and USA. One of these took place in Gujarat following the massive earthquake there in January 2001. Thirteen young adults from Gujarat, nine from other Indian states, and ten from Canada, Hungary, Japan, South Africa, UK, and the USA took part in an international interfaith project to help restore a mosque in a Muslim village, and to rebuild a temple in a Hindu village. The original temple had been totally destroyed

Work at the mosque

and the mosque partially damaged in the earthquake.

One of the young participants, PAULA, from the USA, wrote: The physical work was very powerful for me, being able to give of my time and spirit are things that I value. Learning about different religions was also very moving. I believe that religions, faiths, or just ways of being are really interesting to know about because you learn what motivates people, what keeps them strong, and what their answers to the big questions are. The things I will remember for the rest of my life were the small things during the trip. I loved the bus rides, talking and singing with everyone. I loved the spontaneous dancing that would sometimes happen. I loved that at every meal we would pray together. I loved the conversations I had with the other participants, that weren't planned. I loved all the laughing that we did as a group and how close I felt I came to everyone. The part that changed my life was the people I met. They are what made the trip so absolutely amazing to me. The work we did was very powerful, but the friends I made, I will have for life.

ANOTHER RFYN PROJECT took place in the Philippines in 2004: Some of the participants belonged to the Aromanon whose spiritual site had been visited during the April 2003 tour when it was seen that they worshipped on the bare earth in their communal hall. After consultations, it was decided that it would be a great offering to the tribe if the bare floor of the worship space were concreted. The chief and his wife were very pleased to host an interfaith group of young adults, but first they had to perform a ritual before the participants' arrival, to ask permission from their ancestor spirits. Once they considered that this had been granted, the project plan was finalized.

The young adults travelled quite a distance to get to the hall, and the only access was on foot. In order to formalise the gift of our service, a sheet of white cloth and some betel nut were presented according to the traditional symbolism of the tribe. Sand and other materials were carried to the hall on a bullock cart and by the young adults. We were joined there by other young adults from the tribe and the chief's family and helpers. It was great not only to achieve something concrete by the end of the afternoon, but also to share in discussions with young people from the community. Finally, the chief and his wife performed a special ritual of thanks, attended by the participants in a sacred place near the tribal hall.

RFYN: After the hard work, the fun!

Kashif Shahzada at the E-learning trial, IARF 2002 Congress

Sandy: In 2002, when I was working on some interfaith e-learning for the Network of International Interfaith Organisations, ZARRIN CALDWELL, then IARF's research co-ordinator, contributed the religious freedom component for that.[8]

Zarrin wrote, 'Sometimes, in fact often, the rights of different groups conflict. The scenario (below) is drawn from real-life religious freedom situations in different countries and shows how complex it might be to determine who has the right to do what.'

What is the best balance of rights and responsibilities?

Zarrin Caldwell

- SCENARIO ON RELIGIOUS FREEDOM -

The majority of the population from Country A is from one dominant faith. As such, this faith's institutions have some influence over the government's policies and education programmes in the country. While the country's Constitution guarantees religious freedom, some minority and ethnic groups operate in the country. They are required, however, to have state authority to function. Under this policy, places of worship must conform to established zoning laws.

Members of one minority group have been holding 'house church' meetings because they do not have enough financial resources to have their own centre. This group claims they are not breaking any criminal laws and have a right to both religious freedom and private meetings in their own homes. Parents in the neighbourhood, however, have complained to the authorities that minors are attending these meetings, are being 'brainwashed' by their teachings, and being encouraged to convert.

Some members of the dominant faith in Country A have raided a few of the 'house church' meetings and threatened the participants.

Your group is representing an international organisation that is to issue advice to the parties concerned about how to resolve this conflict. What kind of brief statement would you make?

Some questions to reflect on:

Q. Does the government have the right to break up these meetings and/or declare them illegal? If so, on what grounds?
Q. What responsibilities does the minority faith group and/or members of the dominant faith have to the community?
Q. Is there additional information in this case you would want to ask for?

Q. Are there creative solutions to the above problems that would bring people together rather than create more divisions?

SHLOMO ALON, currently an IARF trustee, Chair of the Interfaith Encounter Association and Chief Supervisor of Arabic Language and Middle Eastern Studies at the Ministry of Education in Jerusalem, wrote this profile of inter-religious work being done in Israel to help resolve religious freedom issues:

Interfaith dialogue was established in Israel in the late 1950s by a small group of visionaries. Despite decades of commendable interfaith activities, the need for a real dialogue between Jews, Muslims, Christians and others in our region is nowadays needed even more. There is an urgent need to supplement existing interfaith efforts, to draw ever larger numbers of individuals into the circle of interfaith dialogue and to widely implement interactive models for encounter that can effect true and lasting change in the outlook and attitude of participants.

In light of the above, a group of concerned long-time interfaith activists formed the Interfaith Encounter Association (IEA) in the summer of 2001. We care for a society in which the otherness of the other is not only accepted, but truly understood and respected and Freedom of Religion is a very important value. The IEA is guided by the following basic principles and goals:

- Equal representation of all faiths;
- Equality of the genders;
- Outreach to individuals from all faiths, age groups, walks of life and levels of society;
- Outreach to individuals across the religious-secular and political spectrums;
- Continual recruitment through committed activists;
- Implementation of interactive programs that effectively change outlooks and attitudes, such as extended weekend seminars and ongoing study groups;
- Continual development of new models for effective encounter;
- Ongoing evaluation of all strategies and programs.

The IEA is dedicated to promote real coexistence through inter-religious dialogue. We believe that, rather than being the cause of the problem, religion can and should be a source of solution for the conflicts in the region.

IEA representative Shlomo Alon (right) sharing peace building ideas with participants from India and Pakistan at The Goldin Institute for Peace and Reconciliation Conference in Amritsar, India in 2005.

We do not believe in the blending of all traditions into one undifferentiated group, but in providing a table where all can come and sit in safety and ease, while being fully who they are in their respective religions.

IEA includes now thousands of affiliates from all walks of life in its central circle of activity - the population Israel. In the Israeli-Palestinian circle of the Holy Land we work in cooperation with different Palestinian organizations across the Palestinian Authority. In the circle of the Middle East the IEA plays a major role in the Middle East Abrahamic Forum, together with organizations from Egypt, Jordan, The Palestinian Authority and Cyprus. We have special projects for women, youth interfaith encounter and many cross-cultural Study Visits.

As Theodor Herzel, the visioner of the Jewish Homeland said, more than 105 years ago:

If you really want it, it will not be a legend but a reality!

At the IIC's Education for Peaceful Living conference in 2000, a young woman from Canada, PAMELA WILSON (picture below/r), painfully reminded those present that our religions have not lived up to their high ideals and that all kinds of freedoms, including religious freedom, have been negated by them.

She demonstrated visually how the churches' residential school system in Canada had abused her First Nations people. A volunteer conference participant, representing a young First Nations person forced to attend such a school, was first bound around the eyes. She was told, you can no longer see your people, they are dead to you. Then her legs were bound. You cannot leave this place; you cannot go home. Then her mouth was bound. You can no longer speak your language. Then the whole body was bound. You can no longer practice your culture or religion. Pamela wept as her story unfolded. When the young people were 18 they were sent back to the reservations where they used similar methods to raise their own children so creating a cycle of abuse that still reverberates through First Nations communities with devastating effects.

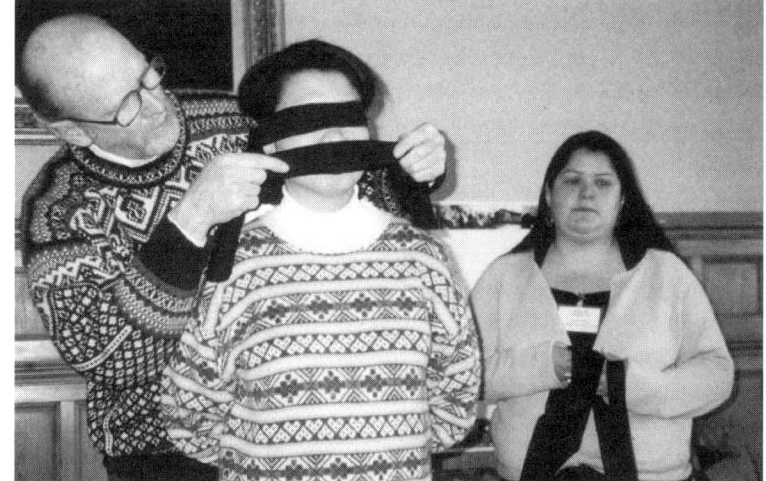

The following examples, from the 2002 IIC conference on religious freedom, describe situations in two countries where religious freedom has been seriously denied and accompanied by religious violence.

PUNJAB: In India, a volunteer led organisation, FATEH (Fellowship of Activists Embrace Humanity), has been established to help the rehabilitation of Punjabi Sikhs who have suffered from religiously motivated violence and torture.

Navleen Kaur told the story of a visit she and others made to a village household in the Punjab where the 22 year old son had returned home from dental school one weekend only to be arrested by the police and taken away for questioning. The policeman in charge admitted they had probably made a mistake but they took the boy anyway. His parents had saved for 20 years to give him an education and neither were political activists. The boy was not even a committed Sikh. Fifteen years later the mother had still not accepted that her son would not come home. The father, after some years, saw a photo of the policeman in the paper announcing his promotion to a post in Delhi, and set out to find him. Poor and powerless, he finally managed to meet the officer who eventually remembered the boy. Indeed, he had not been an activist, but too bad, he nevertheless still ended up in a river.

Navleen explained that this attitude to Punjabi Sikhs, many poor and illiterate, is not uncommon. Other minorities suffer in the same way. The killings and torture have left many broken families, children without fathers, and widows evicted from their husband's family home. For many this situation is a 'silent nightmare.'

TIBET: Nick Gray's stunning and moving documentary film, *Escape from Tibet,* tells the story of a group of Tibetans escaping across the high Himalayas into Nepal and then on to Dharamsala in India. Two young brothers are especially featured, Kelsang and Lobsang Rinchen. The film tells a living story still without a happy ending as thousands more Tibetans, young and old, are com-

Kelsang and Lobsang in Oxford with Reynaldo Mariquoe (centre) of the Mapuche peoples

pelled to attempt the treacherous mountain pathways to escape the aggression and suppression meted out by those who occupy their land. Kesang Takla of the Office of Tibet, London, pointed out that religious and cultural freedom in Tibet for Tibetans is non-existent and institutions like the Human Rights Commission do nothing to support those freedoms. Trade with China has a greater priority. Interfaith groups can play an important role in influencing governments to enact the ethical codes they espouse and put principles before profit.

Kesang Takla

BRITT STRANDLIE THORESEN, on behalf of the members of the Council for Religious and Life Stance Communities, tells us about the interfaith situation and responses to religious freedom in Norway, a country that has a state church:

After some initial dialogues, the idea gradually matured that what was needed here was a national forum for interfaith dialogue and cooperation that would embrace as many religious and life stance communities as possible. The attempt was made to include all major religious and belief groups in Norway and, in 1996, The Council for Religious and Life Stance Communities was founded. Representatives from eight major belief communities came together in the quarters of a Muslim congregation. It was a very special occasion when one by one their leaders rose and said: 'Yes, we want to be part of the proposed interfaith council in Norway.'

The goals of the Council for Religious and Life Stance Communities are to promote mutual understanding and respect between different religious and humanist communities through dialogue, to work towards equality between various religious and humanist communities in Norway based on the UN Covenants on Human Rights and on the European Convention on Human Rights, and to work internally and externally with social and ethical issues from the perspective of religion and humanism.

A key word is dialogue – dialogue without a hidden agenda. The agenda

Sikh-Bahai Dialogue: Jaswant Singh with Britt

of such dialogues does not include proselytizing, it does not aim for comprehensive consensus, and it does not strive for agreement in theological matters. In Norway, where the state church has enjoyed a near monopoly in public theological and moral discourse, the minorities will not so easily trust a decision taken by the religious majority on their behalf. Mutual trust is grounded on co-operation and in the possibility of making oneself heard. All issues where religious faith and humanism have significant social repercussions are discussed by the Council, including questions about human rights, genetic research, euthanasia, educational policies, the role of media in society, contested court and administrative decisions etc. The Council hosts interfaith seminars and, hopefully, it will inspire scholarly research.

In January 2004 a major step was taken by the Government of Norway asking the Cooperation Council to perform a joint marking of the tsunami as so many with different religious backgrounds were suffering. In the Town Hall of Oslo, His Majesty the King, the Queen, the Crown Prince and the Crown Princess, together with nearly a thousand people, were gathered to listen to children reading from their texts about hope and comfort. It was all linked together with music from the different areas of the world and shown on national television.

So far the Council has hardly conducted purely theological dialogues. But it has discussed how to make authors of school textbooks give a better and more correct presentation of each religion or belief. And the Council has addressed a host of issues of particular concern to religious communities e.g. advised against modernization of the spelling of religious terms, protested against a proposal from a political party to forbid circumcising baby boys, and requested that political parties not use religions or beliefs as tools in their electoral campaigns. The Council has also pointed out that it is unsatisfactory that Norway gives only a four years residence permit to most Muslim, Jewish, Hindu or Buddhist clergy coming from abroad, whereas Christian priests who can document a higher education have no problem getting residence permits lasting more than four years.

The Council for Religious and Life Stance Communities in Norway is still very much occupied with the new mandatory school subject, 'Knowledge of Christianity and information about other religions and beliefs.' The aims of the campaign for freedom of belief in Norwegian schools have not yet been achieved and the struggle is still being waged against majority political decisions.

Religion and belief are powerful tools, and in the wrong hands can lead to bitter, bloody, and prolonged wars. In Norway we have been spared such calamities. But, in our history we have ample experience of another troublesome aspect of religion and belief: Intrinsic in religions and other comprehensive normative traditions is the temptation of excluding outsiders from equal public status and from equal respect, as persons and as communities. Our recent experience is that religion and belief can also serve as a basis for eliminating animosities and for the strengthening of understanding and cooperation across ethnic, ideological and religious divides.

Our experience in Norway also demonstrates that the modern state has an important role to play if our goal is to nurture the potentials of religions and life stances for dialogue, reconciliation, and mutual understanding and respect in society at large. The state is responsible for the space between and around the communities of faith, for protecting their exercise of confessional freedom, and for safeguarding the rights of individual human beings to enjoy real freedom of religion or belief.

The Center for Studies of Holocaust and Religious Minorities in Norway has two main fields of interest: the Holocaust on the one hand and religious minorities on the other. Within these two fields of interest the Center will contribute with new research, education and information activities, exhibitions and conferences. Moreover, it is the explicit aim to be a meeting-place for people who want to participate in the enduring controversy concerning all kinds of religious, racist and ethnic motivated repression. The Center of Studies of Holocaust and Religious Minorities officially opened in 2006 in the former residence of the Norwegian Nazi leader Vidkun Quisling. Once a house of shame it will now - as a matter of historical irony - be filled with activities in contrast to its former role.

Britt also tells us about the formation of the OSLO COALITION ON FREEDOM OF RELIGION OR BELIEF:

In 1997 the Council for Religious and Life Stance Communities in Norway was approached by a group of academics from Norway and abroad and some prominent Christian religious leaders who wanted to organize a large international conference in support of Freedom of Religion or Belief. The Council for Religious and Life Stance Communities was invited to host what became *The Oslo Conference on Freedom of Religion or Belief.* The plans were ambitious. Supported by the Ministry of Foreign Affairs in Norway and later also by other European Communities, the Oslo Conference took place in August 1998. It was a success. More than 200 religious leaders, academics, experts, and resource persons participated. At the conclusion of the conference the *Oslo Declaration on Freedom of Religion or Belief* was unanimously adopted, identifying directions for future action. In accordance with the Declaration, the Oslo Coalition on Freedom of Religion or Belief has been established as a non governmental and internationally responsive organization. It is a new international network consisting of experts and representatives from religious and life stance communities worldwide. Academics are one important group, so are representatives from NGOs, from other international organizations, and from civil society. The activity of the Oslo Coalition is based on the Oslo Declaration on Freedom of Religion or Belief. As a follow up the Coalition has worked out a strategic plan for development and practical support for Article 18 of the Universal Declaration of Human Rights.

The Oslo Declaration on Freedom of Religion or Belief

Whereas the Oslo Conference on Freedom of Religion or Belief, meeting in celebration of the fiftieth anniversary of the Universal Declaration of Human Rights, reaffirms that every person has the right to freedom of religion or belief;

And *whereas* participants in the Oslo Conference have accepted the challenge to build an international coalition and to develop a strategic plan of action to achieve substantial progress in and give practical support to the implementation of Article 18 of the Universal Declaration of Human Rights, Article 18 of the International Covenant on Civil and Political Rights, and the 1981 United Nations Declaration on the Elimination of All Forms of Intolerance and of Discrimination Based on Religion or Belief;

Therefore, we the participants in the Oslo Conference:

Recognize that religions and beliefs teach peace and good will;

Recognize that religions and beliefs may be misused to cause intolerance, discrimination and prejudice, and have all too often been used to deny the rights and freedoms of others;

Affirm that every human being has a responsibility to condemn discrimination and intolerance based on religion or belief, and to apply religion or belief in support of human dignity and peace;

Consider the founding of the United Nations and the adoption of the Universal Declaration of Human Rights to be watershed events, in which the world community recognized for the first time that the existence of human rights transcends the laws of sovereign states;

Confirm that Article 18 of both the Universal Declaration of Human Rights and of the International Covenant on Civil and Political Rights together with other instruments create both a mandate for freedom of religion or belief and a universal standard around which we wish to rally;

Recognize that the U.N. has made significant accomplishments in strengthening this universal standard by passage of the 1981 U.N. Declaration on the Elimination of All Forms of Intolerance and of Discrimination Based on Religion or Belief, by the appointment of a Special Rapporteur to monitor its implementation, and by further defining freedom of religion or belief in the General Comment on Article 18 of the International Covenant on Civil and Political Rights;

Recommend that the U.N. Commission on Human Rights change the title of the Rapporteur to Special Rapporteur on Freedom of Religion or Belief;

Urge increased financial and personnel support to the U.N. to implement the work of the Special Rapporteur and his recommendations;

Request the U.N. High Commissioner for Human Rights to develop a coordinated plan to focus resources of the United Nations, including all specialized agencies and bodies such as UNESCO, ILO, NDP, and UNHCR on problems involving freedom of religion or belief;

Call for UNESCO to expand work for peace through religious and cultural dialogue and encourage intensified co-operation with UNESCO in this field;
Urge scholars and teachers to study and apply the Universal Declaration of Human Rights and the 1981 Declaration as universal standards on freedom of religion or belief and as a way to solve problems of intolerance and discrimination caused by competing beliefs;
Challenge governments, religious bodies, interfaith associations, humanist communities, non-governmental organizations and academic institutions to create educational programs using the 1981 Declaration as a universal standard to build a culture of tolerance and understanding and respect between people of diverse beliefs;
Further urge U.N. member states to use the 1981 Declaration and other relevant instruments to mediate, negotiate, and resolve intolerance, discrimination, injustice and violence in conflicts where religion or belief plays a role;
Support research and development of other informational resources and methodologies for collecting information, monitoring compliance and initiating comparative country studies to strengthen the work of the United Nations and protect freedom of religion or belief;
Urge the organizers and sponsors of the Oslo Conference, in consultation with Conference participants:

- to review the discussions and recommendations of the Conference, with the purpose of creating an 'Oslo Coalition on Freedom of Religion or Belief,' inviting support and participation by governments, religious or belief communities, academic institutions and non-governmental organizations; and
- to develop a strategic plan of action and seek funding to carry out programs and projects based on its recommendations, in cooperation with the United Nations system.

Oslo 15 August 1998

Britt signing the Oslo Declaration of 1998 on religious freedom. Bishop Gunnar Stålsett of Oslo is standing beside her.

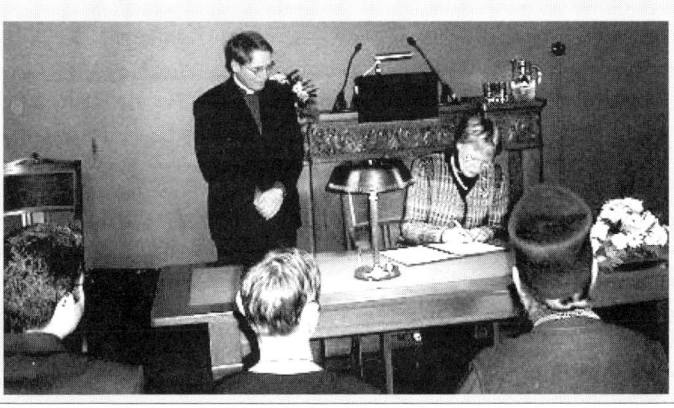

> *REAL FREEDOM: Take a good look at yourself. All truths are within you. To look for truth outside yourself is to search for water outside the ocean.*[9]
> Master Seongcheol (1912-1993)

SUMMARY

Religious freedom is a big issue. It isn't just about the rights of faith minorities in distant countries. It's also about the rights of faith communities everywhere in a balance with the rights of other groups, like the media, who want to express their right to free speech in ways that are sometimes very painful to people of faith. The lack of cohesion between these two rights too often leads to violence. Meru Devidasi and Andre Porto have written in this book (Role of Religions and Civil Society chapters respectively) about recent examples of this when cartoons of the prophet Muhammad (PBUH) printed in a Danish newspaper and then copied across Europe caused great distress world-wide to the Muslim community, leading to deaths in the violent and disturbed protests that followed the publications.

Rights must be accompanied by responsibilities. A balance has to be achieved. Relationship building between people of different faiths and between those with religious and secular beliefs can help establish forums for dialogue and debate and lead to a consensus and balance for the protection of all. If people of faith can be confident and stand together, they can address issues together and support each other at difficult times. Maybe then it would also be easier to respond to crises in less reactive ways. People who have worked for communal harmony in areas often disturbed by religious differences and fears have found that building such trust and solidarity can help withstand the forces unleashed when times get tough and provide alternative resolutions.

Working together for the religious freedom of all and balancing this with religious responsibilities may prove to be two of the most significant activities for a maturing interfaith movement in the days and years ahead.[10]

Peace begins with me.

Chapter VII   **PEACE**

THE GOLDEN RULE[1]

BAHA'I: Blessed is he who prefers his brother before himself.
Tablets of Bah'a'ullah, 71

BUDDHISM: A state which is not pleasant or enjoyable for me will not be so for another; and how can I impose on another a state which is not enjoyable to me?
Samyutta Nikaya, V

CONFUCIANISM: Do not do to others what you do not want them to do to you.
Analects 15,23

CHRISTIANITY: All things that you would that others should do to you, do you even so to them.
Matthew 7,12

HINDUISM: This is the sum of duty; do naught unto others which would cause you pain if done to you.
Mahabharata XIII,114

ISLAM: No one of you is a believer until he desires for his brother that which he desires for himself.
An-Nawawi, 40 Hadith, 13

JAINISM: A person should treat all creatures as he himself would be treated.
Sutrakritanga 1.11.33

JUDAISM: You shall love your neighbour as yourself.
Leviticus 19,18

NATIVE AMERICAN: Respect for life is the foundation.
The Great Law of Peace

SIKHISM: Do not create enmity with anyone as God is within everyone.
Guru Arjan Devji 258, Guru Granth Sahib

ZOROASTRIANISM: That nature only is good when it shall not do unto another whatever is not good for its own self.
Dadistan-i-Dinik, 94, 5

INTERFAITH

Discussing peace in Northern Ireland at the 'Religion, Community and Conflict' event.

INTRODUCTION

Religions are directly or indirectly implicated in many conflict situations. At the same time, many religious people, directly or indirectly, are actively trying to resolve such situations. How do religions contribute to conflicts? How can people of faith turn that around and contribute to peace and community cohesion?

When you look at struggles around the world, it becomes clear that land and its ownership are often at the heart of the divisions: who owns it; how can it be shared; who has to leave it; will having our own country make us safe? A quick glance through history's pages reveals how tenuous is any grasp on land and how fleeting is any sense of security brought by it. Borders constantly waver; ambitions endlessly embrace them; and humanity relentlessly flees over them.

When you look at the world's religions, you see something similar: this belief is ours; it is the right one; we will defend it at all costs; it must also cross borders to reach you and fill your lands, for your good. Religions too can have narrow boundaries for those who interpret them with narrow visions. Yet, in each religion, there are also strong messages of peace and inter-connectedness. The Golden Rule is at the heart of all of them. If these messages are implanted in each of our traditions then perhaps we cannot blame religions for problems in the world today. We can only look at the way religious people are living their faith.

Sometimes it seems peace activists are the angriest people we know! If the Golden Rule does not reign over the earth it could be because it does not reign in us. Peace begins at home. Jiddu Krishnamurti said 'Society is not different from me.'

We are the society we seek and if we want it changed, if we want to be happy and undisturbed by wars and worries, then we have to be peaceful. We have to look again at our religions and drink deep of the resources there that bring us to peace.

But what about the original critique, that religions cause the problems in the first place so why bother with them?

SIMON KEYES, Director of St Ethelburga's Centre for Reconciliation and Peace, puts it this way:

Everyone knows that religion causes wars. Friction between the Roman Catholic and Protestant varieties of the Christian message of peace dominated over two hundred years of European history.16th century France, for instance, endured thirty years of bloody civil war in which one denomination attempted to exterminate the other. Henry IV called an end to the slaughter in 1598, but it wasn't too long before Louis XIV was to declare Protestantism illegal once again. This didn't have much to do with the humble heart of true Christianity, of course. It was naked religious politics, one social group pursuing its worldly interests over another, invoking an exclusivist theology to identify friend and foe.

But that's history, isn't it? Modern wars are about economic conflicts, not theology. 'People of faith' are the good guys who demonstrate to an aggressive world what peace and freedom are all about, surely?

St Ethelburga's, a small mediaeval church in London, was destroyed by a huge bomb in 1993 (see picture), planted by the IRA to disrupt the City of London. It's been rebuilt as a Centre for Reconciliation and Peace with a mission to promote understanding of the relationship between faith and conflict. We're finding that it is a complex, and highly topical, equation.

It's not just a problem of people abusing scripture to justify violence - be it the suicide bomber or 'God tells me to' political leadership. Conflicts in the Middle East and, sadly still, Northern Ireland, demonstrate that religious sectarianism still defines some communities' sense of their identity by excluding people who believe differently. In places like Sudan, Nigeria, Pakistan and India the fault lines between different faiths are loaded with potential violence.

I believe that the single biggest issue for members of any religious tradition today is to come to terms with the fact that there are many different and mutually incompatible 'stories of faith' in the world. As these

Participants at the Euro-Mediterranean Civil Forum on Dialogue of Cultures and Civilizations, Crete, 2003. IIC representative and peace activist, David Partridge, has asked them to vote against the Iraq war. As you can see most – but not all – were happy to do so! Won't it be good when so many hands from around the world are also raised with a resounding 'Yes' for interfaith!

become detached from the cultural and geographical anchors that have previously kept them apart, the need for this work increases.

Religious pluralism is not just about being a good neighbour. It presents a major challenge to personal faith. If my interpretation of 'I am the way, the truth, and the life' means that I consider my belief is superior to yours, then will we ever be able to love each other fully and give each other freedom? If my revelation supersedes yours, why should I tolerate your decadence? If I am 'saved,' what incentive is there for me to avert Armageddon?

True faith transcends this kind of polarisation, when it is liberated from exclusivism, literalism, patriarchy. We need to guard against a lazy syncretism that short-circuits the integrity of different religious traditions. But this should not deter us from reframing how we articulate our faith so that we can embrace other people who see earth and heaven quite differently. Without this, faith will remain a source of conflict, rather than a resource for promoting the peaceful coexistence of the human family in all its glorious diversity.

MARCUS BRAYBROOKE shares this reflection on how interfaith can be a forum for 'Sharing Our Joys and Sorrows:'

Of the many inspiring interfaith gatherings that I have been privileged to attend, one of the most moving was a conference on 'Creative Responses to Suffering,' which I organised for the World Congress of Faiths (WCF) in 1979.[2]

Instead of summarising the teaching of their religion on suffering, each speaker shared his personal experience of suffering and how his faith had strengthened him to cope with it. Rabbi Hugo Gryn, for many years vice-chair of WCF, whose teenage years were spent at Auschwitz, told, almost for the first time, his harrowing experiences. On Yom Kippur, the Day of Atonement, 19 July 1944, Hugo fasted and hid among a stack of insulation boards, and wept for hours crying and asking God's forgiveness. 'Then I seemed to be granted a curious inner peace... I believe God was also crying. And I understood a bit of the revelation that is implicit in Auschwitz. It is about man and his idols. God, the God of Abraham, could not abandon me, only I could abandon God.' 'The creative response to suffering,' Hugo told the conference, 'must be compassion.'[3]

Fr Benedict Ramsden, an Orthodox priest, also spoke of his own experiences of suffering and went on to talk about 'the central doctrine of Christianity that the cost of the pain of the world has been borne by a man who was God.' Donald Nicholl warned of the superficiality of much religious talk on the subject. 'Suffering,' he said, 'is unique to each of us and has as many faces as there are human beings.'[4]

Remembering that conference, recalls memories of how many wonderful and inspiring people, of every faith, it has been our blessing to have known. At its deepest, interfaith fellowship is the meeting in friendship of people who have been inspired by their faith. The fruits of faith are a love and compassion that transcend all barriers.

There is a place for the 'official' dialogue, where representatives of religious communities meet and discuss together. But there is a deeper meeting, which WCF has always tried to encourage, where we come together in friendship as human beings. We share our experience of the Divine and support each other in the struggle to be true to our deepest convictions and to work together for a world that more fully reflects the loving purposes of God.

'Do you know what causes me pain?' That is the question our interfaith sharing should enable us to answer, as the recent statement 'Welcome and Unwelcome Truths Between Jews, Christians and Muslims' suggests.[5] To be able to answer this, we need great empathy and to experience as deeply as possible each other's beliefs, devotions, hopes and fears. In this way we discover in the depth of our being our common God-given humanity, which is obscured by the enmities and divisions in our world. But when we see each

Marcus Braybrooke with an interfaith group in Delhi

other person as a brother or sister, a child of God, we will seek their welfare as much as our own. This is why deep interfaith fellowship has the potential to heal the world's divisions and to help us create a world of lasting peace and justice.

I would like to close this reflection with these two texts.⁶

Lord open our eyes, that we may see you in our brothers and sisters. Lord, open our ears, that we may hear the cries of the hungry, the cold, the frightened, the oppressed. Lord, open our hearts, that we may love each other as you love us. Renew in us your spirit. Lord, free us and make us one.
Mother Teresa

O Lord give me strength that the whole world look to me with the eyes of a friend. Let us ever examine each other with the eyes of a friend.   *Yajurveda.*

Prof XINZHONG YAO, a Confucian scholar, shares this personal reflection on the role of religions in addressing issues of conflict:

For more than twenty years I have been devoted to interfaith and inter-philosophy in a scholarly way, and my main interests are in the communication and dialogue between Chinese and Christian traditions, a central concern for many Chinese intellectuals in the modern era. As a Chinese scholar, my perspective is to a great degree determined by my own cultural and philosophical background, taking an inclusive rather than exclusive approach to other religious and non-religious traditions, with an attempt to examine the philosophical roots of interfaith problems.

For me, religions are, at least partially, responsible for many historical and contemporary conflicts. Modern religious leaders and scholars tend to explain away the association of religion and violence from the perspectives of 'the social roots of religion,' claiming that the undesirable image of religion in conflict is due to the 'unjustified association of religion with nationalistic, political and economic interests.' It is true that religion cannot be separated from its social ties, and the tension between social groups is no doubt one of the most important reasons for the religious involvement in conflict.

However, this does not exempt religious doctrines and practices from sharing responsibility. It has been widely acknowledged that religion is a 'primary cultural marker distinguishing groups in conflict' and, in distinguishing one from others, religion cultivates and nurtures a

Xinzhong (l) in dialogue with Dr Ram Prasad, a Hindu scholar, at IIC's 1997 Annual Autumn Lecture.

strong religious identity. Religious identity provides the sense of security for individuals and groups, and religious communities and value systems are an important source of the sense of belonging underlying the meaning of life.

However in a religious context it is often the case that security is achieved at the expense of equality and belonging is acquired in a course of separation. Identity is the product of consciously drawing lines between people, and the boundary-drawing function develops through faith-oriented doctrines and specific religious practices, which if not supervised properly, could become one of the chief drives for a particular group of religious people to go to conflict: in the active pursuit of drawing a line between 'believers' and 'non believers,' between 'this' and 'that' faith, some religious leaders and followers tend to treat the former as 'the self' while the latter as the 'alien other.' The efforts in extending the 'self' group results naturally in a fierce identity competition, in which a religious person with a strong sense of identity and belonging would stand up for his/her own identity or if necessary, fight for it, treating all others who have an 'alien' identity' as 'opponents.'

Therefore, to reduce tension between religions, to transform the hatred of our 'enemies' to love and reconciliation, the steps we must take are to stop seeing those who are not in our own faith as the 'aliens,' not to draw too clear a line between 'us' and 'others.' Is this possible? While admitting that the tendency to draw lines is embedded in religious doctrines and practices, we must also see that there are rich resources within all religious traditions that, if applied appropriately, would enable us firstly to have a balanced view of 'us' and 'others,' secondly to counteract the urge to view 'others' as 'aliens' or potential enemies, and finally to strive for peace and harmony.

These three steps, for me, constitute an interfaith perspective on conflict and reconciliation.

Three steps being taken: Professor Paul Knitter, Maha Ghosananda and Dr Irfan Ahmad Khan leading local people and members of the International Peace Council to the village of Acteal to support the community and the Chiapas peace process.

INTERFAITH

> **FROM THE UPANISHADS:**
> *Lead us from Darkness to Light, from Death to Life.*
> *Lead us from Falsehood to Truth, from Hate to Love.*
> *Lead us from War to Peace.*
> *Let Peace fill our hearts, our World, our Universe.*
> *Peace, Peace, Peace.*

THOMAS MATHEW, IARF Vice-President and its South Asian Coordinating Committee Chairman, writes about the special experience that moved and inspired him to work for peace:

The visit to Hiroshima in the year 1988 remains alive in my mind, and I believe that it will remain so ever with me. The visit was part of a study tour to Western Japan organized by the Asian Rural Institute, Japan, where I was a student in the disciplines of Rural Development and Social Service.

The Peace Museum in Hiroshima was more eloquent to us than all tongues across the world, and more informative than all what is said, written and read about the damning holocaust in Hiroshima, caused against a cross-section of humans and the environment by other so-called humans for what ever reason the history debates about. The dead have gone. The survivors are there, who are the living exhibits and sobbing witnesses to the rest of the world and to the futurity of history, much more to the hearts of anyone asking: do we wish one more Hiroshima-like event to happen any time, anywhere, for any reason?

Our Institution student team visiting Hiroshima was drawn from different parts of the Globe. In the evening, we chanced to hear a descriptive explanation of the tragedy from a surviving, but badly affected lady. It was not easy at all for her as deep emotions choked her voice, and neither was it easy for us to hear her words and watch her body language, exhibiting the magnitude of

Thomas and group at the Hiroshima Peace Memorial Park

Hiroshima victim, Miyuki Kamasawa, inaugurating a peace conference at Trivandrum, India in 1997

suffering and sorrow that can be caused by the anti-thesis of Peace - War.

Cruel as it might appear to trouble the shattered survivor before us with questions and doubts, the student curiosity in us was too strong to resist, and she readily started giving answers and explanations. The suffering survivor of the Atom Bomb, that had rudely jerked the world conscience, and at the same time compelled a global re-thinking about the safety of the Earth and Her Children, instantaneously came out with an answer to a question I asked her, with some reluctance, at the end of the meeting: 'Do you harbor animosity to the Americans?' (43 years after the Bombardment). The answer: 'NO.' All human beings are one, valuable and equal. In all wars and wartimes common humans suffer, are murdered and tortured. Therefore, all those who love human beings must rally against War. No religion or belief teaches murder, homicide, mayhem or torture, but every one of them teaches love, mercy, sympathy, compassion, peace and therefore, everyone has to work to ensure another Atomic or other war never happens again, anywhere, any time in future.

The transcending words from one who lost every thing, and everyone at the age of 14, through no fault of her own, one who is above the worldly emotions of enmity, revenge, retaliation, religious fanaticism etc, were surely in the realm of Spiritual Heights. And, we students came back to our respective abodes and concerns filled with admiration.

This experience and encounter ignited my conscience to some sort of restlessness, and the outcome was a few questions to myself - what is my role in this world? What can I do preventively to avoid man-made catastrophes to the human race on account of War, Religion etc? How could I promote peace? Having been born and brought up with a background of love towards humans and other creations, I was internally forced to find suitable answers for these questions and to turn to humble but appropriate actions.

I came back to my home country, India: so far seven Hiroshima-Nagasaki survivors have been brought to India. With the help of these living martyrs I could explain to lakhs of people, through direct contact, and more through media like audio, video, TV, press, photo exhibitions, seminars etc, about the never repairable or curable damages of an atomic or other war to the world and the humanity at large. Lakhs of students in more than three hundred Schools and Colleges across and outside the country viewed the photo exhibitions and took anti-atomic weapon/war pledges. Many people of goodwill from Japan have sent in about a thousand Hiroshima - Nagasaki Photo Panel Packets that have been given for the use of school libraries in India and in Sri Lanka.

Multi religious congregations of the Hibakusas (survivors of the atomic bomb attacks) prayed univocally and unanimously for world peace and thousands of children and youngsters belonging to almost every religion known to the world pray and shout: 'We want no war.'

The opportunities being created for the thousands with all imaginable diversity, praying united for world peace and no war, gives new inspiration to go ahead.

BRIAN WALKER, Chair of Religions for Peace in the UK, provides a profile of their work and shares this account of how he became involved.

I am a practicing Christian, who became committed to inter faith dialogue whilst working in West Africa, with the war-ravaged people of Sierra Leone. There, following a decade of Rebel War, in the world's least developed country, where life expectancy at birth is 34 years and income is less than 80p per day, Muslims and Christians are working together for reconciliation and sustainable peace.[7]

For years, religious leaders worked in vain to persuade the rebels to stop the violent conflict: the terror, the killings, the machete amputations, the devastation. Then, in the late nineteen-nineties, with the help of Religions for Peace (International), leaders from both faiths risked their lives by driving into the tropical rain forest together to meet with the rebels and help them transform their conflict by peaceful means. The religious leaders included Bishop Dr J C Humper, who had already had his home in Bonthe destroyed, and Imam Sheik A B Conteh, a target of rebel fighters, who had previously escaped death disguised as a woman.

Today, those same leaders form the Inter Religious Council of Sierra Leone (IRCSL). Inspired by the Holy texts of their own faith and recognizing the values of those espousing traditional African religions, they all work together for reconciliation between ex-combatants, rehabilitation of child soldiers and reconstruction of their shattered homes, towns and economy.

Religions for Peace UK has formed a concordat with the IRCSL, for mutual help and support in working to build a culture of peace by peaceful means in Africa and in Europe. Religions for Peace (UK) now offers a programme of talks, workshops and on-going support for communities of faith, inter faith and no faith across the UK, who wish to understand and experience conflict as a positive opportunity for durable peace. This programme, 'Conflict Transformation for Peace,' uses research from experience in Sierra Leone to build upon the United Nations programme 'Conflict Transformation by Peaceful Means (the TRANSCEND Method).' The importance of women in peace building is firmly recognised and *Women of Faith Transforming Conflict: A Multi-Religious Training Manual* is freely available from us.

Other work includes our partnership in the Bill and Melinda Gates Foundation 'Hope for African Children Initiative,' a pan-African effort created to address the enormous challenges faced by millions of African children who have either been orphaned by AIDS or live with parents who are sick or dying from AIDS-related illnesses. Work also continues with the UK Consortium on AIDS and International Development Working Group for Orphans and other Vulnerable Children (OVC), seeking to provide support worldwide for OVC affected by HIV/AIDS and their carers.

Religions for Peace, known worldwide as World Conference of Religions for Peace (WCRP), is the largest international coalition of representatives from the world's great religions who are dedicated to achieving peace. We currently work across four continents, in 55 countries, including some of the most troubled regions: Bosnia-Herzegovina, Indonesia, Iraq, Israel, Kosovo, Liberia, North Korea, Rwanda, Sierra Leone, Sudan. International programmes include: close collaboration with UNICEF (The United Nations Children's Fund); the first ever Global Network of Religious Women's Organisations; commitment to disarmament and security; promotion of human rights; and peace education.

Membership of Religions for Peace (UK) is free to individuals over 18 years and organisations interested in furthering our work. Help us achieve our mission:

a world of justice, a world at peace, a world in harmony.

Brian in Sierra Leone

It is important to keep in mind that organisations function in different ways according to the contexts in which they are situated. There may be many constraints and challenges as well as dynamic opportunities to understand and explore. What might be the incentive and priorities for an interfaith organization in your area? What might be the difficulties you could meet? Reflecting on this may help your thinking about the limitations and possibilities others encounter.

Dr YEHUDA STOLOV of the Interfaith Encounter Association, Israel tells us about 'Interfaith in Action' in his volatile part of the world:

The Interfaith Encounter Association tackles in its work, mainly in the Holy Land and the Middle East, two main themes - building bridges between communities for peace, and conflict transformation. It sees the first as an essential component of the second and builds both of them through interactive interfaith dialogue.

Looking closely at the situation in the Holy Land, especially when bringing into account its small size, some 100km total, leads to the understanding that peace can not be sustained here without wide and massive grassroots transformation of the conflict's human relations aspect, from prejudices and fears into mutual understanding, respect and trust. Such transformation can be induced from a growing sense of a joint community, with shared interests, among the mainstreams of our communities and from their realizing that fostering inter-communal relations of friendship with respect for the differences is a more effective way to nurture the unique identity of each community than isolation.

This transformation of inter-communal relations can be achieved by the formation of 'community cells' in neighbouring communities, exemplifying the desired relations and attracting more and more people until they encompass the whole community. In order for this process to be successful and effective, the interaction in each of these 'cells' has to be both deep and powerful and positive. Interactive interfaith encounter, in which participants actively engage in a deep conversation about their faith and faith-based practice, is a most powerful tool for such interaction. The existential meaning of the issues ensures people, whether religious or not, come to the conversation from a deeper place in them. Through the conversation many similarities are revealed and, perhaps most important, differences can be talked about and accepted in a non-threatening way. Participants are trained in accepting others in their otherness and not to condition friendships by agreements.

Neme Ghazawi and Yehuda in friendly dialogue at an interfaith encounter retreat. Neme coordinates an interfaith encounter group in Netanya-Qalansawa.

This line of thought led us, a group of concerned long-time interfaith activists, to establish in the summer of 2001 the Interfaith Encounter Association (IEA), dedicated to the promotion of this process. In practice the IEA organizes more than 100 encounters a year, in three geographical focuses:
IN ISRAEL its main effort is to develop more interfaith encounter groups in neighbouring communities. So far we have formed 14 such groups – from the Upper Galilee in the north to Eilat in the south – and we are currently in the stages of forming 8 more. When funding permits, we organize weekend retreats in a specific area in order to start or enhance a group in that area.
IN THE ISRAEL-PALESTINIAN context we work in cooperation with 7 Palestinian organizations – from Nablus and Jenin in the north to Hebron, Gaza and Khan Younis in the south. So far we have organized 14 joint retreats of interfaith encounter and now begin to plan also for on-going groups, similar to those we have in Israel.
IN THE MIDDLE EAST we work to develop regional interfaith encounter and cooperation. We do that under the auspices of the Middle East and North Africa Region of the United Religions Initiative, with partners from Egypt, Iran, Jordan, The Palestinian Authority, Lebanon, Tunisia and Turkey. We are now planning for an Israeli-Jordanian on-going group in the south cities of Eilat and Aqaba.

Those who wish to get involved are first of all invited to visit our website, especially the reports page, and subscribe to receive updates from our various activities. Obviously those who live in the region are welcome to join our activities but also those who live in other parts of the world are welcome to participate in our global support network and join and initiate groups of Friends of IEA.

MONICA WILLARD, United Nations NGO representative of the United Religions Initiative, shares her commitment to the International Day of Peace:

The United Nations began observing the International Day of Peace (IDP) in 1982. Although it was initially observed in September for the opening of the General Assembly, a 2001 resolution established the fixed, annual date of September 21. This resolution also calls for the International Day of Peace to be observed with a global ceasefire and non-violence. These UN Resolutions invite nations and people to honour a cessation of hostilities for the duration of the Day and to promote peace education, observances, celebrations and public awareness for peace.

Seeing the world's current conflicts, we have a long way to go to accomplish these goals. Most of us will never be at a negotiation table that creates a

Mrs Nane Annan, wife of Secretary General Kofi Annan, has been at the UN Student observance for IDP since it began in 1997

INTERFAITH

Students send their messages of peace to every country of the world using the World Peace Flag Ceremony.

ceasefire. Yet everyone can promote the International Day of Peace. Think of what could happen if September 21 was fully observed as a Day of Peace, ceasefire and nonviolence. Preparing for this annual date would begin a process that involves partnerships, dialogue and shared projects. Peace education would be part of the educational curriculum. People would be encouraged to think and act with more courtesy, care and compassion. After all, how can you call for peace and not look at how you talk to your family or act at work?

Now think even bigger. Imagine the various religious and spiritual traditions using September 21 to pray collectively for peace in our world, our countries, our communities, our families and in our hearts. Grandfather Harry Bird from the Lakota nation used a quote that sums up this potential. He said, 'A heartfelt prayer is more powerful than an atom bomb.' Let us commit to harness this power for peace by using September 21 annually for prayers, mediations and vigils. Whatever your faith practice or tradition is, you would know that you are connected with millions or even billions of other people praying together for peace.

The International Day of Peace offers great potential for new partnerships. Having a shared purpose and date established by the UN encourages people from different cultures, faith traditions, ages or geographical regions to collaborate on joint projects. You can contact your local and national government to ask them to proclaim September 21 as the International Day of Peace in your community and country. For sample proclamations, ideas and information please go to our website.

The spirit of peace is contagious! Once you consider how you can get involved with the International Day of Peace, reach out to others and build a local coalition. The possibilities are endless. Have fun, but take it seriously! That's what will make it an annual event.

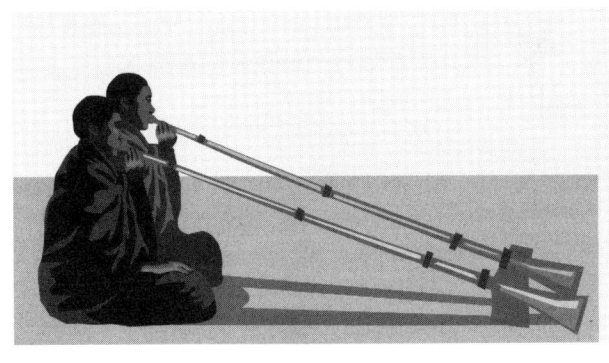

> Although it is difficult to bring about peace through internal transformation, this is the only way to achieve lasting world peace. Even if during my lifetime it is not achieved, it is all right. The next generation will make more progress.
>
> HH Dalai Lama

INNER PEACE

As people of faith it is vital that we do not forget our faith in striving for interfaith goals. It is only too easy when enveloped in organizational affairs, stress and targets to forget the impulse that started us on our interfaith journeys. When we forget, our work may also suffer, from a loss of inner dynamic and become just another job, just another struggle for money, status, and security.

Dr KARAN SINGH (pictured left) shares his insights into the inner developments needed for interfaith to progress and endure:

Peace and harmony have been sought by humanity ever since the dawn of civilisation. And yet the whole of human history, from the very earliest times, is replete with wars and violent conflicts from the tribal right up to the international level. All religions preach peace, but in fact religion has been one of the major sources of violent conflict down through the centuries, and remains so even today. Science was supposed to help establish peace, but it has created increasingly deadly weapons of mass destruction, so that a single nuclear warhead now packs explosive power equal to one thousand of the bombs that obliterated Hiroshima and Nagasaki half a century ago. Communism, socialism, capitalism, democracy - all claimed the desire to establish peace, but all invariably waged war. Even now, dozens of local and regional conflicts are raging around the world, and thousands perish every month as a result.

As against these negative approaches, however, all the great spiritual traditions of the world tell us that there is, deep within our consciousness, a creative power that, if invoked and nurtured, can bring about a benign transformation in our thoughts and behaviour. In the East it has been accepted for thousands of years that the outer personality is simply an ever-changing and temporary habitation for an inner, immortal spark - call it the soul, the Atman or whatever. In India there has developed over the last thirty centuries an entire science of introspection and inner development known by the generic term

> **DR KARAN SINGH:**
>
> *In all work in the interfaith movement we must never forget the importance of our own individual inner aspirations.*
>
> *We have to move through prayer, through meditation, through study, through devoted work, towards the true centres of our being.*

Yoga, a psycho spiritual discipline designed to unite the divinity immanent and the divinity transcendent, of which the outer physical exercises known by that name in the West are merely a small part.

With the development of depth psychology in the West, particularly with C G Jung who must be ranked as one of the most creative thinkers of the 20th century, and with the unique heritage of Zen masters in Japan, modern psychology has at last realised that our conscious minds are simply like the surface of an ocean, constantly buffeted by waves and typhoons, harbouring in its depths numerous creatures, friendly as well as hostile. The spiritual and mystic traditions of humanity are informed by the belief that there resides deep within us a divine spark that is capable of being fanned into the blazing fire of spiritual realisation. As the seer of the Upanishad proclaims, 'I have seen that great Being shining like a thousand suns beyond the darkness. It is only by knowing this that we can cross the ocean of darkness and death.' This quest constitutes our spiritual challenge as human beings endowed with an unquenchable thirst for the greater reality pervading our everyday consciousness.

This inner spiritual link is the true foundation of the interfaith movement. It binds the entire human race into a single family, cutting across all barriers of nationality and religion, caste and creed, sex and social status. What the Hindus call ântarik shânti, Buddhists the Bodhi Chitta, Sufis the Noor-I-ilahi, Chinese the Tao, and Christians 'the peace that passeth understanding' is, therefore, the first prerequisite in our quest for peace and a creative interfaith dialogue.[8]

Dr STEPHEN FULDER of the organisation Middleway in Israel describes an example of interfaith action that involves awareness of this inner transformation that must take place for lasting change:

For several years, in a program called 'The Transformation of Suffering,' we brought groups of Israelis to Nablus for deep dialogue with Palestinians over a weekend. Sitting together we used deep listening and sharing of each other's pain to touch each other and break down hate, stereotypes and labelling. In one weekend, a life-changing experience is possible and we saw it again and again. The soldier who cried while talking about a newspaper slogan describing the actions of the Israeli army as 'shoot and cry,' which made us all cry with him, the Palestinian woman who spent 10 years in an Israeli jail for carrying a letter, who announced that she succeeded to eliminate any speck of hate from her heart.

After the intifada, we could not go to the Palestinian areas and we wanted to do something more visible, so I started a program of peace walks and a new organisation called 'Middleway.' This too used a more spiritual approach to peacemaking. It was based on the dharma yetra peace pilgrimages of the Buddhist monks in East Asia. The Walks include Jews and Arabs walking very slowly, in silence and steadiness. We walk through the towns and cities of Israel. Our message is our presence, radiating kindness, steadiness and quietness, showing that peace is possible. We give out cards reminding people of the values of non-violence and compassion, and encouraging the reduction of hate and fear. At every place we go we meet local people, sit in circles for sharing and reconciliation. Sometimes we combine this with humanitarian assistance where we can, for example arranging for the importation and planting of thousands of olive trees which had been cut down by the army.

Walking in peace, for peace.

We are deeply influenced by dharma wisdom and the Buddhist teachings of an intimate, attentive and compassionate engagement with the changing flow of life. We try and address the roots of violence and conflict through our activities. For this reason we do not carry out obviously political campaigns or demonstrations which contain seeds of violence and do not aid the underlying climate. Instead, we emphasise and show how peacefulness can contribute to peace, how respect and acceptance of the other reduces violence and conflict and increases healing and happiness in divided communities. We are concerned with means as well as ends, with our inner experiences as well as outer change.

SR MAUREEN of the Brahma Kumaris World Spiritual University also reminds us of the importance of inner spiritual development for the future integrity and growth of the interfaith movement in her reflection on 'The Spiritual Dimension of Dialogue:'

I have been an active member of the Brahma Kumaris (BK) World Spiritual University for nearly 30 years and almost from the beginning of my spiritual life with the university I became involved in interfaith work. I was living at our newly opened BK centre in Edinburgh and went over to Glasgow to visit a place called the 'International Flat.' I had no idea what this was, but as soon as I entered from the cold, unwelcoming staircase of the tenement block, I walked into another world. It was a sort of all faiths social bash! I just enjoyed seeing the happy faces around me. At that time I had no idea what a wonder and a challenge it is to bring people of different faiths together. At many events, in the UK and around the world, I have witnessed people from very diverse backgrounds creating true friendships.

There is something that transcends even our religious labels and helps us to appreciate each other as human beings, and to honour the being within, that gives each of us individual expression in our life. An individual cannot be put into a box of what a good Christian, Buddhist, Muslim or Jew should be like, each of us is unique, created and moulded by our relationship with God and our understanding and practice of what we have learned from life's experiences, including religion. This understanding has helped me a lot in dialogue. I wish to connect with the person, the being, and relate to them as a friend, a brother, a sister. This is the spiritual dimension of dialogue without which all other dialogue is meaningless. Although many separate religion and spirituality, my experience is that a truly religious person is deeply spiritual. Religion is about how you live your life.

The former Prime Minister of India, Mr Narasima Rao, emphasised this when he said, 'The problem is that people do not know enough about their own religion. If people knew about their religion, there would never be conflict, but it is very convenient not to know too much about your own religion.' The event where he spoke this was in celebration of The Year of Interreligious Co-operation and Understanding in 1993, commemorating the first ever interfaith event, the Parliament of the World's Religions in Chicago a hundred years before.

In the UK, I had the privilege of being part of a team organising the UK launch of the year. Working with a committee of 22 people from 12 faiths can have its interesting moments, but the togetherness was exceptional. Those who spoke at the event and shared in the ceremonies showed a way forward by their lives and their presence. The event, from 10am until 10 pm, included addresses from religious leaders, theatrical presentations, workshops and a gala performance with well-known artists. The trust with which we had worked permeated into the atmosphere of the whole day.

I am always fascinated by watching and listening to people of faith, not so much to their words but to their hearts. Some do 'play a role' - they are in dialogue because it is the expected thing to do, but their motives are more

Interfaith dialogue at the BKS Global Retreat Centre (Maureen 3rd from left)

> **PENNY FAUST:**
>
> Peace for me means knowing that people are willing and wanting to live together in harmony. After all, that is what the Torah (God's Law) teaches us; in giving it, God provided the framework for people to live alongside each other, not necessarily in total agreement – it would be a very boring world if there was no argument – but in sufficient tolerance to allow others to live the way that they want without hurting them or wanting to change them. Peace at that level reflects the message of Torah that we should 'love our neighbour as ourselves' (Lev Ch 19).
>
> And on a more personal level, peace is my acceptance of the need to live in this world, making the best of what life throws at me, both the good and the bad. The whole duty of humankind, says the prophet Micah (Ch 6), is 'to do justly, to love mercy and to walk humbly with thy God.'
>
> If each one of us tries to achieve that, then we shall be at peace.[9]

connected to their own pride or position. Others genuinely wish to understand and connect with others or seek answers to burning questions.

Young people especially interact without any pretence. At the Asian meeting of the World Youth Summit in 2004, a young Indian man addressed a panel of religious leaders: 'You create the wars and we, the young people, become your pawns – can you give us a model by which this no longer happens?' I remember the look on that young man's face – he was expressing the frustration of his generation that is inheriting a world of division and conflict. He was not apportioning blame, he was asking for a way forward. This is where dialogue demands of us to move us out of our comfort zones and to act.

I have had two great mentors in interfaith work. The first is definitely Dadi Janki, my own spiritual mentor. She is an extraordinary woman, filled with God's love, who at the age of 90 travels the world with incredible energy and vision. She has always encouraged me in interfaith work and has taught me how to be unlimited in encountering another. She never allows me to set limitations for myself. The second person is Rev Marcus Braybrooke, from whom I have learned about quiet diplomacy and sensitivity in relating to people of faith. Marcus is a loving bridge builder through the total respect he gives to everyone without exception.

Exploring the spiritual dimension of dialogue is really where my heart is. In October 2005 we held a dialogue for about 40 religious leaders and people of faith from all over the world, at the headquarters of the Brahma Kumaris in Mt Abu, India. With the theme 'The Inner Voice of Peace' we aimed to bring the leaders into silence and inner contemplation together, as a preparation for deeper dialogue. The themes we explored included: *What is the inner voice of peace calling me to do? What does it mean to live a spiritual life today? What is a compassionate heart? How does silence or inner stillness enhance my spiritual life? How can we help to create societies of peace and dignity?*

We took the group to beautiful places on the mountain to meditate in silence and asked them to converse in pairs interspersed with periods of silence. Some chose to sit with their partner for 45 minutes of uninterrupted silence. The result was an atmosphere of peace that was tangible. As people talked there was no more posturing, no comparisons, dare I say it, no ego – it really became a loving dialogue of the heart. This is the area of dialogue I believe it is crucial to build on as such experiences will be drawn upon in times of need. They last not just for a few days but for a lifetime. Humanity's survival depends on it.

FR PAOLO DALL' IGLIO shares with us a vision of Christian-Muslim fraternity that is unfolding in the Syrian desert and that encompasses both the material and the spiritual:

In the Monastery of Mar Musa (1300 meters high, founded in the 6th century in a wild valley, in the desert north of Damascus, with frescoes of the 11th century, and restored by a new monastic community at the end of the 20th century), the three priorities of Prayer, Manual Work and Hospitality are focused on the inter-religious perspective: that of building a positive Christian-Islamic relationship. It constitutes an essential aspect of the spiritual vocation of all monks and nuns here. The choice of the Arabic language for the social and liturgical life of the monastic community is deeply tied to this vocation.

This perspective of deepening inter-cultural and inter-religious collaboration is possible because of the help of numerous organizations as much as friends. We have established a growing library at the monastery featuring classical texts on Christianity and Islam and also work on human relationships

Deir Mar Musa Monastery

in order to deepen the understanding of our inter-religious human context. A special section is dedicated to Louis Massignon (1883-1962), a major scholar in oriental studies, whose meditation and exemplary life continues to inspire our monastic community; he was a very important disciple of the recently beatified Charles de Foucault (1858-1916), the famous hermit of the Algerian desert.

In this Syrian multi religious society, the monastery is also engaged in organizing workshops and seminars, which will assist the exchange of experiences and ideas, both in fields of biodiversity and environment, as well as interfaith and inter cultural dialogue. Moreover, the monks and nuns of Deir Mar Musa have assumed responsibility for the Monastery of Mar Elian in Qaryatein, 50km northeast of here, on the way to Palmyra.

At this time, an international team is planning to set up a permanent route (mainly for pilgrims on foot) that would be named 'Abraham's Path,' as a sign of the desire for reconciliation between the children of the Patriarch. The aim is to create a route from Urfa and Harran in Turkey, then through Syria (with a stop in Deir Mar Musa), and going to the Holy Land through Jordan reaching Jerusalem and finally ending in Hebron, in Arabic al-Khalil (God's friend), place of the Patriarch's tomb. The dream which grows up in hearts, everywhere in the world, is a path for all believers, from any tradition, who could walk together, hand in hand, in the brotherly and mutual enrichment with the children of the biblical-koranic Abraham tradition.

In conclusion, we would like to share with you our concern not to give up the non-violent fight for peace and justice: effort, spiritual jihad, with patience and consistency. The fact is that we are, in Syria, right in between Iraq and Palestine-Israel, in an oasis so fragile and exposed. It is only if we throw ourselves faithfully over any belonging that has become frozen and rigid – pushing each other forward, with a strong desire for harmony and beauty – that we will meet as brothers and sisters, allies, companions.

PACTIFISM

The daily news, politicians and people seem to be imprisoned in an endless historical stream of aggression, revenge, macho-ism and destruction; perhaps it's more about fear, and a lack of self-confidence.

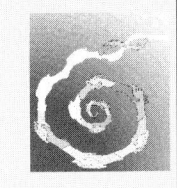

What we are missing in most political leaders are the examples and ideals set by Gandhi, the Dalai Lama and others. People call these pacifists, often not realising that, to be like Gandhi and the Dalai Lama, you need to be very strong, active, brave, and willing to risk your life, lose friends, everything. That's why I prefer the term Pactifism - peace, action and pact.

Exemplary people like Gandhi and the Dalai Lama always try to achieve the best, not only for themselves or their own group of people, but also for their opponents. They also see their opponents as fellow human beings and never try to denigrate them.

Only this allows a sustainable, peaceful solution of conflicts to evolve, a mutual approach, a pact.

Jael Bharat

SUMMARY

Peace is the great - and elusive - need of our times. We all want it, for ourselves and for others. As you have read here - though you rarely read it in the news-papers or hear about it in any media form - people of faith and interfaith organizations are everywhere working for the end of conflict, for harmonious relationships between peoples, for community cohesion, for greater understanding and cooperation, for peace. They work very hard for this, often in dangerous places. Take them all away and we would notice the difference.

But they won't go away, they will not cease their efforts, because they believe in what they are doing and they have faith that it will and does make a difference.

Faith and action, iman and amal, shradda and karma: all our faiths offer us the resources we need for the right balance to bring our right faith into right action.

Then we will fulfil our dharma, our reason for being here, and so be a blessing of peace to all.

PEACE at PETRA

We were in Amman, Jordan, for an international interfaith event.
One day we took an excursion to Petra.
Those of you who know Petra will remember how noisy and busy it is.
Jael and I were on our way back up, walking. We turned a corner.
There, surrounded by those tall pink rocks, we were suddenly totally alone.
Not a person, not a sound. No bird song, horse neigh. No-thing stirred.
We were embalmed in absolute silence, profound stillness.
It was mystical; ancient yet forever new.
We were blessed by it for perhaps a minute before the world began again.

Sandy Bharat

> What will it really be like, living together?

Chapter VIII

LIVING TOGETHER

INTRODUCTION

People of all races and religions live side by side today in many of our major cities. Some people take this evolution even further by marrying someone of another faith and culture. Some move into communities where people of different faiths, from different countries, try to live together in peace and harmony. Some live with two religious traditions, balancing each other, both bringing meaningful spiritual insights.

This is not always as easy as it might at first seem. Any of you who have a friend with a different religious world-view and a different cultural conditioning will know that the first affectionate responses are often followed by the need for deep reflection on major differences. Living with these differences and learning from them is a great blessing as well as a challenge for those able to undertake this journey.

In one sense, everyone has to develop from such interaction in some way or other as everyone is different. Those who explore such differences in marriages or residential communities have a very intense experience. Here are reflections from two people who have experienced, in different ways, marriage to someone of another faith.

Buddhist Vihara and Christian Church side by side in Oxford.

HEATHER AL-YOUSUF writes: It is human nature to form attachments, to connect with other human beings. Interfaith marriages are in a sense a natural consequence of people of different faiths living alongside each other in one society, especially where, as in Britain today, law and custom give the individual the right to choose his or her own marriage partner.

When my husband and I married twenty years ago we didn't think of ourselves as part of a wider phenomenon: the delicate and sometimes painful process of working out how to live together and raise our children with our two faiths (Shi'i Islam and Anglican Christianity) as somehow part of the package seemed a very private matter. Our compromises, the sometimes critical perspectives on beliefs and practices of both faiths from the vantage point of the outsider often made us marginal in our own communities and troubling to our wider families. Religion is grounded not just in belief and inner experience, it is also crucially about belonging, common assent and practice: our hybridity, our belonging to both but also to neither exactly, tended to make us apologetic and defensive. We felt that our experience was just something strange, perverse even, about us.

Then gradually we became aware that we were not the only ones. About seven years ago I joined a group for people in marriages like ours set up by Brother Daniel Faivre. Simply meeting and talking in a context where both faiths were recognized, where the dilemmas of interfaith couples were shared and understood was wonderfully therapeutic. It also helped me see the 'work' that interfaith couples do privately in their own lives in the context of a wider interfaith project. Trying to respect and make room for a partner's faith in an interfaith marriage relates to the deep respect and recognition of the other which interfaith activity promotes. Successful interfaith marriages, like interfaith work, may even demonstrate in practice the qualities of generosity, tolerance and empathy that transform faiths from appearing to the other as mere particularist symbols of difference into channels of wisdom and communication.

Even as faiths are in conflict on the world stage and, for some, faith identities become ever more defensive and polarized, marriages between people of different faiths continue.

> A man madly in love with his beloved went to knock at her door.
> Through the closed door, she asked: 'Who is there?'
> He answered: 'It's me!'
> She said: 'There is no room for both you and me in the same house.'
> Upon hearing this, the man left and went to the desert where he spent his time in meditation.
> Some years later, he came back and knocked at her door again.
> The voice of his beloved asked: 'Who is there?'
> He answered: 'It is yourself!'
> And the door opened.
>
> From MUHYI AL-DIN IBN 'ARABI (1165-1240)

I'm doing some work now with Rosalind Birtwistle and others in the Interfaith Marriage Project which provides sources of information and contact for people in interfaith marriages of all kinds - whether they feel a bit isolated, or are struggling with disapproval and guilt, or feel torn between respecting the requirements of faith and their partner's integrity, or feel overwhelmed at the compromises they've had to make - or indeed feel positive and celebratory: the aim is to support couples and families. The Muslim/Christian marriage support group still meets twice yearly in London, and we'd like to expand to other areas in the future.

Inter faith marriages may be troubling to society at large and to faith communities in particular, but they are not going to stop happening. As the numbers involved increase, it's time perhaps for our societies and faith communities to start looking sensitively at the experience of both partners in interfaith marriages and their children. There may even be things to be learned from them.

PAUL KNITTER and his wife Cathy experienced a different situation when she converted to Buddhism after many years of marriage. Paul writes about being 'Wedded to Dialogue:'

There is a lot of talk nowadays about what a difference it makes when interreligious dialogue is based on interreligious friendship. People from different religious traditions can understand each other and respect each other much more deeply when they are friends who really care about each other than if they are just acquaintances who share common concerns. Such a claim can't be proven; but it can be experienced.

I certainly have experienced it. That's because I have many and valued friends who walk religious paths different from mine. But it's especially because one of those interreligious friends happens to be my wife. You might say that I am wedded to interreligious dialogue.

About ten years ago, my wife, Cathy Cornell, decided to move from her Roman Catholic Christian path and practice to that of the Buddhist Vajrayana tradition. To some extent, that was because of the many abuses and inconsistencies she witnessed in the Catholic Church (especially in regard to the human rights of women); but much more so, it was because the content and practice of the Dharma spoke to her more coherently and engagingly than did Catholic doctrine and liturgy. While she still has a great respect for Jesus and the Gospel, she has taken refuge in the Buddha, the Dharma, and the Sangha. And so, I found myself married no longer to a Catholic, but to a Buddhist.

Although I certainly miss her at my side at Mass (though she does accompany me occasionally, when a certain very 'inclusive' Jesuit priest is the celebrant), I must say that her conversion has enriched our marriage in ways I never expected. My primary friend – my spouse, my fellow-parent, my lover – was now a 'religious other.' Our relationship over the past years has made powerfully and excitingly clear to me that friendship with a religious other makes interreligious dialogue both necessary and possible. This is true, I believe, of any interreligious friendship. It is especially true of an interreligious marriage.

Paul in dialogue with Maulana Dr Farid Esack, IIC Annual lecture, Oxford 1996

Because I love Cathy, I certainly accepted the fact that she was now a Buddhist. And such acceptance was much more than mere tolerance. I was happy that she was a Buddhist – because I witnessed that she was happy to be a Buddhist. So I accepted her religious otherness; indeed, I affirmed it. I did not want to change it; I did not want to try in any way to reconvert her or even to 'include' her in my Christian understanding by picturing her as 'deep down still a Christian.' But neither could I leave it there. I could not just accept and affirm her religious otherness; I had to engage it.

That meant I had to enter into a dialogue with her. I had to try to understand why she was so happy to be a Buddhist, what it was that moved her and satisfied her in her Buddhist practice. That was the easy part. In engaging her otherness, I also felt impelled to try to make clear to her why I remained a Christian, even a Catholic (now with a Pope who as Cardinal had chided me for not holding to Catholic doctrine!) That's what friendship between two different religious people does. It wasn't enough that Cathy accepted or even understood intellectually why I chose to follow Jesus as a Catholic; I wanted her to see why it was good for me; I wanted her to affirm, and rejoice, that I was still a Christian, even though that was not the choice she made. So I had to talk to her about why I believed what I believe. I had to dialogue with her. Dialogue became a necessity.

But it also then became a real, enriching possibility. This is the part that's hard to explain. Maybe here we are touching the beauty and mystery of love and friendship. In feeling the need to explain my religious experience and beliefs to her in a way that she could see how good it was for me, I found new ways, new words, new comparisons, even new connections with Buddhism by which I could express what I wanted to express. In trying to communicate why I'm still a theist, why Jesus the Christ is essential for me, what I experience the risen Christ to be – I came to what I guess I can call new symbols, new connections, new implications of my Christian faith-experience.

And in this process I realized that I was coming to understand myself, my Christian identity differently – I dare say, more deeply or more engagingly. Here, I guess, was the real fruit of dialogue: in trying to understand and communicate with Cathy, my religious other, I was being changed, maybe even to some extent transformed, in my own religious identity.

Marriage is only one way to be interreligious friends. But for me it sure has been one of the most demanding, and rewarding.

MARY PAT FISHER shares these thoughts from her experience of living together in community:

I've been living since 1990 at Gobind Sadan outside New Delhi, and I feel that I'm in paradise, for so many kinds of people are living, working, and worshipping here as members of one family. Under the inspiration of our great teacher, His Holiness Baba Virsa Singh, we are Sikhs, Hindus, Muslims, Christians, Jews, and Buddhists, of all ages, castes, and various countries. Our devotions to the same one God Who is known by many names go on around the clock in places such as our eternal sacred fire, our temples to Indian deities, our Darbar Sahib where reading of the Guru Granth Sahib goes on perpetually, our mosque where hundreds of Muslims pray, our Sh'ma Place, and our Jesus' Place. We also celebrate the holy days of the great prophets, all with the same joy. Babaji teaches us that they have struggled and sacrificed to help us all; they have never come to divide us. Babaji does not believe in conversion; he helps people to find God by going deeper into their own religion.

In addition to the joy of living among many different kinds of people, we experience the joy of a peaceful environment, with many organic gardens of flowers and vegetables. We live simply and support ourselves mostly by farming. So powerful and tangible is the spiritual presence that people who come here feel they have entered an oasis of peace and healing. Indeed, many people are healed here, by prayers and service, often being relieved of ailments that doctors cannot cure.

Gobind Sadan is thus far little-known among the general public, but leaders from India and abroad - scientists, scholars, government officers, religious leaders, and social workers - often visit to receive Babaji's blessings and guidance. We have a special compound for our foreign guests, with its own enclosed gardens.

> **GURU NANAK**
>
> *Since I joined the company of holy ones, the feelings of other-ness have vanished.*
> *I have no enemy and I do not even feel others as others.*
> *I have indeed befriended all.*
> *Whatever God does I accept cheerfully, this is the advice I received from the holy ones.*
> *God awakes in everybody, and Nanak says: By realizing this he feels joyous and happy.*
> *Nanak says that one should remain in high spirits and the grace of His name, and always wish well-being to humanity at large.*

Praying together at Gobind Sadan's shrine to Jesus. Mary Pat is in the centre of picture.

Otherwise, we live mostly in simple village fashion. Guests are encouraged to join in the perpetual devotions at the sacred fire, to eat in the free community kitchen, and to participate in volunteer work so that they can experience the joy of mixing with many kinds of members of our human family, as well as experiencing the divine presence in this spiritually charged and blessed atmosphere. Because we do not engage in fund-raising, this unique place is not well known. Our great challenge is how to let the world know that under Babaji Virsa Singh's inspired guidance, people of all religions are living together quite happily here, and also that by hard work and faith in God, anything is possible. Many people talk about interfaith understanding; we live in the midst of it.

There are other ways of 'living together' too, for example by appropriating different religions for different conditions or by combining two religious traditions or practices into our spiritual lives. In Japan the former is perfectly normal. Many people there turn to Shinto, Buddhism and Confucianism for different moments in life. Increasingly individuals too define themselves by two traditions, for example as Buddhist-Christian or Hindu-Jain, feeling that one alone cannot fully express their religious understanding. Many people might think of themselves as members of one religion but find the rituals or methodologies of another very helpful and harmonious. There are new terminologies like interstitial theology and interspirituality to express these realities.

Dr RUWAN PALAPATHWALA of the Centre for Social Inquiry, Religion and Interfaith Dialogue in Melbourne helps us reflect on living with two religious traditions and the challenges this involves:

Many people find it inconceivable to live with two religious traditions and associate fear, apprehension and heresy with it. The purpose of this brief essay is to outline

> **LIVING TOGETHER IN HARMONY:**
>
> *Hundreds of years ago the Parsis came by sea route to a king on the west coast of India and requested from him a piece of land to live on.*
>
> *The king who was endowed with uncommon wisdom ordered a cup full of milk to be placed before the head of the Parsis and said:*
> *You see, my country is already like this. Where can I accommodate you?*
>
> *The head of the Parsis, who was equally witty, poured some sugar, put it into the cup of milk and addressed the king:*
> *O king, you see how well the sugar has dissolved in the milk without causing it to get spilt. I assure you, Your Majesty, that we too will live with your people just like the sugar in the milk.*[1]

why it is so and provide a template to triumph over such resilience. The inhibitions we associate with living with two traditions emulate various aspects of three significant quests which provide the basis for human existence. I name them quests because human existence is a dynamic flux of reality which is driven by three fundamental meaning-seeking experiences:

1) the puzzlement every human being experiences of being here on earth – the first fundamental quest of wondering for self: 'where am I from?'
2) one's angst of having to face a world that is characterized by change and decay through one's own experience of it through birth, old age, disease and death – the second fundamental quest of asking self: 'why me?'
3) one's conscious and subconscious search for a meaning-giving substance in which one may find an explanation to the wonderment of being here and its experience so that one may overcome the predicament of life and ascend over its fate – the third fundamental quest of asking self: 'where to from here?'

This meaning-giving substance is that which we call religion and the embodiment of that substance is what we call a 'religious tradition' – a framework and a practical outworking of a religion in real living. The framework through which people are invited to see the world and take account of their place in it is the 'worldview' of a religious tradition. The outworking of the substance of the tradition is the culture of a religious tradition. The 'outworking' of the substance of the religion falls into two main domains: ritual and daily living. Ritual is the act by which people connect with the Divine Depth of the meaning-giving substance and daily living is the demonstration how one makes sense of the conundrum of being human.

When the issue is looked at this way we may begin to understand many questions related to living with two religious traditions. For instance, it helps us to understand how people belonging to a culture that has been shaped by one religious tradition express provincialisms that divide, i.e. ways of being that

The scholar, Raimon Pannikar (centre in white), lives in three traditions—Christian, Hindu and Buddhist. Here Raimon meets with some members of the Donnington Grove Interfaith Groups, founded by the late Dr Michael Hooker (next to RP, right) that met regularly for many years at a venue run by Shi'tennoji, a Japanese religious group.

subconsciously guide sentiments such as patriotism, racialism, ethnicity and identity and finally actualises in a person's identity as a Christian, a Buddhist, a Hindu, a Muslim, and so on.

It is obvious then that people do feel frightened, suspicious and apprehensive of a religious tradition which is not one's own. Then, what does it mean to live with two traditions? It provides a template for us to realise that: a) truth is not monolithic; while truth is One it manifests itself in the world in many forms like a ray of sunlight through a prism; b) two traditions provide two complementary paths into the Divine Depth which is the one meaning-giving substance to all life; and c) traditions are not all that be but truth is.

This is how one young woman in the Philippines has experienced growing up with two, often conflicting, religious traditions. YVONNE GUMAYAT PANGSIW (*right*), a member of the IARF's Religious Freedom Youth Network, shares with us her reflection on 'My Different Journey to Interfaith:'

A mountainous place called Kalinga with different tribes, different dialects, different practices and beliefs, there I was born and raised, in a family wherein my father is a great believer in free religious practices and beliefs. Thus joining the IARF group did not make my parents doubt for me to accept, welcome and be a part of it! I did not only accept this but I tried to invite my family to be a part of it for I believe this will enlighten us, especially in our culture.

Still I remember my childhood days were spent in a very different way so that to describe to most of you who haven't been to the Cordilleras would be very foreign to imagine. I was raised in a society where my grand-parents, my great grand parents, believed in many *anitos*, spirits which ruled our lives and even today, everywhere I go, I am being guarded by my *arongans* or angels. They are the ones that give us luck, give us sickness when they are forgotten, in a society that is full of rites and rituals. Though we already call ourselves Christians, we adhere to what our old folks tell us. We respect them so much that we enjoy their advices, whatever problems this may create for our Christianity.

A pause during a trust building walk in Kalinga.
Half of the group are blindfolded and trusting the other half to lead them safely.

We grew up in a somewhat old-fashioned society where all our actions were being watched, even the way we dressed. We were told: 'You are a daughter of a nurse so you should always be neat; You are a daughter of a priest so you should look and talk in a holy way; You are the fruit of an announcer so be expected to know all happenings; You are a Kalinga, you must be brave.' These were just some of the expectations I had to keep thinking of.

Not only that but in Kalinga, tribalism is a practice that I wish I had not grown up with since fear is everywhere because of the misinterpreted *Bodong* (Law of Pagta). This has become so commercialized that if a tribe is weak and commits a mistake, it is punished to the fullest but if the tribe is popular, there is less penalty imposed. This affects the ways we identify with others. When I went to college, I did not want to let others know what high school I attended, the province where I came from, but later on I saw the value and beauty of the Bodong, the culture I have. I saw that it is really respectful just like a fraternity in school with a motto 'one for all, all for one.' I began to accept and became proud to be an indigenous member of the Kalinga tribe.

To summarize, I am still struggling to come out from the shell of conflicting identities that my background has conditioned in me. And I know that our interfaith work will help bring me out of that shell.

Dr ELIZABETH J HARRIS also reflects on 'Drinking from Different Wells' and the challenges of drawing deep from more than one religious tradition:

In 1999, Voies de L'Orient (Eastern Paths), a Roman Catholic organization in Brussels, held a conference on 'Drinking from Several Wells' to explore the experience of people who see themselves as belonging to, or drawing from the wisdom of, more than one religion. The title appealed to me. The concept of drinking from different wells is more evocative and fluid than the more familiar phrases of dual or multiple belonging, hyphenated religious identity or religious bilingualism. 'Wells' are linked with depth, purity and the sustaining of life. They are also loci for social interaction, conversation and laughter.

For the last twenty years, I have drawn from both Buddhist and Christian spiritual wells. In 1986, in my mid-thirties, I travelled to Sri Lanka to study Buddhism. I was a Christian who had already been converted to the urgency of building good interfaith relations in Britain. I was a member of my local inter faith group - in Harrow - and the World Conference on Religion and Peace. 'Study' is perhaps the wrong word to describe what I did in Sri Lanka, for I did not see myself as an academic 'in dialogue' with Buddhism. I wanted to immerse myself in the religion so that I could glimpse how Buddhists see the world. As well as academic study, therefore, I meditated with Buddhists, took part in acts of devotion and went on pilgrimage. Above all, I built friendships. Later I learnt a name for what I did, 'passing over in order to come back.'

One can only 'pass over' to another religion if one lets go of previous religious conditioning as much as possible. And this has a cost for it can challenge the very roots of one's identity, self-worth and composure. For the religions of the world are not the same. The Theravada Buddhist world-view is different from the Christian. To enter it, for instance, I had to bracket the concept of God. At

Liz (middle) in Japan on the Rissho Kosei-kai - International Interfaith Centre Dialogue Tour with Yukako Nakamura and Anne McClelland

times I felt disorientated and unsure. Yet, in retrospect, I can say that the fruit of what I did was totally positive. I was never seriously tempted to become a Buddhist. But Buddhism entered my mind and heart, alongside Christianity. Both religions began to exist within me in creative tension.

I can say now that my primary identity is still Christian. I have doubts that a person can ever be both 100% Theravada Buddhist and 100% Christian. That would be to reduce the differences between the two religions too much. But 'Buddhist' responses to situations sometimes come into my mind before 'Christian' ones, and what I have learnt about my own mind and heart through Buddhist meditation cannot be quantified.

I would not recommend 'passing over' to another religion to everyone. Some forms of inter-religious encounter demand a strong sense of identity on all sides. However, for the few, 'passing over' can be a positive experience. Those who do it will never 'come back' to the same place. They will come back changed and enriched - and convinced that the world needs wisdom from different religious wells if it is to work towards wholeness for all.

Dr JOHN TAYLOR (below) describes an experience he had of how combining traditions brought interfaith healing:

In a suburb of Yaoundé, Cameroun, there was a signpost 'Mallam Yusuf, Healer in the name of Jesus.' In 1976, this simple compound was visited by participants in a World Council of Churches conference on dialogue with traditional religions. They came not only from many parts of Africa but from other continents too. Mallam Yusuf, a practising Muslim, explained that his Christian parents had not understood the gift of healing that he felt he had inherited from his traditional grandparents. The Muslim community was more accepting and he felt inspired by the Muslims' recognition of Jesus as both prophet and miraculous healer. Mallam Yusuf went out into the streets and rescued abandoned or lost children whose mental illness had led them to lose contact with their families. Having identified those families he offered free therapy and even housing for the children in terms of traditional pharmacology and a loving, caring environment. The local hospital was amazed at his results. Visiting 'healers' among the conference delegates, from as far apart as the Pacific and North America, compared their healing methods with his and the African healers rejoiced to see autism being successfully treated by a healer from Oklahoma.

The coming together of traditional, Muslim and Christian spiritualities and healing ministries confirmed for me the importance of a dialogue that is at once spiritual, cultural and practical. Indigenous cultures that have been so often despised by monotheists can provide salutary lessons in caring and healing. Usually we have compared the best in our own tradition with some excess or failing in the other tradition, for example, if we are Christians, we have compared Mother Teresa's witness with a Hinduism untouched by Mahatma Gandhi's compassion, or the dedication of medical missionaries with malign sorcery.

The Yaoundé meeting drew attention not only to the need for dialogue, respect and co-operation between people of different faiths, but also to the possibility for an 'inner dialogue' where people can discern in their own personal or communal identity not only the tradition with which they are usually 'labelled' or to which they give their full allegiance, but also other traditions which have contributed historically to their doctrines and practices. Inculturation in different continents may give many different but coherent expressions to Christian belief; the same may be true in other faiths, as the Muslim Mallam Yusuf exemplified.

Dialogue does not necessarily hide or weaken one's sense of identity but it may reveal complexities of indebtedness and of new possibilities for openness. Dialogue is not an exercise of compromise or dissimulation but an adventure in discerning truth wherever it is to be found. Dialogue with our neighbours can lead us to a deeper dialogue with One whom we may address as God or to a deeper awareness of the Ultimate.

Rabbi RACHEL MONTAGU shares her experience of learning about other traditions and what it has taught her about her own:

When I was a child we had Austrian Catholic neighbours. One bit of home that their mother insisted on was a real Austrian Christmas tree, floor to ceiling and covered in sparkling thread. Some weeks before Christmas we were welcome at their house to help ice and decorate biscuits to be sent to family in Austria. Then they would come and keep us company while we lit Chanukah candles. When I'm asked what drew me to work in interfaith dialogue, I suspect my sense that religious joy is something to be shared originates in the spicy biscuit smell in their kitchen and the glow of candlelight on both families' faces.

While I studied in Jerusalem, I was inspired by all I was learning about Judaism but I wanted to learn about the experience of faith of Muslims and Christians in Israel too. So I joined an interfaith dialogue group called Hope run by a Catholic sister who had lived in Israel for many years. Perhaps I am too much a child of the diaspora to live happily in an all-Jewish environment. Later I went to two series of Jewish-Christian-Muslim conferences in Bendorf, Germany, one for students and one for women. There I learned that Jews share certain ideas with Christians but that different aspects of Jewish experience and thought resonate with those of Muslims and Islam. Also I learned that women of all three faiths have things in common across the religious boundaries. Now I belong to a Jewish and Christian Women's Theology group that is invaluable to me as a place to relax and share ideas with colleagues,

Informal Jewish-Christian Dialogue at an IIC conference:
R/L
Brian Pearce,
Harold Kasimow,
Kusamita Pedersen.

many of whom are also often a resource for others and need somewhere that nourishes us.

After I came to work at The Council of Christians and Jews and suddenly found interfaith work was my profession as well as an absorbing interest, I read an essay by George Lindreck who said: 'God may intend Jews and Christians to hear very different messages through one and the same text.'[2] This fascinated me. When teaching Biblical Hebrew I always try to emphasise the multi-layered possible understandings of the Bible. Now here was someone saying that Judaism and Christianity's different readings may be God's intention rather than a sign of the world's imperfection. We can relish what the Chief Rabbi Sir Jonathan Sacks called 'The Dignity of Difference' and by sharing those differences in dialogue with each other we can celebrate our God-given diversity.

The Philippines is a country where it has not always proven comfortable for people of different faiths to live together, where tensions between religious communities have soured relations in some parts of the country. There is another, more positive, story to be told.

ANGIE GRAPA, an International Council Member and National Coordinator in the Philippines for the International Association for Religious Freedom, shares with us the joys of working for interfaith and the challenges of bringing together people from different and divided religious communities:

For almost 18 years now, my work with young people has never ceased to amaze me. There is always a new challenge that comes along. The greatest challenge that I ever faced was when IARF Philippines held an Educational Tour for young people in April 2003. It was not just an ordinary tour. Participants included members of the ten major tribes of Indigenous People, the four major groups of Muslims from Cotabato in Mindanao, and Christians and Universalists from the Visayas. Mindanao was a dreaded place for us people from the Visayas. There were so many negative stories about the people and order situation there. It was scary. How was I going to invite participants from the Visayas?

The circumstances surrounding the participants in that pilgrimage were divisive, and conflict could have erupted any time because they came from different religious and cultural backgrounds. Not only that, there were already a lot of biases and prejudices existing among them. The situation was volatile and I really found that difficult to handle. The participants had to travel, eat, sleep and do things together for one week. At least they must have enough trust to be able to cooperate with one another.

Sharing with the Imam during the interfaith pilgrimage

I had apprehensions because that was the first time I ever handled that kind of group composition.

Something had to be done to create a peaceful atmosphere of unity among all of them in spite of their differences. So I designed modules for team building that included self-awareness, communication, and leadership exercises. These training modules were done with the participants in between visits and in the evenings. Twenty six young people came to participate in the tri-people pilgrimage. The group visited different worship places in Cotabato in Mindanao, and Negros and Cebu in the Visayas. They became closer with one another day by day. Friendships were forged and barriers were overcome so that in the end they were already one big happy family.

The result was amazing! The journey, along with the interactions with one another in the different activities, opened their eyes to the fact that there were indeed misconceptions about each group and these were corrected. The realization of many young lives unfolding in a more interacting, accepting and tolerant way is more than enough reason to be happy.

We followed that pilgrimage with further training in other parts of the country. The results have always been positive. If only people are given the same opportunity as these young people had I believe that, in the future, peace among different religious groups can be attained and to know that I am a part of this global movement is very fulfilling!

ANDREAS D'SOUZA of the Henry Martyn Institute (HMI) also writes about living together communally and the difficult, dangerous journey this often entails:

Hyderabad (Deccan, India) is famous for its pearls, Nizam's Jewels and communal riots. The deep-seated hatred between Hindus and Muslims has often erupted in violent riots, killing innocent people, destroying property and disrupting normal life. After more than a decade's work experience in this conflict prone area I have come to believe that interfaith dialogue does not mean discussion on doctrines or dogmas or on what differentiates us but rather building relationships which are healing and reconciling. Creating space for the divided communities to intermingle and interact on a humanitarian basis has succeeded in transforming relationships from hatred to friendship, from doubt to trust, from alienation to closeness. No doubt the road from enmity to loving relationships is long and arduous. But persistent focus on praxis (action-reflection) brings people together and leads not only to peaceful coexistence but also to pro-existence sometimes even at the risk of one's life. Let me illustrate this point with an example.

During the horrible genocide in Gujarat in 2003 when more than 2000 Muslim men and women were killed, women were raped and children and women were burnt alive, the old city of Hyderabad felt the repercussion of this violence. Fear of reprisals had gripped the city. In the HMI run project areas we had taken extra caution, especially during the nights. On one of those evenings in the tension filled old city three Muslim women were in the act of prostration performing their evening ritual worship. Their men were either in the mosques or out working. They heard frantic knocking on their door. Opening the door they found a group of Hindu women and children begging them to take them in. Their area was invaded by a group of angry Muslim youth seeking revenge for the Gujarat atrocities. The Muslim women quickly ushered the Hindus inside their home. The angry youth surrounded the house and demanded that they hand over the group. The brave women called out: 'No, these are our sisters and our children. You will have to kill us first before you touch them.'

The above story is illustrative of the results of building relationships that transcend narrowly defined boundaries of caste and creed. It did not matter for these praying Muslim women to which faith the women who came for help belonged. They saw precious lives of their neighbours in danger.

When we speak about interfaith we speak about building relationships that transform the lives of people and not just dialogue. I believe that 'dialogue,' which implies discourse between two or more, often tends to be an intellectual exercise. Though discourses, exchanges, discussions are necessary for mutual understanding and relationship building we cannot stop there. We need more than discourse, more than exchanges. We need actions leading to building healthy relationships, which implies involvement, respectful commitment to the other, that transcends all the human made barriers while fully safeguarding one's own faith commitment. I believe it is this involvement and commitment that, while safeguarding my individual authenticity, will simultaneously guard the authenticity of my partner.

Muslim and Hindu Sisters meeting together

HE Prof Dr HAMID AL-RIFAIE, President of the International Islamic Forum for Dialogue (IIFD) in Jeddah, Saudi Arabia shares with us his perspective on dialogue with the religious 'other' in a more formal setting:

In 1992 a high ranking Islamic delegation visited the Pontifical Council for Interreligious Dialogue (PCID) in the Vatican-City where we met the late HH John Paul the Second and held an extended meeting with the staff of the PCID headed by HE Cardinal Francis Arinze, President of the PCID at that time. In the beginning of the meeting I asked for permission to address those present on behalf of the Islamic delegation and said:

'We did not come here to convert you into Islam in spite of the fact that it is our desire to do so, since we wish all the people to follow the faith which we believe in; and we hope that you will not try to convert us into Christianity; although we know that it is the desire of your hearts to have all people follow the faith that you believe in. Why then are we here? We are here because we feel that human progress is in danger, and our religion calls upon us and motivates us to do our best to guide the human procession into one of justice, peace, prosperity and safe co-existence among human communities. Are you ready to contribute in achieving these noble human goals?'

They said: 'Yes, of course we are ready.' At the end of the meeting the Muslim delegation and the PCID signed an agreement to start regular annual meetings for discussing issues of mutual interest.

Both the International Islamic Forum for Dialogue and the Pontifical Council for the Interreligious Dialogue have continued to activate the agreement by holding annual meetings which are alternately arranged between them. During more than fifteen meetings they have examined many important topics such as:

- Religion and human dignity
- Religion, human rights and duties
- Religion and the family and child

Dr Al-Rifaie addressing the late Pope John Paul II and members of the Islamic-Catholic Liaison

- Responsibilities of men and women in society
- Status of women in society
- Justice and human dignity
- Rights and duties of the citizen
- Human dignity and rights in war
- Religion and the dialogue of civilizations in an era of globalization
- Building of the culture of dialogue among generations
- Religion and the building of societies
- Protection of the environment and human security.

A joint declaration was signed by both sides and released at the end of every meeting detailing the points on which they agreed. Similar agreements have been signed between the IIFD and many international organizations throughout the world including: The National Council of the Churches of Christ in USA; The Middle East Council of Churches - Lebanon; The World Supreme Council of Buddhists - Taiwan; The National Center of the Russian Glory - Moscow; The Middle East Institute for Peace and Development - New York; The World Council of Public Friendship - Sudan.

The above-mentioned experience has confirmed that dialogue is the shortest path to mutual understanding between the followers of the religions, cultures and civilizations. Also it is the best and the most practical way of discovering the common ground in the framework of our religious, cultural and national diversity.

During my long experience in the field of dialogue I found that people all over the world recognize and respect religious and cultural diversity, in the same manner as they acknowledge and respect religious and cultural particularities. But what is still absent is a common world culture which may help us to work together to bring justice, peace, prosperity, sustainable development and safe co-existence among the human communities.

So I call upon all the wise people, thinkers, scholars, politicians, and experts from the followers of all the religions, cultures and ideologies to come to a round table debate to contemplate together what are the principles, values and thoughts which are suitable for a common world culture.

Israeli and Palestinian:
Learning to live and laugh together near Nablus.

SUMMARY

When we hear the world news it seems that people do not find living together at all easy – not at home, not in local or religious communities, not nationally, regionally, or internationally. Everywhere the media confirms strife, tensions, and violent disagreements.

In this chapter a few contributors have shown it is possible to buck that trend, to change the conditioning. It is possible to live together. It may not be easy but it is possible and these contributors have shown some of the ways they are developing to help achieve harmony at home and outside the home.

Maybe in future interfaith activists can find more effective strategies to encourage the media to include positive stories in the news outreach, to give hope to others, to provide models for change, to build a network of people committed to living together in peace and harmony. Some are already working hard to achieve this (see Simon Cohen's reflection in the Youth chapter).

> **DR ELIZABETH AMOAH**
>
> *As I was growing up as a child with Methodist parents in my village, we lived in a large compound house with other members of the 'extended family.'*
> *My maternal grandmother, a strong, powerful and influential person in our life, lived with us.*
>
> *Unlike my parents, my grandmother was a devoted member of the Anglican Church in the village but she continued to practise as a traditional healer. On several occasions when I accompanied her to the thick forest to collect therapeutic herbs and plants, I observed her pouring libation to the gods/goddess and ancestors, etc, before collecting the plants.*
>
> *We had tenants who were also committed Muslims. We played with their children and we sometimes ate together.*
> *I had an aunt who was a traditional priestess of one of the several divinities in the village. At times she invited us to share meals with her in her room, at the corner of which was a shrine.*
>
> *Some of my cousins were married to Muslim men so they moved to the 'Zongo' where there were predominantly Muslims.*
> *There was scarcely any problem with regard to religious differences.*[3]

Where is it going?

INTRODUCTION PART III

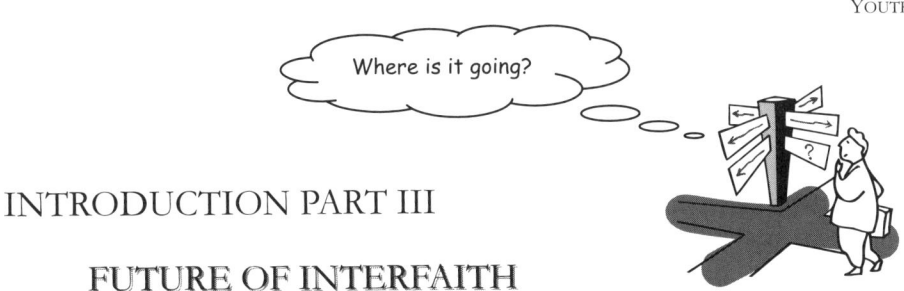

FUTURE OF INTERFAITH

Young Europeans from minority communities at interfaith workshop, Coventry 2000.

CHALLENGES

Is the interfaith movement keeping up with new developments? For example, civil society now routinely takes on interfaith, often with better resources and wider impact.

What is the role of religions in interfaith developments? Can anyone represent a religion? If not, why limit engagement to religious people only, especially when that means, as it so often does, only religious people from mainstream organizations and faith communities. Do religious affiliations hold back collective action that would benefit many more? Is it time interfaith action moved out of the constraints of faith based initiatives and become more humanistic, people of faith and secular people working together for the common good of all life?

What about young people? If they are the future, what is their vision? Can they make the changes needed? What are they saying and doing about interreligious relations now?

In this final part of the book, we will explore what some experienced activists, some fresh young activists, and some former activists have to offer on the future of interfaith.

NEVER TOO YOUNG TO START INTERFAITH!
Our grandson Dylan Gosai, (left) and Jonathan Fry, when they were one years old, in their International Interfaith Centre T-shirts

CHAPTER IX

INTERFAITH YOUTH

INTRODUCTION

Young people are already making a significant contribution to interfaith work. Ten years ago the participation of youth lit up interfaith events that were mostly peopled by elders. Now most organisations try to include youth programmes in their developments and some organisations are specifically youth oriented.

One of these is the Interfaith Youth Core (IFYC), built on the vision of Dr EBRAHIM (Eboo) PATEL and his close associates. Eboo was in Oxford for some years on a Rhodes scholarship, doing a doctorate. During this time he was an active IIC trustee as well as developing the Interfaith Youth Core.

He taught at both the interfaith evening classes we organised and this is what JOANNA JECZALIK wrote about his impact on one of them, *Interreligious Dialogue,* which he co-tutored with Peggy Morgan and Norman Solomon. The picture (opposite page) shows Eboo teaching on the other course, with Joanna on the far right.

Eboo showing us his doctorate in the IIC office

Joanna: I found the 10-week course quite challenging on a personal level. I realised that engaging in interfaith dialogue is by no means a theoretical exercise, but a deeply practical and, in some ways, uncomfortable pursuit. Issues of faith are sensitive and touch many parts of our emotional and intellectual world-view. Prejudices you never thought you had bubble up to the surface and have to be exposed to the light – perhaps for the first time. By the end of the course I had no doubt that this pioneering work in developing ways of setting up peaceful and constructive dialogue will have an enormous impact on conflict resolution throughout the world.

Through all three of the tutors I gained a better insight into the issues and challenges facing inter-religious dialogue but one particular section engendered a new realisation. Ebrahim Patel was covering the subject of 'Practical dialogue for daily life in plural societies` in the eighth week. He asked all the course delegates to choose a personal symbol of their particular faith tradition and to discuss this in pairs. Each delegate was then asked to describe his or her chosen symbol and explain what it meant to them. The ensuing discussion was fascinating. Symbols ranged from a lighted candle to a particular stained glass window to music, chanting God`s name, air and nature, the cross bearing the words 'Father forgive' that was made out of the ruins of Coventry cathedral and others. Each person's feeling for their chosen symbol was deeply personal and had a powerful spiritual resonance that was particular to them. I was struck by Eboo's summing-up of this session: 'There are a variety of symbolic languages that have been given to us.'

Eboo teaching at IIC's Introduction to Interfaith course in Oxford

Suddenly I saw the diversity of religions and their expressions in language, art, music, poetry etc. as an extraordinary gift. In a way, it seemed to me, that our world and its universe provides us with an almost infinite number of keys to the door that opens onto spiritual enlightenment. My focus on Interfaith work changed subtly in this moment. I realised that religions would overcome their differences, not by superficial displays of unity, but through understanding, embracing and enjoying the wealth of ideas, cultures, philosophies and civilisations that they all, in their different ways, offer to all of us.[1]

EBOO and PATRICE BRODEUR, from the University of Montreal, introduce us to the theme of their book: *Building the Interfaith Youth Movement*.[2]

Forty years ago, in a book titled *Where Do We Go From Here: Chaos or Community*, Martin Luther King Jr. introduced an image called 'the world house:' The great new problem of mankind [is that] we have inherited...a great 'world house' in which we have to live together - black and white, Easterner and Westerner, Gentile and Jew, Catholic and Protestant, Moslem and Hindu ....Because we can never again live apart, we must somehow learn to live with each other in peace.[3]

Today, King's words seem prescient. At the dawn of the 21st century, the United States is the world's most religiously diverse nation playing a central role in a global era characterized by increasing religious conflict. Our book is based in America with the understanding that its editors, authors, and topics are part of 'the world house.' Brodeur's notion of the 'glocal'⁴ provides a conceptual lens through which this dynamic can be understood. The local is where the global happens. For example, a medium-sized peaceful Montreal high school discovered that thirty of its students had either been child soldiers themselves or had witnessed warfare first hand. Though they now dress and behave outwardly like other young people, their experience of organized violence shapes their understanding of everything from video games to high school cliques. Glocal describes the combined dynamics of global influences on our respective local contexts and, in turn, the impact of our local behaviors on these global influences, wherever we happen to be in the world. Glocal therefore also characterizes both the context of this book, a new religious America, and its content.

Patrice in action

Diana Eck

Our book seeks to understand the emergence of a global interfaith youth movement through the unique lenses of a rapidly changing US religious landscape, what Eck has called 'A New Religious America.'[5] While many of the immigrants from this post-1965 era fashioned social lives outside of the American mainstream, their US-born and raised children study algebra in public schools, play basketball at YMCAs, major in sociology at Ivy League institutions, kick rhymes in urban hip hop ciphers, walk police beats in leafy suburbs, join medical staffs in small-town hospitals and participate in American life in every other conceivable way. The United States is faced with the challenge that Wilfred Cantwell Smith raised when he lived during the 1940s in the religiously diverse city of Lahore, located in present-day Pakistan, of how 'to learn to live together with our seriously different traditions not only in peace but in some sort of mutual trust and mutual loyalty.'[6]

There are no easy answers to this challenge. A number of social responses have emerged. One response is that of the extremist movements characterized by bigotry and bias. They are telling new Americans, often in violent ways, 'We don't want to live together with you.' A second response is to assume that people do not bring their faith identities into social situations, and therefore religion need not be a part of public discourse. A third response is to view religion as one more element in an individualistic, laissez-faire culture, and to watch with detached interest as people mix-and-match religious identities. A fourth response is to recognize that people's religious identities impact everything from their private lives to their community institutions to our public square, and understand that a religiously plural society, if it wishes to have harmony amongst its various religious communities, must be proactive about dealing with matters of religious diversity.

We, of the emerging interfaith youth movement, not only hold the fourth position; we act from it. While religiously diverse young people interact in classrooms, playgrounds, and shopping malls everyday, unless those interactions intentionally deal with matters of religion, they also cannot be considered truly interfaith. Too often, in our everyday encounters in spaces that bring together people of diverse backgrounds, perhaps felt most acutely in schools, the religious dimensions in the lives of our younger generation remains, at best, silent, and at worst, rejected.

Learning to talk about the variety of religious identities, among many other kinds of overlapping identities, requires active and self-reflective interfaith activities. These activities must be integrated into a wide set of both formal and informal programs. They can result in the promotion of pluralism, that is, a philosophy that seeks to foster inclusive practices in all spheres of any diverse society. The challenge of how to manage these diverse identities so as to promote a healthy pluralism is being faced in all countries that have a high degree of ethnic and religious diversity, which represents the majority of the world's nation-states. This challenge may be more acute, however, in societies with high immigration levels.

The goal of this book is to begin building a knowledge-base in the field of interfaith youth work. This book is situated at the intersection of six academic disciplines and their respective applied fields: religious studies, sociology, education, youth studies, community studies, and leadership studies. Authors were selected not only for their role in building interfaith youth projects, but also because they represent a new generation of scholar-practitioners in the emerging academic field of interfaith studies.

One of our goals in the interfaith movement is to empower each other to pioneer new cooperative and transformative learning paths at the same time as we make room for critical self-reflection through which scholarship can be produced as another tool for empowerment. Our hope is that this book will serve both as a guide to those who want to organize interfaith youth activities in their own local contexts as well as an invitation to join the community of people building this movement.

We move on in this special chapter dedicated to the contribution young people make to interreligious relations with an introduction to some of the people and activities of the organization founded by Eboo and others.

DAN STEINHELPER (left) gathered together some of the thoughts, experiences and understandings of young people in the USA, Nepal and Jordan who are connected to

THE INTERFAITH YOUTH CORE (IFYC)

MOLLY HOISINGTON is a member of the Chicago Youth Council of the Interfaith Youth Core. She reflects:

Growing up as a Jewish kid in Utah a big part of my Jewish identity was inevitably influenced by my experience as a religious minority. Sometimes I struggled and was baffled by my position: I couldn't explain exactly the ways that my bat-mitzvah experience was so important to me any better than I could truly understand what was so similarly engrossing about my friends' churches activities. My mom posed a single question to me that articulated how I could grow from all this struggle. She basically asked me how I would choose to represent myself. She pointed out that I might be the only Jewish kid that many people in Utah would ever get to know. Because of this she said I should be especially conscientious of the way I represent my faith.

The first time I seriously considered her question was as I packed my bags to move to Chicago at the philosophical age of fifteen. I realized that I almost certainly wouldn't be the only Jewish kid in my new environment in Chicago. Nevertheless, I didn't want to give up on the view of my religion I had developed. I had learned to value the universal aspects of Jewish philosophy. I had grown up feeling a special responsibility to understand my religion in a way that connected me to the world at large.

I've found that I especially appreciate Jewish values that emphasize life, learning, and love for family as well as a broader community. But these values are not uniquely Jewish. They are essentially human. The more practice I get as a 'representative' of Judaism the more I get the impression that I'm sharing a message that my friends are already familiar with, only in different packaging.

One value that I am particularly fond of is the stubbornly optimistic view that says it is possible to change the world for the better (Jews call this concept Tikkun Olam). I love meeting people who have caught the fever of this optimism. My favorite way to cross a supposed cultural barrier is by sharing an experience that is grounded in this contagious idealism. While I do a service project I feel that the good deeds of my actions compound upon themselves. I get a sense of completeness when I consider this symbiotic relationship. The idea that I can expand my perspective of the world at the same time as I make the world a better place to grow up in is my favorite idea in the world.

The more I think about it, the more I love my mom's question. She emphasized how religion doesn't need to be confined to the time I spend in synagogue. It is natural that I should feel my identity as a Jew blur into my identity as a human being. The time when I experience this blending in its most intense manifestation is when I am doing something active to change the world and thus inescapably changing myself. I feel swept away by spirituality when I am active in the broader community, and that is when I feel proudest of the Judaism that I am voicing to the world.

USRA GHAZI, a facilitator on the Chicago Youth Council of the Interfaith Youth Core, tells us about 'A Faith Odyssey' she recently experienced:

The year was 2001. The class was Western Civilization. A wide-eyed sophomore ecstatically looked around the classroom to see if the others had also witnessed the moment of truth - a moment of pure and unadulterated discovery of cosmic proportions. She wouldn't know what to call it then, but the 15-year-old Muslim girl believed that she had uncovered evidence of doctrinal beliefs that linked three very different contemporary faith communities within one covenantal ancestry. After having read about, and seen documentaries exploring the history of the Jewish and Christian communities, that girl became aware of an Abrahamic lineage. What she thought she'd discovered though, was really something they never decided to teach. As a teenage Muslim being raised in an increasingly pluralistic society, that day was the first time I learned to learn on my own - the day I learned to believe as a believer with Christians, Jews, and people of other faiths.

Later that day, I tried to explain my discovery to others. I attempted to engage my friends in a dialogue about the peculiar history we shared with others, but to no avail. I was perplexed. Why was it that people of faith didn't act towards others, especially those from diverse faith communities, as one and the same? I decided that people just didn't care. They must have other priorities as high school students. What I realized years down the line was that it isn't that people don't care - they just don't understand.

Thinking back, I particularly remember praying the afternoon prayer, Dhur, after school in an empty classroom one day and feeling embarrassed that I couldn't respond to the questions being posed to me by the teacher who had to lock up. 'Um, excuse me...I really need to lock this room. Can you please, uh, do that elsewhere?' After I concluded the prayer, I apologized and explained. After refusing to shake the hand of a male school Dean of students, I recall feeling unbearably awkward as he asked me, 'So, if Ali [the president of the Muslim club] just told you his grandma passed away, you're saying you wouldn't give him a warm hug?' I apologized for the awkwardness and explained. On more than one occasion, when a teacher asked if my different colored head scarves represented a different religious belief or theme, I laughed. Then I apologized for being rude, and explained why I didn't expect such a question.

In an educational institution, a public school in which I felt like a pariah unless I was consistently explaining about myself, I didn't blame my peers for not knowing. I didn't hold contempt against my instructors for putting me on the spot. I realized that my connection with Jewish, Christian, Hindu, Buddhist and other religiously inclined peers was weak because we'd been socialized that way. I realized that my discovery of the Patriarch Abraham was because they don't teach much about Ibrahim's Jewish and Christian children in Sunday school. They must not be teaching children much about Isaac's brother Isma'il, and his descendant Muhammad, in Synagogues and Churches. And the separation between Church and State did a swell job of keeping us from sharing these commonalities at school. By the time I helped organize our high school's first ever Interfaith Dialogue (my senior year), it was as if the veils had been lifted. The pariahs had a safe haven to discuss their views. After the program, private conversations dwindled on until they kicked us out of the building. I made a secret promise to myself that never again would I allow the lack of knowledge of others to be misunderstood as intolerance.

And, it seems that finally, the secret is out.

ANAS AL-ABBADI works with the Jordan Interfaith Action Cooperation Circle and shares a personal reflection on interfaith youth service:

Interfaith dialogue work and youth work shaped my life and gave me a new perspective to see things. I really see things in a different way now. Some of my colleagues in Jordan, they wonder, 'Why are you doing this?' And I asked myself several times this question. Watching the different conflicts, rising up every now and then because of mistrust or misunderstanding or lack of information about the other culture, makes me more and more insistent about what I am doing now. I believe, through my past experience, that there will be no conflicts in our world if we only give each other the time and the space to express ourselves. Through learning about different religions and different cultures, I found no single religion which asks for violence. What I found is that all religiously motivated violence was only raised because of a personal interpretation and lack of knowledge and understanding.

'The other,' who is the other? If we all tried to find a definition of who is the other, our world will be a much better place. This is why we organized in Jordan a regional conference about 'The other in my tradition.' Misconceptions, paradigms and stereotypes can be the fuel for any cultural violence. All of this can simply be avoided by cultural exchange, meeting the other, and learning about the other. I really love what I am doing, and I will keep doing it.

Young people expressing themselves at the Art and Religion Contact-Making Seminar, organised by the Jordan Interfaith Action Cooperation Circle in Petra.

Moving on to Nepal, SATYATA SHRESTHA, a member of the Youth Society for Peace, Nepal, writes:

Nepal is the constitutionally declared Hindu kingdom and birth place of Lord Buddha, therefore, Hinduism and Buddhism are practiced simultaneously with great faith and trust. Also, there has never been conflict or clash in the name of religion throughout the history of Nepal. All the religions are well respected and appreciated in their own ways because we believe in the principle of 'Unity in Diversity.' I believe that all the religions preach the same messages but in different ways and by different means. Above all, the religion 'Humanity' is the greatest religion and it is the only Dharma.

Nepalese women fasting for the longevity of their husbands.

JAGANNATH KANDEL, a founding member of the Youth Society for Peace, writes this:

People respect each other as humans, not on the base of their religion, Hinduism, Buddhism, Christianity or Islam. All the religions are treated and respected equally. Whether with a handshake or with a 'Namaste' people do it with their heart. Family members have a strong bond with each other and it's possible only because of true love and respect for each other. Whether the low land of 'terai' or the highest peak of the world, Mt Everest, people view both of these places with the same eyes of equality. Whether the preaching of non-violence and peace in the *Light of Asia*, the life of Gautam Buddha, or the stories to teach the true successful living in the great epics like *Tripitaka*, *Ramayana*, and *Gita*, people listen and internalize all with equal importance in their life.

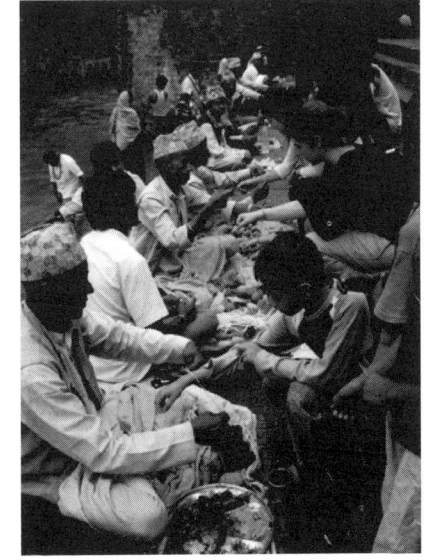

Devotees receiving sacred thread on the auspicious occasion of Rakchhya Bandhan.

INTERFAITH

The following poem is a collaborated effort between the Chicago Youth Council (CYC) and nationally-renowned poet Kevin Coval. The CYC members performed the poem at the Chicago Mayor's Interfaith Prayer Breakfast in the fall of 2005. The CYC is a group of high school and college students who participate in an intensive, interfaith, leadership-development, service-learning program in the Chicago area. [7]

~~~ CHICAGO STORY ~~~

Umar	I come from Dirt with divine winds a box beats within me
Usra	PIB Colony, Karachi, Pakistan. a three story building with no roof surrounded by trees of a bitter fruit, hot summer days, playing cricket in the narrow street
Rehman	the 2800 block of Logan Boulevard, a family so large counting them is like counting grains of sand. my family, possesses slightly more personality, but seems to lack the drive to disperse, forever tethered to the home of our birth
Elliot	Eastern Europe? Romania and Poland? places that have never meant much to me, a spattering of old-world stories, I only half remember
Patrice	mom is from North Carolina, my father Virginia. my mother's father, Dr. Perry P. Little finished morehouse college in the same graduating class as Dr. Martin Luther King Jr.
Lauren	Irish and proud of it. go Notre Dame, go to Ireland, go drink a Guiness, whatever you do it better be of the Emerald Isle to be a true McBride.
Umar	from Canaan to Bacca peace is sent from Mecca through the oasis onto the rest of the land an illiterate man lyrical with his Arabic chanting what the pharaoh did in arrogance. Uncle Moses came from Hebrews so I must respect my people Abraham spoke Hebrew so I must respect my people
Rehman	my mother Roman Catholic from Manila, my father a Pakistani Muslim. hybrid "Cruslim" identity. Eid and Christmas, days during which I could receive gifts, declaring *I'll believe in anything if presents are involved*
Patrice	Good Friday, Easter, Christmas, reading the Bible as a family, baptism, communion every first Sunday, prayer meetings on Wednesday nights. My faith became more than the traditions learned at an early age. it became real to me.

Elliot	a house called Conservative, but only affiliated with Reform and Orthodox, a youth movement called pluralist, my own ideology Reconstructionist. so I'm officially confused. and fascinated. and passionate. and loving...
Usra	Ramadan mornings, a woman singing praises of the prophet on the AM dates, spicy fruit salad, samosas, breaded dumplings in tangy yogurt, break fast, 5 times daily prayers, counting 33 times, 33 Times, 34 times on the segments of our fingers the words Subhanallah, Alhamdulillah, Allahuakbar, God is the greatest
Lauren	treating members of your family, the clerk at the 7-Eleven, the man selling Street Wise on the corner of Belmont and Sheffield. my faith lies in the capacity to love, the capacity to smile. the capacity to help people cleanse these waters to reveal the pure hidden form of human nature - mindfulness
Umar	indisputed evidence my heart tells me I had better sense between the medicine and the rhetoric my mind confides in the present day for heavens sake justice runs through the family tree the way we handle beef Kosher, Halaal and now organic meat with no preservatives dervishes formed in circles like ciphers i feel nervousness secreting saliva most of our days spent in congregation praise the Creator i am a traveler chose Chicago to be my destination
Rehman	where on sleepless nights I solace in the cacophony of the city; comfort in the rattle of the Red Line:
Usra	in apartments with names difficult for the super to pronounce. the Nasirs in 5C, Husseins in 1D, Ghazis in 5A, chicago
Patrice	where we were discouraged to move to 16th and Drake. where I witness gang wars. our house in the line of a bullet that came through our picture window. God's grace. a pastors family of 6 lived for 6 years unharmed
Usra	where Karachi can be found on California Avenue
Patrice	where I made it my goal to do whatever I could to effect change in the youth of Lawndale. picking up the pieces, preserving the family & love felt in the community. Chicago,
Elliot	where a White Sox victory gives way to elementary school celebrations,

	and homemade Sox t-shirts replace school uniforms for a day. blue, colared shirts lie in a heap at home, and fourth graders come to school wearing old, white t-shirts penned with sharpies late the night before – penned with 'White Sox,' 'Konerko,' Jenks,' 'Guillen,' 'Chicago' –
Lauren	where Everyday is new, but some things remain - CTA trains run, newspaper stands open, and you can get a cup of coffee on every downtown corner;
Usra	assalamu alaikum sister at least once a month from a stranger, in Chicago
Elliot	that turns Illinois blue at election time where in four or eight or twelve years – we'll send our superstar Senator over to the Oval Office, and boast that he is from our backyard, – Chicago
Rehman	where it's not quite a melting pot, but rather a salad bowl with pieces coarsely chopped and mixed,
Lauren	where we're all here because we love this city, and we all help to create it,
Umar	where tourists ride chariots CTA el n' underground bound toward freedom like Harriet these are my people got the love to carry it just like the books and stories of generations before me we human beings tryin' to write our own stories just like the religions and traditions of generations before me young people of faith tryin' to tell our own stories...

Back row: Mariah Neuroth, Umar Khan, Kevin Coval, Elliot Leffler, RehmanTungekar, Usra Ghazi, Patrice Casey.
Front row: Umnia Khan, Lauren Menger, Chicago Mayor Richard M. Daley.

YOUTH AROUND THE WORLD

Other organizations also include and support young people and make good use of their energy, integrity and commitment. Here are reflections from some of those special young activists.

PHILIP RIZK, a Gaza Project Officer for the Foundation for Relief and Reconciliation in the Middle East, shares this reflection on how the needs of humanity bring God down to earth for us all:

This past week I was at one of the harbors in the southern part of the Gaza Strip, where we are running an economic regeneration program for the fishing community. I recall noticing a man, dressed in rags, standing on the beach facing southeast without even a prayer rug lying before him in the sand. In the background loomed the fishermen's storerooms, the tin roofs riddled with rusty holes from years of being rained on without repair. The makeshift walls barely standing upright, an assortment of metal, wood and stone. These fishermen have not worked in five years; I don't know how they survive. Somehow they do and here, this lone fisherman stands and worships his maker.

Another prayer comes to my mind as I reflect on this place I have begun to call home. It is the prayer of a sick grandmother and her husband. With their children and grandchildren they live, tucked away in the back corner of an olive tree grove on which they work. Here I had come with my pastor and another member of the church to deliver them a box of food to help them through the month. Before we left this Muslim family my pastor prayed that God would bless them, would heal her and show them mercy. To every request prayed, the old man, kneeling with his hands outstretched before him, would utter a quiet 'oh Lord.' His wife beside him, who had just returned from the hospital the previous day, likewise centered all her attention in reverence to her God. Despite the medicines lying next to her in the dirt that she could barely afford, despite the nearby rooms with asbestos ceilings that leaked in the rain, despite her hungry stomach she knew that the One that had created her was attentive to her plight.

The Amoudy brothers on the shores of Khan Younis in the Gaza Strip.
After years of the Israeli army prohibiting them to reach the sea and their boats, the brothers are hoping to rebuild their prior vocation.

I sit here reflecting on these encounters. In them I have met with God so deeply. It is at this human stage that differences of religion, of dogma, of theology, all these things that divide us, matter least. It is this spiritual dimension, this human need of food, care, prayer and community that I encounter a Muslim as no different than a Christian like myself. I am not implying that differences of creed, of tradition and faith don't matter but it is in moments such as these that I see how God could have come to this earth, differing from us in every way, divine coming to human. God came for the needy, for the weak, for the suffering, for us all. And we are to go and do the same.

TRICIA DEERING, Senior Communications Manager for Habitat for Humanity's Europe and Central Asia Area Office, sends us this report about special young builders:

We love getting our hands dirty! Young Muslims and Jews in the USA, and Catholics and Protestants in Northern Ireland are doing it. Japanese and Romanian teens jumped onboard. Armenian students and their Ugandan peers are in on it. Muddy shoes and paint-splattered smiles abound in these diverse groups, and they all have one more thing in common: They love volunteering for Habitat for Humanity!

HFH is a nondenominational Christian charity dedicated to eliminating poverty housing. Active in nearly 100 countries around the globe, HFH invites youth – and those of all ages - from all faiths, and ethnic backgrounds to join the mission – and help build decent family homes. To date, more than one million people are living in HFH homes families helped build, and pay for through no-profit mortgages. HFH youth from around the globe report newfound friends, rich cultural exchanges, and spiritual inter-faith experiences as they unite in the struggle against poverty.

In Northern Ireland, one volunteer sees Habitat for Humanity as a way to bring peace to a fractured community: 'For me, it is being a tool in helping Catholics and Protestants come together. I am doing it for God and to help people have a better home and better way of life.'

In the Philippines, Japanese and Korean students joined forces. Says Mariko from Japan: 'At first I thought it would be hard to work with the Koreans, especially since I didn't know the language, but now they are like my brothers and sisters. It's great to work together and share cultures.'

Thousands of youth volunteers team up for fundraising events, spring-break builds, and advocacy campaigns like the annual 'Act! Speak! Build!' week.

Students joined a challenge in Tennessee. The Rev. Larry Mathis of Knoxville dared a group of

Tricia joins in!

A happy Habitat team taking a break from all that hard work.

international students to buy a week's worth of groceries with $20 – for a mother with three small children. Says Vesta of the Czech Republic, 'It's really tough. If you use your money the wrong way, you might not eat.'

Eye-opening educational experiences abound, as one Canadian university student reports after building with her family in Costa Rica. 'Houses made out of rusted corrugated tin sheeting, scraps of wood and street signs...no electricity or running water, and garbage was scattered everywhere. Children were playing in the dirt next to clothes hung on barbed wire fences to dry. I had no idea that people lived in such poverty,' says Sally. 'I know that not everyone has the opportunities that I have had - to go to university, to travel. But with Habitat for Humanity, I know my family is helping to better the lives of people in need.'

Youth volunteers become active participants in trying to make the world a better place. Says James, a student from Rhode Island, USA: 'My favorite moment occurred when I was nailing the plywood roof to the trusses. There was a real roof on this house that would protect a family from rain, heat, and cold. It was a great feeling.'

Join the mission!

Like Dan Steinhelper of IFYC, RAMOLA SUNDRAM of the International Association for Religious Freedom also made a tremendous effort to bring some stories together to celebrate the work being done by IARF's RELIGIOUS FREEDOM YOUTH NETWORK. One of those stories comes next in this chapter. Two others, Yvonne and Angie's reflections, are in the Living Together chapter and Ramola's own contribution is in the Organising chapter. Read more about the Network itself in the Religious Freedom chapter. Diversity!

One of the RFYN members, WOODROW C MAQUILING Jr, known to friends as 'aR-aR,' tells us about his interfaith journey in the Philippines, a country often troubled by religious conflicts:

Not so long ago I got my first invitation to be part of a youth project aptly called 'Tri-People Interfaith Tour.' Tri-people because the fellowship tried to gather young people coming from the three major spiritual factions in the country - Christians (Catholics and Protestants), Muslims, and Indigenous Peoples (IP).

Being quite naïve about the project, I was eager to accept the invitation. This was something new to my system and I thought I should give it a try. There and then I went on to inform my parents about it. They were very reluctant about the idea that their son would be in an interfaith fellowship with Protestants, Muslims, and IP's (Indigenous Peoples). Our family is orthodox Roman Catholic (largest religious faction in the Philippines) and we have quite a number of biases against spiritual factions other than our own – for example, Protestants and other Christian denominations are lost sheep of God which need enlightenment that only the Catholic way of life can truly provide, that these newly sprouted Christian fellowships are Satan disguised etc. Moreover, rumors tell us that Muslims are traitors, barbaric, destroyers and IP's are the same and also branded as witches, uneducated, and uncivilized.

All these prejudices formed the misconceptions about others that fuelled the apprehensions of my parents about my participation. Nonetheless, I explained and persuaded them that I will join as a representative of Roman Catholic youth, which was really true, and that my participation would somehow help dispel the false impressions held by other spiritual factions about Catholics. My willingness was in the hope that I may be able to share our way of life. In the same manner I was keen to learn about and understand the spiritual values and practices of others.

As well as my family's hesitant consent, I also needed the blessing of our Bishop in the Diocese. Accompanied by my papa, we went to meet him at the Cathedral. With raised eyebrows, he had similar reactions to my parents. He then asked me numerous questions regarding the organization (IARF) initiating the project and yet I couldn't tell more than my minimal understanding of that. Things got increasingly blurry yet the good Bishop gave his cautious blessing after having reiterated the prejudices I mentioned above.

For almost three years now, from the time I started my interfaith journey,

The interfaith team and friends after concreting the floor of the spiritual hall of the Aromanon tribe.

> ### EQUANIMITY
>
> The Zen master Hakuin was praised by his neighbours as one living a pure life. A beautiful Japanese girl whose parents owned a food store lived near him. Suddenly, without any warning her parents discovered she was pregnant. This made her parents very angry. She would not confess who the man was, but after much harassment she at last named Hakuin. In great anger the parents went to the master. 'Is that so?' was all he would say.
>
> When the child was born, the parents brought it to Hakuin, who now was viewed as a pariah by the whole village. They demanded that he take care of the child since it was his responsibility. 'Is that so?' Hakuin said calmly as he accepted the child.
>
> He took very good care of the child. He obtained milk from his neighbours and everything else the little child needed. A year later the girl-mother could stand it no longer. She told her parents the truth - that the real father of the child was a young man who worked in the fish market. The mother and father of the girl at once went to Hakuin to ask forgiveness, to apologize, and to get the child back again. 'Is that so?' Hakuin said as he handed them the child.[8]

numerous changes have come into my life. One is the developing spiritual realization of my own faith because it was only during these times that I really learned to appreciate this. It was in an interfaith setting where I became closer to God, where I had this special connection with Him. More than anything else, I was able to comprehend that none of the prejudices that people held were true.

My horizon became unlimited in such a way that I see life as a beautiful gift and the way to enjoy it is to nourish our own faith and nurture the understanding of the spirituality of others. Experience has its way of telling me that there's no monopoly of truth and as such all spirituality constitutes the whole truth. This reminds us that God communicates to humankind in various ways and in the same manner humankind gives diverse responses.

Over the years, some family members have teased my interfaith involvement to the point that my parents scolded me, almost believing that I shifted religion. Yet, it fascinates me how time has managed to mitigate the misconstrued impressions of my family and of our bishop. None of their worries concerning me shifting religion proved to be right. Recently, I attended the birthday party of the only living Cardinal in our country. I happened to have a brief conversation there with our bishop concerning my interfaith involvement. Surprisingly, he's more open now with my activities. My parents too are gradually softening their approach to interfaith. In one instance, when a party was held at home, my parents allowed me to invite a group of pastors (friends in interfaith fellowship) to join in.

After all, life is all about sharing…

YOUTH IN THE UK

REBECCA HATCH from Save the Children tells us about the new youth project she coordinates:

Diversity and Dialogue brings young people from different faiths together. We develop projects that encourage young people to share their beliefs and values and to work together to change society for the better.

Young people can be reticent about sharing their beliefs and values. Those who do not consider themselves religious may be particularly unused to and uncomfortable with discussing their own moral codes. However, if we want to create a society where those from different faiths and backgrounds can understand and respect each other, then it is vital that children develop the skills to talk openly about their different religions and ethics.

In our work we have been trying out new ways to get young people working together. Over the summer we worked in partnership with the British Museum and a team of 17 young people from seven different religions. Curators helped them to investigate how different faiths and cultures have lived together through history. In parallel, they discussed their own religions and the opportunities and challenges of living in a diverse city like London.

The group then created a trail around the Museum, writing their own interpretations of the artefacts. They selected objects that they felt could teach us lessons about how to live in a multi-faith society successfully. To view an online version of the trail, please visit the website of the British Museum (see Resources).

Diversity and Dialogue was conceived at a meeting of Christian, Jewish, Muslim and secular NGOs. Discussion of events in the Middle East led to talk of the negative impact of global conflicts on religious communities in the UK. Anti-semitic and Islamaphobic attacks have risen as a direct result of world events. Their conclusion was a commitment to run an interfaith education project – Diversity and Dialogue.

The project has used global development issues to unite different religions – as a counter to the global conflicts that have divided them. People from any faith or none can unite to campaign for trade justice or universal education and healthcare. During the British Museum project, for example, I counted Make Poverty History white bands around the wrists of young people from five different faiths.

We are currently working with students from three Manchester schools, who have come together to produce short films on different Millennium Development Goals.

Participants in our Liverpool Community Spirit and Faith in our Community projects

Engaging in global development is a unifying and reflective experience and we think it has a significant role to play in promoting interfaith dialogue.

More information and ideas from the project can be found at our website. The partner organisations are: CAFOD, Christian Aid, the Citizenship Foundation, Islamic Relief, the Jewish Council for Racial Equality, Muslim Aid, Oxfam, Save the Children and World Jewish Aid.

JAYNI GUDKA (below), a young Jain who took part in Diversity and Dialogue's event at the British Museum, writes this reflection on why multifaith events are important and how they can contribute to co-operation and co-existence in our world today:

Unity. The United Kingdom. 'United Kingdom,' what does this mean? What is it that we should stand united for? Stand united against?

Multi-faith is as important now in the 21st century as ever. Living in this diverse city of London, which has faced such severe destruction, is it still important to live in a society enriched with the vibrancy of different faiths and cultures, or is it a reason to segregate from others to form divisions amongst ourselves?

Should we, the citizens of one of the most powerful cities in the world, one of the most powerful countries in the world, the 'United Kingdom', create boundaries of intolerance and prejudice? Should the lack of knowledge of the environment around us promote violence instead of creating awareness for our personal and social growth towards mutual respect and understanding? What makes us British? Is it the fusion of the faiths from all areas of the world, carefully entwined with the vibrancy of global friendship and consideration? Is it the union of individuality and commonality where uniqueness is part of the culture, something encouraged and to be proud of? Or is it just simply the celebration of diversity?

So let's start with 'diversity,' the diversity within London. Is this an unimportant topic? We hope not. Over the last couple of years we have discovered that 'diversity' in fact goes to the heart of what the London community is all about.

Community identity is no longer straightforward, if indeed it ever was. Dynamics of young and old, ethnic groupings, gender roles, peer pressure, wealth and poverty, dishonour and respect, networks and boundaries, are what make communities. We cannot afford to ignore this diversity amongst us. Neglected or suppressed, diversity becomes the occasion or excuse for prejudice, discrimination, hatred, despair, as events in Oldham, Bradford and elsewhere have reminded us. Multi faith events not only help us to promote our diversity, but highlight the good that it does for our society at the same time. They incorporate the extension of knowledge with the chance to create solutions to problems which may have occurred due to the lack of this knowledge.

Jayni and the team.

They also enforce the compassion that we must have towards one another, which is shown to us through religion and faith from throughout the world and throughout history, where mistakes due to prejudice and cruelty have had devastating effects. To prevent such incidents from happening again, and to ensure that a harmonious environment is created and maintained, these multi faith programmes are vital for this city, country and world.

Whilst helping with this multi faith project (at the British Museum), we were asked the question 'How can people of different faiths have a common identity?' Whilst we were discussing this, people commented on the core principles of the World Religions being the same. They compared values such as truth and compassion, which were common foundations to all the religions. This got me thinking....

People of different faiths may not want a common identity, not because they are against the beliefs of others and do not want to join together to form one identity of mutual friendship, but because it's the vibrancy that different faiths and cultures bring to London that make it an interesting place to live in, and although we stand united in the want to stop all prejudices, united in harmony, we remain individual and unique in our own identities.

Also in London and referring to the same destruction mentioned by Jayni, LOUISE MITCHELL, Youth Officer with the Council for Christians and Jews, expresses how interfaith shaped her response to the London underground bombings of July 2005.

7:30am and the usual barely controlled pandemonium hits King's Cross Station. People stride purposefully, eyes to the floor, tickets in hand, hoping to avoid the pitfalls of confused tourists and dysfunctional ticket barriers on their way to the tube. Yet, though this routine is well established, in the last few weeks a change has come over rush-hour London.

On board the tube, commuters no longer feel able to stay within their usual metro-lined vacuums. When the carriage doors open, surreptitious glances from behind newspapers vet the oncoming passengers for tell-tale signs of terrorist intent. Is he carrying a bag? Does he look nervous? Is there any possibility that he could be - MUSLIM?

Underground in London, 7 July 2005.

The bomb attacks that destroyed the lives of so many Londoners shook, too, the relationship between the different cultures that constitute cosmopolitan London society. Muslims, already eyed warily following 9/11, have become the focus of London's fear; the entirety of Islam seemingly reduced to the terrorist actions of a tiny violent minority. Moreover, it is not just Islam that has been hideously distorted. Readers of newspapers as diverse as the Metro and the Independent write letters suggesting that the atrocities of July 7 prove religion to be violent and fascist; they offer hope that in the next generations such bigoted ideologies will become obsolete. Terrorists, then, seem to have become an official face of religion. So what can be done?

Well, for a start, religious communities have to begin communicating amongst each other. The reductive equating of religion to terror reveals that when any religion is threatened religion in general comes under threat. As such, those of us who believe in the importance of religious values need to unite to show the positive side of our beliefs. We need to understand other faith communities in order to protect our own.

Secondly, we have to communicate with people outside of a faith structure. Interfaith work cannot just be kept within people of faith. There has to be dialogue also between people of faith and people not of faith so that both groups can begin to understand where the other is coming from. This is often much harder than interfaith work as there is often no framework at all from which to work. Yet, it is equally important.

Finally, and most problematically, we have to communicate with people within our faiths who share our belief but not our ideals. It is not good enough to dismiss things we don't like in our own religion as not really being part of that religion. Extremism is a marginal part of all religions and we cannot afford to write it off as something entirely foreign. If we reduce interfaith work to 'nice people talking to other nice people about nice things' we have missed the point. We have to engage with people whose opinions we don't like in order for dialogue to be significant.

THE MAIMONIDES FOUNDATION

As part of its work towards a Jewish-Muslim dialogue, the Maimonides Foundation initiated the interfaith football programme. It involves over 120 Muslim and Jewish schoolchildren aged 9-12 playing football in mixed faith teams for three Sundays. Partner in this scheme, the Arsenal Football Club hosts the children and provides coaching at their football ground in Highbury, London.

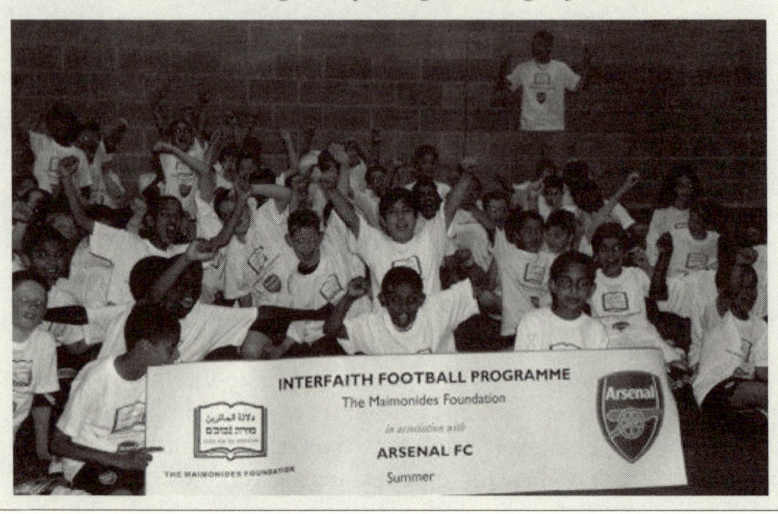

Commuting daily, I, too, pass surreptitious glances at fellow passengers. I, too, sit tensely in my seat hoping that only old age pensioners with zimmer frames board my carriage. At the moment, the fear of another terrorist attack does emphasise the differences between racial and religious groups. It is our job to make the effort to understand ourselves, our communities and 'other' groups better in order that these differences can really be celebrated rather than feared.

After such events the Press play an important role. With his special interest in the media, SIMON COHEN of *global tolerance* shares his vision of interfaith:

Traditional interfaith activity does not particularly interest or inspire me. If I invite you to attend a conference about the importance of interfaith and you accept, the chances are that you are already receptive to the idea of bringing people of different faiths together under an umbrella of mutual tolerance and respect. I really empathise with you, but you do not concern me.

The people that concern me are those who base their values and opinions about religion and interfaith entirely on what they see or hear in the media. Malcolm X once said, 'The media's the most powerful entity on earth. They have the power to make the innocent guilty and to make the guilty innocent, and that's power. Because they control the minds of the masses.' It is a sad truth of modern society that people hear, for example, 'Islamic fundamentalism' and they

Simon Cohen

HRH Prince Charles opening an interfaith meeting place, 'the Tent' at St Ethelburga's on 4 May 2006. Simon Cohen and global tolerance handled all of the media and PR for the event, reaching over 200 million people across the world.

think Islam and terrorism are directly related. This ignorance fuels the fire of fundamentalism and religious tension that interfaith activity tries to extinguish. In the absence of a mass exodus to the public library to find the truth about religion, only improved and more creative media coverage of religious and interfaith issues will help. Then, and only then, will traditional interfaith activity swim with the tide of the public consciousness and not against it.

After my theology degree and several years in the media industry, I set up *global tolerance*, a public relations and media training organisation for faith groups. I wanted to harness the potential of the media to have a positive influence on the public's perception about religious and interfaith issues. The first thing we did was launch the first ever national conference on religion and the media, in which we brought to the forefront the challenges and opportunities for the media and faith communities to improve the coverage of religion. We are launching the first national interfaith football tournament, with young people from different faiths playing on the same team, as well as interfaith eating experiences in restaurants. All of our productions are geared towards achieving maximum mainstream media coverage for religious and interfaith issues that are usually reserved for the back pages.

Our media training and public relations advice for faith groups is at the core of our work. In November 2005 we handled the public relations for the UK visit by Rajmohan Gandhi, grandson of Mahatma Gandhi. The campaign for the peace activist reached over 100,000,000 people, with coverage secured in some of the top media names in the world. We achieved this through an understanding of the media, an appreciation of what our story really was, media contacts and perseverance. We advise and train all faith communities and organisations that have an ethos of building bridges rather than burning them.

We run several websites (see Resources under *global tolerance*) including the leading online resource for religious tolerance in the UK. We also design and build websites for faith and interfaith groups.

INTERNATIONAL INTERFAITH CENTRE (IIC)

When we were at the International Interfaith Centre we organised just one specifically youth only project though we tried always to include young people in all our programming. The specific youth project took place in our last year at the IIC and was called Through Another's Eyes (TAE).[9] The whole idea was based on a project of the same name originally organised for twenty youth, Arabs and Jews, by Givat Haviva. They have since run a similar project specifically for women.[10] Each participant was given a camera, introduced to someone from another faith community or culture and invited to make a photographic record of what happened during their encounters, to see the world through another's eyes.

THROUGH ANOTHER'S EYES

The Oxfordshire incarnation of the project, initiated by Sam Wintrip and developed and co-ordinated by Henry Wai, brought together eight local teenagers from seven different faith backgrounds to increase understanding, respect and appreciation of each other's religions and to develop photography, writing and cooperative skills in a fun way. In addition to group meetings, some of the participants also took part in visits to local interfaith communities that we organised in the same period. Photos were taken that illustrated some aspect of each person's personal faith as well as their interfaith experiences during the project. The best of these, as chosen by the group, then formed an exhibition in Oxford Town Hall, part of the IIC's 10th Anniversary Interfaith afternoon.

Henry Wai

As one participant, Gracie, explained: I really enjoyed being part of the interfaith project. I learnt that different religions share many common goals. I found out how powerful and relevant religions that I thought old and out-dated can be. I got a chance to meet other young people with true and motivated faith, and realized the religious diversity in my community that I didn't see by just looking at the surface. I had a lot of fun and I'd recommend to other people to go out and have a proper look at the rich and colourful faiths and cultures all around them.

Another participant, Ellie, commented: To say that I enjoyed the interfaith project does not seem

Some of the Oxfordshire TAE group

to quite explain the experience. It was a brave and original project that, despite my reservations, proved that a small group of strangers can develop a relationship of mutual respect and trust, produce a thought-provoking display, come up with a lot of diverse ideas AND have fun together! Visits to places of worship made me optimistic and helped change my views, in a positive way, in our capacity to share our religious beliefs. And finally, not to detract from the photography, but the group co-operated in such an honest way, and genuinely liked spending time together. Altogether, heart-warming, mind-opening and indescribably rewarding.

Preparing the exhibition

INTERFAITH IN ACTION IN A GLOBAL CONTEXT

Another important IIC youth gathering was during our symposium, organised for the 1999 Parliament of World Religions in Cape Town. The first task of the young people involved was to interview representatives from the twenty-five organisations who participated in this event. The aim was that this would diminish the possibility of a 'sales' only approach and bring out some of the deeper aspects of each organization's profile. Brave young people! However, during the final session they had to endure this ordeal themselves when the interviewers became the interviewed![11]

BISHOP BILL SWING, founder of the United Religions Initiative, described this when he wrote about our Young Ones.

On a brilliant early Cape Town summer afternoon, the Interfaith in Action in a Global Context Symposium began its final period of work. Fortunately, the session featured some of the young adults who had been involved throughout the three-day program of focused panels. The Rev. Dr. Robert Traer expertly guided and probed through a discussion of the place of interfaith in the lives of these young adults and where they will be five years from now.

The Swings at the Symposium

First named people, Yashika, Megumi, Ramola, Matthew, Andre, Nava, Satish and Ebrahim came from distant places like Japan and Brazil as well as

Paul, Megumi, Nava, Matthew, Ebrahim, Ramola, Yashika, Andre, and Satish with Bob Traer, far right.

the local South Africa. They are usually involved in media or are social activists or are pursuing PhD's. Though young in years they had a depth of experience in and wisdom about interfaith activity.

Some wondered if the word 'Interfaith' was necessary since they had lived life where faiths naturally integrated and no special word was needed. Perhaps by naming it we might lose it or make it too self-conscious. As a matter of fact, the word 'interfaith' sometimes kept their friends at a distance because their friends' parents suspected some kind of proselytizing. Others had scars from colonial religions and now were cautious lest a kind of colonial interfaith movement develop.

These young adults were knowledgeable, educated, passionate about the subject, independent and thorough in approach. A new day has arisen in interfaith leadership as these outstanding young adults no longer wait as add-ons but instead are charting their own interfaith courses of action.

Here is an extract from the notes of Dr PAUL TRAFFORD, who closed this session with a Buddhist reflection:

Bob Traer began to interview members of the panel with the question, 'Does Interfaith work re-inforce traditions?' Yashika responded by saying that one can start more with the values of goodness, compassion, and social liberalism coming together. Then one can draw in the understandings of the various faiths. Nava said that the Parliament had strengthened her belief in humanity: the encounters were an educational experience. For Megumi, interfaith work had strengthened her respect for the dignity of life, and had become an opportunity for critical self-examination. Matthew Smith was interested in the processes of interfaith and argued that organisations were important to facilitate this. Ramola, responding to a question about her experience of the Parliament, felt that it had been a valuable opportunity, providing a rich exchange with local people and their stories. Andre recounted how, for him, the large interfaith gatherings organised by the United Religions Initiative were a great inspiration and helpful in counteracting what he called 'globalitarisation' (a neatly coined phrase referring to the excessive control wielded by large corporations in 'global markets'). Satish saw the need to change our consciousness as a primary act which can then influence the events we attend.

INTERFAITH LECTURE AND WORKSHOPS IN BUDAPEST

In 2002 we were asked by the International Association for Religious Freedom to organise the interfaith lecture and workshops component at their Congress held in Budapest, Hungary. Dr Harriet Crabtree of the Inter Faith Network of the UK gave the main lecture and one young respondent, who was taking part in the IARF Young Adult part of the Congress, was MORSE FLORES, a member of the Ibanag/Kalinga tribe. He described his interfaith experiences in the Philippines:

Morse Flores

In terms of religious beliefs in my country, there are three main belief systems. First is Christianity (including all it's various denominations). As we all know, except for East Timor which gained its independence this May, Philippines is the only catholic country in Asia where more than 70% (of the total 80 millions Filipinos) are Christians. Muslims comprise 10% (around 10 million). Indigenous Peoples account for more than 10% (15-18 million) throughout the Philippine archipelago.

Recently, my country has been on the front-page of various daily broad sheets and news broadcasts in connection to the conflict in the south (Island of Mindanao). It is a conflict deeply rooted in religion and politics together. Since childhood I have been hearing from some elders and friends that I have to avoid this place and this kind of people. Being identified from the South (Muslim) is equated with being a criminal, secessionist, fundamentalist, terrorist, and other negative connotations, which demoralize a person's humanness. This is also true about the Indigenous People. We are actually written in Philippine history books as head-hunters (savages), uncivilized people who need to be educated and cultured. In the same way, our views of Christians are as bad as theirs about us.

Why do we look at each other like this? It is because this is the way our elders told us. Even our educational system (which is of course very biased) taught us to be like this. It's a shame to say

Morse, front/second left, with his music group, United Rhythm

but it is true. Most of the prejudices of the young people are actually bestowed upon them by their own elders. This is the main reason why even young people, young as we are (from the three main groups), cannot talk freely. Indeed the bad perceptions that we have for each other boil from the deepest part of our hearts. Since these bad stigmas were learnt from the people whom we look up to, it is indeed very hard to change but we must. In Manila, we were able to develop an Interfaith Course for three months during the summer vacation. The dialogues were conducted every Saturday and Sunday. We even held our mass and rituals in the same venue. Young representatives from the three groups came together in one place and discussed everything in our minds. During the first month, we had speakers from the Christian faith who shared with us their Christian values and way of life. The second month, it was those from the Islamic faith who talked to us about their Muslim culture and traditions. The third month was reserved for the Indigenous People like me who gave very colourful participation during the three months long Interfaith Dialogue.

So what are the greatest lessons that we learned from that programme? We came to realize that religion, in the past and in some cases at present a source of conflict, can actually be a source or instrument for Peace.[12]

INTERFAITH WORKSHOPS AT COVENTRY 2000

MINORITIES OF EUROPE asked us to organise the interfaith workshop component of their special Coventry programme. This is what Sandy wrote for the IIC Newsletter after the event:

Values have No Boundaries: Action for the New Millennium was the theme of Coventry 2000, a four-day event held in Coventry, UK in August 2000, organised by Minorities of Europe. As part of the diverse programme the 200 young participants from minority communities throughout Europe could choose from five mainstream 'rivers': gender, sexuality, disability,

Interfaith group at Coventry 2000

European organisations, and interfaith. Forty of them - from Portugal, UK, Ireland, Latvia, Sweden, Finland, Germany, Uzbekistan, Russia, Hungary, France, Lithuania, Romania, Greece, Italy, Estonia, Croatia, and Poland - chose the interfaith programme that the International Interfaith Centre had been asked to co-ordinate.

Our co-ordination team included people from six faith traditions and several interfaith organisations: Inter Faith Network for the UK, World Conference on Religion and Peace (WCRP), International Association for Religious Freedom (IARF), World Congress of Faiths (WCF), Coventry Multi-Faith Forum and the IIC. We decided to hold each of the four three hour river sessions in different religious centres in Coventry to maximise the interaction between local communities and the young people, many of whom had not had the opportunity for such contacts. The centres were also chosen to reflect the daily themes ie. diversity (Hindu mandir), equality (Sikh gurdwara), solidarity (Jewish synagogue) and action (Muslim mosque).

Group discussions, role-play, art and music during the interfaith river embraced a wide range of subjects, including introductions to ten religious traditions and the four themes of Coventry 2000. The first small group enquiry revolved around our understandings of the divine. This was perceived in many ways: as the knower and the unknown; as energy and light; as creator, personal and impersonal; as the reality hiding behind all different beliefs and as the power creating all the different beliefs; as emptiness and as the image of ourselves; as universal and rather particular; as an infinite circle with overlapping spheres where beliefs touched each other in the divine presence; as something to be loved and feared; as source and sustainer, gender free and self-existent, full of paradox and mystery. Somehow, despite the diversity of description, there was a shared understanding that this divine paradox was at the centre of everything.

It was exciting to discover that the Finnish participants in the interfaith river were not blond haired and blue eyed, as might be expected, but Muslims originally from Somalia; those from Poland were Ukrainians; the Romanians were Bahai's etc: all minorities in some way or another in their countries. Many of the young people in our river had experienced prejudice of some kind: dietary, ethnic, religious. These tensions were not left 'at home'. During the overall Coventry 2000 programme the gay and lesbian participants felt others were discriminating against them, that they were not in the safe place they'd expected but threatened by homophobia. Religious aspects of the overall programme also brought some critique against the interfaith team that was thought to be responsible for this imposition (we were not). Dealing with these issues highlighted the value of such events and the opportunities they provide for intense and educational encounter.

The new generation of European young leaders are not prepared to be voiceless but demand full participation in the issues that concern them.[13]

FROM CONFLICT TO TRUST: INTERFAITH EXPERIENCES AND POSSIBILITIES

We had four special young guests at the 2001 IIC conference (see picture above, l/r Vladimir Mandic, Ines Babic, Ghada Issa and Dotan Arad.). Here are some extracts from a report written by Sandy for the IIC Newsletter.

The conference began movingly with two young people, Ghada Issa, a Palestinian Muslim from Hope Flowers School in Bethlehem, and Dotan Arad, an Israeli Jew and Yeshiva student from Jerusalem, standing together to offer prayers for peace.

The next morning Ghada and Dotan joined with Vladimir Mandic, a student from Serbia, and Ines Babic, a young teacher from Croatia, to share their experiences of trying to move from conflict to trust. Peter Brinkman from the International Peace Council questioned them and found that 'they left us with a new and arresting understanding that peace is a process - not a search for a quick or easy solution. Conflict erodes and destroys trust at every level. To restore it requires a painstaking and patient commitment that will endure all the by-products of conflict - fear, anger, resentment, and unresolved pain and suffering.'

Vladimir told us he had been studying in Kosovo when the NATO bombing started and had to return to his town in Serbia on the border with Kosovo that was then also bombed by NATO. He reminded us how grateful we should feel to live in a safe area without the frightening sound of explosions around us and without the economic distress caused by the resulting destruction. He told us how Serbs and Croats share a common language but need visas to cross each other's borders. Vladimir felt that the roots of conflict were not connected to religion - Serbia had been communist - and that religious communities should show their commitment to peace-making as all religions teach not to kill.

Ines took this one step further by stating that it was time for those who were witnesses to the conflict rather than participants to come forward and do something. With others she had formed groups for all ages to begin to reflect together on ways forward and the rebuilding of relationships. This takes time and it's too early to expect peace and inter-religious dialogue to be part of this healing. You cannot expect children born in the traumatised and impoverished refugee camps to look positively at the 'other' until these conditions have been addressed. If they want to go home they have to be able to co-exist and then the process towards seeing the 'other' as human again can begin. This requires both intrafaith and interfaith development. 'The former takes me back to my tradition and uncovers the important components and content of my own faith as a basis to work from. The latter tackles some issues within the wider community, highlights the diversity but also reminds of the common ground - a great start on the long way from conflict to trust.' Interfaith alone does not help where religious identity and nationality are inter-linked. It is first essential to see one's own religion and religious practice in a new way.

Dotan pointed out that although he and Ghada live 20kms apart they cannot cross the border to meet. They had to meet in Oxford. Dotan had met a Sufi in the Ghaza Strip who had made a deep impression, allowing him to see the 'face of God' in the 'enemy.' When this happens you have to adapt your view of the 'other' and, unlike many Israelis, Dotan had chosen interfaith as an option for peace, a way to learn to live together. A religious person is often perceived as fanatical - this stigma has to dissolve. Religious power should be used to build peace and to establish religious rather than secular authority in the disputed holy places. A religious person is patient, working with God for long-term solutions rather than short-term fixes, and all the conflict partners in the Middle East believe in God. Dotan acknowledged the Israeli side as stronger with concomitant responsibilities but argued that weakness is not always the same as truth and that Palestinians also need to understand that Jews have suffered, in the past when stateless, and now in Israel. People from his home area had been killed and his mother worries if his father will come home at night. For Jews, Israel was their country long ago and is the only 'safe'

> Conference on children's rights held in Nazareth in 1999.
> We attended this event and were surprised to learn that child brides for old men were often chosen by the men's mothers to ensure strong helpers in the household.

place in the world. Like Palestinians, they need a secure place. Being blown up at bus stops leads Israelis to see all Palestinians as terrorists. There is a need to find ways for Palestinian and Israeli children to meet together, for sport for instance, to help humanise the 'other.' Dotan thinks that inter-religious dialogue could build bridges between people where there is disagreement at political level. Both sides are religious or give respect to religion so it could be a key to dialogue. 'I pray that wisdom will win the emotions and we, the two nations, will learn to live together, peacefully, in our little holy land.'

Ghada felt that two peoples or two religious communities sharing the land is not the problem if equal respect is shown for each other's rights. Forcing people into refugee camps by taking or destroying their homes is not evidence of respect. Ghada works with Muslim and Christian Palestinian children teaching peace and democracy programmes but it is hard to convince children to love the 'other' when they have spent the night in air-raid shelters, live under occupation in severe conditions, have poor employment and economic prospects, live in a state separated from its various parts by checkpoints and concrete roadblocks, and who have had fathers and brothers killed. Equal rights have to become a reality in order to move forward from conflict to trust. Hope Flowers School tries to offer new views to replace old aggressions, using sport, agriculture, science and handicrafts to bring Palestinian children into joint programmes with Israeli children. The school also brings together rabbis and imams and priests for interfaith dialogue and to teach that to the children.

As Peter reflected, these young people 'left no doubt as to their courage, insight and commitment to peace. Interfaith experiences and possibilities, all agreed, provide a core of hope. The caveat, however, also came across loudly and clearly: work in the trenches of conflict is intensely personal and relational and requires an interfaith commitment to work shoulder to shoulder on the ground.'[14]

Peter Brinkman

SUMMARY

We have read how some young people are contributing to and advancing the interfaith agenda. If you are a youth and this has inspired you, do contact your nearest interfaith group. They will welcome you.

Check the national coordinating bodies like the Inter Faith Network for the UK and the North American Interfaith Network
to find out if there are groups in your area.
Check with the United Religions Initiative to see if there is a co-operation circle in your area and with Religions for Peace
to see if they have a local group.
Both organisations - and many others - are active around the world.
If there is no group, start one!
Any of the organisations mentioned above will help and support you. Look in the Resources section at the end of this book
for further options.

You are the future of interfaith.
What you bring to dialogue and activities will help
shape the present and the coming years.
You are needed. Get connected.

A special 'young' lunch time in the IIC/IARF office: From l/r Andre Porto, Josef Boehle, Zarrin Caldwell, Eboo Patel, Ramola Sundram and Joanna Jeczalik.
Colleagues from five countries and five faiths.

INTERFAITH YOUTH

*My faith is in the younger generation,
out of them will come my workers,
they will work out the whole problem.*
Swami Vivekananda

> Can my community share our light with the world?

Chapter X

THE ROLE OF RELIGIONS

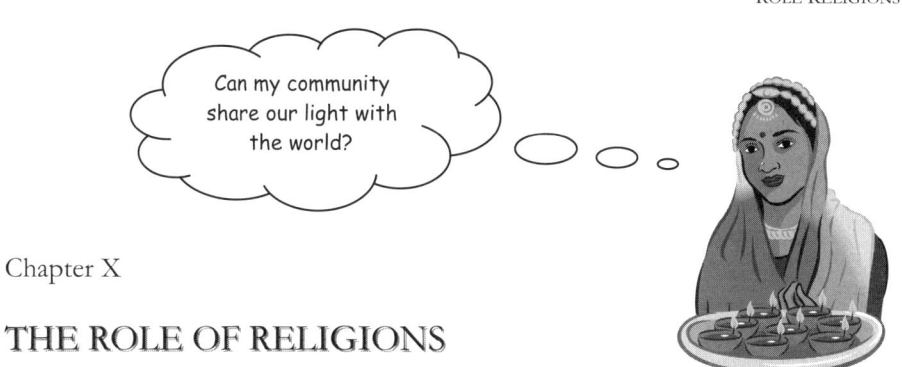

QUESTIONS

Specifically oriented interfaith dialogue and activities, thus far, only touch a small percentage of religious people and have little hope of reaching into secular society. So, as civil society increasingly brings people of faith together through varied programmes and initiatives that have a broader outreach than just inter-religious enquiry, are interfaith organisations being left behind, becoming redundant, stagnant, limited by their competitiveness, stifled by their struggle for funding, less effective, out-dated, un-mindful of or even unsure what their task now is? Is the focus on religions just too narrow, a restriction that civil society is not burdened by? If religions are ultimately limited and divisive in what they deliver, why then give them so much exclusive attention?

Interfaith activity will probably always span many levels but still the question remains: what is it really for, what is the role of religions, what do we and other species sharing this world with us really need to be happy and peaceful? Is there a more universal and unifying aspect on which to focus to

---

SWAMI VIVEKANANDA said:
This is the message of Sri Ramakrishna to the modern world: Do not care for doctrines, do not care for dogmas, or sects, or churches, or temples; they count for little compared with the essence of existence in each man, which is spirituality; and the more this is developed in a man, the more powerful is he for good. Earn that first, acquire that, and criticise no one, for all doctrines and creeds have some good in them. Show by your lives that religion does not mean words, or names, or sects, but that it means spiritual realization. Only those can understand who have felt. Only those who have attained to spirituality can communicate it to others, can be great teachers of mankind. They alone are the powers of light.[1]

Sri Ramakrishna

bring greater understanding and co-operation in the world?

We may dream that interfaith will help to decrease suffering on this planet; suffering caused, for example, by conflicts in which religions often play a role. We may hope that the dialogue between religions could have a special potency to prevent and/or end wars. But is this true? Or is the comparison of religions with universities more factual? Any dialogue between Cambridge and Oxford, for example, however productive it might be, will often be accompanied by competition, which shows itself via most aspects and individuals who are linked to these universities. The competition goes on even into the old age of students who left university many years before. Competition can lead to conflicts. As long as individuals who finished their university education keep an immature attitude - I am from Oxford and so have received the best education, which makes me better than others - and/or remain attached to one university rather than just being grateful for the education they received, will there not be narrowness of heart and spirit and seeds for division and conflict?

To decrease suffering on this planet, do people of religion need to be able to take off their label? Religion has helped us, like universities, to get some knowledge or qualification but does there come a time when we have to leave them behind, to start life in broader human society, experience the realities, learn and develop ourselves? Might it be that to decrease competition, conflict and suffering, the setting of interfaith dialogue is inadequate? If human society aspires to become more mature/civil, does the dialogue have to be taken out of the context and power of religions, and representatives of religions? Do individuals need to become brave enough to leave behind identification with labels of nationality, religion, race etc. before being able to enter a real dialogue in respect and love for the other? Do we have to go beyond religions?

As long as interfaith activities encourage people to 'belong' to their traditions, will their impact be as enclosed as the boundaries the labels bring with them? Is the purpose of religion to tell each other all about what we believe in this or that tradition or to understand how what we believe can return us to our true Selves? Can we change the world other than by example?

The DALAI LAMA once said:

There are two primary tasks facing religious practitioners who are concerned with world peace. First, we must promote better interfaith understanding so as to create a workable degree of unity among all religions. This may be achieved in part by respecting each other's beliefs and by emphasizing our common concern for human well-being. Second, we must bring about a viable consensus on basic spiritual values that touch every human heart and enhance general human happiness. This means we must emphasize the common denominator of all world religions – humanitarian ideals. These two steps will enable us to act both individually and together to create the necessary spiritual conditions for world peace.[2]

ROLE OF RELIGIONS

In 2001, Marcus Braybrooke, quoting Anne Frank, reflected, that: 'Nobody need wait a single moment before beginning to improve the world.' This thought is as relevant now as then, even if different world events might currently dominate our reflections. Marcus wrote:

On September 11th, a young Muslim from Pakistan was evacuated from the World Trade Centre where he worked. He saw a dark cloud coming towards him. Trying to escape, he fell. A Hasidic Jew held out his hand, saying, 'Brother, there's a cloud of glass coming at us, grab my hand, let's get the hell out of here.'

People of all faiths have held hands to support and comfort each other and to join together in prayer. Can we continue to hold hands as we shape a world society in which all people share to the full the precious gift of life?

Those who were killed in America on September 11th and those who have been killed in Afghanistan will not have died in vain if their cries of anguish are also a wake up call to us to urgently tackle our world's problems.

The dangers of religious exclusivism and extremism, against which we in the interfaith movement struggle, are now clear for all to see. We should seize this moment to urge all people of faith to re-examine their teaching and practice to root out all that divides believers from each other.

We should emphasis the importance of spiritual and moral nurture in the home and in schools and colleges. Beyond our religious and interfaith circles we need to share, with politicians and economists and all who shape the future, our vision of a world society based on understanding and co-operation.
The responses to the tragic events of September 11th have defined 'goodies' and 'baddies' in the old language and actions of confrontation and enmity. But violence at best only suppresses aggression and breeds future conflict.

The experience of interfaith and peace groups active in areas of conflict is that bitter hatred can only be healed by listening. Slowly we begin to hear the other's pain and grievance just as they may hear our sorrow. By acceptance and forgiveness we can free ourselves from the chains that bind us to a bitter past.

The Dalai Lama said that two responses to the terrible events of 11th September 2001 were possible. One came from fear, the other from love. 'If we could love even those who have attacked us, and seek to understand why they have done so ... we would become spiritual activists.' For this to happen, he says, we need Divine help and mutual support to grow in inner peace and wisdom. Each of us can contribute to healing the world.

As Anne Frank wrote in her diary at the age of fourteen, 'How wonderful it is that nobody need wait a single moment before beginning to improve the world.'[3]

> **TAO**
>
> Do you think you can take over the universe and improve it?
> I do not believe it can be done. The universe is
> sacred. You cannot improve it. If you try to change it,
> you will ruin it. If you try to hold it, you will lose it.
> So sometimes things are ahead and sometimes they are
> behind; Sometimes breathing is hard, sometimes it comes
> easily; Sometimes there is strength and sometimes
> weakness; Sometimes one is up and sometimes down.
> Therefore the sage avoids extremes, excesses, and complacency.

WENDY TYNDALE made these observations about the role of religions at the International Interfaith Centre's 10th Anniversary Dinner in 2003:

There are many people who see religion as a force for divisions and for destruction in the world, and they have their reasons: The Hindu nationalist movement in India is about power, profit, discrimination and violent coercion, but is this what the Vedas teach us? There are Christians and Jews who support the most merciless type of capitalism, but who heard Jesus saying we should store up as much grain as possible in our own barn and then shut the door? And where in the Hebrew scriptures are we told to exploit our neighbour to our own profit? And we know from the discussions since 11 Sept 2001 that the Islamic conception of jihad has nothing to do with terrorism.

The desire of the inter-faith movement is to return to the original spirit and vision of our different religious traditions and to promote an agenda for peace and justice in the world, even if this often means working with people on the margins of their faith communities rather than with those in power. [The] interfaith movement is not merely a strategy to change the world for the better. Unless we take time, open spaces, listen, celebrate together, meditate and pray, we shall be caught up in the very dynamic we are trying to change. It is all about the paradoxical situation of being in the world but not of it.

One day the Buddha was walking along in a beautiful place with his disciples and he said: 'This would be a good place to build a temple' (or in some translations a 'sanctuary'). One of his followers then plucked a blade of grass and planted it in the earth. 'The sanctuary has been built,' he said. The Buddha smiled.[4]

Two former General Secretaries of the International Association for Religious Freedom (IARF), Robert Traer and Andrew Clark, also pose some challenges and ask questions about the role of religions in interfaith encounter.

ROBERT TRAER, IARF General Secretary from 1990-2000, writes that religion is personal:

> Before I began interfaith work I taught world religions. With a Ph.D. in comparative religion, I thought I was quite knowledgeable about the history of religion and the differences between the religious traditions. As I took part in interfaith activities, however, I soon realized religious people live 'outside the boxes' that textbooks use to distinguish one religion from another.
>
> After meditating with two Buddhist nuns in Seoul, I was astonished when they began to play Gregorian music while we had tea. 'Why are you playing Christian music?' I asked. 'We like it,' one of them replied. 'It's very spiritual.' The nuns said they were friends with Catholics, who operate a leprosy clinic where some of their lay Buddhists volunteer. Catholics welcoming Buddhist volunteers? Buddhists inspired by Christian songs about God? My study of world religions did not prepare me for such sharing and friendship by members of different traditions.
>
> In England I met a Catholic sister, who was also a Zen roshi. Her ministry has involved teaching meditation to prisoners, for years in the Philippines and then in the United Kingdom. She saw no conflict in being both a Christian 'religious' and a Buddhist teacher.
>
> A Muslim friend in Bangalore, India invited Christian neighbours to his house before Christmas to share what Jesus meant to them all. The Qur'an reveres Jesus as a prophet but asserts that he is not the Son of God, as Christians claim. Yet, with Christian friends an Indian Muslim celebrated the virgin birth of Jesus and the significance for both Muslims and Christians of the teachings of the man the Qur'an calls 'son of Mary.'
>
> In a Muslim village near Calcutta illiterate women were asked by a field worker for the organization I directed to consider how they could dispel some of the antagonism between their village and nearby Hindu communities. The women decided to celebrate the Indian holiday of Diwali, except for making an offering to 'idols' as Hindus do. The Muslim women saw they could identify with their Hindu neighbours without compromising their religious teachings.
>
> In Israel I have gone with members of Rabbis for Human Rights into the West Bank to assist Muslim Palestinians in planting their fields and pruning their olive trees, despite threats and violence by nearby Jewish settlers. Jews seeking

Jews with Palestinian landowners enjoying a meal together

Rabbi, soldiers and Palestinians landowners are negotiating about plowing land near Hebron

justice for Muslims by resisting other Jews, who are taking Palestinian land because they believe God has given it to the Jewish people.

This last experience should remind us that even remarkable acts of interfaith cooperation in our time have not helped end the many harsh conflicts within religious traditions as well as between different religious communities. As long as Christians, Muslims, Jews, Hindus and other religious persons support the use of violence to defend their way of life, we should refrain from characterizing the teachings of their 'religions' as peaceful. Instead, we should be honest and acknowledge the violent histories of our religious traditions. We should be humble and admit how little we all have done to understand why religious convictions are so often expressed in exclusive and judgmental ways.

When I think about 'religion' now, I think first of persons who are religious. I am critical of any statement about any religious tradition that takes the form of 'Islam believes' or 'Judaism holds' or 'Christianity proclaims' or 'Hinduism teaches.' Muslims believe, Jews hold, Christians proclaim, and Hindus teach, as do Buddhists, Sikhs, and members of other religious traditions.

We are all responsible for the teachings of our religious traditions and for the moral character of our communities. We have much to learn from one another, much to improve in our own teachings and practice, and much to share.

ANDREW CLARK, IARF Secretary General from 2000-2005, enquires what is the point of interfaith encounter?

The argument in the liberal establishments was actually won over a decade ago, and their religious leaders opened their doors to encounter with 'the Other.' The ethos of interfaith is growing rapidly but amorphously to support its new religious subculture. There are a few exceptions where the other religion or belief appears to be exploitative, dangerous or a personality cult.

Religious freedom thus has to be circumscribed by a concept of religious responsibility, and the International Association for Religious Freedom has taken an initiative to open the debate on what that concept of responsibility might entail. In due course it needs to be extended to the really difficult areas such as religiously justified violence, self-immolation, extreme ascetic practices, séances and the ritual slaughter of animals (possibly including the Christmas turkey.)

What then should I ask of my own tradition, the Religious Society of Friends (Quakers)? Should we not base our inter-faith multi-logue on the proposition that we have intrinsic difficulties in our Quaker faith and practice? We clearly do not have 'the whole Truth.' We need help to develop our Quakerism, or to evolve onto some new, deeply discerned spiritual path, nevertheless rigorously tested using our own disciplines. The point of interfaith encounter being mutually to share our vulnerability and searching. The danger being: an implicit endorsement of tendencies towards religious syncretism, with religious tenets, truths and insights used like Lego blocks subjectively to build whatever meets an individual or group's current needs.

Let us take some simple examples of where interfaith encounter can boldly go. Most religions are determined or guided by sacred texts that were written hundreds if not thousands of years ago. They may not exist in their original form, only as copies or translations. How can they be used reliably to designate or proscribe our behaviour today? We actually have common problems as believers with the 'infallibility' or even reliability of our scriptures...Similarly with the implications of modern scientific discoveries. More problematically, we may be faced with the fact that our young people are either losing interest

SWAMI AGNIVESH

Egotism and the new religion of the Market are sweeping the global world ignoring all human and environmental concern.
It is a world where only the share-holder value and profit dominate and where we religious leaders stand by and do nothing or next to nothing...We don't live up to the standards we preach. We like to be in league with the powerful, the famous and the mighty and ignore half of our brothers and sisters or feed them with some future heavenly reward or some better rebirth in a future life. What is the use of quoting holy books if they do not translate into action?...
No system of injustice and of exploitation can subsist unless we religious leaders give the moral and ethical platform for it...
We are at the beginning of a new millennium. Humanity has all the resources and the means to eradicate some of the worst problems that humankind is suffering from. Can we give the world a spiritual and social orientation that is truly uplifting, humanistic and universal?
Can we refrain from our sectarian outlook and find a common platform to contribute our share for a better and more peaceful world?
And finally, can we give half of humanity, the women, a rightful place in the religious field? [5]

August 2004: Andrew with IARF flag protesting in support of Tibet outside the United Nations, New York, before going inside to attend the Millennium Peace Summit (from which the Dalai Lama was excluded).

in religious discipline of any kind, or are unwilling to recognise any relevance in traditional religious structures and hierarchies.

Currently, interfaith dialogue is usually dysfunctionally polite. We cannot point out each other's strengths and weaknesses because, without being asked to do so, it could be interpreted as an attack. We are afraid to ask and share our doubts. The point of interfaith encounter, however, is not to put up a good show and fly our flag in a spiritual rainbow environment, it is to identify and seek out truthful, critical allies. This process admits the possibility that no individual faith tradition currently encompasses answers commensurate with its own supreme claims about knowing the Truth, and its ability to guide the spiritual destiny of the human species.

> ACCOUNTABILITY:
>
> At the end of the day Allah will not ask me
> what I achieved in life, or whether I changed the world.
> I will only be asked about whether I did what I could do.
> That's the only question that will be asked of us.
> You were given so much time, so much money;
> these are the talents that I gave you.
> What did you do with them?
> Not whether you changed the world's problems.
> Whether you brought about gender equality, interfaith understanding, harmony,
> solved the problems of the Balkans, Jews and Muslims.
> You won't get asked any of these things.
> What did you do with what I gave you?
> That's all that we are responsible for.
> And so we are accountable to God at the end of the day, and that's it.[6]
>
> Maulana Dr Farid Esack

CANON ANDREW WHITE has strong words about the role of religions in bringing about the peace they preach in his reflection, 'Inter Faith on the Front Line.'

I spend most of my days in Iraq, Israel and Palestine. Places where religion does not always play a positive role. In fact it may be said that religion plays a decidedly negative role. It is no good just saying that religion is all about peace, mercy and tranquility. It is not and has never been. Religion has power and power can be used creatively or destructively. Sadly in history it has often been used destructively. From the time of the crusades when Christians caused mass destruction and death in the name of the Cross to the recent terrorist activities in London, New York and daily in Baghdad. Too often religions are not prepared to face up to the huge atrocities that take place in their name. The most influential writing on this subject is by Oliver McTurnon who recently wrote the book *Violence in God's Name*. In it he shows how this has taken place over thousands of years involving all major religions.

If we are going to allow religion to take the positive role that it should in our life we first have to be aware of it potential negatives. I have the strange reality of being the only cleric in the Anglican world who cannot usually go to his church. St George's Baghdad is just too unsafe to visit at the moment. The Church is surrounded by razor wire, bomb barricades, and armed guards. Not what you normally expect for a place of worship but it is precisely because it is, that it has become the target of attacks. Churches, not to mention the Shia holy shrines, are all targeted places of aggression. This is because religion has gone very wrong. It has abused the power it has, thus become a source of violence and aggression rather than peace. If religion is to be the source of peace then it has to realize that the creation of peace is the very thing that power needs to be used for. It is not easy. Peace is a difficult thing to maintain and must always involve the respect of the other.

Interfaith activity is no longer the activity of a few nice liberals in suburbia, drinking tea and eating smoked salmon bagels. It is now a matter of life and death. In all the areas where I work there is an increase in violence in God's name.

Andrew (centre) in Iraq with Ayatollah Hossain Al Sader and other clerics

INTERFAITH

Andrew with children in Baghdad

If we are to change this and make a real difference in our world faiths must talk to each other and engage to make a difference. We must engage with each other in the most difficult situations. This is what my colleagues are doing in Baghdad, Jerusalem and Gaza City. It is very dangerous, at times staff and colleagues have even been killed because they dared to talk to and even befriend the other. Here in the Middle East interfaith activity is not the quest of the weak, but the strong, courageous and brave. People can and do change. One of my closest friends and colleagues, Sheik Tal El Sider from Hebron, was once bombarded at a press conference for working with the 'Zionists.' At the end of the tirade he took the hand of the Rabbi next to him and said, 'He is my brother, we will walk together until we find Peace.' At this one of the media personnel shouted at him 'well what do you think you are doing then?' He replied 'I am walking this path, pulling up the thorns and planting flowers.' The sheik was one of the founders of Hamas but has given up the way of violence and puts all of his energy into making Peace.

Even as this reflection from Andrew arrived in our computer, the violence Andrew wrote of was finding new victims in Gaza as Win Burton, her husband and daughter were kidnapped there. Win was a long-term employee of the Churches Ecumenical Council and Soul for Europe. A keen interfaith activist she attended meetings of the Network of International Interfaith Organisations as an observer and initiated a European version of it. She and her husband recently completed their work in Brussels and were about to move back to Britain when this happened. Their daughter Kate was working in Gaza with a human rights project there and Win and Hugh were visiting her over the Christmas period when they were kidnapped at gunpoint and disappeared.

Win Burton

> A challenge from Professor RAVI RAVINDRA:
>
> *In my judgment, there is something wrong with interfaith dialogues.*
> *When the East-West or interfaith dialogues are too much bound by the past, the dynamic nature of cultures and religions, and above all of human beings, cannot be appreciated. If one has never met someone from another culture or religion, interfaith or inter-cultural conversation is obviously a good idea.*
> *But I wish to suggest as strongly as I can that interfaith dialogues are at best a preliminary stage of human to human dialogue and can even be an impediment to a deeper understanding. A dialogue of cultures and worldviews, in which the parties involved declare their adherence to one or another faith or culture, can fix these faiths and cultures into the entities that they were.*
> *In fact these cultures and religions are alive and dynamic and are undergoing large and serious transformations right now.*
> *An inter-pilgrim dialogue, which is of necessity somewhat trans-cultural, trans-religious and trans-disciplinary, is needed to move into a future of a larger comprehension.*[7]

At such a difficult and dangerous moment, it was clear to see the benefit of interfaith cooperation. Immediately contacts in the region were brought into concerted action to find and save the family. Two days later they were freed, unharmed. The contacts that make this kind of action possible are not established overnight. They are the result of continuous relationship building through many years, the product of hard won trust and mutual respect, strong enough to withstand the pressures that would seek to destroy them. It is a pity, with such negative press about religions in the media most often, that to protect the delicate negotiations, the input from interfaith organisations to the resolution of this crisis, could not be openly revealed. As Win herself put it, 'It's been wonderful how the faith communities have been involved in the whole process, able to negotiate and make contacts on a quite different level from the formal governmental ones and I'm sure, unlock doors and bend hearts as a result.'[8]

In a rather different but inter-related UK environment, Rev FERGUS CAPIE of the London Inter Faith Centre writes on inter faith - a view from within the Church of England:

While British society continues to be arguably largely secular in spirit, if increasingly - especially in our cities - mixed faith in practice, there is a sense in which it is still officially Christian in terms of structure. The Church of England is by law established, with the Queen as its head in matters temporal and the Archbishop of Canterbury in matters spiritual. As such, many of its responsibilities are for society at large, for those of all faiths and none. My post - as an Inter Faith Adviser within the Diocese of London - was created to help address questions such as what it may mean to belong to a traditionally exclusivist and missionary religion in a now secular and many faith context. Historically, within the British Isles, contact with the religious 'other' had been somewhat at arms length, through the missionary movement. Now, through the pattern of immigration, with Hindus and Muslims and Sikhs and others as our neighbours, colleagues, friends - what were to be the church's changing and developing theologies and strategies for mutual engagement?

My own work in London NW6 has included the setting up of London Inter Faith Centre, a place for meeting, study and dialogue among the world's religions. I think it would be fair to say that until 9/11 this type of work was often considered 'suspect' by many in the life of the church. What was this business of 'dialogue' all about? Did it amount to compromise? Post 9/11 there rapidly developed an acknowledgement that, as the late Sheikh Dr Zaki Badawi once said to me, 'we talk or we fight.' Dialogue developed teeth; inter faith became 'legitimate' in day to day practice, just as significant work had been done theologically within Christianity to enable Christians to understand its legitimacy and need, in theory.

And in very recent years inter faith has gone from 'suspect' to 'legitimate' to 'de rigeur' - being ever more mainstreamed and integrated in the life of society. Many of us would want to thank Sandy and Jael for their determined and continuing work through the more frontier years, towards helping create the climate and infrastructure of the present situation, in which it is readily acknowledged that a person or community's faith identity can be central to life and a matter of enrichment rather than threat to others outside their own bounds.

London Interfaith Centre during a visit from Prince Charles

We here at London Inter Faith Centre (a one man band at the outset but now a team of four paid staff and also with many different faith colleagues) would certainly wish to pay tribute to all that Jael and Sandy have done in this crucial area of interpersonal and inter community relations - to the end that we may all learn from one another as we seek to grow into a single society, rather than a series of competing communities.

DR MICHAEL BARNES SJ, from the Centre for Christianity and Interreligious Dialogue (CCID), spoke of the role of religions in this way:

My suggestion is that religions are to be understood as 'schools of faith' which seek to educate a particular group of people by introducing them to the

Panels from the Faith Zone at the London Millennium Dome

collective wisdom of the group. Such a 'school' properly conceived, looks in two directions at once, like every school: towards the group itself and the traditions which it seeks to enhance and preserve, and to the wider world beyond the group with which it hopes to encourage an imaginative dialogue.

It is all too easy, in a multi-faith world, to seek to reconcile the conflicting truth claims of different religious traditions by attempting to rewrite them in the light of some overarching universal vision. The more demanding challenge is to work within and between living traditions. It is not to seek to extract from them some supposedly timeless ethical essence, but to enable religious communities to re-read, not to re-write, their own stories and to learn from each other.

Essentially Inter Faith Dialogue is such a re-reading - a common enterprise in which, at a number of different levels, schools of faith learn to co-operate. For this to work, communities have to be given sufficient space and encouragement to reach down into their own fund of collective wisdom and to rediscover their own strengths and sources of energy. At the same time, if they are not to become alienated from wider society (and wider society not to be alienated from them), this has got to be done consciously in relationship with whatever they take to be 'other' - whether other communities of faith or secular society.[9]

SIDNEY L SHIPTON OBE, Coordinator of The Three Faiths Forum, tells us about the Forum's work:

I am not an academic but a non-practicing lawyer working in the voluntary not-for-profit sector for many years. Since 1997 I have been the Co-ordinator of the Three Faiths Forum – Muslim/Christian/Jewish Trialogue - although I have been involved in interfaith activity for many years, in fact, since my student days and I believe passionately in this work.

The Three Faiths Forum was set up in January 1997 by Sir Sigmund Sternberg, Sheikh Dr M A Zaki Badawi KBE and Rev Dr Marcus Braybrooke. The major activity of the Three Faiths Forum is to promote understanding and mutual respect between the three Abrahamic monotheistic faiths: Islam, Christianity and Judaism. To realise this, The Three Faiths Forum works at several levels. First, it has an Advisory Board, where approximately 50 representatives of Islam, Judaism and Christianity come together every couple of months to hear reports and to act as a think tank. The second level is possibly the most important, namely the local or regional level. That is to say, at grass roots, since the good relations between the leadership of the Muslim, Christian and Jewish communities does not always percolate down to the local level. Local groups are therefore a priority. The third level on which we work is through our Medical Group, where Muslims, Christians and Jews involved in medicine and medical matters come together to discuss controversial matters such as abortion, euthanasia, mental health, genetic engineering and other similar subjects. A new field of activity in the last couple of years has been our endeavours to promote and form Three Faiths Forum groups in universities.

The Three Faiths Forum holds joint meetings with other organisations, for example, with the Royal Society of Medicine when the late Sheikh Dr. M.A. Zaki Badawi KBE spoke on organ transplants; with the Globe Theatre Education Department, where a well attended seminar on 'Shakespeare and Islam' was arranged; with St. Ethelburga's Centre for Reconciliation and Peace, where a joint meeting was held with the Muslim Council of Britain; with the Immigration Advisory Service on the problem of asylum seekers.

While our main activity is to bring Muslims, Christians and Jews together at the grass roots level, there is also the objective of mutual problem solving on issues like animal rights and animal slaughter, anti-Semitism and Islamophobia, and Faith Schools. In recent years the Foreign and Commonwealth Office has begun to send visiting delegations to meet the leadership of the

Three Faiths Forum Advisory Board Meeting L/R: Sheikh Dr M A Zaki Badawi, John Battle MP, Sir Ian Blair, Sir Sigmund Sternberg, Sidney Shipton

Three Faiths Forum and to hear presentations on the activities of the Forum. For example, following a visit from an Albanian delegation, the first ever Interfaith Conference was held in Albania. Delegations from Bulgaria, Ghana, Cameroon and Iran have participated in such discussions with the Three Faiths Forum at their request. Leaders of the Three Faiths Forum have visited Paris, where an Interfaith seminar was held at the British Embassy. In Belgium, meetings took place in the European Parliament and were hosted by the German Ambassador with a view to establishing a forum in Belgium.

DENA MERRIAM, Initiator and Convener of the Global Peace Initiative of Women, tells us how she was drawn into interfaith service and what it has taught her about the role of religions in 'The Hindu Who Changed My Life.' This Hindu, as we have found, has inspired many on the interfaith path.

I have been involved in interfaith work for the last decade, and when I stop to think of the origins of this work for me, I realize it was my encounter with my Hindu teacher some thirty-five years ago. I never met Paramahansa Yogananda in the flesh, but for all of my adult life, he has been the central figure of my life guiding me in all aspects of life, through the ups and downs, teaching me the even mindedness and universal principles of right living that are the essence of all religious traditions.

I recently re-read some of Yogananda's talks, dating back to the mid 1930s, and was again amazed at how advanced and far-sighted he was. He spoke then about the universal principles of all religions, saying that he did not limit himself to any one religion or country, but was a citizen of the world and proponent of the one faith, the one universal Divine source. These are the very principles that must come forward today if we are to end the increasing sectarian and religious divides. Yogananda taught me the unity of religions, a message of greater relevance today than when he spoke it.

My encounters with Yogananda's teachings taught me to look to the essence of religion, not the outer rituals or even belief systems, but rather to see into their core, their source. This is the true meaning of interfaith. I didn't realize it then. Through this universal lens, I began to study many of the different religious traditions, and found more in common than was different. I developed a great appreciation and love for each of the traditions. It was not until much later that I officially became involved in interfaith work, but I see now that the foundation was laid long ago as I studied Yogananda's teachings and began to practice them in my daily life.

I realized early on that the vision of universality has always been part of Hindu culture. Hinduism does not preach an exclusive worldview. It embraces all prophets and teachers. It allows for numerous paths to reach the Supreme. It incorporates the concept of incarnation and endorses both the formless and the form. In stark contrast to what most people still believe today, the Vedic tradition encompasses a monotheistic worldview. All is one, and one is all. There is no other. In fact, it is the most purely monotheistic worldview that I

> *All paths are to God, because, ultimately, there is no other place for the soul to go. Everything has come out of God and must go back to Him.* [10]
>
> Paramahansa Yogananda

have encountered. When I say this at interfaith conferences today, people do not know how to respond. They are conditioned to view Hinduism as a 'polytheistic' religion. I question our interpretations of 'monotheism' and 'polytheism.'

In the West, some people interpret their religious traditions as presenting a rather defined concept of Divinity, but Hinduism avoids this. Within the Hindu worldview, all things, all interpretations are possible. In fact, it is very compatible with science. I learned from Yogananda that 'underlying both science and religion are universal principles that govern all creation.'[11] This thinking was very advanced for the time. Science is only just now beginning to uncover some of the truths taught by the sages of old.

Ironically, it is through my Hindu teacher that I came to know and love all religions, to understand the universality of religion, and to know that the essence of it all is oneness – a oneness of mind, a oneness of consciousness, a oneness of creation. This is the special contribution that Hinduism can and must make to the world community during this time of increasing religious strife and misunderstanding. This awareness of our oneness can help us overcome the misperception of division that is one of the root causes of suffering in our world today.

Like Ravi Ravindra previously, MATT WEINER of the Interfaith Center of New York, recognises some challenges to interfaith and shares his thoughts about the ways religions have to engage with each other today:

There is something wrong with the interfaith movement, and funny enough it is not conservative religion. As a liberal social activist interfaith organizer, it took me some time to figure this out. I assumed, like those around me, that the goal was to be clear and vocal about our basic arguments to create a paradigm shift. Indeed, the work of interfaith appears as integrated and straight forward as it does noble. All religions are salvifically valid, progressive social and political values are a given, and we should move everyone in this direction.

I came to Harvard Divinity School with these ideas in mind. I took the right courses in ethics and theology, and even lived in Emerson's room: chosen over larger and brighter rooms in Divinity Hall for the obvious, if romantic, reason that Emerson embodied both a progressive political and theological approach, as well as the exploration of other faiths for one's personal spiritual development.

Then I went to work for the Interfaith Center of New York where we succeeded in convening diverse religious leaders. Everyone was proud of the diversity, the basic consensus of our views towards each other's faith and world politics, and the proof that there was a local and global agreement on an interfaith blueprint.

But something was wrong: while we apparently had the world's religious diversity, everyone was religiously and politically liberal. We talked about 'common ground' and 'social norms' but were talking to ourselves. So we invited conservatives to join our prayer and dialogue programs. But they were not interested. The few who did come were ultimately not welcomed by our liberal majority because, well, they remained conservative. Again we switched strategies. This time we created non religious programs for grassroots religious leaders that would serve basic community needs: education about health care access, domestic violence, immigration, and the court system. The programs were not theologically or politically bent. They just provided information that religious leaders, as social advocates for their communities, desperately needed.

The plan worked. Chinese Buddhist monks and Christian evangelical Latinos who refused to dialogue about theology came to programs on immigration rights. Hasidic rabbis and Arab Muslims that would not come to a prayer service or discuss the Middle East attended our programs on health care access. The Vodoun priests who keep their faith quiet and the African American Baptists who couldn't be bothered with interfaith because they had 'real problems' attended programs on the court system. Why? The consensus was that religious leaders who focus on helping their own communities recognize a pragmatic need to do so with leaders of other faiths in the public square of this great city.

In our new interfaith framework, there is an awareness of genuine difference – a difference that is not going to go away, with a dynamic that often remains persistently uncomfortable. Yet, while most of these religious leaders had never worked across faith lines before these initiatives, they overwhelmingly find that they can.

Matt with Ratan Barua, a Bangladeshi Buddhist activist, at his tourist shop, two blocks from ground zero.

Our organizational focus has also changed. We went from serving communities who were primarily upper middle class, to a more inclusive economic range; from an intellectual focus, to grappling with problems 'on the ground;' and from abstract discussions of world peace or spiritual exploration to neighborhood issues.

Although we have succeeded in engaging hundreds of religious leaders in interfaith, I had not anticipated it complicating my own understanding of what it means to be an interfaith organizer. Switching from an advocacy model that assumed a theological and political position to one that invites all comers and forces people to find organic partnerships brings out hidden creativity and latent rigidity in unsuspecting ways - in all of us. My journey from Emerson's room to grass roots interfaith on the ground has not pulled me personally to the right. But I have found that finding ways to work with and not always against those you disagree with, while not compromising views, is a difficult exercise of singular importance.[12]

MERU DEVI DASI of ISKCON and the Vaishnava Communications Institute, reflects on religions as the real challenge to secularism:

Many religious people feel today that modern secularism should be challenged; however, I would suggest that religious fundamentalism is not the most constructive way to put forward that challenge. Religious fundamentalism, or a politization of religion, tends by its own nature to create an even sharper secular fundamentalism as a reaction. This could be seen in the controversy over the Danish cartoons depicting the Prophet Mohammed. Some would say that this controversy denoted a clash of civilisations; but looking at it more critically, it seemed more like a clash of fundamentalisms (if not extremisms).

Extreme reactions will hardly provide constructive solutions to a clash of values; on the contrary, they often tend to polarize peoples' positions. If we look at the discussions surrounding religion in the European Constitution, they partly reveal how easy it is for such a polarization to occur. What I would like to suggest is that an effective dialogue can only develop when we have found a

*Meru (standing) with Rasamandala Das (seated, left)
talking to a visiting interfaith group at the Oxford Centre for Hindu Studies.*

way to deal with the root-causes of secularism within our individual theologies.

The Catholic theologian Pannenberg writes that secularisation was never intended to be an emancipation from religion: it was conceived as a pragmatic solution to civil war and unrest in Europe.[13] His advice for his own religion is to find unity amongst its various branches, but *more* importantly, to incorporate the idea and practice of tolerance in its understanding of *truth*. This is a crucial point that concerns all religions, even though many eastern traditions have historically emphasised respect for other faiths.

In interfaith dialogue the challenge is the dialogue itself. Dialogue necessitates a willingness to hear a person from another faith, and to give respect to someone we may not agree with. However, an even greater challenge is to accommodate another faith in our own understanding of truth, of what is truly important. Without this it might be hard for religion to take back its place in the public arena.

There may be many good reasons for a lack of will to accommodate other religions, but Pannenberg is pointing us to an extremely important factor. If our understanding of what is real and truly good does not include respect and tolerance towards other faiths it will be 'quite unreasonable to expect modern culture to reconsider the exclusion of religion from the public square.' Pannenberg is not trying to lead us to a relativistic position, but rather to an authenticity of spirit.

The real challenge to secularism therefore is reasonable, cooperative and genuinely spiritual religion. When religions can find a genuine way of not only tolerating, but also understanding and respecting other faiths, then secularism will not be the only tenable position for society. In fact, it will not even be the most reasonable position to take.

SUMMARY

Maybe, for the most beneficial future, religions have to give up their institutional powers and status and focus more on training adherents to expand beyond narrow tribal boundaries into a spiritualised humanitarianism, a unity of Spirit, mature at last? Of course, that can't happen until we all want that more than anything else. Religions are only collections of people who use them. We share a collective responsibility. Each one of us is an active ingredient in the future, and in the role of religions in that future.

DON CUPITT

We find that we are most profoundly moved by the most transient beauties: water, spray, rainbows, clouds, flying insects, birds, shadows, flowers, moments of love or friendship.
Absolute certainties and eternal verities leave us cold.
We don't want to hear about them, because in the religion of Being the deepest religious feeling is evoked by the most fleeting phenomena.[14]

INTERFAITH

O Brother, Sister!

When I was forgetful, my true Guru showed me the Way.
Then I left off all rites and ceremonies,
I bathed no more in the holy water:
Then I learned that it was I alone who was mad,
and the whole world beside me was sane;
and I had disturbed these wise people.
From that time forth I knew no more how to roll
in the dust in obeisance:
I do not ring the temple bell:
I do not set the idol on its throne:
I do not worship the image with flowers.
It is not the austerities that mortify the flesh
which are pleasing to the Lord,
When you leave off your clothes and kill your senses,
you do not please the Lord:
The person who is kind and who practices righteousness,
who remains passive amidst the affairs of the world,
who considers all creatures on earth as his own self,
He attains the Immortal Being, the true God is ever with him.

Kabir says:
He attains the true Name whose words are pure,
and who is free from pride and conceit.

From: *Songs of Kabir*
(LX5) [15]

What is all this interfaith then?

Chapter XI

ENGAGING CIVIL SOCIETY

INTRODUCTION

The interfaith environment is changing. Until quite recently the only resource for finding out about other faiths or for organising interfaith activities was the interfaith organisations, whether at international, national or local levels. Now, civil institutions, governments, multi-nationals, most organised bodies are themselves engaged in interfaith communications and co-operations. Social cohesion has become both a secular and religious imperative. Although, initially the first port of call for relevant information was the nearest interfaith organisation, now governments, NGO's and others are developing their own interfaith components.

One example of this, a secular initiated local urban project that managed to create a great deal of community and religious interaction, was the Community World Cup event that took place in Oxford in June 2004. This was a five-a-side football competition for thirty-two different nations organized by the Oxfordshire Fire and Rescue Service in partnership with Street Dreams, a community cohesion group.[1]

Although the World Cup was developed as a community cohesion project rather than directly as an interfaith one, yet still it fulfilled that brief by bringing together young people in the area from diverse nationalities and religions for a common interest – football - through which other factors could also be explored. One young participant said he had met people and learned about other cultures and religions in a way that he had not imagined possible. Indirectly then the success of this venture – now planned as an annual event - challenged the relevance of interfaith organizations. The organisers of the project had personnel and finance resources beyond the scope, thus far, of the dedicated but small Oxford Round Table of Religions group.

When we were in Germany, meeting colleagues there to organize an interfaith event, we met a group working with Balkan refugees. They had found religion far too sensitive a topic for discussion amongst the people they helped, even though it was very important to many of them. Through establishing a

> *The thesis I want to propose to you is quite simple and, I suspect, controversial: that global responsibility can serve as the common ground for interfaith dialogue. That's a rather simple assertion, which is based on another simple, though frightening, reality: given the degree of suffering that pervades and tortures our world today - human suffering due to the way some humans are treating other humans and ecological suffering due to the way humans are treating the planet - we face a crisis such as our species and the planet have never before faced. It is a crisis that threatens not only life as it exists but also life as it will exist.* [2]
>
> Prof Paul Knitter

cultural society where all could safely reconnect with each other, trust gradually built up and created a space for religion to be addressed.

One of the critiques of interfaith sometimes is that it is preaching only to the converted. By going straight to the point it only attracts those who are already interested in interreligious dialogue. It does not reach the other parts, the majority, of the faith communities. Gathering together around a topic or project of mutual concern to a broader group can prove a more gentle, less threatening way of coming together for enhanced communication and cooperation.

Another challenge and change in the interfaith environment is the development of faith networks in unprecedented well-structured ways. Until quite recently the interfaith group or organisation was the source of information for contacting different faith communities. Now many faiths have their own nationally organised networks that can be contacted directly. These have also resulted in prompt, collective responses to particular community threats. Once quiet and seemingly passive minority faith communities have become organised and competent respondents to global events and media attacks. So it might seem that faith communities and civil society can act together now without mediation by interfaith organisations.

However, different religious groups and faith communities also need to develop relationships and act together with civil society for the common good, so interfaith organisations remains a valued and essential part of community cohesion at all levels. They have to work with secular institutions to eradicate poverty, design new economic models, and develop peaceful solutions to aggressive situations. The input to and impact on the United Nations of religious and spiritual bodies is increasing. We are people first and as people we create our world. Spiritual people can bring perspectives to this creation that can benefit all.

> **From the ZOROASTRIAN tradition:**
>
> *With obeisance I pray, with hands uplifted for this, O Mazda. I beseech of Thee that my actions toward all may be performed in the Divine Righteousness and with this I implore from thee the understanding of Thy benevolent Mind wherewith I can bring solace to the Soul of Mother Earth.*

BRIAN PEARCE, Director of the Inter Faith Network for the UK, shares his experience of inter faith and wider society:

When I first became interested in the late 1970s in relations between different faiths, I was primarily concerned with how, as an Anglican Christian, I should understand theologically the presence in our world of different faith traditions. At the time I was working in the British Civil Service in Whitehall. When I subsequently found myself helping to initiate conversations about ways to increase the profile of inter faith work I found my Civil Service background more relevant than I might have expected as proposals emerged for a new organisational framework, which in due course became the Inter Faith Network for the UK. It links a wide range of organisations with an interest in promoting good inter faith relations in this country and includes among its member bodies national representative organisations of the main faith communities; national and local inter faith organisations; and educational and academic bodies. When the Network was established in 1987 it had around 60 bodies. It now has over 110. This increase reflects the significant expansion in inter faith activity across the last 20 years, although the foundations of this had, of course, been laid well before that.

I would pick out two aspects of this developing inter faith landscape as having been of particular significance. The first is that engagement with other faiths has now risen firmly up the agenda of all the major religious traditions in Britain as elsewhere. In the past, faith communities saw inter faith activity as being of only marginal concern and, indeed, to some extent, a suspect activity! But now there is a mainstream recognition that inter faith dialogue can be rooted with integrity in loyalty to one's own tradition, while being open to the insights of others and working for the common good with people of other faiths, based on values which we find we hold in common.

The second aspect is the increased engagement here in Britain between government, public bodies and faith communities at both national and local level. This is in part a reaction to events in recent years, including the disturbances in northern cities and towns in the summer of 2001, the terrorist attacks in the United States in September of that year and the London bombings in July of 2005. All of these have made government more interested in finding ways to promote community cohesion and to tackle extremism. But it has also come about in part because government has come to see faith communities as having an important role in serving their local communities more widely; and as being the bearers of 'values' which help to provide some of the 'glue' which is needed to hold our society together.

Previously, there was some hesitation on the part of public authorities about the extent to which it was appropriate to engage with faith communities (and uncertainty as well on the part of faith communities about their engaging in the political process). Prior to the events of 2001 which I mentioned, the Inter Faith Network was working with the Local Government Association and relevant Government departments to prepare guidance for local authorities

Brian in dialogue at an IIC conference with Myra Laramie, a Cree Elder of the First Nations people of Canada.

which was published in early 2002. This tried to set out a constructive framework within which local authorities and faith communities could engage with one another. It was followed in 2004 by a review set up by the Home Office of the arrangements for consultation between central Government and faith communities. By then a new Unit had already been set up in the Home Office to focus on work relating to faith communities, which had previously been handled there as an aspect of race relations. A new funding scheme, the Faith Communities Capacity Building Fund, has provided central Government funding to strengthen faith community and inter faith organisations in their work in contributing to community cohesion.

In 1987 there were some 24 local inter faith organisations. In 2001 there were around 100 and today there are over 200 (and the number of national inter faith organisations has also increased). Many of these new local initiatives have come about in order to provide some framework for contact between local authorities, public bodies and faith communities, but there is still a focus in local inter faith work on promoting encounter and mutual understanding in addition to engaging in the 'public square' in this way.

So the landscape of engagement with government, at national and local level (and also regionally) has altered dramatically in recent years. There are very positive aspects to these developments but there is also a need to ensure that faith communities and inter faith organisations retain their independence and integrity and do not become drawn into a process of over 'governmentalisation.' The right balance between independence and engagement needs to be found on both sides.

This burgeoning new relationship between government and faith communities has taken secularists (and those for whom religion should by now have been on its way out!) by surprise and has caused them some disquiet. It is evident that the intensification of dialogue between different faith traditions has not been accompanied by a similar deepening of the dialogue between those within our society who have a formal religious commitment and those who do not. Arguably, this will become the most important dialogue of the 21st century. As in inter faith dialogue, we need to look for the meaning behind the 'languages' we use and to see how far, despite sharp differences, there may be more common ground than we expect in our understanding of the characteristics of the universe of which we all find ourselves a part and of how, in the light of this, we should deal with one another in our shared life together.

GLOBAL RESPONSIBILITIES

Here are a few examples of the ways the interface between interfaith, faith and civil society is being explored. They are just introductions to a much broader scenario that is daily developing in most parts of the world with as yet unforeseen possibilities and outcomes.

Poverty and development

Poverty is still a huge problem despite the dedicated work of numerous individuals, agencies and governments. As we write the Make Poverty History Campaign is gaining momentum and influence as people around the globe reflect on ways to end the suffering of the poor. Development has been through many phases and its implementation is always under review as experts become more sensitive to the riches – moral, religious, communal - inherent in even the poorest community when considering solutions to economical disadvantage.

WENDY TYNDALE has been active for many years in the arena of religions and development. She was a primary contributor to the World Faiths Development Dialogue (WFDD) until her recent retirement from it. The aim of WFDD, established in 1998 as an initiative of James Wolfensohn, then President of the World Bank, and Lord Carey, then Archbishop of Canterbury, is 'to facilitate a dialogue on poverty and development among people from different religions and between them and the international development institutions.' Its focus is on 'the relationship between faith and development and how this is expressed, both in considering decisions about development policy and in action with impoverished communities all over the world.' Here is a reflection from Wendy on that relationship between faith and development:

> The majority of the poorest people in the world see all human activity as falling within the divine or eternal ordering of the universe. Since they make no separation between the religious and the secular, religion is necessarily a source of inspiration and wisdom both with regard to what 'development' means as well as how to go about it. Indeed very many people of different religious traditions would say that an essential ingredient of development must be people's own individual inner spiritual development if they are to be successful in transforming the societies around them.
>
> Many development workers have a negative view of religion, as anti-developmental, oppressive to women, a divisive force in many communities, stuck in out-dated traditions, and even with violent potential. Their observations are not groundless. Religious leaders can be authoritarian and resistant to change and in many countries, from Northern Ireland to India and the Middle East, we have seen how religion can be used manipulatively for political purposes. Highly controversial, too, is the practice that began in the era of largely Christian colonial missionaries but still goes on today, of offering development in exchange for conversion to a particular religion. Many people who have

Awakatan Women.

benefited educationally from attending mission schools, for instance, look back on the experience with mixed feelings, aware of the advantages their education has given them but also regretting having been uprooted from their own indigenous beliefs and practices.

The most positive models of development involving religions are usually found in communities of people with a deeply-grounded faith of their own but who are also genuinely open to others. An example among many is a group of indigenous Mayan women who act as midwives in villages around the town of Aguacatán in the western highlands of Guatemala and have a collective project of growing flowers and strawberries together. Although started by a small indigenous Presbyterian church, the group has welcomed both Catholics and followers of the ancient Mayan spiritual tradition. This is a courageous and visionary step in Guatemala, where the 'Evangélicos' have been pitted against Catholics and Mayan spirituality has been feared and despised by Christians of all shades for centuries.

One of the main contributions of religions to development is the understanding they bring that a rational/technological approach alone does not fit every situation, nor can 'development' be reduced to results that can be counted, weighed and measured, let alone to progress seen in purely economic terms. There are countless examples of very poor people strongly resisting programmes of economic development that run counter to their beliefs: Taoists in China have objected to tourist hotels being built on sacred mountains, Ugandan slum dwellers have been horrified at the burial grounds of their ancestors being used for new housing and Mayan people in Guatemala have blocked roads and bridges in order to stop mining companies tearing open their Mother Earth.

Development agencies have to look beyond the purely economic and pragmatic if they want to connect with the impoverished people they seek to serve. Religion is far more than a merely cultural or sociological phenomenon. Development workers who dismiss Islam, for instance, as a patriarchal and tyrannical force with regard to women, fail to understand the space and nourishment that millions of Muslim women find in their religious tradition, even while they may often be at odds with the attitudes of its leaders.

Indeed, one of the greatest challenges for religious people working in development today may be to work from within the institutions to which they belong to help to make them more open to change, often by returning to the original 'fire' that galvanised people when the religion began. Religious leaders at all levels still exert huge influence. If more of them were ready to cross the barriers of their different traditions and to join together to stand up for the interests of the poor, to denounce corruption and exploitation and vigorously to promote a different set of values as a basis for the ordering of our world, many changes might be brought about – changes for which inspiration could well be drawn from the practice of many faith-based grass roots communities.

Economics

KAMRAN MOFID introduces us to the initiative he started: Globalisation for the Common Good: An Inter-faith Perspective on Globalisation.

In 2002, in Oxford, a small and humble movement, Globalisation for the Common Good, came into being. This movement is for 'Rekindling the Human Spirit and Compassion in Globalisation.' We wanted to have an alternative to the current dominant economic/free trade globalisation and to make globalisation good for all. Our movement found many dedicated and committed friends around the world. From Oxford we went to St. Petersburg, Russia, then to Dubai. In 2005 we were in Kenya, in 2006 we were at Chaminade University, Honolulu, Hawaii and in 2007 we meet in Istanbul.

Globalisation for the Common Good Mission is to promote ethical, moral and spiritual values into the areas of economics, commerce, trade and international relations amongst others, as well as personal virtues, to advance understanding and action on major global issues by civil society, the private enterprise, the public sector, governments, and national and international institutions, leading to the promotion of collaborative policy solutions to the challenges posed by globalisation. We are committed to the idea that the marketplace is not just an economic sphere, 'it is a region of the human spirit.' Whilst considering the many economic questions and issues we should also reflect on the Divine dimension of life, and should, in contrast to what is practised today, be concerned with the world of heart and spirit. We view the problem and challenge of globalisation not only from an economic point of view, but also from ethical, spiritual and theological perspectives.

We affirm our conviction that a genuine inter-faith dialogue and co-operation is a significant way of bringing the world together; leading to the

An Inter-faith Perspective on Globalisation for the Common Good, Inaugural Conference, Oxford, 2002.

creation of a harmonious environment needed to build a world of peace, justice and prosperity for all. The call for Globalisation for the Common Good is an appeal to our essential humanity to deal with some of the most pressing concerns of peoples the world over.

Religion has always been a major factor in the growth of human civilisation. Business and wealth creation, when they are for a noble reason, are blessed and vital for human survival. Bringing religions and business together for the common good will empower us with humanity, spirituality and love. It will raise us above pessimism to an ultimate optimism; turning from darkness to light; from night to day; from winter to spring. This spiritual ground for hope at this time of wanton destruction of our world, can help us recognise the ultimate purpose of life and of our journey in this world.

At the 1999 IIC Annual Lecture, 'Values and Transformation: Changing World Economics,' KISHORE SHAH described the dialogue in this way:

Andrew Rogerson, the World Bank Representative for United Kingdom and Ireland, began with a description of the important lessons that the World Bank had learnt through experience as it tried to fulfil its goal of poverty eradication with a sense of mission and professionalism. The World Bank has just gone through a major exercise, listening to the 'Voices of the Poor,' getting a first hand view of how the poor perceived poverty, its causes and the efforts being made to address poverty issues. The result has been a 'wake up call,' a heightening of the sense of urgency to achieve results and the need for changing strategies to be able to achieve results. The World Bank has learned through experience that technical solutions and finances are not sufficient for achieving success. A holistic, multifaceted approach that takes power relations and cultural values into account has become a must. Equity issues will also have to be brought to the fore. And no solutions are likely to work unless they are locally owned. A recent survey has shown that economic reforms advocated by the international aid community have worked only in those countries where they are locally owned, where the governments themselves are convinced of their need. On the other hand, bribes by the international community to promote reforms have been failures.

Andrew then explained how the World Bank was trying to put new approaches into place by assisting governments in developing countries to develop their own strategies. The new approaches are rooted in more humility and underline the need to develop greater understanding. The Comprehensive Development Framework (CDF) being piloted in about a dozen countries was an important step in this direction. The CDF process begins with identifying priority needs for the next fifteen to twenty years, and developing strategies to meet these needs with various institutions, from international to grassroots, acting in co-ordination. Changes are not likely to happen overnight and provide a major challenge for economists who are not used to dealing with intangibles such as culture and values. It is in this context that Andrew Rogerson felt that a dialogue between faith groups and the World Bank has become necessary. No technical agency, he said, could make changes on a significant scale ('scale up') without making alliances. The faith communities, who often are natural advocates for the poor and have an impressive repository of grassroots experience, can help the World Bank by bringing in the missing perspective and to understand the intangibles.

Satish Kumar, Editor of *Resurgence* and the Programme Director of Schumacher College, began his response with a narration of his experience when he crossed the border between India and Pakistan in the early stages of his World Peace March. Friends and relatives who had come to see him and his colleague off at the border were concerned about the reception they would get in enemy territory and urged them to take a few days supply of food with him. Satish Kumar, putting his trust in God and people, refused to do so, fearing that 'packets of food would become packets of mistrust.' To his delight he discovered that his trust was well placed. A young man who had heard about the March from a passing traveller was waiting to receive them with garlands on the other side of the border.

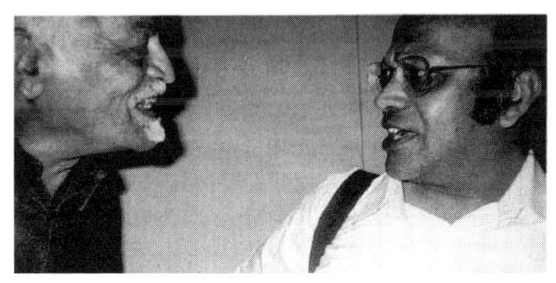

Satish Kumar with Kishore Shah.

Development was a term coined by economists that divided the world into two, the industrialised nations, where everything was compartmentalised, and the developing nations, that had to strive to become industrialised. It was a notion that failed to recognise that the so-called developing countries could aim for a different goal. Similarly, he emphasised that it was wealth and not poverty that was the root of the problem. He cited examples, of Jesus administering a 'vow of poverty' and Buddha and Mahatma Gandhi accepting the principles of voluntary poverty, to stress his point. The problem, he said, is not poverty but injustice and inequality. There was enough for everyone's need but not enough for everyone's greed. Unlimited economic growth which fuels the greed needs to be challenged. The concept of economic growth, which has become a 'mantra' for economists, itself needs to be challenged. The concept of growth needs to be replaced with that of sharing, caring and daring.[3]

Education

One of the seminars we initiated when at the International Interfaith Centre was 'Faith Schools and Social Cohesion: An Interfaith Discussion' at the House of Lords in November 2002. Sam Wintrip, IIC staff, was a great help and the Bishop of Oxford at that time, Rt Rev Richard Harries, was our host. The issue of faith schools, which the UK government supports, was and is a hot topic in the UK. Do they divide religious communities or do they give them self-respect and so promote community cohesion? We had a good turn out for the event and after the presentations there was a lively debate with the diverse and well informed audience. Here are some extracts from Sam's report.

Sam Wintrip

SAMUEL WINTRIP:

> Baroness Ashton from the Department for Education and Skills noted that faith schools, which make up 30% of all the country's schools, are wanted by parents and communities across the religions. There is no evidence to support the claim that faith schools contribute to social segregation. Rather, positive relations and co-operation between different faith schools could be seen as integral to community cohesion.

Canon John Hall, Chief Education Officer at the Church of England Board of Education, was mainly in agreement, underlining the need for faith schools to nurture good relations with other schools, both religious and 'secular.' Suha Yassin (a student from Copthall school in North London) also agreed, but suggested that there should be wider provision of state-supported schools teaching faiths other than Christianity.

Navleen Kaur (Head of Sikh Studies at Guru Nanak Sikh School) maintained that a curriculum infused with religious teaching allowed students to explore their beliefs and cultural backgrounds more fully, an opportunity they would not have in most state schools. A deeper exploration of one's own beliefs and history produces young people who are willing and able to serve as responsible and knowledgeable ambassadors for their own faiths within the forum that is British multicultural society.

Also in support of faith schools, Fiona MacTaggert (Member of Parliament for Slough) told an interesting story from the floor. In her own constituency, she has noticed that in multicultural schools where there is still a shortage of teachers from ethnic minorities, white Christian or secular teachers do not have the linguistic skills or relevant social and theological know-how to tackle the circulation of extremist religious literature and the activity of groups that promote it. Thus, the setting of a faith school may in fact be less nurturing for extremism than a more regular, secular, multicultural school.

Meeting at the House of Lords, London, chaired by Bishop Harries

Ted Cantle (chair of the government team that reviewed the situation in Oldham, Burnley and Bradford following the 2001 race riots) reported that, based on his findings in those towns, the phenomenon of 'white flight' from inner city areas tends to lead to monocultural schools due to their location alone, and that it was this kind of segregation and lack of contact between the various groups in the communities that led to a complete absence of social cohesion. It should be the obligation of all schools, faith-based or otherwise, to encourage a broader intake of differing racial groups, and to commit themselves to activities that contribute to the formation of positive links between community groups.

Dr Owen Cole (religious education specialist) maintained that faith schools are actively selective, and pointed to Liverpool, Glasgow and the East End of London as examples where even the slightest encouragement of division along the lines of faith has proven disastrous in the past. Faith schools are expensive, requiring a denomination to supply 10% of the initial start up cost for a school, and it could be difficult for religious minority communities to gain the wider communal support required to set up their own faith schools, limiting choice to well-funded Christian or under-funded secular education.

Thikra al-Khrsan, a student from the Al-Zahra Muslim school, expressed her worry that single faith schools fail to prepare young people for a multicultural university environment, but went on to say that race-related bullying could often be a factor that encourages young people of faith to seek out an environment where they are amongst the majority. Rabbi Jonathan Wittenberg believes the answer lies in multifaith schools, where students would be able to study and discuss ideas with others of different faiths, but where they will also have the opportunity to study their own faiths deeply to an extent not offered by state secular education. David Rollason (Head of RE at Plashet School) described his school as a place where people value and respect each other. All religious holidays are observed as closely as possible and students are given the option of attending different faith based assemblies.

Some maintain that school is not the place for spirituality and that there should be a strong distinction made between religious education and religious formation. Factors such as race-related bullying and the desire to be amongst a community of people like oneself seem to be perennial obstacles to a truly cohesive pluralist society. School is the place where so many of society's ills are somehow seen to develop in the next generation, and so should be the first and foremost place to tackle such problems.[4]

INTERFAITH

> **From the Global Ethic**
>
> We must strive for a just social and economic order, in which everyone has an equal chance to reach full potential as a human being....
> We must move beyond the dominance of greed for power, prestige, money and consumption to make a just and peaceful world.

The Global Ethic Exhibition at the St Mungo Museum of Religious Life and Art, Glasgow.

Professor IAN MARKHAM writes about the interfaith educational experiment he is engaged with at Hartford Seminary in the USA and how this brings together all kinds of people to learn together:

The fact that God made the world with many diverse faith traditions is one that I have always taken seriously. But it was only when I moved to Hartford Seminary, Connecticut, that I was forced to think through the challenge of diversity for theological education.

About one third of the students at Hartford Seminary is Muslim. The rest are Christians of every type, with an occasional Jew or Hindu adding to the variety. As a Seminary, we are committed to formation: we are not a religion department in a secular university. We want to shape the leaders of our faith communities. So we start our classes with a prayer; we have a weekly chapel worship for the entire community; and our curriculum includes courses in preaching and counselling. In some respects we look like a regular Seminary; in other respects, we are entirely different.

Hartford Seminary is an experiment. Is it possible to teach leadership formation in an interfaith environment? Naturally there are lots of challenges. First, we need to offer sufficient courses so that a person is grounded in his or her tradition. Part of the reason for our specialism in Christian-Muslim relations is to ensure that we can provide training in these two traditions. We have three faculty members in Islamic Studies (two of whom are Muslim) who provide many of the courses in Islamic Studies. Second, we need to find ways to worship in public that don't undermine the integrity of the traditions represented. We have learnt that endless conversation about 'whether we can worship together' is not as helpful as simply embarking on an attempt to do so. The

Ian with Sandy Bharat

Hartford Seminary

practice is often easier than the theory. From the Quakers, we have learnt the value of silence. And both Christians and Muslims can conclude a prayer to God 'in thy Holy name,' which respects the Trinitarian structure of Christian prayer. Third, we have to live with a wide spectrum of opinion. Classes have to embrace the evangelical who believes that salvation depends on faith in Christ to the Muslim who believes that homosexuality is a symptom of the depravity of the West. Naturally, these classes also include significant numbers of non-Christians and gay, lesbian and transgendered students.

There are many rich ironies. The evangelical Christians often find themselves forming an alliance with the Muslims against the mainline and liberal Christians; on certain social questions, they are often in agreement. It is the conservative Roman Catholics who understand the importance of fasting in the Islamic tradition. And observant Muslims find the liberal members of the United Church of Christ church very puzzling: to confine conscious religious observance to an hour on Sunday and to deny certain key beliefs (e.g. the Virgin Birth of Jesus) seems to a Muslim both inadequate and dishonest.

When one lives dialogue, it has challenged all my assumptions and expectations. It isn't smooth. Toleration is essential: there is much that is said that provokes strong disagreement. Yet there is a beauty in it all. Individuals have their faith renewed; the challenge of faithfulness in another tradition can often make a person more faithful in his or her own tradition. The Qur'an has a beautiful verse that explains that God could have very easily created one nation or one community; but God did not do so. In other words, God delights in this diversity. At Hartford Seminary, I am starting to understand how beautiful the world becomes when we live in the middle of this diversity.

Now for a teacher's perspective on the link between interfaith, education and citizenship. Dr RANVIR SINGH, Head of RE and Citizenship Coordinator at Cranford Community College, Hounslow, UK, writes about what he has learnt from Interfaith Relations in a London Comprehensive School:

Many years ago I dabbled in 'interfaith.' I gave talks at the International Interfaith Centre, Oxford; was part of the Next Generation at the Parliament of World Religions in Cape Town and had the honour of meeting the Dalai Lama; joined the executive of the World Congress of Faiths; helped organise the 'Faith in Action' programme at the Sacred Space at the Rio+10 UN Summit on Sustainable Development at Johannesburg, and even attended the Millennium Summit of Religious Leaders at the United Nations.

I also dabbled in human rights. I attended the Hague Appeal for Peace, made presentations to the Working Groups on Minorities and handed in a 200+ page report to the Working Group on Transnational Corporations at the United Nations in Geneva, briefly headed the NGO Media Forum at the 2nd Prepcom and addressed the whole assembly in that role, and led the delegation that lobbied and drafted paragraph 67 of the Declaration Against Racism in 2001.

Ranvir Singh

The two worlds embraced along three fronts: Sikh teachings, the present and the future. According to Sikh teachings, the only 'religion' is spirituality; all else is exoteric, priestly bunkum. However, this spirituality is not other-worldly, since God's Presence/Name/Numenon fills life. The Creator and creation are one. Sikhs call this doctrine of the mystic-revolutionary or saint-knight, *meeri-peeri* (spiritual riches-material riches). Inter-faith and human rights seemed like the two balancing *kirpans* (swords) on the *Nishan Sahib* (Sikh flag). Quite apart from this calling, at that moment I was representing Sikh interests and, in line with Sikh philosophy, working for others in need. But something was becoming clearer to me. In the interfaith world, people were crying out for youth involvement; in the human rights world, for human rights education. Education seemed the key to unlocking the potential of the future. However, what kind of education?

It is safe to say that much education takes place outside the classroom. Families, friends and the media have a large (and not always positive) impact on young peoples' perceptions about the 'other.' Students come to school with biases against each other (Muslim fundamentalists, Sikh enemies of Islam, Hindu idol worshippers, Christian white racist imperialists) that are not evident in the daily, very friendly, interaction of these students. It is true to say that these biases only influence the behaviour of a minority; it is also true to say that they colour the views of the majority.

Citizenship and Religious Education cannot be about religious instruction in a multi-cultural society – we are not surrogate priests, Brahmins, Mullahs, or gianis (scriptural interpreters). It cannot be about teaching mutually contradictory certainties. For me, it is a study of individuals and ideas that can inform our choices: it is about 'learning from' rather than 'learning about' religion. However, the glass needs to be part empty before it can be re-filled. It is about learning how to recognise our existing thoughts and feelings and allow them to

Ranvir explaining Sikhism at a gurdwara to an interfaith youth group from Eastern Europe

be challenged by 'others.' The teaching of 'doubt' and how to bridge the chasm is a more worthwhile skill than buttressing sand castles of certainty on the beach of globalisation.

An ever-shrinking globalising world in which young people have made no systematic study of each other, and in which they are apathetic, is one that is scary and depressing to contemplate. Working in interfaith and human rights was beginning to lead me to such conclusions after another round of listening to 'the usual suspects,' whether in London, Geneva, or New York. Happily, nothing could be further from the truth. Children like to find out about other children, and care passionately about animals, world poverty, and women's rights. More to the point, they want to do something about all of these things. What can be more exciting than offering such an opportunity?

What brighter thought than that all of them will grow up having accomplished some act of interfaith and global Citizenship? Certainly I never did. Many of them will carry on these traits through their life, and some of them may grow up to work full-time at this work. Perhaps they, in turn, will pass the torch to another generation to work with young people, the future of our faiths and our world.

HOWARD SHIPPIN

Neve Shalom/Wahat al Salam, is an example of racial and religious co-existence in Israel/Palestine. Equality rather than integration is the primary focus, a democratic rather than pluralist model which allows the community residents to maintain separate identities whilst working and cooperating together.
Jewish and Arab (Muslim and Christian) families live in community and have developed bilingual school systems for the children with outreach to the neighbouring region. The educational influence extends through the School for Peace which brings together, in home villages, 16 and 17 year olds from different communities for a residential encounter to learn about the other side and to break down 'enemy' images.[5]

The Environment

At the first ever Autumn Lecture organised by the International Interfaith Centre in 1994, Professor SEYYED HOSSEIN NASR spoke about the environmental crisis and its religious dimensions:

Seyyed Hossein Nasr

The religious dimension of the environmental crisis is much too serious to neglect, especially since the crisis is a global one...Today, the crisis is not confined to the West, although you all know that every child born in the so-called highly industrial societies uses something between fifteen to thirty times as much of the earth's resources until he or she grows up as a child who is born and brought up elsewhere. But in the destruction of the globe everyone is sharing together, from Muslims to Hindus to Buddhists to followers of the primal religions in the Polynesian Islands or Africa, to Christians, Protestants, Catholics, to agnostics and atheists. It is one of the very few things in which the whole of the globe is sharing.

[It] is one of the great paradoxes that we fight about everything else, but we are agreed upon how to go about destroying the globe. Dissenting voices belong to a very small number of people and what they say is usually taken as a noisy nuisance and when action is taken, it is mostly cosmetic. We therefore have a great paradox consisting in the fact that this problem, which is of the most vital concern to the whole of us, is one that we share but agree only not to solve. Instead, we are only accentuating it from day to day and leading ourselves to the point where it will become finally insoluble.

It is into this situation that the religions of the world, not wanting to fall behind one another, have come now forward to join hands with each other and also with secularist forces in making statements about the environmental crisis. We have already had the Assisi Declaration named indirectly after St. Francis of Assisi, among the best known of Christian saints, who spoke so often about the importance of nature. At the conference in Assisi, representatives of all of the religions came together to make an ethical declaration about the protection of the earth, a declaration which has unfortunately done practically nothing to change either the views of the World Bank or of the various

---

Prof SESHAGIRI RAO

Nature is our friend, not an enemy. We are born and live and play in the lap of nature and receive sustenance from her. Our debt to Nature is immense. We need to discharge our debt by giving back a fraction of what we have taken from her. Nature is not to be exploited or conquered, but to be nourished and cherished. We should develop a friendly and responsible relationship with nature.[6]

countries selling arms or of factories bellowing smoke into the atmosphere. It just made people feel better for a while. We must consider why this is the case, and why we must face in all honesty so much apathy in these matters.[7]

That case is still being considered, more than ten years after Prof Nasr's warnings. Declarations are still being made; activists, religious and secular, work hard to diffuse the crisis but it grows. Even in the face of this growing threat to all life forms, the will to change direction seems too much for governments, too often concerned with short term voting strategies than painful long-term solutions. Yet we all share the responsibility. We can blame no-one else.

Globalisation

MEHBOOB SADA, Director of the Christian Study Centre in Pakistan, shares some thoughts about interfaith and globalization from his perspective:

Mehboob Sada

The diverse affiliations of faith in human society have emerged from different geographical, historical and cultural contexts. They are the common cultural heritage of human society. Religious and other communities, especially today, cannot afford to exist like islands or travel along parallel lines. They need to inter-relate and interact with each other. Dialogue and harmony among religious communities envisages opening up towards people of other religious affiliations, in a spirit of good will, respect and collaboration, while being firmly founded in one's own faith. A deeper understanding of one's own faith coupled with ever growing consciousness of one family with other communities necessarily evolves into a spontaneous interaction with people of other religious traditions. The mission of dialogue and harmony is declared as establishing friendly relations with persons of different faiths and to celebrating a culture of working together for a better society.

Today's globalized world hosts various religions and they are increasingly coming into contact with each other. Therefore they have to respect their mutual inter-relatedness and the resulting attitude with one another. In order to respect and build relationships dialogue is the key to a peaceful and harmonious society. Dialogue helps in building relations and it is a continuous process rather than a specific event. Dialogue is an encounter of different beliefs/disbeliefs, suggesting that our different faiths can be purified and strengthened by the challenges of understanding what the other does not believe in.

The tectonic events of the past few years, including September 11 and the war against terrorism in Afghanistan, Iraq, and beyond, have dramatically affected Muslims and their attitudes toward Non-Muslims in general and the United States in particular. However, some of the dynamics that are influencing the environment in Muslim countries and especially in Pakistan are also the product of trends that have been at work for many decades. The terrorist acts on the United States on September 11 and subsequent Terror War dramatically disclose the downsides of globalization, the ways that global flows of technology, goods, information, ideologies, and people can have destructive as well as productive effects. The disclosure of powerful anti-Western terrorist networks shows that globalization divides the world as it unifies, that it produces enemies as it incorporates participants. Samuel Huntington in *The Clash of Civilizations* and *The Remaking of World Order* explains that culture provides unifying and integrating principles of order and cohesion and from dominant cultural formations emerge civilizations that are likely to come into conflict with each other, including Islam, China, Russia, and the West. On Huntington's model, religion is 'perhaps the central force that motivates and mobilizes people' and is thus the core of civilization. But the reality has proved otherwise.

The attacks on the twin towers in US and the subsequent war against terrorism has changed the geo-political situation in Pakistan as well as in the world. The image of Muslims as terrorists was wrongly portrayed by the media and that led to some unusual repercussions. There is no alternative to dialogue in the current scenario as inter-religious distrust and enmity have become so entrenched that many perceive harmony as but just a dream. The situation worsened very rapidly after 9/11, not only in Pakistan but also in the West, especially in the USA. The social interaction between people that had been living peacefully for years turned into animosity. The teachings of Islam and Muslims were portrayed as terrorist, which created problems for the Muslim residents of the USA.

In order to improve the situation of distrust and conflict in the USA, the Presbyterian Church of USA organized the Inter Faith Listening Project in which I, with my Muslim Scholar friend, Dr. Aslam Khaqi, visited the different states in USA. During our visits different lectures were delivered to the Churches, Islamic Centers and mosques, followed by detailed question and answer sessions. This exercise proved very useful in removing or reducing the misconceptions that were created by the different groups for their vested interests. The lectures were conducted in New York and Texas. We also visited the Houston Graduate School of Theology and various other locations throughout the country.

The hosts and organizers of the Inter Faith Listening Project were very friendly and cooperative, which helped in making the stay very useful, not only for us but also for the audiences. Dr. Khaqi at the end of the project said, 'I am converted at heart' and was so impressed by the attitude of the organizers that he is planning to open an Inter Faith Dialogue Centre in Islamabad. Inter Faith Listening Project through the use of simple rules of communication helped in bridging the gaps between the people living in the North and South. Listening to other people's views and interacting with them helps in reducing biases and prejudices. I am extremely grateful to all those who gave me an opportunity towards this cause. I hope that this century will see universal peace, progress and prosperity. This dream seems difficult to be true but it is possible if we pursue cooperation and collaboration while respecting each other.

In an interview on BBC's Radio 4 the UK's Chief Rabbi, Sir JONATHAN SACKS, spoke of the effect globalization was having on some Jewish communities. Here is an extract from that report.

Conflicts around the globe had begun to have uncomfortable repercussions for some Jewish communities in Europe. 'This is all a kind of tsunami of anti-Semitism which is taking place a long way from this country but (of) which Europe seems unaware.' While the Jewish experience of Britain was generally good, British Jews were experiencing a globalised anti-Semitism through satellite television, e-mails and the internet. He claimed anti-Jewish feeling was on the rise in European countries such as France. 'A number of rabbinical colleagues throughout Europe have been assaulted and attacked on the streets. We've had synagogues desecrated. We've had Jewish schools burnt to the ground - not here but in France.'

Figures from the UK-based Community Security Trust, which monitors anti-Semitic incidents and advises the Jewish community on such matters, said it had seen a huge rise in incidents last year. Some 532 anti-Semitic incidents were recorded by the trust in 2004, 83 of which were physical assaults. Sir Jonathan added that he was concerned that more was not being done to change attitudes.[8]

Dr JOSEF BOEHLE

Religions and politics at the beginning of the 21st century are shaped by and responding to massive global changes. After a long dominance of the Western secular model in international relations we find that Western based paradigms, including the relation between religion and the state, are increasingly questioned. The impact of globalisation processes and the resurgence of religious movements have strengthened the quest for complementary approaches to *exclusively* nation-centred, confrontational 'realpolitik' and *purely* secular diplomacy. Religious actors play an increasing role in multi-faceted crises in a fast globalising world, highlighting the need for a more objective and in-depth understanding of religious identities, of local and regional particularities, that could inform new national and global policy solutions. In addition, we need more inter-religious education projects and also international institutions which are fully able to cooperate on humanitarian issues with a wide variety of constituencies, including diverse faith communities.[9]

An open perspective:
Window to the desert; Mardin, Turkey.

ANDRE PORTO in Brazil reflects on the marginalization felt by so many in the world today as a result of globalisation:

As the final deadline for submitting this text approached I couldn't resist delaying my writing until the very end in order to be able to re-collect perspectives and follow-up the historical cartoon crisis (February 2006) ignited by cartoons originally published in Denmark portraying Prophet Muhammad hiding a bomb inside his turban. As this is written protests are still going on in many cities worldwide and the growing tension between Islamic and western secularized Christian countries doesn't seem to be dissolving. It is not every week that you hear a moderate Islamic prime minister such as Abdullah Badawi, from Malaysia, pointing out so explicitly, 'The demonisation of Islam and the vilification of Muslims, there is no denying, is widespread within mainstream Western society,' and then get astonished by an Italian minister suggesting the Pope initiates a new crusade against Islam after a Catholic Priest was shot dead in Turkey. Turbulent times when more than ever interfaith solutions, networking and mediation are needed.

How do we avoid the clash of civilizations trap? Already on the cover of Brazil's biggest weekly magazine is 'War of Civilizations,' referring to the cartoon storm. It is so simple to say and easy to buy it. But there is another divide that is more real, since civilizations are too mixed up anyway, which is defined by the neo-colonial map ruled out by WTO, IMF, GE, Warner, VISA, Nike, and other multinationals. Worldwide, in general, the media, academia and governments are biased and prejudiced against the diversity and cultural richness of the world beyond the Rich North. Here in Brazil, in Africa, Asia, as well as in any poor or migrant neighborhood in rich countries, there is a solid sentiment of being constantly disrespected, under-valued and exploited. The cartoon became a powerful symbolization for so much accumulated disrespect and aggression in a world where the so called 'civilized' fabricate lies to justify wars and bloody, insane, illegal military interventions. The Rich North keeps enslaving in-debt countries, torturing prisoners and being the biggest polluter, warming up the planet ready to make all Life extinct in sacrifice to the altar of ultimate inconsequential consumerism (with no excuses asked!) The imperial karma of humanity is now creating a backlash in a world where walls and borders are being dissolved (elementary in globalization as contradictory as it is). And we are all guilty! There are no good and bad guys. 'The one who hasn't sinned throw the first stone.' Each one of us has a share in poisoning the Sacred. There is only one humanity after all.

A new vital myth/vision, such as the collective mission of saving Life, may spring out of the interfaith movement. The perennial bridges and partnerships we are able to build up will become transcendental symbols to counter-part the widening chasms. Spiritual citizenship, simplicity, doing good, being wise, sowing seeds of peace, active participation in the community, care for the environment and respect for spiritual, cultural and ethnical diversity should be practiced and exemplified by all of us. Reconciled.

TRAVIS REJMAN, Director of the Goldin Institute, gives us this profile of an organisation engaging many dimensions of civil society for a better world.

The mission of the Goldin Institute for International Partnership and Peace is to provide a global platform for activists, organizations and communities from all sectors of civil society to share and develop the knowledge, skills, tools, networks and inspiration needed to create a peaceful, just and sustainable future.

Through an annual forum, the Institute brings grassroots peace activists together from current and potential Partner Cities to consider the methodologies, tools and mutual support needed to enhance the movements for peace, justice, and sustainability in their communities. These encounters and conversations are the cornerstone of the emerging Partner Cities Network.

At the inaugural 2002 Goldin Institute in Chicago, over 60 interreligious organizers from over 25 cities in the Middle East, North and South America, Europe, Africa, and Asia gathered together to share with fellow practitioners about the dynamics of their local contexts, to learn better practices for dialogue and engagement, and to help lay the foundations for the nascent yet vital and growing Partner Cities Network. In 2003 the Goldin Institute focused specifically on the theme 'Social Cohesion in the Midst of Diversity and Migration.' During the week of October 19 - 25, 2003, teams of organizers from around the world gathered at the Cova de St. Ignatius in Manresa, Spain, to discuss innovative and practical ways to build community in the midst of diversity. Interest in joining the network of Partner Cities is welcomed.

Goldin Institute colleagues and friends Chicago 2002

Spirituality and Religion at the United Nations

BAWA JAIN, Secretary General of the World Council of Religious Leaders, reflects on an historical interfaith event that took place at the United Nations in August 2000: 'There Came A Day....'

Despite the best efforts of individual religious and spiritual leaders from different parts of the world, the human family is still unable to prevent the eruption of horrible acts of war. Terrible conflicts have threatened and impacted the lives of millions of people in various parts of the world. There continues to be a growing conviction that new measures must be sought to arrest violent conflict. It was for this purpose – to find new ways of preventing hostilities and ensuring peace and security – that the world's most prominent religious and spiritual leaders were asked to assemble for The Millennium World Peace Summit of Religious and Spiritual Leaders in August 2000. During the Summit's preparatory stages, Kofi Annan expressed the view that 'This gathering of the world's pre-eminent religious and spiritual leaders in a united call for peace will hopefully strengthen the prospect for peace as we enter the new millennium.'

Over 2,000 religious and spiritual leaders, along with other participants from more than 120 countries, assembled for the Summit. It was unique, for the first time in history they came together on one platform in the great Sanctuary, The General Assembly Hall of the United Nations, with the common purpose of fulfilling two of the stated goals: to sign a common Commitment to Global Peace and to create a Council which could be available to the United Nations and Governments of the world in our common effort to achieve World Peace.

Increasingly, matters of war and peace have rested with the United Nations. What better place for the world's religious leadership to gather to give their blessings than in the Hall where so many of the world's conflicts have been addressed; where nations must come together to seek to redress the unacceptable conditions of poverty that plague the human community; and where new commitments to preserve and restore our planet must be made for the sake of future generations.

At his opening address, United Nations Secretary General, Kofi Annan, expressed the view that 'This Summit of religious and spiritual leaders is without doubt one of the most inspiring gatherings ever held here.'

The question was posed: Why hold the Summit at the United Nations, a political body that has no involvement in matters of religion? The answer was simple. Many of the conflicts in the world then – and today – have been among different religious and ethnic groups. Often these conflicts have been waged 'in the name of religion.' By holding the Summit at the United Nations, we were searching for ways to foster peace 'in the name of religion.'

The religious traditions and the United Nations share a common mission: to work to improve the human condition, seek peace and security for the entire world's people and reduce religious tensions. The Millennium Summit

Bawa (centre) with Kofi Annan and some participants of the Millennium Peace Summit.

explored ways that religious and spiritual leaders and the UN could work together more effectively to achieve these goals.

After the Summit convened on August 28th and 29th at the United Nations, religious leaders continued to engage in two-day working groups at the Waldorf Astoria Hotel to devise special initiatives to address regional conflicts, poverty and environmental issues, the reduction of human and societal tensions through the elimination of poverty, common action to preserve and enhance the environment, and cooperative measures for addressing the threats to peace in zones of conflict.

A number of remarkable outcomes resulted from the historic Millennium World Peace Summit, including the signing of the Commitment to Global Peace by all the leaders present; creation of The World Council of Religious Leaders in Bangkok, June 2002; co-founding of the Religious Leaders Initiative of the World Economic Forum, to bring moral and spiritual counsel to the major challenges of our time, including globalization and to redress the growing economic divide; a partnership with the United Nation's High Commission for Human Rights to bring religious and spiritual voices to combat intolerance and racism; the establishment of a Global Commission for the Preservation of Religious Diversity in New Delhi, India in November 2001; and a 3L (Look, Listen and Learn) meeting of senior leaders from religion and government with the aim to have a better understanding of the very complex and ancient conflicts in Israel/Palestine.

It has been my great fortune to meet many of the world's religious and spiritual leaders who have dedicated their lives to achieving global peace. It is an honor to share their pursuit of peace and mutual understanding. For me, personally, this was the realization of a life-long dream and that was a vision of my Spiritual Father, the Jain Monk, Acharya Sushil Kumarji Maharaj, that one day these leaders would join efforts with the United Nations to carve a true path to peace.

Acharya Sushil Kumarji Maharaj

Dr GERARDO GONZALEZ from Chile shares with us his path into interfaith. His major work involves a project dedicated to creating a spiritual forum for world peace at the United Nations:

Although I still feel young in my heart, I have been walking my life for almost seven decades. Along the last 40 years of my life I had the opportunity to live in different places of the world - among them Paris, Hanoi, Katmandu and New York - and to visit many others, as international officer of the United Nations. To be in touch in those places with an amazing diversity of cultures and religions allowed me to discover that Humankind is more complex in spiritual terms than the uni-dimensional religious environment where I lived my childhood and adolescence.

Actually, I was born in an observant Roman Catholic family (one of my uncles was a Jesuit priest) and in a country where at that time around 90 percent of the population identified themselves as Catholic. I went to Catholic schools run by the Jesuits and from 18 to 25 years old I was a Jesuit myself, starting studies to become a priest. All that happened before the Vatican II Council, which produced a Copernican revolution within the Catholic Church, particularly as far as its relations with other Christian churches and other religions are concerned. So, I was taught that 'there is no salvation outside the Catholic Church' and in secondary school we had a course of 'apologetics' where we learned how to defend our faith from the poisonous teachings of the Protestants.

I started opening my mind, heart and soul to other religions rather late in my life, when I went in 1985 with my family to live in Vietnam and my wife decided to become a Buddhist. Three years later we moved to Nepal where we met Lama Gangchen, a Tibetan Buddhist monk, who became the spiritual guide of my wife and my personal friend. His openness and respect for the people of other religions was an inspiring example for me. It was only in 1995 that I became actively involved in the cause of interfaith dialogue and cooperation for peace thanks to Lama Gangchen. He came to visit us in Santiago with the idea of promoting the creation of something like a 'spiritual United Nations.' Then I helped him to transform that intuition into a proposal for the creation of the 'United Nations Spiritual Forum for World Peace.' Three years later we started a project aimed at transforming that seed-idea into a collective proposal, supported by a wide array of spiritual leaders, religious institutions and interfaith organizations.

The way in which I presented in 1999 the concept of a 'spiritual forum' to the participants of a seminar in Geneva expresses clearly my vision of interfaith dialogue and cooperation. I said: 'Allow me to start with a powerful image. Close your eyes and visualise a wide field at night illuminated by a tenuous light produced by many oil lamps spread around. They are made of different materials: iron, bronze, stone, glass, clay. They are different in size and shape. They are burning different kinds of oil. But they have in common that each one of them produces a beautiful flame. Imagine now that these lamps start moving closer to each other, forming a circle, none of them in the centre. And see now how the light coming from all these lamps melts in a common shinning light, while their shape and the unique colour of each individual flame remains intact. This is how we anticipate that the UN Spiritual forum will be: The place for different spiritual energies strengthening each other in the common goal to build up a genuine peace in the world.'

This text helps to understand what is for me interfaith dialogue and cooperation (ID&C) and why I have devoted my life to this cause.

Firstly, ID&C is feasible and makes sense when there is a common cause, which in this case is peace. I realised that when we focus on the doctrine, belief systems or cosmo-vision, the differences among the large variety of religions, spiritual traditions and emergent spiritual movements active in the world are usually deep and difficult to overcome. Actually, most of the religiously motivated violence in the history of Humankind has been caused by differences in doctrine, with the self-proclaimed 'orthodoxes' persecuting and even killing the 'heretics,' or the dominant religious communities forcing the dominated minorities to convert to the 'true religion.' Instead, when we focus on their value systems and ethical paradigms, we find a lot of similarities and convergent trends. Consequently, if interfaith dialogue focuses mainly on shared values - such as justice, solidarity, respect and love - common goals will easily emerge, calling for cooperation among individuals and communities professing different faiths or following diverse spiritual traditions. So, in the above vision, the light of the lamps must be understood as spiritual energy - the transforming power of love - rather than the possession of the 'truth.'

Secondly, an important condition for a productive ID&C is mutual respect. Large and small communities, people belonging to old religions and to emergent spiritual movements, treat each other respectfully. Being in a circle with an empty center means that nobody is heading or dominating the others. All are united because they are inspired in common values and share common goals. Actually - this is my personal view - what we respect in ID&C are not

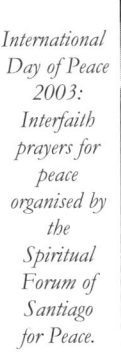

International Day of Peace 2003: Interfaith prayers for peace organised by the Spiritual Forum of Santiago for Peace.

necessarily the beliefs of the others, but their right to remain in the religion or spiritual tradition of their parents or to chose a new one or no one. Because we respect the religious freedom of our partners, we approach respectfully to their respective faiths, with an open heart ready to find admirable teachings, which can enrich our spiritual life. So, speaking from my own Christian faith, appreciation of diversity in nature, in culture and in spirituality as a marvellous gift of God is a basic condition for cultivating ID&C.

These are some of the principles that I have learnt while practicing ID&C for already ten years at the local level in our Spiritual Forum of Santiago for Peace, with the participation of people from 14 different spiritual traditions and linked to 23 value-oriented organizations; and at the world level, within the United Religions Initiative, with its more than 280 cooperation circles, as well as in the Partnership Committee of the project 'Towards the creation of a spiritual forum for world peace at the United Nations' to which I am devoting now the best of my energy and love.

An Integrated Approach

Dr VINYA ARIYARATNE, Executive Director of the Sarvodaya Shramadana Movement of Sri Lanka, writes about interfaith dialogue for peace and re-awakening in Sri Lanka:

Sri Lanka has a plural society of several different ethnic communities numbering 19 million. The majority of the Sinhalese are Buddhists by religion with others belonging to Hindu, Islamic and Christian faiths. For over two decades Sri Lanka has been in the throes of violent conflict, in which there have been major military battles, killings of civilians, severe human rights abuses and destruction of economic infrastructure. The Sarvodaya Shramadana Movement of Sri Lanka has been in the forefront of peace building and conflict resolution in the country.

Founded in 1958, Sarvodaya is the largest non-governmental people's self help development movement in the country, with over 15,000 villages as participants – nearly half the rural population of Sri Lanka. 'Sarvodaya' is a word from Mahatma Gandhi that means 'the awakening of all' and 'Shramadana' means 'sharing of time, efforts and labour.' Sarvodaya empowers communities to take charge of their own destinies and build their own futures based on self-help and self-reliance. Sarvodaya has a vision of a new social order: a society with no poverty and no affluence, based on principles of truth, non-violence and self-sacrifice, governed by ideals of

Uplifting consciousness

participatory democracy in which basic human rights are supported and the basic needs of all are met. With a staff of more than 1,500 plus thousands of volunteer workers, Sarvodaya has a strong organisational structure, extensive outreach that covers all areas and ethnic groups in Sri Lanka, and a proven history of exceptional accomplishments.

In the current context of armed conflict and violence in Sri Lanka, Sarvodaya envisions development and peace in terms of three interlocking spheres: consciousness, economics, and power.

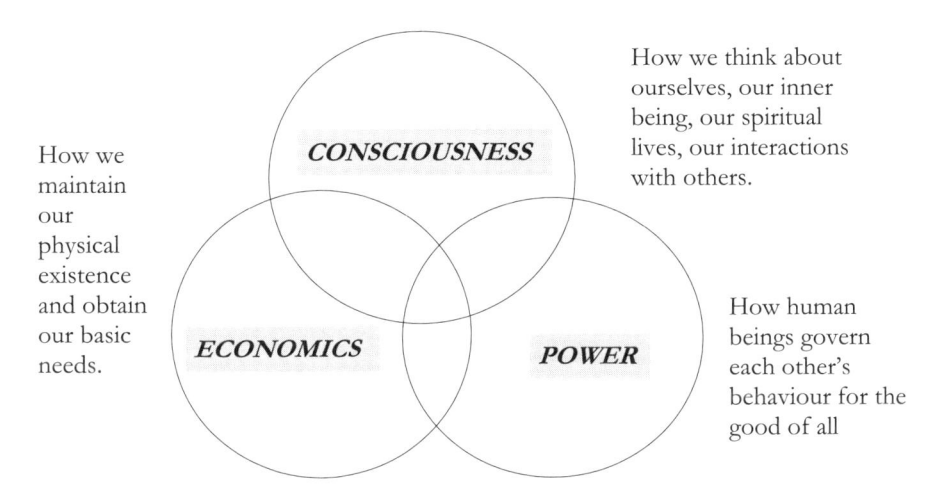

CONSCIOUSNESS — How we think about ourselves, our inner being, our spiritual lives, our interactions with others.

ECONOMICS — How we maintain our physical existence and obtain our basic needs.

POWER — How human beings govern each other's behaviour for the good of all

Whilst we know these three spheres need to be balanced in order to create a healthy society, we should of course keep in mind that we divide life into these spheres for the sake of analysis, which is in reality, not compartmentalized. They are inter-twined, inter-related and inter-dependent.

By consciousness, we mean our spiritual and cultural area, nature of our inner being, how we think about ourselves, the way we make our relationships with our own selves and with others and the environment. As to the economy, we talk about how we maintain our physical existence and fulfil our basic human needs. When we speak of power, we think of how we make decisions and execute them.

Interfaith dialogues to build interfaith understanding are among the key activities of Sarvodaya peace initiatives under the consciousness sphere actions. In a highly polarized society, differences of the religious communities exacerbate ethnic disunity. People in general do not understand the basics of each other's religions. The absence of open dialogues between religious leaders and academics further contributes to religious disharmony. During the last 20 years, since the time the conflict in Sri Lanka took a violent turn, Sarvodaya has conducted hundreds of inter-religious dialogues at community level involving particularly the youth. Also, dozens of peace meditations, where religious leaders and laypersons from all religions participated, were conducted. We could see the impact of these actions. Whenever there were ethnic tensions, those who took part in these activities took leadership to collectively intervene as multi religious groups and diffuse the situation.

In conclusion, we see interfaith understanding through dialogue as an essential component in peace building and in the 're-awakening' of the community.

JOHN BARNABAS LEITH, Secretary for External Affairs, National Spiritual Assembly of the Bahá'ís of the UK, shares his thoughts on the need for unity:

My spiritual life as a child and teenager began in the Church of England. After I left school in 1965 I encountered the Bahá'í faith and found it to be my spiritual home. The Bahá'í scriptures unequivocally teach us to associate with the people of all faiths 'in a spirit of friendliness and fellowship,' so interfaith activity naturally and easily became an important part of my life as a Bahá'í.

Initially my interfaith encounters were sporadic and informal. It was when my family moved to the Oxfordshire market town of Abingdon in 1987 that my interfaith journey began in a more systematic fashion. I became part of a delightful interfaith dialogue group in Abingdon. It was there that I began to realize just how inspiring dialogue can be and how enriching is the fellowship that grows in such groups.

After my election in 1993 to the National Spiritual Assembly, the UK Bahá'í community's national governing council, I started to represent the UK Bahá'í community in a range of national and international interfaith bodies. One development I have found particularly exciting and fruitful is the growth in multi-faith collaboration in service to our fellow human beings. I am part of two multi-faith organizations: the Multi-Faith Group for Healthcare Chaplaincy; and the Faith Based Regeneration Network. Both have made significant achievements in public life. Although the faith communities involved in these multi-faith organizations do not engage in direct dialogue, collaboration in service leads, in my experience, to deeper mutual understanding, trust and regard.

Religion, having been driven to the margins of public life in the 20th century, has emerged in the 'public square' – for good and for ill – in a most unexpected way in the 21st. The world needs the spirit of religion as never before to help resolve its most intractable problems. But unfortunately, religion is getting a bad press because of those who claim religious justification for murder, rape and terrorism. The work being done by local, national and international interfaith organizations plays an essential part in demonstrating that the reality of faith is not fighting but love, not intolerance but respect, not self-seeking but a focus on the good of humankind.

The Bahá'í approach to creating a society in which people of different faiths and ethnicities live together harmoniously and in prosperity starts from the view that there is one human race who worship one God. This is not to deny the diversity of humanity, the different understandings of the divine transcendent, or the particular practices of each of the faiths. Indeed, diversity is of the essence of human life. Unity without diversity descends into a dead uniformity, a kind of spiritual and cultural death; but diversity that is not rooted in a deeply felt human unity and solidarity always risks turning into separation.

It is my belief that disunity is not a symptom but a cause of the spiritual disease that has brought the world to its present plight. If this is so, then building unity must be the starting point for dealing with the disease and not the end product of an indefinite process of knocking off the world's problems one by one (a process akin to tilting at windmills). If the interfaith movement is willing to accept unity as its foundation – the unity of God/the divine/the transcendent (however you think of or name whatever it is that is beyond us and for which we yearn), the unity of the human race, and the underlying unity of religion – then it will be able to counteract religious extremism more effectively, make a meaningful contribution to the struggle of the diverse religions to draw closer together, and play its part in freeing the spirit of religion to help cure the world's spiritual sickness.

Barney with Shafiqur Rahman, Muslim Chaplain at The Royal London Hospital.

This is an urgent matter. 'The well-being of mankind, its peace and security, are unattainable,' Bahá'u'lláh urges, 'unless and until its unity is firmly established.'

SUMMARY

In the last few years especially the world has woken up to the relevance of interfaith relationship building. Governments, NGO's, business, no one doubts any more the need for religious communities to be engaged in the big issues of our time. Prof Hans Kung has been proven quite correct in his dictum that there would be no world peace without peace among the religions. Love them or hate them, they have to be acknowledged and although they may cause some problems here and there they also contain within themselves rich resources to address and rectify the problems that affect everyone everywhere.

With this new 'popularity' comes new responsibilities and challenges. Experienced, mature interfaith organisations can make significant contributions to the aspirations of people from religious and secular communities, from government and education, from business and NGOs, who want to understand each other better and work together for the common good but don't know how to start that process.

> [Perhaps] we should recognise that the clash in the
> world today is not between civilisations, cultures,
> religions or nations,
> but rather between forces inside each heart,
> between fear and faith,
> between fear – or hate – and acceptance.[10]
>
> Rajmohan Gandhi
> London 23 November 2005

11 SEPTEMBER 2001
The event that woke many up to the relevance of interreligious dialogue:
3 Nuns viewing a wall covered with missing notices after the
September 11th terrorist attack on the World Trade Center, New York City.

Listen everyone, to the sound of the future.....

Chapter XII

INTERFAITH FOR THE FUTURE

We have looked at many aspects of interfaith and heard from many of its key players. We have explored some of the challenges to interreligious momentum in the current era. We have learnt a little about the vision of some young interfaith activists. What can we make of it all? What is the future of interfaith?

No doubt interfaith activities will be as plural as the religious communities who make them possible and continue in a variety of ways, as now. Maybe new vision is needed too to adapt to ever changing circumstances – to the increasing interaction with secularism, to the hands-on approach of governmental institutions, to the rising conservative religious right, to the weakening religious centre ground, to a perhaps stagnating, rather too easily satisfied understanding of what could be achieved, with real faith, in the future.

Dr CHANDRA MUZAFFAR of the International Movement for a Just World reflects on flourishing together:

> Born and bred in one of the most complex multi-ethnic societies in the world, I became deeply conscious of the importance of inter-religious harmony at a very young age. Even as a primary school pupil of nine or ten, I was writing essays about how Malaysians could contribute to national unity.
>
> Many years later as I began to study Islam, the religion of my choice, I realized that dialoguing with people of other faiths, working with them on the basis of shared principles and, indeed, establishing a bond with them rooted in our common humanity, were integral to the teachings of the faith. I became a passionate advocate of a universal, inclusive approach to the religion - as against a particularistic, exclusive understanding of Islam - which would guarantee justice to all, without distinction. Justice, I discovered, was an essential prerequisite for fostering inter-religious harmony.
>
> Both as an academic and as an activist, I have, in my own modest way, attempted to promote better understanding among different religious communities in Malaysia and in the world at large. By making people aware of those

fundamental spiritual and moral values that they share - while coaxing them to respect differences in doctrine and ritual - I hope to bring them closer together. It has not been an easy task.

The vast disparities in power between different religious communities especially in the global arena; entrenched vested interests associated with religious and political elites; and centuries old ignorance and prejudice constitute formidable obstacles to inter-faith empathy. They can only be overcome through more equitable distribution of power and wealth, on the one hand, and the eradication of ignorance and prejudice, on the other. Neither the wielders of power nor the purveyors of prejudice will yield to either justice or truth without a fight.

But those of us who are committed to a harmonious universe where there is justice and respect in the relations between different communities will have to continue the struggle with even greater determination and resolve. For we know that in an increasingly borderless world where different religious communities are forced to interact with one another, there is really no alternative to living together in peace and harmony. Either we flourish together or we perish together. Surely, God in God's Eternal Mercy and Compassion would want us to flourish together.

Chandra speaking at the Inter-Civilisational Dialogue organised by the National University of Malaysia and Soka Gakkai Malaysia in Kuala Lumpur on 26 October 2002.

WENDY TYNDALE gives this assessment of the strengths and weaknesses of interfaith activities thus far and what she feels could be helpful for future developments:

Strengths:
- The very existence of interfaith activities is a strength. If we do things together, whatever they are, we both show others that collaboration is possible and also get to know other faith traditions better through the people we work with. Interfaith work hasn't just stayed at the level of top leaders.
- Work done at the grassroots level of people working with the poor, with young people from different communities, through different inter-faith circles/committees in many countries in the world and with the hotchpotch of people who arrive at the massive meetings of organisations such as the Parliament of the World's Religions and the United Religions Initiative is all useful as a way of incorporating more people

into understanding better what other faith traditions are about.
- The different interfaith organizations span a wide range of activities: education, youth, spiritual sharing, development, peace and reconciliation, inter-cultural activities - and so on.
- There is joint theological thinking going on with a focus on particular issues, such as faith and 'development' in the countries of the South/the globalisation agenda.

Weaknesses:
- There is a risk of interfaith dialogue lapsing into 'clubby circles' in which bonds of friendship among the privileged few who can attend international conferences may be formed but without any specific focus. This could result in the dialogue failing to turn into transformative action in our societies and thus, implicitly supporting the status quo.
- The interfaith work is still very largely led by people and organisations from the Christian West. Is this because Christianity feels solid enough to play a leadership role? Is it because the West has the money and resources to do it? Is it because there are western agendas that are suited by such activities?
- Interfaith worship tends still to be rather artificial with people from different religions 'taking turns' or prayers so concocted to please all that they skate over any depth of spirituality. However, this is not always the case and the very fact of joint worship is a huge step forward that has not

---

Maybe this Sioux story shows us something fundamental we still have to learn?

The Creator gathered all of Creation and said, 'I want to hide something from the humans until they are ready for it. It is the realization that they create their own reality.'

The eagle said, 'Give it to me, I will take it to the moon.'

The Creator said, 'No. One day they will go there and find it.'

The salmon said, 'I will bury it on the bottom of the ocean.'
'No. They will go there too.'

The buffalo said, 'I will bury it on the Great Plains.'
The Creator said, 'They will cut into the skin of the Earth and find it even there.'

Grandmother Mole, who lives in the breast of Mother Earth, and who has no physical eyes but sees with spiritual eyes, said, 'Put it inside of them.'

And the Creator said, 'It is done.'[1]

Wendy (r) in dialogue with Dr Josef Boehle, Birmingham University and Sr Joan Kirby, Temple of Understanding

been accepted yet by the majority.
- Interfaith work is carried out solely by the 'progressive' sectors/people of the different religions, leaving out the majority who either are indifferent to other faiths or think that they are mistaken.
- Each interfaith organisation is still too concentrated on defending its own turf.
- There has been no serious evaluation of interfaith work.

What needs to be done in the future:
- We need to strengthen joint work being done on social and political issues, so that the interfaith movement is seen to have something relevant to say to people in their daily lives.
- We need to be stronger on evaluating work which has been done as a basis for planning future action.
- More thought needs to be given to why the interfaith movement is led by Western Christians and how this might be changed. It is a vital point, as we need to be very aware of the dangers of being used for agendas which are not our own.
- We need to get together to see how our resources are being used and whether a merger of some of the organisations might not be a good idea.
- Holding onto the specificity of the different religions, we need to ground interfaith work deeper into the spirituality of the different faith traditions involved. There have been fears expressed that the interfaith movement is beginning hardly to be distinguished in character from the secular NGO one. The need to find better ways of worshipping together is part of this point.
- Somehow, and this is very difficult, we need to find ways of talking to people who find interfaith activities a threat or a sacrilege.

CRITICAL MOMENTS IN INTERRELIGIOUS DIALOGUE, a World Council of Churches conference held in Geneva in 2005, also engaged with this question, the future of interfaith and what is still needed to be done. Some panellists at the closing plenary shared these thoughts:

Msg CHIDI DENIS ISIZOH from Nigeria, a member of the Pontifical Council for Interreligious Dialogue, believes an enlargement of the dialogue community is essential. 'If you learn something and keep it for yourself, you are selfish and useless to the community, but if you share it, you become a worthy member of it.'

Rabbi EHUD BANDEL from Jerusalem, vice president of the International Council of Christians and Jews, feels that self-critique in the spirit of humility is most needed. 'We need to engage in soul-searching, examining our history and asking ourselves whether we have lived up to what we preach.'

For Professor ANANT RAMBACHAN, a Hindu scholar from Trinidad, understanding the problems caused by violence is crucial. 'There is a crying need for our traditions to passionately reject violence inflicted in the name of the state, religion or ideology.'

Anant Rambachan.

Professor TARIK RAMADAN, a Muslim author and university lecturer based in Geneva, concluded, 'Our current discourse of love and peace is often perceived as naïve and simplistic. We need to reconcile ourselves with the complexity of our world, moving away from simplistic statements and building local spaces of trust to counter the new global ideology of fear.'

Venerable BHIKSUNI CHUEHMEN SHIH, a Theravada Buddhist monk from Taiwan and chief executive of the International Buddhist Progress Society, stressed the need for 'building positive friendships, understanding and cooperation.' Indeed, this is the foundation for anything that might follow.[2]

SRI SWAMI SATCHITANAND

We cannot have communion with God without having communion with our fellow beings.
Many people say to me: The world is going to collapse at any moment.
I do not think so. I consider this a transitory period.
We are witnessing a great change.
I see a very bright future for humankind and I really feel we are going to see a better world.
I have confidence in the international interfaith movement.
I believe in the people who are sowing the seeds of health and happiness, of peace and goodness.
This world is going to be filled with people who love each other, care for each other, and together build peace through better understanding.[3]

ASAF HUSSAIN, from the University of Leicester, reflecting on the situation in the UK, suggests making a fresh start:

In the contemporary world interfaith dialogue is necessary, for a lot of misunderstanding has spread abroad. This also affects British society, for different faith communities exist here and hostilities abroad affects or can affect them in this country. What therefore needs to be stressed to the faith communities is that they are settled in Britain, which is a different context from those elsewhere. Hostilities from abroad should not be transferred to Britain. In fact, a fresh start should be made in understanding other faiths for not only is the context different but one faith community's history with another is also different.

A fresh start would begin by judging the people of other faiths for what they are and without preconceived notions. Preconceived notions often distort the view of people from other faiths by stereotyping them. That should be completely avoided. It is possible that this kind of new start may even stimulate a positive change in the opinion of other people from different faiths. But where the context involves bad history between two faiths, that history cannot be easily erased. For example, in the Indian context, many Hindus can never forgive the Muslims for their history there or for their destruction of Hindu temples and the building of mosques over their remains. Many Hindus will always feel that burden. It is not surprising then that during the BJP rule, all Muslims were considered 'invaders.' This led to massacres in Gujarat that were fuelled by hatred. Also, the politics between the two countries of India and Pakistan, usually hostile or distrustful of each other, will make the average person feel the same way about people of the other faith. But in Britain since the communities have settled here, and there are many British born Hindus and Muslims, they don't have a history of hostility in this country and that should be capitalized upon.

Peaceful co-existence and new understandings of the other faiths is necessary within the new context. In fact such views can be so propagated that the people of the faiths hostile to each other in their countries of origins can learn the lesson that generalizations are wrong. Although this may not be an easy task it is worth trying.

Muslim-Hindu dialogue in the UK
Yahya Michot,
Oxford Centre for Islamic Studies,
and Shaunaka Rishi Das,
Oxford Centre for Hindu Studies,
exploring new understandings.

HUMAN BEINGS
by ADRIAN MITCHELL[4]

look at your hands
your beautiful useful hands
you're not an ape
you're not a parrot
you're not a slow loris
or a smart missile
you're human

not british
not american
not israeli
not palestinian
you're human

not catholic
not protestant
not muslim
not hindu
you're human

we all start human
we end up human
human first
human last
we're human
or we're nothing

nothing but bombs
and poison gas
nothing but guns
and torturers
nothing but slaves
of Greed and War
if we're not human

look at your body
with its amazing systems
of nerve-wires and blood canals
think about your mind
which can think about itself
and the whole universe

look at your face
which can freeze into horror
or melt into love
look at all that life
all that beauty
you're human
they are human
we are human
let's try to be human

dance!

> **DAG HAMMERSKJÖLD at the Dedication of the United Nations Prayer Room**
>
> Man has reached a critical point in history,
> where he must turn to God
> to avoid the consequences of his own faulty thinking.
> We must pray, not a few of us, but all of us.
> We must pray simply, fervently, sincerely and with increasing power
> as our faith grows....
> The ability of every individual to seek divine help is a necessary link
> in the golden chain of harmony and peace.
> You can help change the world by your prayers and prayerful actions.

DIANE WILLIAMS, Chairperson Emeritus, the NGO Committee on Spirituality, Values and Global Concerns (NY) at the United Nations, shares her thoughts about how spirituality at the United Nations will affect the future of interfaith and world peace:

> 'Unless there is spiritual renaissance, the world will know no peace.'
> *Dag Hammarskjöld, 2nd UN Secretary-General*

The United Nations was built on spiritual principles and universal values such as peace, human rights, human dignity, human worth, justice, respect, good neighbourliness and freedom. Many of the key founders of the UN and those in leadership positions there today also use spirituality and values as a guiding force.

The Dumbarton Oaks Conference, which took place in San Francisco in December 1944, began to address the formation of a United Nations Charter. The key countries that were addressing the UN Charter listed 12 major functions of the UN. One of these functions was to be the seeker of freedom. And, in defining this term, it said that for humans to attain ultimate freedom the UN not only had to promote material growth but also spiritual growth. This spiritual consciousness was behind the formation of the UN and on October 24, 1945 the UN Charter was officially recognized and the United Nations came into being.

UN Secretary General, Kofi Annan, once stated: 'For many of us, the axiom could well be: we pray, therefore, we are. At the heart, we are dealing with universal values. To be merciful, to be tolerant, to love thy neighbor... there is no mystery here. Such values are deeply ingrained in the human spirit itself. It is little wonder that the same values animate the Charter of the United Nations, and lie at the root of our search for world peace.'

On October 27, 2005, at *Spirit of the United Nations* - a celebration of the UN's 60th anniversary organized collaboratively by the NGO Committee on Spirituality, Values and Global Concerns (NY) at the UN and the Values Caucus in partnership with the UN Department of Public Informations, the UN

Staff Recreation Council and several other organizations - the President of the 60th General Assembly spoke of the essential role of spirituality and values at the United Nations. From its founding until the present time spirituality and values have played key roles in solving global challenges by using a foundation of universal values and by transcending the boundaries of religion, ethnicity, gender and geography to build a culture where we, the peoples of the world, can address together our common global concerns in a holistic, positive and transforming way and 'live together in peace with one another' – thus realizing the core objectives and universal principles stated in the United Nations Charter and the Universal Declaration of Human Rights.[5]

There are many efforts and groups that aim to bring more purposely the spiritual and values dimension into the UN, including the Values Caucus, the Spiritual Caucus and the NGO Committee on Spirituality, Values and Global Concerns at the UN in Geneva and in New York. Civil Society is also promoting interfaith cooperation through UN groups such as the Committee of Religious NGOs and the United Religions Initiative UN Cooperation Circle. Currently there is an initiative called the Tripartite Forum on Interfaith Cooperation for Peace, an open-ended consultative group composed of representatives of UN Member States, the United Nations system and non-governmental organizations, that focuses on interfaith dialogue and cooperation. The activities of the Forum are mutually reinforcing and inclusive of related initiatives and programs of the United Nations and are designed to foster mutual respect, tolerance and friendship between people, cultures and religions.

In a world that is plagued by ethnic and religious conflicts these UN committees, caucuses and initiatives are coming together in the spirit of partnership, cooperation and unity to live the values in the Charter of the United Nations and to find solutions to today's pressing global concerns. As a member of the UN community for over the past decade, I have observed that what happens inside the UN eventually begins to ripple out into the world…into the local and global community…into the homes, schools, the media, houses of worship and every aspect of society. Therefore I am confident that our collective search for interfaith cooperation for peace will soon be a reality.

Diane Williams (l), Chairperson Emeritus, and Maria Malaman, Councilwoman, of the NGO Committee on Spirituality, Values and Global Concerns at the United Nations (NY)

MUSSIE HAILU from Ethiopia shares with us his vision for the future of interfaith as the pathway to peace-building:

Can you imagine a world where there is peace among religions? Where people from a diversity of religious and spiritual traditions and from all sectors of society gather at common tables all over the world to pursue justice, healing, and peace with reverence for all life? Where there is a spiritual partner of the United Nations? Where local actions are connected to form a global presence? Where the wisdom of faith traditions is revered and where the deepest values of people are respected and put into action for the good of all? I can - and it is that vision that leads me to the path of interfaith work.

More than ever, our world needs the healing touch that religious and spiritual traditions can bring. It needs the message of love and peace, and the confirmation that all of us belong to one human family. To create peace, harmony, unity and a better future for all is not something which we can leave to guiding institutions like the United Nations and other international organizations or governments. It must also be the concern of different religious and faith leaders around the world. The impact various religious and faith traditions can have on the world has the potential to be far more reaching than any government or institution. The core beliefs of religious institutions - love, unity, peace, forgiveness, harmony and living for the sake of others - have the potential to build bridges of lasting peace and harmony, especially when people of faith work together to understand and appreciate what unites them as well as what is unique and different.

An organization that is dedicated to promoting such interfaith understanding is the United Religions Initiative (URI). As I learned more about URI, I understood that its purpose would not be to create one unified world religion, but to provide a place for people of faith to understand and explore the challenges of global interdependencies. Reports show that over half of the world's armed conflicts are not between nation-states at all, but between groups of differing ethnic and religious groups. Though I was born, grew up and still am an Ethiopian Orthodox Christian, I have due respect for all religious and faith traditions. To me religion is like the hand of God with different religious and faith groups like God's fingers. The hand cannot function properly without the fingers working together.

The idea of URI is now deeply rooted in my heart and life. The great peace-maker and teacher, Gandhi, who is a role model for me and for many others, made a plea for a new mode of relationship between people of diverse faiths. He called not just for nonviolence and tolerance, but also for a commitment to openness and learning whereby people would actively seek to know the deepest and best in each other's religious wisdom, knowledge, and spiritual practice. He called it a 'reverence for other faiths.' To me, Gandhi was one of the pioneers of interfaith work in our world. Inspired by the work and teaching of Gandhi, I welcomed the idea of URI and was privileged to attend the first summit at the birthplace of United Nations in San Francisco, California.

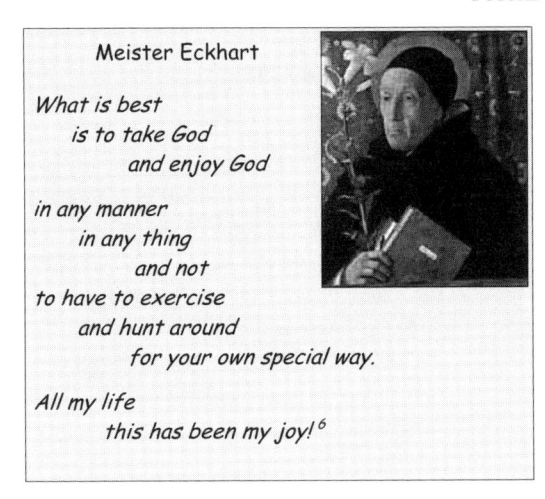

> Meister Eckhart
>
> What is best
>   is to take God
>   and enjoy God
> in any manner
>   in any thing
>   and not
> to have to exercise
>   and hunt around
>   for your own special way.
> All my life
>   this has been my joy![6]

Following this, I returned to Africa and was inspired to promote interfaith activities. As a result of this experience, I understood the importance of engaging people at the grassroots level to expand interfaith work. In 1998, we organized a regional interfaith conference for sixty men and women, young and old, representing fourteen faith traditions from eight East African countries. The seeds of the interfaith movement, planted in Africa during this meeting, sprouted in different parts of Africa. The result is that there are now many interfaith groups in Africa engaged in promoting religious understanding and tolerance. Soon after, over a hundred and twenty eight representatives from twenty nine URI cooperation circles in Africa met in Nairobi, Kenya, for three days for the first ever URI Africa Regional Assembly. Participants came from Burundi, Ethiopia, Democratic Republic of Congo, Kenya, Malawi, Mozambique, Rwanda, Uganda, Zambia, and Zimbabwe. Driven by our overall compelling desire for peace and development, we participated in appreciative inquiry interview conversations and we shared personal stories. Through this assembly we become closer to each other and designed a plan of action to work collectively to promote religious harmony and a culture of peace in Africa.

In Addis Ababa, Ethiopia, I started an interfaith organization along with like-minded colleagues from different faith groups in the county. The organization is called the Interfaith Peace Building Initiative (IPI) and it is a member of URI. To date, we have organized a number of peace workshops and conferences as well as activities that promote understanding and dialogue. The IPI is now a driving force for peace in the country. It is the first interfaith organization in Ethiopia. IPI called on various religious institutions to work together to prevent conflict and promote cultures of peace and tolerance in Ethiopia. The Interfaith Peace Building Initiative has been bringing together youth from various religions to hold a dialogue on current social issues so as to encourage

INTERFAITH

> **MOST REV DR ROWAN WILLIAMS Archbishop of Canterbury**
>
> *Whether it's our neighbours on the streets of Deptford or our neighbours in Pakistan or Sri Lanka or Central Africa, what we can all do is to try and close the gap that little bit further: to let people know that they're not suffering alone.*
> *We still have to look for the big solutions, the long-term aid and support, the problem-solving plans.*
> *But let's start with what anyone can do, anywhere; never mind the success, simply act and speak as if people were worth taking seriously.*[7]

them to contribute to the peace and development of their country and shape their own future.

It is my own experience working on interfaith issues internationally, regionally and as a pioneer in my own country that allows me to say with strong voice that Interfaith is the Pathway to Peace. I have not only learned a great deal by engaging in the work of interfaith, but I have also grown more spiritually aware while remaining committed more than ever to my own religion and tradition.

I know and believe deeply that promoting interfaith understanding will help all of us move from fear to trust, from falsehood to truth, from hate to love, from disrespect to respect, from unnecessary competition to cooperation, and from war to peace. If all religious traditions of our world could come together under the banner of interfaith for peace and harmony, there would be peace, love, compassion, mercy, forgiveness, justice, reconciliation, respect and dignity for all, leading us to a culture of peace and a better world. Interfaith is the pathway and the road map.

May the day come when all of us as citizens of this world can stand together and respect each other regardless of differences in colour, religion or ideology, and that young and old, men and women, rich and poor, black and white, people from all corners of the earth, from all beliefs and cultures join their hands, minds and hearts to celebrate life and thank the creator of the universe and mother earth. May peace prevail among different followers of religions. May peace prevail on Earth!

SHAHZAD SYED, a young journalist from Pakistan, gives us his take on how present situations are just a phase influenced unduly by misguided politics. Remove this and peace and harmony will prevail. Here is his perspective on peace, conflict transformation and the challenges of communalism:

For the past known history, there was no major incident of communal or sectarian violence in that part of world where Pakistan is presently located. There was complete harmony and peace in that region and the communities, regardless of their religious beliefs, particularly sectarian beliefs, lived in complete peace and with mutual respect and traditional tolerance. Conflict on the basis of religious, communal and sectarian difference was the product of politics. The division of India on a communal basis led to communal riots, fought, with sticks and knives at the village or street level. There is still communal conflict between the countries that emerged from partition, now fighting with tanks, jet fighters and probably nuclear arsenals in the future.

In Pakistan itself, sectarian clashes or violence are also a product of politics, the kind used brutally following the Islamic Revolution in Iran and which some Muslim countries have accused of being exported to other countries. After these allegations, right or wrong, other Muslim countries started fencing against the Iranian brand of revolution by containing the influence and power of sects represented in particular societies. History since the 1980s shows conflicts patronized by State functionaries at the local or lowest level to settle scores or engage communities in non-issues while imposing dictatorship and denying the people their democratic rights. Our society witnessed attacks on our mosques, churches, Imam Bargahs (Shi'ite religous places) and other places of worship using suicide bombers that killed innocent people in their hundreds at a time when they were busy with their prayers.

We have no evidence that the people engaged in their prayers were attacked and killed for any crime. It is an example of the post-Iranian Revolution phenomenon where State functionaries, for political reasons, patronized sectarian violence. Otherwise, there was no conflict among different sects and people. There were hundreds of examples of people from all the different sects taking the dead and injured to hospitals and donating blood, just to save as many human lives as they could. This caused frustration among those who perpetrated the heinous crimes against humanity as a whole.

No doubt our society is passing through a conflict expressed through sectarian violence in the shape of suicide bombing and attacking the places of worship but it is confined to a very limited number of people with vested interests. On the whole, there are no bitter feelings among the people thus the

Religious leaders, women, children and journalists (Muslims, Christians, Sikhs, Hindus, Baha'is) on 28th Feb, 2006 opposite the UNO building in Islamabad, Pakistan. They have come together for a protest, organised by Shahzad, against the blasphemous cartoons about the prophet Mohammed (PBUH).

> **PARAMAHANSA YOGANANDA**
>
> *Let us pray in our hearts for a League of Souls and a United World. Though we may seem divided by race, creed, color, class, and political prejudices, still, as children of the one God we are able in our souls to feel brotherhood and world unity. May we work for the creation of a United World in which every nation will be a useful part, guided by God through man's enlightened conscience.*
>
> *In our hearts we can all learn to be free from hate and selfishness. Let us pray for harmony among the nations, that they march hand in hand through the gate of a fair new civilization.*[8]

conflict is short term and for a particular phase of our political history and has no roots in the beliefs of people from different sects.

The transformation of society into an ideal one is not a difficult proposition in our case as the conflict is artificial, imposed on the people using dubious means. Once this particular phase of our political history is over and states normalize their relations or achieve a natural balance, then the whole of society will be transformed, regaining its traditional strength of harmony, peace and tranquility.

THE SPECIAL ROLE OF WOMEN

Women are an important part of any global or interfaith future, a crucial factor too often neglected in the past. As long ago as the 1893 Parliament of the World's Religions in Chicago, one woman participant, Mrs JULIA WARD HOWE (*picture l*, writer of the Battle Hymn of the Republic), addressed the issue of women in religion. She said: I think nothing is religion which puts one individual absolutely above others, and surely nothing is religion which puts one sex above another. Religion is primarily our relation to the Supreme, to God Himself....And any religion which will sacrifice a certain set of human beings for the enjoyment or aggrandizement or advantage of another is no religion.... Any religion which sacrifices women to the brutality of men is no religion.

Of course, it is people from religious communities that take part in interfaith so the attitude of a religion to women affects the outflow of interfaith. Brutality may not be an issue but true inclusiveness remains elusive in many religious traditions. This has been reflected in the interfaith arena but many organizations now strive to be more inclusive and to include the contribution of women in their programming. More and more organizations are being led by women.

One of these is the GLOBAL PEACE INITIATIVE OF WOMEN

MARIANNE MARSTRAND writes:

The Global Peace Initiative of Women (GPIW) is an international, multi-faith network of women leaders who come together to stimulate peace building and reconciliation efforts in areas of conflict and post-conflict. These women, from the religious, government and civic sectors of society, share two primary goals: to bring alternative resources, be they spiritual, economic or educational, to aid in healing conflict; and to relieve the social and economic stresses that lead to violence.

GPIW: Lighting a candle for the present and the future.

The organization was founded on the premise that women today have a special contribution to make in finding alternatives to violence. Our work aims to foster respect for all peoples on Earth and for the Earth's natural environment. We highlight humanity's shared values, even as we profoundly appreciate the diversity of human culture and belief. We realize the importance of transmitting such values to the next generation. Thus, in our sacred work, we place special emphasis on cultivating interfaith understanding and developing leadership in young adults around the world.

The Global Peace Initiative is a partnership of women and men who see the urgency of tapping into the resources of women, and listening to their perspectives as we try together to create a more caring and compassionate world community. Some of our programs include 'The Women's Partnership for Peace in the Middle East,' that brings together Palestinian and Israeli women to develop activities that create a greater movement toward peace; a Summit in 2006 of Iraqi and US Women leaders to interact in the spirit of goodwill and compassion, leading to renewal and healing; and The Sudan Youth Peace Dialogue that will bring together young adults from the South, the North and the Darfur regions to seek ways of putting behind the many years of conflict and begin a positive future for their country.

Some of the participants from the Women's Partnership for Peace in the Middle East Dead Sea Summit, 2003.

INTERFAITH

> **HARRIET CRABTREE**
>
> *Inter faith dialogue and encounter is enormously important. It can make a real difference to our societies and to our wider global community. Men and women of different faiths can and must find ways to live in respectful harmony, able to talk honestly about differences but to build societies rooted in values held in common among the faiths. In face of the threat of prejudice and the entwined evils of religious and racial bigotry and conflict we have a challenge to work for understanding and peace. And in face of the global scourges of poverty, war and limitation to freedom for many peoples and individuals, we have a united challenge to find ways for our faiths to work in every land where they are present to make common cause for justice and peace.* [9]

Sandy: I remember attending a women only event in London some years ago that involved participants from all spheres of influence, not just religious. In the afternoon, following round table discussions, fifteen or so women were called to the central microphone and given one minute to explain their vision, project or organisation. Every one did it in the time allotted. Every one was clear. Some even had time to be inspiring! I still remember the impact of Scilla Elsworthy of the Oxford Research Group. In stark contrast was another event Jael and I both attended, organised by a specialist interfaith organization. Instead of an intimate setting the speakers were divided from their audience by a stage. Here, day after day, arrived a succession of elderly men intent on making everyone wait for their lunch! Some days the morning schedule was extended by two hours as speakers went well beyond their allotted time. On one day a young woman also graced the platform. She was scheduled last to speak and by the time her turn came participants were as usual clutching their stomachs and fantasising about food. Some began to leave the hall. Worst of all, just before the young woman stood up to make her offering, the men preceding her apologised and said they had to leave for another appointment.

A reflection on the contrast between these two events might be helpful.

Two young women making a difference Pamela Wilson from Canada and Martha Qumba from South Africa on their visit to us at the IIC office.

His Holiness the Dalai Lama with the Young Generation at the 1999 Parliament of the World's Religions, Cape Town

THE DALAI LAMA has been an active interfaith campaigner despite his high status as spiritual and political leader of the Tibetan people. In a letter to Juliet Hollister of the Temple of Understanding, he wrote:

> I appreciate any organization or individual people who sincerely make an effort to promote harmony between humanity, and particularly harmony between the various religions. I consider it very sacred work and very important work.
>
> It is my strong belief that the key message of all the world's religious traditions are the same....It is a message of love, of the importance of cultivating forgiveness and understanding, and of brotherhood and sisterhood.

Regarding the great richness in the diversity of religious traditions, His Holiness said:

> Within the world, among human beings, the spiritual inclinations and interests of individuals are so diverse that we need diverse spiritual traditions to be able to fulfil the needs of this richly diverse humanity.[9]

On World Tibet Day in 2001, the Dalai Lama gave this message on the importance of interfaith:

> [All] the major religions of the world have the same potential to transform people into better human beings. The common messages of love, kindness, tolerance, self-discipline and a sense of sharing are in some ways the foundation for respecting the fundamental and basic human rights of every person. The world religions can therefore contribute to peace, harmony and human dignity. That is why understanding and good relations amongst the different religious traditions of the world are so important.

> The final reflection comes from a distinguished and
> experienced Muslim interfaith educator from the Middle East,
> HRH PRINCE HASSAN OF JORDAN.

Sandy was privileged to be present on 4 June 1995 when Prince Hassan gave the first non-Christian sermon ever to be delivered at Christ Church Cathedral in Oxford. Of all the hundreds of enthusiastic people present she happened to be sitting next to the one protestor! As the Prince stood up so did the protestor! The Cathedral 'heavies' moved in and soon dragged him, yelling his exclusivist theology, from the scene. This person was clearly not in tune with the future unlike Prince Hassan whose message encapsulates much of what you have read and proffers a cohesive vision for the future of interfaith relations and the future of humanity. He writes:

Looking back will historians record the first quarter of the 21st century as the era of the second great monotheistic wars? At times it is hard to think otherwise. The predicted theory of an unavoidable 'clash of civilisations' between backward, authoritarian Middle Eastern regimes and modern western democracies of the end of the 20th century, permutated rapidly, following the tragic events of 9/11, into a widely-held and dangerous view that there is an inevitable clash between the Islamic and other monotheistic faiths. Though we may not wish to acknowledge it, this in turn has given rise to a deeply entrenched, almost subconscious 'clash of monotheisms' mentality that pervades all sectors of society and that is driving rifts into pluralist, multicultural societies across the globe.

Simultaneously, we are currently witnessing a series of alienations within all sectors of society: rich, poor; educated, uneducated; the participating, the disenfranchised, excluded or marginalised – all of whom, through globalisation, are fully aware of where they miss out on the one side, or of what they have to fear on the other. In this context, religious dogma and political ideology become so inextricably intertwined as to make of the disenchanted easy prey for those with extremist ideologies, whilst simultaneously prompting an intensification of hard - as opposed to soft - security reactions that merely exacerbate the problem, and erode the very civil liberties that underpin the freedom of the modern civil societies they purport to sustain. Together they erode the middle ground.

This centripetal breakup can be avoided, but it requires commitment, imagination and flexibility. Our task, as I see it, is to provide a contract of generations with both our own children and those as yet unborn; a contract, based on humanitarianism, hinged on an ethic of human solidarity, which can provide both guidelines and hope for the future of human relations, and indeed, of the very planet itself.

But our future depends not only on finding technical solutions to the problems we face, but also on reaching a consensus about the ethical basis of our response. Each one of us is no more, but also no less, than a human being. To emphasise our common humanity is not to deny or to belittle the importance of transcendental concerns, rather it is simply to recognise that no single definition of the truth is universally accepted. Whilst there may be different cultures in the world today, all have contributed to universalism, and the values that we share today have a sound basis in the myriad traditions. Our common humanity must be our starting point as we learn to live with multiple perceptions of the truth. This, of course, entails educating future generations to respect human dignity, diversity and the multitude of faiths. But we need to go further and to educate ourselves.

In this context it is important that we gain a better understanding of religion itself and crucially, disentangle religion from faith. Religion is not faith. As Reza Aslan put it: 'Religion is the story of faith' – and we all have our own stories and should respect each others stories, inclusive of their pain. The problem, he notes, arises 'when faith, which is mysterious and ineffable and which eschews all categorisations, becomes entangled in the gnarled branches of religion.'

In an age when the spectre of fundamentalisms threatens to tear our fragile human unity apart and stereotyping seems to blunt any hope of our recognising our common humanity, I remain convinced that even the deepest disagreements can be resolved through dialogue and mutual respect. There may not be any simple answers, but with courageous re-examination of the Holy texts, there are possibilities of meaningful meetings of minds at the religious level.

Prince Hassan

Recent events have highlighted the desperate need for deeper comprehension and understanding of the faiths and cultures of each other. What we are seeing in the world today, whether in Iraq, in the Middle East or indeed in Europe, marks a very difficult turning point with human, moral and religious dimensions. There has to be a universally acceptable moral authority that is above politics.

The key to meeting the challenges of the future lies in changing conventional ways of thinking and it is my firm belief that: through a reconsideration of security - social, economic and cultural - through proactive steps to stimulate the evolution of a culture of participation in genuine civil society, and likewise through proactive steps to create a culture of peace through education for rights and responsibilities, it is possible to find culturally sensitive solutions, based on an ethical consensus, to global problems; in brief, through the formulation of a legal-ethical-moral template to which all can adhere.

Let us transform our understanding of our individual faiths from a force for conflict to a source of conflict resolution, and show a sceptical world the power of faith to unify and enlighten through a dialogue of civilisations. Violence and terror are all too often born out of political and economic despair. Peace is born of hope. Surely we can give our children the very thing that they symbolise to us: hope for the future.

THE MUSIC OF THE SPHERES
From the music of the spheres:
The sentience of the mighty Whole,
There came a chord
That swelled to climax
And to Light
Pouring in the great lasered harmonies
To this struggling Earth
As piercing shafts of inspiration:
Renewing the lost human Ideal…

Eric Gladwin

- NOTES
- IMAGE ACKNOWLEDGEMENTS
- CONTRIBUTORS
- INTERFAITH PERSONALITIES
- RESOURCES

NOTES

DEDICATION PAGE: Paramahansa Yogananda, *Where There Is Light: Insight and Inspiration for Meeting Life's Challenges*, Self-Realization Fellowship, Los Angeles, U.S.A. PP 41-42.

CONTENTS: Last page: Quote from *www.positivetones.com*

CHAPTER 1: ORIGINS

1. Sri Mata Amritanandamayi, Address to the Millennium Peace Summit of Religious and Spiritual Leaders, at the United Nations, New York, on August 29, 2000. For full text, see *www.ammachi.org/amma/international-forum/millineum2000.html*
2. Kofi Annan, UN Secretary General, Address to the Millennium Peace Summit of Religious and Spiritual Leaders, August 29, 2000, UN General Assembly Hall, New York. For full text, see *www.commongood.info/Annan.html*
3. For full text see Swami Vivekananda, *The Universal Religion*, Ramakrishna Vedanta Centre, Bourne End, 1993.
4. Marcus Braybrooke, *Pilgrimage of Hope: One Hundred Years of Global Interfaith Dialogue*, SCM Press, London, 1992. See also John Henry Barrows, Ed, *The World Parliament of Religions*, Parliament Publishing Co, Chicago, 1893.
5. 'Looking after one another: The safety and security of our faith communities.' Copies available free with A4 stamped, self-addressed envelope from the Inter Faith Network for the UK, 8A Lower Grosvenor Place, London SW1W 0EN, or download at *www.interfaith.org.uk*
6. For more about the Network, see *www.interfaith-centre.org* and *www.interfaithstudies.org/network.html*. All the Network organisations at time of writing are listed in Resources. However, it is changing/expanding so check with IIC for latest situation.
7. K L Seshagiri Rao, Editor in Chief, Encyclopedia of Hinduism and Professor Emeritus, University of Virginia, Address to the International Ministerial Conference on the Dialogue among Civilizations, Delhi, India, 9 & 10 July 2003.
8. Alan Race, *Interfaith Encounter: The Twin Tracks of Theology and Dialogue*, SCM, London, 2001.
9. The interview can be seen in full in the Faith and Interfaith video series, available from International Interfaith Centre, 2 Market Street, Oxford OX1 3EF, UK or online from *www.interfaith-centre.org*. We had the privilege of interviewing John Hick, Keith Ward, Yehuda Stolov, André Porto, Chandra Muzaffar and Farid Esack for this series.
10. Paramahansa Yogananda, *Whispers from Eternity*, Self-Realization Fellowship, Los Angeles, U.S.A. P 3.
11. Swami Satchidananda, quote published at *www.interfaithstudies.org/interfaith/inspiration.html*

12. Lord Navnit Dholakia of Waltham Brookes OBE, extract from Foreword to Sandy and Jael Bharat, *Touched by Truth: A Contemporary Hindu Anthology* (Sessions of York, 2006). Info at *www.spiritualityfordailylife.com*

CHAPTER II: RATIONALE

1. Told in Satsvarupa Dasa Goswami, *Prabhupada: He Built A House In Which The Whole World Can Live*, Bhaktivedanta Book Trust, Los Angeles, 1994.
2. See International Interfaith Centre Newsletter 11.
3. Extract from Wendy Tyndale, 'Globalising God: the New Internationalism,' published at *www.interfaithstudies.org/otherthemes/globalgod.html*
4. Extract from John Hick, 'Is Christianity the only true religion, or one among others?' Talk given to a Theological Society in Norwich, England. Published at *www.johnhick.org.uk/article2.html*
5. Extract from Anant Rambachan, 'What difference does religious plurality make?' published at *www.wcc-coe.org/wcc/what/interreligious/cd34-09.html*
6. Richard Thompson's report on 'From Religious Fundamentalism to Interfaith Dialogue' seminar in International Interfaith Centre Newsletter 11.
7. John Hick, 'On the Practice of Meditation', International Interfaith Centre Newsletter 12.
8. Dom Peter Bowe, 'Keeping Faith with Interfaith: Searching for God in a Pluralist World.' Paper given on the Retirement of Dr Michael Hooker from Donnington Interfaith, 27 April 2001.
9. For example, Interfaith Seminaries at *http:newseminary.org* and *www.interfaithseminary.org.uk*
10. The Brahma Kumaris might be a good example of this. Read about them at *www.bkwsu.com*
11. Speech by Nelson Mandela upon receiving the Juliet Hollister Award, 5 December 1999, at the Parliament of the World's Religions, Cape Town, South Africa. For more about Juliet Hollister, see *www.templeofunderstanding.org/newSite/whoWeAre/history.php*
12. Extract from Dr Harriet Crabtree, 'Inter Faith Dialogue and Encounter,' lecture given at the IARF Congress, Budapest, August 2002.
13. Sr Maureen Goodman, reflection on IIC conference, 'Building Community – Living Together, Working Together.' See IIC Newsletter 9.

CHAPTER III: EXPERIENCING

1. Huston Smith, interview at *www.motherjones.com/news/qa/1997/11/snell.html*
2. Extract from Dom Peter Bowe, 'Searching for God in a Pluralist World.' 27 April 2001.
3. International Interfaith Centre Newsletter 9.
4. International Interfaith Centre Newsletter 16.
5. Albert Nambiaparambil CMI, *Pilgrims on the Seashore of Endless Worlds: Experiences in Inter-Faith Dialogue*, Asian Trading Corps, Bangalore 2002, revised 2005.
6. Marcus Braybrooke, 'My Vision,' *One Family*, newsletter of the World Congress of Faiths, October 2005.

7. Extracts from David Partridge, 'Why I Pray at the Mosque,' *Church Times*, 26 November 2005.
8. For full text of Sensei Ross' article, see *http://www.chicagozen.org/articles/interfaith.html*
9. Full texts for all these experiences can be found in the IIC booklet, Oxford Interfaith Projects 2003.
10. Albert Nambiaparambil CMI, *Pilgrims on the Seashore of Endless Worlds: Experiences in Inter-Faith Dialogue*. P149.
11. Paul McKenna, Scarboro Missions, Canada. Find out more at *www.scarboromissions.ca*

Chapter IV: organising
1. Text © Inter Faith Network UK: *www.interfaith.org.uk* Copies of this and many other informative documents can be bought from the Network at 8A Lower Grosvenor Place, London SW1W 0EN, UK.
2. There are many interfaith calendars. See, for example, *www.interfaithcalendars.org* and *www.festivalshop.co.uk*
3. A useful resource is Jean Potter and Marcus Braybrooke, Eds, *All in Good Faith: A Resource for Multi-Faith Prayer*, World Congress of Faiths, 1997.
4. Daniel has published many interfaith books, including *Resources for Multi-faith Celebrations*. For more details, see *www.westminster-interfaith.org.uk*
5. Diversiton – respecting diversity in the workplace. See *www.diversiton.com*
6. Extracts from Rev Ryan's report of Religion, Community and Conflict conference.
7. Extract from Robert Traer, 'Truth is Healing.'
8. John Henry Barrows, Ed, *The World Parliament of Religions*, Parliament Publishing Co, Chicago, 1893.

Part II: interfaith issues
1. Network Joint Statement is published at *www.interfaith-centre.org*

Chapter V: diversity
1. For the full interview, see IIC's *Faith and Interfaith* video series, as above.
2. Traditional story. This version is from *www.kissedbyanangel.com/twoangels*
3. Tao Te Ching, translation by J H McDonald, in the public domain, at *www.wisegorilla.com/images/taoism/TaoTeChing.html*
4. Paramahansa Yogananda, *Whispers from Eternity*, Self-Realization Fellowship, Los Angeles, U.S.A. P 19.

Chapter VI: freedom
1. Full report at *http://www.oikoumene.org/index.php?id=2252&L=0*
2. Prof Arvind Sharma, 'Religious Freedom: A Hindu Perspective,' Testimony provided to the *United States Commission on International Religious Freedom*, 18 September 2000.
3. 'Religious Freedom in the World: A global report on freedom and persecution,' Freedom House, 2000.
4. Extract from Dr Crabtree's paper at the 2002 IARF Congress.

5. Booklet, *Visit to Britain by Rajmohan and Usha Gandhi*, Initiatives of Change UK, London 2005. *www.uk.iofc.org*
6. Extract from Karel Blei's keynote speech at the 2002 IARF Congress. Full text available at *www.iarf.net/AboutUs/Congress2002/co_Blei.html*
7. Extracts from *www.iarf.net/AboutUs/Congress2002/co_lw_VolCode.html* Contact IARF for current status of this project.
8. For more about the e-learning project see *www.interfaithstudies.org* The Religious Freedom component is also posted at *www.iarf.net*
9. Real freedom: Master Seongcheol: *www.koreanbuddhism.net*
10. See the developing Universal Declaration of Human Rights by the World's Religions at *www.worldsreligionsafter911.com*

CHAPTER VII: PEACE

1. Guidelines for a Golden Rule Workshop, see *www.scarboromissions.ca/Interfaith_dialogue/guidelines_main.php*
2. Marcus Braybrooke, *A Wider Vision*, 1996, pp103-4. See also *World Faiths*, No 110, Spring 1980.
3. Hugo Gryn, *Chasing Shadows*, Viking, 2000, p 251.
4. Donald Nicholl, *Holiness*, 1987. Quoted in A *Wider Vision*, p104.
5. 'Welcome and Unwelcome Truths Between Jews, Christians and Muslims: A Platform Statement from the Sternberg Centre JCM Group,' reprinted as Appendix in Marcus Braybrooke, *A Heart for the World*, O-Books, 2006.
6. Marcus Braybrooke, Ed, *1,000 World Prayers*, O-Books, 2003.
7. UN Human Development Index at *http://hdr.undp.org/docs/statistics/indices/index_tables.pdf*
8. Extracts from speech given at International Peace Foundation, Bangkok, 20-22 January 2004; adapted for this book by Dr Singh.
9. Penny Faust quotes from International Interfaith Centre Newsletter 18.

CHAPTER VIII: LIVING TOGETHER

1. Retold by Mathoor Krishnamurti, *Mathoor in Britain*, M P Birla Foundation, Bangalore, 2004.
2. George Lindreck, 'Postmodern Hermeneutics and Jewish-Christian Dialogue' in *Christianity in Jewish Terms*, Eds, Tikva Frymer-Kensky, David Novak et al, Westview Press, 2000, p 111.
3. Extract from International Interfaith Centre Annual Autumn Lecture 1998, 'African Indigenous Religions and Interreligious Dialogue' by Dr Elizabeth Amoah, University of Ghana.

CHAPTER IX: YOUTH

1. International Interfaith Centre Newsletter 16.
2. Eboo Patel and Patrice Brodeur, Eds, *Building the Interfaith Youth Movement: Beyond Dialogue to Action*, Rowman & Littlefield Publishers, Inc, 2006.
3. Martin L. King, *The World House* in *Where Do We Go from Here: Chaos or Community?*, Harper & Row, New York, 1967.
4. Patrice Brodeur, 'From Postmodernism to 'Glocalism': Towards a

Theoretical Understanding of Contemporary Arab Muslim Constructions of Religious Others,' in *Globalization and the Muslim World*, ed. by Birgit Schaebler and Leif Stenberg, (Syracuse: Syracuse University Press, 2004), pp. 188-205, esp. 197 for a detailed definition.
5. Diana Eck, *A New Religious America* (San Francisco: HarperCollins, 2001).
6. W.C. Smith: *The Faith of Other Men* (New York: Harper & Row, 1962).
7. Chicago Story: Kevin Coval – www.melekyonon.com. The Interfaith Youth Core organizes and provides support for the Chicago Youth Council. Umnia Khan, the associate with the Chicago Action Program of the IFYC helped to organise work on the poem. Mariah Neuroth is the Director of the Chicago Action Program of the Interfaith Youth Core.
8. Traditional story, published at www.markings.bc.ca/spirit/zen.html
9. For more information see the International Interfaith Centre booklets, 'Through Another's Eyes' and 'Oxford Interfaith Projects 2003.'
10. Find out more about Givat Haviva at www.givathaviva.org.il
11. International Interfaith Centre Symposium at 1999 Parliament of World Religions. See full symposium reports in International Interfaith Centre Newsletter 12.
12. Extract from presentation made by Morse Flores at the 2002 IARF Congress in Budapest.
13. International Interfaith Centre Newsletter 14.
14. International Interfaith Centre Newsletter 15.

CHAPTER X: ROLE OF RELIGIONS
1. Swami Vivekananda, 'My Master.' Two lectures on Sri Ramakrishna delivered by Swami Vivekananda in New York and England in 1896 and subsequently combined. See www.hinduism.fsnet.co.uk/namoma/life_thakur/life_thakur_my_master.htm
2. His Holiness the Dalai Lama, 'World Religions for World Peace,' at www.dalailama.com/page.62.htm#World_religion_world_peace
3. International Interfaith Centre Newsletter 16.
4. For full text, see International Interfaith Centre Newsletter 19.
5. Extract from Swami Agnivesh's address to the Conference of the World's Religious Leaders in the Vatican on 23 January 2002 at Just Commentary, www.just-international.com. See also www.swamiagnivesh.com
6. For full interview with Farid Esack, see IIC's *Faith and Interfaith* series.
7. Ravi Ravindra, 'What calls You Pilgrim?' published by Metanexus, The Online Forum on Religion and Science: http://www.metanexus.net
8. E-mail to Sandy and Jael Bharat, 15 January 2006.
9. Extracts from talk given by Fr Michael Barnes SJ to the Annual General Meeting of the Catholic Missionary Union in September 2001. For full text, see www.cmu.org.uk/articles/art_dia.htm See also www.heythrop.ac.uk/ccid/
10. Paramahansa Yogananda, 'How God is Pulling Us Back to Him' in *Journey to Self-Realization: Discovering the Gifts of the Soul*, Self-Realization Fellowship, Los Angeles, U.S.A. P 51.

11. From SRF's Introduction to Paramahansa Yogananda, *Where There is Light*, Self-Realization Fellowship, Los Angeles, U.S.A. P xii. On the same page Yoganandaji is quoted: '[But] realized souls who understand science as well as metaphysics find no difference at all. They see the parallelism between science and truth because they see the whole picture.'
12. Extracts from Matthew Weiner, 'The Real Interfaith Work: From Emerson's Room to Urban Interfaith on the Ground,' *Harvard Divinity Today*, May 2006.
13. Wolfhart Pannenburg, 'How to think about secularism' in *First Things 64*, June/July 1996: 27:32.
14. Don Cupitt, *The Religion of Being*, SCM Press, 1998, page 62.
15. Rabindranath Tagore, Trans, *Songs of Kabir*, Samuel Weiser Inc, Maine, 1998.

CHAPTER XI: CIVIL SOCIETY
1. Oxford football World Cup, see *www.pluspurple.com/oxford/nations.htm*
2. Extract from Paul Knitter, 'The Eco-Human Crisis: Interfaith Dialogue and Global Responsibility,' International Interfaith Centre Autumn Lecture 1995.
3. International Interfaith Centre Newsletter 12.
4. 'Faith Schools and Social Cohesion: An Interfaith Discussion,' held at the House of Lords on 11 November 2002. See IIC Newsletter 18.
5. Howard Shippin, 'Education for Peaceful Living,' International Interfaith Centre conference. See IIC Newsletter 13.
6. K L Seshagiri Rao, 'Religions and Conservation: A Hindu Perspective,' Lecture for International Interfaith Centre, May 1995. Copies available from IIC.
7. For a full copy of Prof Nasr's paper, 'The Relation Between Religions in the Shadow of the Environmental Crisis,' contact the International Interfaith Centre.
8. Downloaded on 1 January 2006 from *http://news.bbc.co.uk/1/hi/uk/4573052.stm*
9. Extract from Dr Josef Boehle, 'Religions, Civil Society and the UN System: Exploring strategies to enhance interfaith cooperation for sustainable peace' at the Conference on Interfaith Cooperation for Peace: Enhancing Interfaith Dialogue and Cooperation towards Peace in the 21st Century, held at the United Nations on 22 June 2005. *www.commongood.info/boehle.html*
10. Booklet, *Visit to Britain by Rajmohan and Usha Gandhi*, Initiatives of Change, UK, London 2005. *www.uk.iofc.org*

CHAPTER XII: FUTURE
1. Sioux Creation Story at *www.inspirationalstories.com*
2. For more about the World Council of Churches conference, 'Critical Moments in Interreligious Dialogue,' see *www.oikoumene.org*
3. Swami Satchidananada quote *www.interfaithstudies.org/interfaith/inspiration.html*

4. Human Beings' by Adrian Mitchell. Reprinted by permission of PFD on behalf of: Adrian Mitchell. © as printed in Adrian Mitchell, *The Shadow Knows*, Bloodaxe Books Ltd, 2004.
5. For a fuller Spiritual History of the United Nations, see *www.csvgc-ny.org*
6. Matthew Fox, *Meditations with Meister Eckhart*, Bear & Co, Rochester, 1983.
7. Rt Rev Rowan Williams, Archbishop of Canterbury, New Year Message 2006.
8. Paramahansa Yogananda, *Worldwide Prayer Circle*, Self-Realization Fellowship, Los Angeles, U.S.A. P 26.
9. Extract from Dr Harriet Crabtree's lecture at 2002 IARF Congress.
10. 'Dalai Lama Dedicates Interfaith Temple in Indiana' by Dennis P O'Connor, *Religion News Service*. Published at www.beliefnet.com/story/132/story_13223_1.html

IMAGE ACKNOWLEDGEMENTS

Our thanks to everyone who sent their pictures for this book, to Celia Storey for her help with images, and to the International Interfaith Centre for use of its photo archive. Most photos used in the reflections were received from contributors. Many others were taken by Jael during our IIC years. These are now part of the IIC photo archive. Other IIC photographers in this period included Celia Storey, Marcus and Mary Braybrooke, Klaus Glindemann, Shige Wada, and Gwyneth Little. We also wish to express our gratitude to the following for additional images used throughout the book:

DEDICATION PAGE: Mavela Creche Christmas Party 2005: Paddy Meskin.

CONTENTS LAST PAGE: Ripples: Jehangir Sarosh

PREFACE:
Pii: Bridge at Self-Realization Fellowship Mother Center: Carol Jordan

FOREWORD
Piii: Marcus Braybrooke and Laxmi Saba: Marcus Braybrooke, *www.worldfaiths.org*
Piv: Marcus Braybrooke and Dalai Lama: Marcus Braybrooke

CHAPTER 1: ORIGINS
P8: Farid Esack and HIV/AIDS Action at 1999 Parliament of the World's Religions: Celia Storey
P11: IIC Conference participants: Celia Storey
P12: Paramahansa Yogananda: courtesy of Self-Realization Fellowship
P13: Ethiopian religions: Timeless Ethiopia Tour, *www.timelessethiopia.com*
P15: The great sage Vyasa: Public Domain at Wikipedia
P19: Pashupati Nath Temple: Jagannath Kandel
P22: Gishiki Ceremony: Tsubaki Grand Shrine of America
P23: Shumei drummer: Shumei Taiko Ensemble
P24: Jain munis: ©Karoki Lewis, *www.karokilewis.com*

P25: Abdul Bahai: *http://info.bahai.org/article-1-3-0-4.html*
P26: International House of Justice: *www.bahaipictures.com*
P27: Olivia Holmes and Megumi Hirota: International Association for Religious Freedom
P28: Jashan ceremony: Joseph H Peterson, *www.esotericarchives.com*
P29: Zoroastrian clip art: *www.wisegorilla.com*
P31: Wailing Wall: André Porto
P32: Prayers in Morocco: André Porto
P36: Self-Realization Fellowship Lake Shrine Gardens: Carol Jordan.

CHAPTER II: RATIONALE
P45: Holy Land prayers: Eliyahu McClean
P46: Whirling dervish: André Porto
P48: Nelson Mandela: Temple of Understanding.

CHAPTER III: EXPERIENCING
P55: John Hick, Sandy and Jael Bharat: Shige Wada
P64: Three Faiths Walk: Paul Goodman
P65: Isabel Smyth and Ani Lhamo: Ani Lhamo, *www.samyeling.org*
P66: Golden Temple: Margaret Paton
P73: Zen Circle: *www.wisegorilla.com*
P79: HACI/WCRP meeting: Hope for African Children, *www.hopeforafricanchildren.org*

CHAPTER IV: ORGANISING
P 86: Oxford Round Table of Religions: David Partridge
P107: Annual Interfaith Service of Commitment to work of United Nations: Interfaith Center of New York
P108: Participants at Millennium Peace Summit: Bawa Jain and Millennium Peace Summit.

PART II ISSUES
P110: Diversity at the 1999 Parliament of the World's Religions: Celia Storey

CHAPTER V: DIVERSITY
P117: Fr Albert at Hindu-Muslim conference: Vijay Ajmani, Udasin Ashram
P123: Lao Tzu: *www.wisegorilla.com*
P128: Self-Realization Fellowship Lake Shrine and Mahatma Gandhi World Peace Memorial: Carol Jordan.

CHAPTER VI: FREEDOM
P130 & 131: World Council of Churches conference photos: Jacques Matthey
P135: Rajmohan Gandhi: Kevin Lidden
P140: Shlomo Alon in dialogue: The Goldin Institute
P148: Real freedom, Korean rooftops: André Porto.

CHAPTER VII: PEACE
P152: Crete conference participants: David Partridge
P155: Peace Councillors: Marcus Braybrooke.

P168: Deir Mar Musa Monastery: Joel Greenyer, *www.jgreen.de*

CHAPTER VIII: LIVING TOGETHER

P171: Church and Vihara: Ellie (IIC's Through Another's Eyes project)
P172: Ibn Arabi: Fair use, found on many websites
P187: Israeli and Palestinian women: Bob Traer.
P188: Elizabeth Amoah: The Pluralism Project, *www.pluralism.org*

CHAPTER IX: YOUTH

P209: London Underground on 7 July 2005: Adam Stacey, Creative Commons Licence. *http://moblog.co.uk/view.php?id=77571*
P210: Youth football: The Maimonides Foundation, *www.maimonides-foundation.org*

CHAPTER X: ROLE OF RELIGIONS

P223: Ramakrishna Paramahansa: Ramakrishna Vedanta Centre UK
P224: Dalai Lama in London: Paulette Micklewood
P234: London Interfaith Centre: Vivekananda Centre London
P238: Paramahansa Yogananda: courtesy of Self-Realization Fellowship
P242: Kabir: Public domain image. A Company-style miniature painting of Kabir as a weaver, c.1825, from the Central Museum in Jaipur. Source: *http://oldsite.library.upenn.edu/etext/sasia/aiis/mini-paint/company/004.html*

CHAPTER XI: CIVIL SOCIETY

P258: Seyyed Hossein Nasr: *www.worldofwisdom.com*
P265: Acharya Shri Sushil Kumar Ji Maharaj: Public domain image
P271: Barney Leith and Shafiqur Rahman: Multi-Faith Group for Healthcare Chaplaincy, *www.mfghc.com*
P272: Three Nuns: David Finn, Prints and Photographs Division, Library of Congress, LC-DIG-ppmsca-01932.

CHAPTER XII: FUTURE

P277: Anant Rambachan: Peter Williams, World Council of Churches
P277: Swami Satchidananda: *www.swamisatchidananda.org*
P280: Dag Hammersköld: Photo: UN/DPI; *www.sfn.se*
P283: Meister Eckhart: Fair use, found on many websites
P286: Julia Ward Howe: Public Domain
P289: Dalai Lama: Council for a Parliament of the World's Religions
P292: Heaven's Gate: Phil Burdall; Creative Commons License at *www.flickr.com*

CONTRIBUTORS

P304: Patrice Brodeur: Gunther Damper
P312: Eboo Patel: © Eileen Ryan Photography, 2006.

GALLERY

P318: Neville Hodgkinson: Steve Bowrick; Creative Commons Licence at *www.flickr.com*

RESOURCES

P331: Maze: Karol Miles; Creative Commons Licence at *www.flickr.com*

CONTRIBUTORS

AL-ABBADI, ANAS *www.ifyc.org www.uri.org www.jordanyouth.org* 
Founder/Director of Jordan Interfaith Action; Director of United Religions Initiative MENA; Youth and Interfaith Dialogue activist; co-founder and board member of National Forum for Youth and Culture; Trainer on Intercultural Learning. Anas loves working with youth, especially from different cultures and believes they can make the world a better place.

ALLAN, JAMES W *http://aifes.ashmol.ox.ac.uk* 
Professor/Emeritus Fellow of St Cross College, Oxford; University Lecturer in Islamic Art; Keeper of Eastern Art, Ashmolean Museum, 1992-2005; Director of Ashmolean Inter-Faith Exhibitions Service, since 2005; President of the British Institute of Persian Studies. Author of numerous books and articles, including *Persian Steel: the Tanavoli Collection* (2000).

ALON, SHLOMO *www.interfaith-encounter.org www.iarf.net www.uri.org* 
PhD in Arabic Language; Chair of Interfaith Encounter Association, Israel; Head of Arabic Studies, Israeli Ministry of Education; Senior Lecturer at School of Education, Hebrew University; Council Member of International Association for Religious Freedom; Global Trustee, United Religions Initiative; Author, Hebrew-Arabic textbooks and dictionaries.

AL-RIFAIE, HAMID *http://dialogueonline.org* 
HE Prof Dr Al-Rifaie is President of the International Islamic Forum for Dialogue based in Jeddah, Saudi Arabia. He is also Co-President of the Islamic-Catholic Liaison Committee at the Vatican and Assistant Secretary-General of the Muslim World Congress. He has a doctorate in Chemistry.

AL-YOUSSUF, HEATHER *www.mcmarriage.org.uk* 
Heather is a classicist turned arabist, Anglican wife of a Shi'i Muslim and mother of three. She founded the Muslim-Christian Marriage Support Group and is active in research and projects that engage with the particular sensitivities of mixed faith marriage.

ARIYARATNE, VINYA *www.sarvodaya.org* 
Vinya is a medical doctor & Executive Director of Sarvodaya Shramadana Movement, Sri Lanka. He initiated community based, non-medicalized programmes to address psycho-social effects of children affected by separatist war and is the author of *Sarvodaya Peace Action Plan* (2001) and a teacher at the European University Center for Peace Studies, Austria.

BEKRAHDNIA, SHAHIN 
Zoroastrian of the Iranian tradition, teacher of ancient history and classical civilisation, a Justice of the Peace and a legal consultant. She has written and published on Zoroastrianism, including a postgraduate thesis in anthropology on issues of Zoroastrian identity in the 20th century, and is active in inter-faith movements and organisations.

BHARAT, JAEL AND SANDY *www.spiritualityfordailylife.com* 
Jael: Born in Holland as Leendert Plaisier; atheist; widowed 1983; mystic since; farmer 1960/2001; teacher of macro-economics 1971/81; staff at International Interfaith Centre, 1998/2004.
Sandy: Staff, International Interfaith Centre, 1994-2004; Author, *Christ Across the Ganges: Hindu Responses to Jesus* (O-Books, 2007); theology graduate, Exeter; disciple of Paramahansa Yogananda.
Together: Met in Korea, 1996; 5 children and 3 grandchildren.
Books: *Mapping the Cosmos: An Introduction to God* (Sessions 2006); *Touched by Truth: A Contemporary Hindu Anthology.* (Sessions 2006);

BOEKE, RICHARD *www.worldfaiths.org* 
Graduate, Yale Divinity School; Baptist US Air Force Chaplain before becoming a Unitarian Minister. He and his wife, Rev. Johanna Boeke, for 40 years have supported the IARF. Currently Unitarian Minister in Horsham, England, and Secretary of the World Congress of Faiths.

BOWE, PETER *www.douaiabbey.org.uk* 
Benedictine monk at Douai Abbey, Reading for 40 years, for 20 of those animating interfaith dialogue among monks and nuns in the UK and Europe. Chaired Donnington Interfaith Group for many years. Peter is currently helping to establish a town monastery in Douai, France.

BRAYBROOKE, MARCUS & MARY *www.worldfaiths.org www.threefaithsforum.org.uk* 
Marcus: Retired Anglican parish priest; involved in interfaith work for over forty years; President of the World Congress of Faiths; Co-Founder of the Three Faiths Forum; Patron of the International Interfaith Centre; Peace Councillor. Author of over forty books, including *Pilgrimage of Hope* and *A Heart for the World*.
Mary: Social worker and magistrate, Mary has been involved in interfaith matters for nearly fifty years. (She went to a Sunday school at Cambridge Unitarian church). She has worked with adults, children and sick people of many backgrounds & cultures; currently working with kidney patients in Oxford and Swindon.

BRODEUR, PATRICE *www.theo.umontreal.ca* 
Canada Research Chair on Islam, Pluralism and Globalization in the Faculty of Theology and the Sciences of Religions, University of Montreal. Doctorate in Study of Religion from Harvard University. Master's Degree from Institute of Islamic Studies, McGill University. Studied at Hebrew University, Jerusalem and University of Jordan. Active with WCRP.

CAHILL, DES *www.rmit.edu.au* 
Professor of Intercultural Studies, RMIT University, Melbourne; heads Australian chapter of WCRP; represents his country on Asian Conference of Religion and Peace; member of Australian Partnership of Ethnic and Religious Organizations and local police multifaith advisory committee. Current research specialization in religion and globalization.

CONTRIBUTORS

CAPIE, FERGUS *www.londoninterfaith.org.uk* 
Anglican priest whose work has included several distinctive contexts, from prison and boarding school ministry to parish and inter faith work in east and now west London. Present post has involved significant amount of travel to other parts of the world over last decade, engaging with a variety of models of cross-faith contact.

CLARK, ANDREW *www.antislavery.org* 
Worked on relief and rural development projects in Ethiopia, Nigeria, India, Bangladesh and Vietnam. Appointed General Secretary of Quaker Peace and Service (1982-99) and International Association for Religious Freedom (2000-05). Now retired, serves on the Executive Committee of Anti-Slavery International. Would like to improve at Chinese chess.

CLARK, DAVID *www.leicestercounciloffaiths.org.uk* 
Retired Church of England priest. After his curacy in a mining town in Lancashire followed by Precentorship of Manchester Cathedral, he worked for 15 years as an Industrial Chaplain and 13 as a parish priest. Spent his last five and a half working years on Inter Faith relations with the Leicester Council of Faiths while attached to St James the Greater, Leicester.

COHEN, SIMON   *www.faithandmedia.com*   *www.adamandeveit.net*   *www.globaltolerance.com* 
Director of *global tolerance*; interfaith media advisor; freelance writer; ran media training courses at Parliament of World Religions (2004) and World Spirit Forum (2005). Voted one of top young media professionals in UK by Media Week (2003, 2004). Received awards from UnLtd and Millennium Awards Trust as one of UK's leading social entrepreneurs.

DASI, MERUDEVI   *www.iskcon.org*   *www.ochs.org.uk* 
Merudevi Dasi is the European Director of Communications for ISKCON and the Director of the Vaishnava Communications Institute (VCI) in Oxford. The VCI serves as a resource centre for Vaishnavas and other Hindus in Europe, carries out research on religious liberty issues, and actively participates in interfaith dialogue.

DEERING, TRICIA *www.habitateurope.org* 
Tricia Deering is Senior Communications Manager for Habitat for Humanity's Europe and Central Asia Area Office. Tricia worked as a journalist before segueing into PR.

FISHER, MARY PAT *www.gobindsadan.org* 
Mary Pat Fisher is author of dozens of college textbooks, primarily about religions and art. Her bestselling textbook, *Living Religions*, is now in its sixth edition. Originally from the United States, she has dedicated her life to volunteer service in India at Gobind Sadan since 1990.

FOROUGHI, PARVINE *www.bahai.org* 
Born in Iran; English degree, Shiraz University; Master's degree, Library Studies, Loughborough University of Technology. Worked at Middle East Centre, Cambridge, Gulf Studies Centre, Exeter, & Exeter University Library. Member, Exeter University Interfaith Society/Exeter Interfaith Group. Since December 1999, volunteer at Bahá'í World Centre Library, Haifa, Israel.

FRY, EILEEN *www.multifaithnet.org* 
Director, Multi-Faith Centre, University of Derby, and previously Researcher and Project Manager of *Religions in the UK: A Multi-Faith Directory*. Eileen has two Masters degrees, in Counselling and in Social Research; Teacher Diploma holder from the British Wheel of Yoga and studying for a PhD.

FULDER, STEPHEN *www.middleway.org   www.tovana.org.il* 
PhD in medical research; author of 14 books on complementary and herbal medicine; practicing Buddhism for nearly 30 years; lives in Israel and is founder and leading teacher of the Israel Insight Society, combining meditation, Vipassana and dharma; co-founder, Middleway and Akoda, two organisations applying dharma wisdom to social change.

GHAZI, USRA *www.ifyc.org* 
Undergrad at DePaul University, studying Religion, Ethics, and Social Justice. As a Pakistani-American Muslim, strives to implement values of mindfulness, integrity, and community service through her work with the Interfaith Youth Core and various Muslim community organizations in Chicago. Credits her parents with inculcating/ inspiring these values.

GIFFORD, MARK *www.moe-online.org* 
Mark is the Interfaith Director of the community rights charity, Minorities of Europe. He read Theology at Durham and is a qualified solicitor. In his spare time he plays the drums and listens to classical music. He is 30 years old.

GLADWIN ERIC P 
Elder/Poet/Philosopher. Inspired by experiences: A sun-blast in the Libyan Desert 1941, Flare of Light on a starry night 1961. Writing: 500 poems about Eternal Cosmic Unity of Energies giving similar instructions to ALL great Faiths, with the logic of reverencing the Sun which freely gives All, manifest and unmanifest, to Earth. Cares about the dangers of misused Thought energy. Love is needed.

GONZALEZ, GERARDO *www.lgpt.net/lama_forum_it.htm* 
Doctor, Social-Psychology, Sorbonne; international officer, Population and Sustainable Development, United Nations. Now retired. Director of international project, 'Towards the creation of a spiritual forum for world peace at the United Nations;' a founder, Network of International Interfaith Organizations; Coordinator of Spiritual Forum of Santiago for Peace; member of URI Senior Advisory Council.

GOODMAN, MAUREEN *www.ukbkwsu.org* 
Programme Co-ordinator, International Centre of the Brahma Kumaris (BKs) in London since 1991; represents BKs on several interfaith bodies; co-ordinates BK community outreach work in the UK and BK Youth activities internationally; trustee, Janki Foundation for Global Healthcare; travels widely giving workshops and lectures on themes related to personal spiritual development.

Contributors

GRAPA, ANGIE *www.iarf.net* 
Bachelor of Science in Psychology from Silliman University; guidance counsellor, College of Arts and Sciences in same university; trainer in human resource development; currently supervising the implementation of IARF's Human Rights Education project in the Philippines; International Council Member for IARF and National Coordinator in the Philippines.

GUDKA, JAYNI *www.inaphoto.com www.jainspirit.com www.youngjains.org.uk* 
A Level Student in London. Inter-faith and community work recognised in her receiving 'Helping hands around the world' award. Participated in establishment of permanent 'faith trail' at British Museum, to enhance inter-faith dialogue. Part-time writer and photographer for international journal, *Jain Spirit*; active volunteer with a charity named Young Jains; Youth Teacher at a faith related school.

HAILU, MUSSIE *www.uri.org* 
Ethiopian; representative, World Federation of UN Associations to the Economic Commission of Africa and African Union; Country Director, HOPE'87; Special emissary to King Kigali V of Rwanda; Board Chair, Interfaith Peace-Building Initiative. Recipient of a twenty-first century achievement award; Fellow of the International Biographical Association. Mussie's motto is May Peace Prevail on Earth.

HARRIS, ELIZABETH *www.methodist.org.uk* 
Secretary for Inter Faith Relations, Methodist Church in Britain; Honorary Lecturer at Birmingham University; active in inter faith relations for twenty-five years; doctorate in Buddhist Studies in Sri Lanka in 1993. She is author of *What Buddhists Believe* (Oneworld 1998) and *Theravada Buddhism and the British Encounter* (Routledge 2006).

HASSAN, HIS ROYAL HIGHNESS PRINCE *www.riis.org www.wcrp.org* 
At the centre of Middle East Politics and diplomacy for many decades he has won exceptional respect for drawing attention to humanitarian and interfaith issues and the human dimension of conflicts. He initiated, founded and is actively involved in many Jordanian and international institutes and committees; President and Patron of the Arab Thought Forum; Moderator of WCRP; a founder of the Parliament of Cultures; author of seven books, translated into several languages.

HATCH, REBECCA *www.diversityandialogue.org.uk* 
Becky Hatch co-ordinates the Diversity and Dialogue project, led by Save the Children, in conjunction with eight other Christian, Jewish, Muslim and secular NGOs. The project runs activities in London, Birmingham, Leeds and Manchester and is producing educational resources to facilitate more interfaith dialogue amongst young people.

HICK, JOHN *www.johnhick.org.uk* 
John has been writing in the philosophy of religion and theology for over 40 years. He has taught at Cornell University, Princeton Theological Seminary, and the Claremont Graduate University in the USA, and Cambridge and Birmingham Universities in the UK. His main work during the last two decades has been in the interfaith area.

HOISINGTON, MOLLY *www.ifyc.org*

A senior in high school; member with the Chicago Youth Council of the Interfaith Youth Core; volunteer at the Chicago Children's Museum; loves to people-watch, play piano and cello. Largely because of that, loves living in the city, but misses the mountains and the hometown-feel of Utah.

HUSSAIN, ASAF *www.le.ac.uk*

Academic teaching at Institute of LifeLong Learning, University of Leicester. Areas of interest are religions and cultures. His books have been on Islam and Middle Eastern politics, published in Britain, America and Pakistan. Currently he is engaged in studying Islamic Fundamentalism and writing two studies on Islamic Fundamentalism in Britain and Islamic Fundamentalism in Pakistan.

JAIN, BAWA *www.millenniumpeacesummit.org*

Secretary-General of Millennium World Peace Summit of Religious and Spiritual Leaders; Secretary-General of World Council of Religious Leaders; founder of World Movement for Nonviolence; Member, Earth Charter Initiative International Resource Team; Advisory Board of the Center for Religion and Diplomacy; Advisory Board of the Earth Council's Collaborative on National Councils of Sustainable Development; Co-founder of Global Commission for the Preservation of Sacred Sites.

KANDEL, JAGANATH *www.ifyc.org www.hvpuk.org.uk/HVP/index1.htm*

18 years old, BA student at Tribhuwan University, member of the Youth Society for Peace of Nepal. Interested in studying good books, playing music and travelling to new places. An optimist and would like to connect with young people at a global level. The Peace Society, based in Kathmandu, is a forum to bring together young people. Motto: 'There is no way to Peace, Peace is the way.'

KEYES, SIMON *www.stethelburgas.org*

Simon Keyes became Director of St Ethelburga's Centre for Reconciliation and Peace after many years of developing new approaches to homelessness, mental health and crime prevention. He also works as a video maker and is writing a book about walking alone from Budapest to London.

KIRSTE, REINHARD *www.interrel.de*

B. Berlin, Germany, 1942. Studied Protestant Theology and Pedagogics in Berlin, Tübingen and Göttingen. Dr. theol. (Kirchliche Hochschule - Church College of Berlin), Reverend of parishes in Hildesheim and Berlin, school advisor in South Westphalia; Coordinator, Institute for Interreligious Studies and co-founder, with wife, of Omni Religio. Lectures at the University of Dortmund.

KLAES, NORBERT *www.wcrp.org*

Born in Essen (Germany) 1938. Studied Philosophy, Theology and Oriental Studies (Bonn, Innsbruck, Oxford, Varanasi). Professor of Theology in Mumbai and Paderborn; Professor of History of Religions in Würzburg. Works for WCRP as European president and as Co-President of WCRP/International.

KNITTER, PAUL   www.paulknitter.com

Paul Knitter has spent the past 35 years of his professional life in the pursuit of both the academic and practical dialogue among religions. Most of that time was at Xavier University in Cincinnati, Ohio, USA. He is presently pursuing an active retirement.

LEITH, BARNEY   www.bahais.org.uk

Born in 1947, educated at Exeter, Birmingham and Kent universities, married with three grown-up children and three grandchildren. Became a Bahá'í in February 1966 and has been an active member of the Bahá'í community ever since. Currently member of National Spiritual Assembly, and Secretary for External Affairs.

LEWIS, KAROKI   www.karokilewis.com

Born Nairobi in 1967; first class Economics degree; postgraduate Diploma in Photo-journalism. Work is a mixture of travel and reportage used in a number of photographic books on India and in newspapers and magazines internationally. Photography and sound recordings reflect historical, cultural and socio-economic interests. Prize-winner, 2003 and 2004 of Travel Photographer of the Year competitions.

MARKHAM, IAN   www.hartsem.edu

Dean of Hartford Seminary and Professor of Theology and Ethics; Visiting Professor of Globalization, Ethics, and Islam at Leeds Metropolitan University; author of *Plurality and Christian Ethics* (Cambridge 1996), *Theology of Engagement* (Blackwell 2003), *A World Religions Reader* (Blackwell 1999) and many other books and articles.

MARSHALL, VERNON   www.interfaith.org.uk/locallist.htm

Unitarian Minister serving congregations in the Greater Manchester towns of Denton and Dukinfield. Author of *The Large View* (Lindsey Press, 2006) on the relationship between British Unitarians and the World's Religions. He is a member of the International Association for Religious Freedom and a founding member of the Tameside Interfaith Network.

MATHEW, THOMAS   www.iarf.net

Vice President, International Association for Religious Freedom; Chair of IARF's South Asian Co-ordinating Committee; Director, SEEDS, India; Peace representative, World Peace Prayer Society, New York; Board Member, National Council of YMCAs of India. He has academic qualifications in public administration, history, social service and rural development. Thomas is married to Sally and they have two children.

MAQUILING, WOODROW   www.iarf.net

Woodrow is 21, Filipino, born and raised in a Roman Catholic way of life and nurtured in an interfaith spirit. He graduated with an A.B. in Political Science from Silliman University, Dumaguete, Philippines. Woodrow is an Account Executive of ABS-CBN Broadcasting Corporation and Youth Coordinator of IARF-Philippines Chapter.

MAY, JOHN D'ARCY
www.tcd.ie/ise/

B. Melbourne, Australia, 1942. STL Gregoriana, Rome, 1969; Dr. theol. (Ecumenics) Münster, 1975; Catholic Ecumenical Institute, Univ. of Münster, 1975-1982; Dr. phil. (History of Religions) Frankfurt, 1983; Melanesian Council of Churches and Melanesian Institute, Papua New Guinea, 1983-87; Associate Professor of Interfaith Dialogue at Irish School of Ecumenics, Trinity College Dublin, since 1987.

MERRIAM, DENA F
www.gpiw.org

Founder/Convener of Global Peace Initiative of Women; organizer of Millennium World Peace Summit of Religious and Spiritual Leaders; organizing global youth summits around Millennium Development Goals with UN; Masters Degree from Columbia University; served on Advisory Boards of Harvard Center for the Study of World Religions, International Center for Religion and Diplomacy, AIM for Seva and Dharma Drum.

MESKIN, PADDY
www.wcrp.org

Born in UK, moved to South Africa when 5. Taught drama, remedial education, human rights, peace, conflict resolution, Holocaust, HIV and AIDS training programmes. In apartheid years she initiated programmes/projects promoting peace and human rights + crèches for children affected/infected by HIV/AIDS. President of WCRP South Africa. Greatest joy is family, especially three grandchildren.

MITCHELL, ADRIAN
www.rippingyarns.co.uk/adrian/

Oxford graduate, became reporter, freelance journalist, then free-falling poet, playwright and writer of stories. Married, 2 grown-up daughters and 2 sons and a daughter from first marriage. Spends more time writing for children, has six grandchildren. Honorary doctorate from North London University and has been Fellow of many institutions, including Cambridge University, Royal Society for Literature, & Unicorn Theatre for Children.

MITCHELL, LOUISE
www.ccj.org.uk

Youth & Outreach Officer, Council of Christians and Jews. Role includes leading cross faith seminars, helping set up interfaith groups & organising retreats for young adults. Passionate about her work; ran a reconciliation trip to Israel/Palestine to allow participants to engage with political and inter-religious dynamics of area; BA in English Literature; MA in Critical and Cultural Theory; loves music, literature, and is qualified soccer referee.

MOFID, KAMRAN
www.commongoodjournal.com   *www.commongood.info*

Founder, Inter-faith Perspective on Globalisation for the Common Good; Doctorate in economics, Birmingham; Certificate in Education and Pastoral Studies, Plater College, Oxford. Co-author: *Promoting the Common Good: Bringing Economics and Theology Together Again: A Theologian and an Economist in Dialogue.* Co-editor, Globalization for the Common Good journal.

MONTAGU, RACHEL
www.ccj.org.uk

Rabbi and Assistant Education Officer at The Council of Christians and Jews. Teaches Biblical Hebrew at Birkbeck College's Faculty of Continuing Education. She studied at Newnham College, Cambridge, Leo Baeck College, London and Pardes Institute, Jerusalem.

MOSAAD, MOHAMED *www.uri.org*

Dr Mohamed Mosaad is an Egyptian psychiatrist and anthropologist and serves currently as the Middle East and North Africa Coordinator of United Religions Initiative.

MUZAFFAR, CHANDRA *www.just-international.org*

Well-known Malaysian intellectual-activist who has authored a number of books and articles on religion, human rights, Malaysian politics and international relations; President of the International Movement for a Just World and is associated with a variety of other international NGOs concerned with social justice and civilizational dialogue.

NAIK, DEEPAK MBE *www.moe-online.com*

Hindu married to Daksha and with her has a son, Rajay, and a daughter, Avni. In the recent past Deepak has been in financial sales, worked in Equalities for Birmingham City Council and is one of eight founders of Minorities of Europe, a registered charity that works with young people to create a little more harmony in the world.

NAMBIAPARAMBIL, FR ALBERT *www.interfaithstudies.org*

PhD in Philosophy; Director, Upasana in Thodupuzha; Secretary, World Fellowship of Interreligious Councils; organized many interfaith dialogues, including world conferences of religions in 2002 and 2003; involved in many international interfaith activities. Author: *Ethics of R M Hare* and *Pilgrims on the Seashore of Endless Worlds;* Editor: 15 books of Kerala Philosophical Congress and Guidelines for Inter-Religious Dialogue.

OGLIO, FR PAOLO DALL' *www.deirmarmusa.org*

Born in 1954 in Rome, a very young activist in post 1968 leftist movement, a Jesuit by '75 and in the Near East by '77. PhD in theology of Islamic-Christian dialogue from the Gregorian Pontifical University of Rome. Still a student, in 1982, he came to pray in the ruins of Deir Mar Musa and by 84, he leads the restoration and formative youth activity. In 1991, the permanent new monastic community started.

PALAPATHWALA, RUWAN *www.trinity.unimelb.edu.au*

Lectures in the field of religion and culture at Trinity College, the University of Melbourne, and in Asian religions in the United Faculty of Theology of the Melbourne College of Divinity. He is the Director of the Centre for Social Inquiry, Religion and Interfaith Dialogue (Melbourne) and a priest in the Anglican Archdiocese of Melbourne.

PANGSIW, YVONNE GUMAYAT *www.iarf.net*

Member of IARF's Religious Freedom Youth Network. Her indigenous name is Balittaney. She was born in the mountainous area of Kalinga Province in the Philippines. She is dedicated to sharing and exploring the beauty of culture. Yvonne is a graduate of B.S. Nursing and willing to accept any challenging opportunities that offer new ideas for humankind.

PARTRIDGE, DAVID   www.ncpo.org.uk 
Anglican parish priest for 40 years. Since the sinking of the Belgrano battleship during the Falklands campaign he has been involved in the Peace Movement, co-chairing Clergy Against Nuclear Arms (CANA) and the Network for Christian Peace Organisations (NCPO). He now works in Oxford on interfaith matters, especially with Muslims, Christians and Jews.

PATEL, EBOO   www.ifyc.org 
Founder and Executive Director of Interfaith Youth Core. Ph.D in Sociology of Religion, Oxford University (Rhodes Scholarship.) Keynote speech, Nobel Peace Prize Forum and Baccalaureate Service Address, University of Pennsylvania. Co-editor, *Building the Interfaith Youth Movement* (Rowman and Littlefield Press). Ashoka Fellow, a network of social entrepreneurs with ideas that have potential to change the world.

PEARCE, BRIAN OBE   www.interfaith.org.uk 
Director of the Inter Faith Network for the UK since established in 1987 and helped over the previous two years in the process which led to this. Before this, in the civil service from 1959-86, including posts in the Department of Economic Affairs, Civil Service Department and HM Treasury. Born in Yorkshire in 1935 and married with four children.

PORTO, ANDRÉ   www.vivario.org.br   www.uri.org/americalatina   www.iser.org.br 
Social and interfaith activist; volunteer director of Rio Inter-Religious Movement (MIR); Latin American Coordinator of United Religions Initiative. Astrologer and photographer (http:/baudefotos.blogspot.com); main interests lie in spiritual citizenship and strategies to bridge social and spiritual movements. Andre is Brazilian, 35, married and lives in Rio de Janeiro. His spiritual path is service to Creation.

RAMBACHAN, ANANT   www.stolaf.edu 
Professor of religion and philosophy at Saint Olaf College in Minnesota; author of several books, book-chapters and articles in scholarly journals, including *The Limits of Scripture: Vivekananda's Reinterpretation of the Vedas, Accomplishing the Accomplished: The Vedas as a Source of Valid Knowledge in Shankara,* and *The Advaita Worldview: God, World and Humanity.*

REJMAN, TRAVIS   www.cpwr.org/what/programs/dginstitute.htm 
Director of the Goldin Institute for International Partnership and Peace based in Chicago, USA where he lives with his wife Gia and son Maxwell; Integral team leader for the Council for a Parliament of World Religions for many years.

RIDDELL, PETER   www.ukinitiativesofchange.org   www.bax.org.uk 
Member of Initiatives of Change in Agenda for Reconciliation team, creating contexts - meetings, conferences, training programmes - in which people on different sides of conflicts can meet each other in creative atmosphere and discover their 'next steps.' Secretary, British-Arab Exchanges, a charity arranging exchange visits between students and young professionals from Britain and Arab countries.

RIZK, PHILIP *www.frrme.org*

Born in Limassol, both German and Egyptian, grew up in Cairo, Egypt, studied in the USA and is currently Gaza Project Officer for Foundation for Relief and Reconciliation in the Middle East. Studied Philosophy and Theology and plans to continue studies in Middle Eastern and Islamic Studies with a vision to build bridges between the Arab world and the West, focusing on reconciliation, peace making and development.

SADA, MEHBOOB *www.pcusa.org/listening project*

Director of Christian Study Centre, Rawalpindi, Pakistan; many awards, including the Human Rights Gold Medal Award 2002-3; Board member of National Commission for Inter-Religious Dialogue and Ecumenism; editor of Urdu Section of *Al-Mushir* journal; Master's degrees in Education and Literature; teacher in education, harmony and dialogue.

SAROSH, JEHANGIR *www.religionsforpeace.net/Europe*

Zoroastrian. Married with three wonderful children and beautiful wife. President of WCRP-Europe; Founder and executive member of European Religious Leaders Council; member of Governing Board, WCRP-International; Executive Committee member of Inter Faith Network for UK. Chairman of international MRJ group of companies. Interests: Tennis, Riding, Philosophy, Travel, Carpentry and Gardening.

SAWAHATA, YASUTOMO *www.rk-world.org*

Representative of Rissho Kosei-kai Geneva. Graduated from RKK Seminary in 1993 as Dharma Teacher. Participant at many international events, including WCC World Assembly, Millennium World Peace Summit of Religious and Spiritual leaders, Day of Prayer for Peace, Assisi etc. Masters degree, peace and justice in religion, Earlham School of Religion.

SHIPTON, SIDNEY OBE *www.threefaithsforum.org.uk*

Born in London, a solicitor by profession; Co-ordinator of the Three Faiths Forum since its inception in January 1997. He served on the Board of Deputies of British Jews as well as the Executive of the Council of Christians and Jews. Member of the Royal Institute for International Affairs, the Medico-Legal Society, the Law Society, the British Academy of Forensic Sciences, and MENSA.

SHRESTHA, SATYATA *www.ifyc.org   www.hvpuk.org.uk*

19 year old student doing a Bachelors in Business Administration degree at Kathmandu College of Management. Loves travelling, exploring nature and reading inspirational books and autobiographies of famous celebrities. Besides studying, she is involved with the Youth Society of Peace and has been working in the social field for the past three years. Satyata enjoys this very much and would like to continue this.

SINGH, KARAN *www.karansingh.com*

Born heir-apparent to Maharaja, Jammu and Kashmir; Regent and Head of State at 18; elected Sadar-i-Riyasat and Governor. Held Cabinet portfolios of Tourism and Civil Aviation, Health and Family Planning, Education and Culture. Member of the Rajya Sabha. Previous Chair of Temple of Understanding. Author, lecturer, distinguished statesman.

SINGH, RANVIR
www.cranford.hounslow.sch.uk

Dr Ranvir Singh is Head of Religious Education and Citizenship Coordinator at Cranford Community College. Support by the Head Teacher for a range of initiatives provides opportunities for students to actively participate in interfaith and citizenship work.

SMYTH, ISABEL OBE
www.interfaithscotland.org

Associate Secretary, Inter Faith Relations to the Bishops Conference of Scotland; founding secretary, Scottish Inter Faith Council, becoming its first Chief Executive Officer; secretary, Churches Agency for Inter Faith Relations in Scotland; staff member, Centre for Inter Faith Studies at Glasgow University; was member, Inter Faith Network for UK Executive.

SOUZA, ANDREAS D'
www.hmiindia.com

Born in India. Director of Henry Martyn Institute International Center for Research, Interfaith Relations and Reconciliation in Conflict Resolution and Peace-Making. Studied Christian and Hindu theology, Arabic and Islam at Pontifical Institute of Islamic Studies and Arabic language in Tunis; Masters degree in Islam and Christian Muslim relations; PhD in Islamic modern thought from McGill University, Canada.

STALLYBRASS, ANDREW
www.caux.ch   *www.interreligieux.ch*

Member, Caux conference planning team for Initiatives of Change; independent writer and journalist; Managing Director of Caux Books; lay preacher of Geneva Reformed Church; church representative, Geneva Inter-Faith Platform, currently a Vice-President; post-graduate certificate of specialisation in theology, University of Geneva. Swiss wife, Eliane. Passions include reading, kite-flying, singing, and mountaineering.

STEINHELPER, DAN
www.ifyc.org

Intern, National Action Program of the Interfaith Youth Core; student at Divinity School and School of Social Service Administration, University of Chicago, in the dual degree masters program; endorsed candidate for ordination, Evangelical Lutheran Church in America; graduate of Wheaton College, Illinois; interest in faith development among young people.

STOLOV, YEHUDA
www.interfaith-encounter.org

Born in 1961 in Tel Aviv, now lives in Jerusalem and acts throughout the Holy Land. Studied for some six years in 'Merkaz Harav' Yeshiva and holds an M.Sc. in Physics and a Ph.D. in Jewish Thought, both from the Hebrew University of Jerusalem. He is married and father of three children and is the Executive Director of the Interfaith Encounter Association since it was founded in 2001.

STOREY, CELIA
www.interfaith-centre.org

Augmented parental role with cookery and gardening; interested in counterbalancing perception that Christianity is the only true religion. Friendship with Marcus Braybrooke provided the opportunity to assist with centenary events celebrating 1893 World's Parliament of Religions. Co-coordinator, then trustee, of International Interfaith Centre.

SUNDRAM, RAMOLA *www.iarf.net* 
Programme Coordinator for International Association for Religious Freedom. Her interest in interfaith began in her childhood in Singapore, where she had friends from many faith traditions. A former teacher, she particularly enjoys working with young adults and has helped set up the Religious Freedom Young Adult Network.

SYED, SHAHZAD *www.jibnet.org* 
First Pakistani Muslim journalist to initiate work on interfaith dialogue and intercultural harmony. Master of Arts in Journalism and Islamic Studies and History; owner/editor of *Sunehra Daur* (Golden Age) magazine; Chair of the Journalists Information Bureau (JIB) Pakistan, an NGO working for media development, interfaith harmony, education and awareness.

TABICK, JACKIE *www.worldfaiths.org* 
Rabbi of North West Surrey Synagogue in Weybridge and a Vice-President of the Movement for Reform Judaism. She is chair of the World Congress of Faiths, a member of the Inter Faith Network UK Executive and a patron of the Jewish Council for Racial Equality. She is married to Larry, who is also a rabbi and they have three children.

TALIB, MOHAMMAD *www.oxcis.ac.uk* 
Fellow in Anthropology of Muslim Societies at the Oxford Centre for Islamic Studies and at the Institute of Social and Cultural Anthropology, University of Oxford. He is also a leading member of the Oxford Round Table of Religions.

TAYLOR JOHN *www.iarf.net* 
Studied and taught Islamics at Cambridge, Punjab, McGill, Harvard, and Birmingham Universities. After 10 years with the World Council of Churches Dialogue programme, 10 years as Secretary General of WCRP International and 6 years with the Conference of European Churches, he now serves as UN (Geneva) representative of the International Association for Religious Freedom.

THORESEN, BRITT STRANDLIE *www.trooglivssyn.no   www.hlsenteret.no   www.oslocoalition.org* 
Teacher for 10 years; Secretary General of the Bahá'í community, Norway; Member of the National Spiritual Assembly of the Bahá'ís of Norway; member of the Cooperation Council of the Religious Minorities and Life-Stance Communities; member of the Oslo Coalition; board member of the Center of Studies of Holocaust and Religious Minorities of Norway. Britt is married to Lasse Thoresen, a composer and professor of composition.

TRAER, ROBERT *www.christianbible.com* 
1990-2000, General Secretary of International Association for Religious Freedom; 1993-2000, Trustee of International Interfaith Centre. Lecturer in ethics and scripture at Dominican University, California. Author: *Faith in Human Rights: Support in Religious Traditions for a Global Struggle* (1991), *Quest for Truth: Critical Reflections on Interfaith Cooperation* (1999), *Faith, Belief, and Religion* (1999), and *Jerusalem Journal: Finding Hope* (2006).

TRAFFORD, PAUL   www.chezpaul.org.uk   www.dhammakaya.or.th

Born in 1968 to Anthony and Fuengsin Trafford; lived in the UK all his life; formally brought up by English father as Roman Catholic, he also received Buddhist transmission from Thai mother, who trained in the Dhammakaya tradition at Wat Paknam, Bangkok. Paul has followed his mother by engaging in various interfaith activities whilst also pursuing Buddhist practice. Currently a Director of Dhammakaya International Society of UK.

TUCKER, EVA   www.northlondoninterfaith.org.uk

Writer. Her third novel *Berlin Mosaic* (Starhaven) was published in 2005. She is co-editor of *Patterns and Examples* (Sessions 2005), an anthology of essays by Quakers who have experienced the spirit of other faiths. For many years she ran the Hampstead Interfaith Group in her home.

TYNDALE, WENDY   www.wfdd.org

Human rights and development practitioner and campaigner with solidarity groups, as free-lance journalist and with non-governmental development agency. Experience largely in Latin America until joined World Faiths Development Dialogue and began working with people from many different religious traditions in Africa and Asia as well. Author: *Visions of Development: Faith-based Initiatives* (Ashgate 2006).

UCKO, HANS   www.wcc-coe.org

Born in 1946 in Sweden, studied in France, Sweden, Israel, and India; Ordained minister of the Church of Sweden; PhD from the Senate of Serampore, India; since 1989 the Program Executive in the Office on Interreligious Relations and Dialogue of the World Council of Churches, Geneva, Switzerland; editor of the WCC publication *Current Dialogue*.

VAN DYK, ALISON   www.templeofunderstanding.org

BA, Sarah Lawrence College; dual Masters Degree, Transpersonal Counseling and Clinical Psychotherapy Counseling; Director of St. Luke's School Early Child Education Program in South Bronx; Chair and Executive Director of Temple of Understanding; Board member: Hartley Film Foundation, Auburn Media, Child Development Institute at Sarah Lawrence College, & Albertson Memorial Church in Old Greenwich, CT.

WALKER, BRIAN   www.religionsforpeace.org.uk

Diocesan/Deanery Synod member, Church of England; Chair of Religions for Peace (UK); trustee of Religions for Peace (Europe); executive member, World Congress of Faiths; doctoral research in transformative inter faith dialogue in UK and Sierra Leone; consultant for European Commission, helping secure funds to rebuild Sierra Leone's infrastructure; coordinator of Hope and Homes for Children. Married with 4 children and 6 grandchildren.

WEINER, MATTHEW   www.interfaithcenter.org

Program Director of the Interfaith Center of New York. Before working with the center he worked for the Global Forum and for Sarvodaya Shramadana, a Sri Lankan Buddhist organization. He is the author of *Stories for Peace*, a graduate of Harvard Divinity School and is currently working on his PhD at Union Theological Seminary.

WHITE, ANDREW *www.frrme.org www.naamantrust.org* 
Chief Executive Officer and President of the Foundation for Relief and Reconciliation in the Middle East, International Director of the Iraqi Institute of Peace, Anglican Priest in Iraq and International Director of the Israeli and Palestinian Institute of Peace.

WILLARD, MONICA BURKE *www.uri.org www.internationaldayofpeace.org* 
Represents the United Religions Initiative at the United Nations and serves as co-chair for the International Day of Peace NGO Committee at the UN. She is one of the founding members of the Tripartite Forum on Interfaith Cooperation for Peace, a partnership of governments, concerned United Nations agencies, and Non-Governmental organizations. She is married to David and they have three grown children.

WILLIAMS DIANE *www.csvgc-ny.org* 
Chairperson Emeritus, NGO Committee on Spirituality, Values and Global Concerns at the United Nations (NY), Council Member Spiritual Caucus and the United Religions Inititative-UN. UN Representative for the Tribal Link Foundation and the International Association of Educators for World Peace.

YAO, XINZHONG *www.lamp.ac.uk* 
Professor of Religion and Ethics at University of Wales, Lampeter where he has been teaching courses on religions and philosophy since 1991. His English publications include *Confucianism and Christianity* (Sussex Academic Press, 1996), *Encyclopedia of Confucianism* (Routledge, 2003), *An Introduction to Confucianism* (CUP, 2000) and *Wisdom in Early Confucian and Israelite Traditions* (Ashgate, 2006).

YOGI, MINAKSHI *www.ifyc.org www.hvpuk.org.uk* 
18 years old, 2nd year Intermediate Level student, member of the Youth Society for Peace in Nepal. Runs the YSP programme in Dang (about 12 hours from Kathmandu). Interested in dance and reading about the history of Nepal; loves to visit beautiful places, sometimes collects stamps, likes to help youth to do and appreciate good works. She thinks that young people can bring about a true change in society.

YOUSSUF, MUSSARRAT BASHIR 
Student of Tasawwuf (Sufism), living in Islamabad. Professionally, working in development sector for last ten years. Currently a free-lance consultant mainly with World Bank, UN agencies and international organizations. Has been Visiting Fellow at Queen Elizabeth House, University of Oxford, working on subjects related to Sufism. M. Phil and two Masters degrees in social sciences from Pakistan and Austria.

INTERFAITH

Norman Solomon

Helen Fry

Zerbanoo Gifford

Charles Brock

Caca Jacupe

Nancy Traer

Jeremy Braybrooke

Sheila Wilson

Ossama el-Kaffash

Hal French

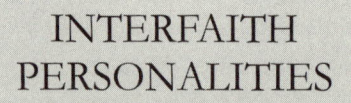

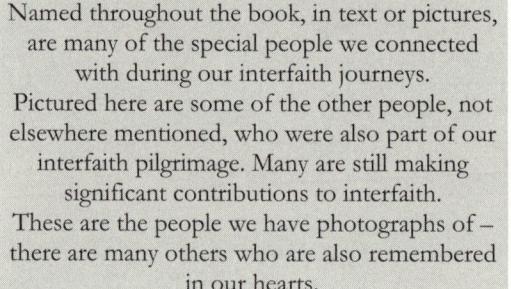

Ursula King

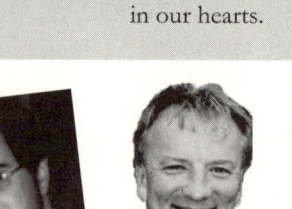

INTERFAITH PERSONALITIES

Named throughout the book, in text or pictures, are many of the special people we connected with during our interfaith journeys.
Pictured here are some of the other people, not elsewhere mentioned, who were also part of our interfaith pilgrimage. Many are still making significant contributions to interfaith.
These are the people we have photographs of – there are many others who are also remembered in our hearts.

Penelope Johnstone

Marianne Rankin

Charles Gibbs

Matthew Smith

Vincent Harvey

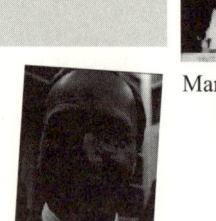

Neville Hodgkinson

David Cheetham

Carmel Heaney

Bhupinder Singh

Jim and Cetta Kenney

Mathoor Krishnamurti

GALLERY

Charanjit Singh    Ajit Singh    Shanti Hettarachia    Keith Ward    Mohinder Singh

Jacques Goulet

Miraj ul-Islam Zia

Michael Taylor

Bill Vendley

Varsana Devidasi

What on earth ......?!

Marshi Anne, Kos Mick and Farre Owt arrive for interfaith encounters of the 3rd kind!

Gwyneth Little

Swami Nirliptananda    Geoffrey Stewart-Smith    Peggy Morgan    Michael Pye    Bruce Gregersen

Yehezkal Landau    Ramesh Kallidae    Jean Potter    Richard Harries    Swami Dayatmananda

FAITH AND INTERFAITH RESOURCES

A sample of organisations, books and journals related to this book.

ORGANISATIONS

ALISTER HARDY/RELIGIOUS EXPERIENCE RESEARCH CENTRE, Department of Theology and Religious Studies, University of Wales Lampeter, Ceredigion SA48 7ED, Wales. www.alisterhardyreligiousexperience.co.uk

ANTI-SLAVERY INTERNATIONAL, Thomas Clarkson House, The Stableyard, Broomgrove Road, London, SW9 9TL UK. www.antislavery.org

AMNESTY INTERFAITH NETWORK, 53 West Jackson, Suite #731, Chicago, IL 60604, USA. www.amnestyusa.org

ASHA FOUNDATION www.asha-foundation.org

ASHMOLEAN INTER-FAITH EXHIBITIONS SERVICE, Beaumont Street, Oxford OX1 2PH, UK. www.aifes.org

BAHAI'S WORLD CENTRE, Akka and Haifa, Israel. www.bahai.org

BBC RELIGION AND ETHICS www.bbc.co.uk/religion/

BELIEF NET www.beliefnet.com

BRAHMA KUMARIS WORLD SPIRITUAL UNIVERSITY, Global Co-operation House, 65-69 Pound Lane, London NW10 2HH, UK. www.bkwsu.org.uk

BRAHMA KUMARIS GLOBAL HOSPITAL & RESEARCH CENTRE, Delwara Road, Mount Abu 307501, Rajesthan, India. www.bkwsu.org

BRITISH MUSEUM - INTERFAITH TRAIL - www.thebritishmuseum.ac.uk

CENTRE FOR CHRISTIANITY AND INTERRELIGIOUS DIALOGUE, Heythrop College, Kensington Square, London W8 5HQ, UK. www.heythrop.ac.uk/CCID

CENTRE FOR SOCIAL INQUIRY, RELIGION AND INTERFAITH DIALOGUE, Trinity College, Royal Parade, Parkville, Victoria 3052, Australia. www.trinity.unimelb.edu.au

CHICAGO ZEN CENTRE, 2029 Ridge Ave, Evanston, IL 60201, USA. www.chicagozen.com

CHILDREN OF ABRAHAM FOUNDATION, Burevägen 18, S-182 63 Djursholm, Sweden. www.abrahamsbarn.org

CO-NEXUS PRESS, Pobox 39218 Solon, Ohio 44139, USA. www.conexuspress.com

COUNCIL FOR RELIGIOUS AND LIFE STANCE COMMUNITIES, Rådhusgt. 1-3, 0151 Oslo, Norway. www.trooglivssyn.no

COUNCIL OF CHRISTIANS AND JEWS UK, 1st Floor, Camelford House, 89 Albert Embankment, London SE1 7TP, UK. www.ccj.org.uk

COUNCIL FOR A PARLIAMENT OF THE WORLD RELIGIONS / GOLDIN INSTITUTE 70 E. Lake Street, Suite 205, Chicago, IL 60601, USA. www.cpwr.org

CRANFORD COMMUNITY COLLEGE, High Street, Cranford, Middlesex, TW5 9PD, UK www.cranford.hounslow.sch.uk

DALAI LAMA, The Office of His Holiness the Dalai Lama, Thekchen Choeling P.O. McLeod Ganj, Dharamsala H.P. 176219 India. www.dalailama.com

DEIR MAR MUSA AL-HABASHI, P.O. Box 178, Nebek, Syrian Arab Republic. www.deirmarmusa.org

DHAMMAKAYA FOUNDATION UK, Wat Phra Dhammakaya, 1-2 Brushfield Way, Knaphill, Woking, GU21 2TG, UK. *International*: www.dhammakaya.or.th

DIVERSITY AND DIALOGUE www.diversityandialogue.org.uk www.savethechildren.org.uk

DOUAI ABBEY, Upper Woolhampton, Reading, Berkshire, RG7 5TQ, UK. www.douaiabbey.org.uk

DOVETAIL INSTITUTE FOR INTERFAITH FAMILY RESOURCES, 775 Simon Greenwell Lane, Boston, KY 40107, USA. www.dovetailinstitute.org

DUTCH INTERFAITH NETWORK www.interreligieus.nl

ELIJAH INTERFAITH INSTITUTE, 10 Caspi Street, Jerusalem, Israel 93554. www.elijah.org.il

FATEH (Fellowship of Activists to Embrace Humanity), Shahpur Gurdawara, 2nd Floor, Dispensary Building, Sector 38B, Chandigarh, UT Punjab. www.fatehworld.org

FOUNDATION FOR HUMAN RIGHTS, 8th Floor Prodinsa Building, 501 Pretorius Street Arcadia, Pretoria 0083, South Africa. www.fhr.org.za

FOUNDATION FOR RELIEF AND RECONCILIATION IN THE MIDDLE EAST, London House, 100 New Kings Road, London SW6 4LX, UK www.frrme.org

GANDHI, MAHATMA www.mkgandhi.org www.gandhiinstitute.org

GENERAL ASSEMBLY OF UNITARIAN AND FREE CHRISTIAN CHURCHES, Essex Hall, 1-6 Essex Street, London WC2R 3HY,UK. www.unitarian.org.uk

GIVAT HAVIVA, Mobile Post, Menashe 37850, Israel. www.givathaviva.org.il

GLOBAL AIDS INTERFAITH ALLIANCE, The Presidio of San Francisco, PO Box 29110, San Francisco, CA 94129-0110, USA. www.thegaia.org

GLOBALISATION FOR THE COMMON GOOD www.commongood.info

GLOBAL PEACE INITIATIVE OF WOMEN, 301 East 57 Street, 3rd Floor, New York, NY 10022, USA. www.gpiw.org

GLOBAL PEACE WORKS, PO Box 316, Yorktown Heights, NY 10598, USA. www.globalpeaceworks.org

GLOBAL TOLERANCE, 123 Whitecross Street, London, EC1Y 8JJ, UK. www.globaltolerance.com www.faithandfood.com www.adamandeveit.net

GOBIND SADAN INSTITUTE FOR ADVANCED STUDIES IN COMPARATIVE RELIGION, Gadaipur, Mehrauli-Mandi Road, New Delhi-110030, India www.gobindsadan.org

HABITAT FOR HUMANITY EUROPE, Karoly krt. 3A femelet I., 1075 Budapest, Hungary. www.habitateurope.org

HARTFORD SEMINARY, 77 Sherman Street, Hartford, CT 06105-2260, USA. www.hartsem.edu

HENRY MARTYN INSTITUTE, P.O. Box 153, Chirag Ali Lane, Hyderabad-500 001 (A.P.), India. www.hmiindia.com

HINDU VIDYAPEETH, PO Box 6807, Balkumari, Lalitpur, Nepal. www.hvpuk.org.uk

HOLY ISLAND PROJECT, Lamlash P.O, Lamlash, Isle of Arran KA27 8GB, Scotland. www.holyisland.org

HOPE FLOWERS SCHOOL, PO Box 732, Bethlehem, Palestine. www.hope-flowers.org

HUSTON SMITH www.hustonsmith.net

IAN RAMSEY CENTRE, 11 Bevington Road, Oxford OX2 6NB, UK http://users.ox.ac.uk

INITIATIVES OF CHANGE INTERNATIONAL/UK www.iofc.org www.uk.iofc.org

INFORM (Information Network Focus on Religious Movements), Houghton Street, London WC2A 2AE, UK. www.inform.ac

INSTITUTE FOR INTER-RELIGIOUS DIALOGUE, 38 Tahery St., Valieasr Ave. Tehran, PO Box: 15875/5934, Iran. www.iid.org.ir

INTERFAITH ALLIANCE: 1331 H Street, NW, 11th Floor, Washington, DC 20005, USA. www.interfaithalliance.org

INTERFAITH CALENDAR   www.interfaithcalendar.org

INTERFAITH CENTER OF NEW YORK, 20 East 79th Street, New York, NY 10021, USA. www.interfaithcenter.org

INTERFAITH CO-ORDINATING COUNCIL OF ISRAEL, ICCI, Pobox 8771, Jerusalem, 91086, Israel. www.icci.co.il

INTERFAITH ENCOUNTER ASSOCIATION, P.O. Box 3814, Jerusalem 91037, Israel. www.interfaith-encounter.org

INTERFAITH LISTENING PROJECT, 100 Witherspoon Str, Louisville, KY 40202, USA. www.pcusa.org/listeningproject/teams.htm

INTER FAITH NETWORK FOR THE UK, 8A Lower Grosvenor Place, London SW1W 0EN, UK. www.interfaith.org.uk

INTERFAITH YOUTH CORE, 1111 N. Wells, Ste. 501, Chicago, IL 60610, USA. www.ifyc.org

INTERNATIONAL ASSOCIATION FOR RELIGIOUS FREEDOM, 2 Market Street, Oxford OX1 3EF, UK. www.iarf.net

INTERNATIONAL CENTRE FOR DIALOGUE AMONG CIVILIZATIONS, 91 Lavasani (Farmanieh) St, Tehran 19375, Iran. www.dialoguecentre.org

INTERNATIONAL COMMITTEE FOR THE PEACE COUNCIL, 2702 International Lane, Suite 108, Madison, Wisconsin 53704 USA. www.peacecouncil.org

INTERNATIONAL COUNCIL FOR CHRISTIANS AND JEWS, Martin Buber House, P.O. Box 11 29, D-64629 Heppenheim, Germany. www.iccj.org

INTERNATIONAL DAY OF PEACE, PO Box 340, Roosevelt, NJ 08555-0340, USA. www.internationaldayofpeace.org

INTERNATIONAL INTERFAITH CENTRE, 2 Market Street, Oxford, OX1 3EF, UK. www.interfaith-centre.org and www.interfaithstudies.org

INTERNATIONAL ISLAMIC FORUM FOR DIALOGUE, P.O. Box 34128, Jeddah 21468, Saudi Arabia. www.dialogueonline.org

INTERNATIONAL MOVEMENT FOR A JUST WORLD, P.O. Box 288, 46730 Petaling Jaya, Selangor, Malaysia. www.just-international.org

INTERNATIONAL SOCIETY FOR KRISHNA CONSCIOUSNESS www.iskcon.org

INTERELIGIÖSE ARBEITSSTELLE / INSTITUTE FOR INTERRELIGIOUS STUDIES, Am Hardtkopf 17, D-58769 Nachrodt-Wiblingwerde (POBox 1201), Germany. www.interrel.de

INTERRELIGIOUS ENGAGMENT PROJECT, 980 Verda Lane, Lake Forest, IL 60045, USA. www.iep21.org

IRISH SCHOOL OF ECUMENICS, Trinity College Dublin, Bea House, Milltown Park, Dublin 6, Ireland. www.tcd.ie/ise

JERUSALEM PEACEMAKERS, Pobox 31894, Jerusalem 91316, Israel. www.jerusalempeacemakers.org

JOURNALIST INFORMATION BUREAU Pakistan. www.jibnet.org

JORDAN YOUTH http://jordanyouth.org/english/#

LAMPETER, UNIVERSITY OF WALES, Ceredigion, Wales, SA48 7ED. www.lamp.ac.uk

LEICESTER COUNCIL OF FAITHS, Pilgrim House, 10 Bishop St, Leicester LE1 6AF, UK. www.leicestercounciloffaiths.org.uk

LEWIS, KAROKI, London/Delhi www.karokilewis.com

LONDON INTERFAITH CENTRE, 125 Salusbury Road, London NW6 6RG, UK. www.londoninterfaith.org.uk

MAIMONIDES FOUNDATION, Nour House, 6 Hill Street, London W1J 5NF, UK. www.maimonides-foundation.org

MALAYSIAN INTERFAITH NETWORK www.malaysianinterfaithnetwork.net

METHODIST CHURCH GREAT BRITAIN, INTER FAITH OFFICE, Methodist Church House, 25 Marylebone Road London NW1 5JR, UK. www.methodist.org.uk

MIDDLE WAY, Israel www.middleway.org

MINORITIES OF EUROPE, Legacy House, 29 Walsgrave Road, Coventry CV2 4H, UK. www.moe-online.com

MONASTIC INTERRELIGIOUS DIALOGUE, St. John's Abbey, Collegeville, MN 56321, USA. www.monasticdialog.com

MULTI-FAITH CENTRE, The University of Derby, Kedleston Road, Derby DE22 1GB, UK www.multifaithnet.org

MUSLIM/CHRISTIAN MARRIAGE SUPPORT GROUP www.mcmarriage.org.uk

NATIONAL SPIRITUAL ASSEMBLY OF THE BAHA'IS UK, 27 Rutland Gate, London SW7 1PD, UK. www.bahai.org.uk

NELSON MANDELA FOUNDATION, Nelson Mandela House, 107 Central Ave, Houghton 2041, South Africa. www.nelsonmandela.org

NEVE SHALOM-WAHAT AL-SALAM, Doar Na Shimshon 99761, Israel www.nswas.com

NGO COMMITTEE ON SPIRITUALITY, VALUES AND GLOBAL CONCERNS AT THE UNITED NATIONS ww.csvgc-ny.org

NORTH AMERICAN INTERFAITH NETWORK www.nain.org

NORTH LONDON INTERFAITH GROUP c/o Hampstead Friends Meeting House,,120 Heath Street, Hampstead, LondonmNW3 1DR, UK. www.northlondoninterfaith.org.uk

NORTHERN IRELAND INTER-FAITH FORUM, 37 Church Street, Warrenpoint, Co Down BT34 3HN, N-Ireland.

OPEN HOUSE, PO Box 26187, Jerusalem 91261, Israel. www.openhouse.org.il

OSLO COALITION ON FREEDOM OF RELIGION OR BELIEF, Universitetsgt. 22-24, No-0162 Oslo, Norway. www.oslocoalition.org

OXFORD CENTRE FOR BUDDHIST STUDIES www.ocbs.org

OXFORD CENTRE FOR HEBREW AND JEWISH STUDIES, Yarnton Manor, Yarnton, Oxford, OX5 1PY, UK. http://users.ox.ac.uk/~ochjs/

OXFORD CENTRE FOR HINDU STUDIES, 15 Magdalen Street, Oxford, OX1 3AE, UK. www.ochs.org.uk

OXFORD CENTRE FOR ISLAMIC STUDIES, George Street, Oxford, OX1 2AR, UK. www.oxcis.ac.uk

PLAT-FORME INTERRELIGIOSE DE GENÈVE, Case postale 3, CH-1211 Genève 20, Switzerland. www.interreligieux.ch

PLURALISM PROJECT, 1531 Cambridge St, Cambridge, MA 02139, USA. www.pluralism.org

PONTIFICAL COUNCIL FOR INTERRELIGIOUS DIALOGUE, 00193 Roma, Via dell'Erba, 1, Italy. www.vatican.va/roman_curia/pontifical_councils/interelg

PROJECT TOWARDS THE CREATION OF A SPIRITUAL FORUM FOR WORLD PEACE AT THE UNITED NATIONS, Via Verde 9440 (Lo Curro), Vitacura, Santiago, Chile.

RABBIS FOR HUMAN RIGHTS, Rehov Harekhavim 9, Jerusalem, Israel 93462. www.rhr.israel.net

RAMAKRISHNA MISSION HQ, PO Box Belur Math 711 202, District Howrah, West Bengal, India. www.ramakrishna.org

RELIGIONS FOR PEACE UK, Hope Cottage, Micheldever, Winchester, SO21 3DG, UK. www.religionsforpeace.org.uk

RELIGIONS FOR PEACE, EUROPE, 18/20 Vale Road, Bushey WD23 2HE, UK. www.religionsforpeace.net/Europe

RISSHO KOSEI-KAI, 2-11-1 Wada, Suginami-ku Tokyo 166-8537, Japan www.rk-world.org

RMIT UNIVERSITY, GPO Box 2476V, Melbourne, Victoria, 3001, Australia. www.rmit.edu.au

ROYAL INSTITUTE FOR INTER FAITH STUDIES, PO Box 830562, Amman 11183, Jordan. www.riifs.org

SARVODAYA SHRAMADANA SANGAMAYA, No 98, Rawatawatta Road, Moratuwa, Sri Lanka. www.sarvodaya.org

SCARBORO MISSIONS, 2685 Kingston Rd., Scarborough, ON, Canada M1M 1M4. www.scarboromissions.ca

SCOTTISH INTER FAITH COUNCI, 523 Shields Road, Glasgow, G41 2RF, Scotland. www.interfaithscotland.org

SELF REALIZATION FELLOWSHIP, 3880 San Rafael Ave, Los Angeles, CA 90065-3298, USA. www.yogananda-srf.org

SENTER FOR STUDIER AV HOLOCAUST OG LIVSSYNSMINORITETER, Villa Grande, Huk Aveny 56, Pboks 1168, Blindern 0318, Oslo, Norway. www.hlsenteret.no

SHUMEI TAIKO ENSEMBLE, 2 Shinen, Shigaraki-cho, Koga-gun, Shiga Japan. www.shumeitaiko.org

SOUTH AFRICAN COUNCIL OF CHURCHES, PO Box 62098, Marshalltown 2107, South Africa. www.sacc.org.za

SPIRITUALITY FOR DAILY LIFE www.spiritualityfordailylife.com

St Ethelburga's Centre for Reconciliation and Peace, 78 Bishopsgate, London EC2N 4AG, UK. www.stethelburgas.org

St Olaf College, 1520 St Olaf Avenue, Northfield, MN 55057, USA. www.stolaf.edu

Stiftung Weltethos (Global Ethic Foundation), Waldhauser Strasse 23, D-72076, Germany. www.weltethos.org

Swami Agnivesh, 7 Jantar Mantar Road, New Delhi-110 001, India. www.swamiagnivesh.com

Taking It global www.takingitglobal.org

Temple of Understanding, 211 East 43rd Street, Suite 1600, New York, NY 10017, USA. www.templeofunderstanding.org

The Festival Shop Ltd, 56 Poplar Road, Kings Heath, Birmingham B14 7AG, UK. www.festivalshop.co.uk

Three Faiths Forum, The Sternberg Centre, 80 East End Road, London N3 2SY, UK. www.threefaithsforum.org.uk

Tibet Government in Exile www.tibet.com

Trinity College Theolgical school, University of Melbourne, Australia. www.trinity.unimelb.edu.au/theologicalschool/

Tsubaki Grand Shrine of America, 17720 Crooked Mile Rd. Granite Falls, Washington 98252, USA. www.tsubakishrine.com

Tsubaki grand shrine of Japan, 1871 Yamamoto Suzuka - Mie, Japan. www.tsubakishrine.com

unesco Association for Interreligious Dialogue, Mallorca, 285, 08037 Barcelona, Spain. www.audir.org

Unicef HQ, Unicef House, 3 United Nations Plaza, New York, NY 10017, USA. www.unicef.org

Unitarian universalist association, 25 Beacon Street, Boston, MA 0208, USA. www.uua.org

United nations HQ, United Nations Secretariat, New York, NY 10017, USA. www.un.org

United Religions Initiative, P.O. Box 29242, San Francisco, CA 94129, USA. www.uri.org

University of Montreal Theology Faculty, 3333, chemin Queen-Mary, Montréal (Québec) H3V 1A2, Canada. www.theo.umontreal.ca

Viva Rio, Rua do Russel, 76-Glória, CEP: 222210-010, Rio de Janeiro, Brazil. www.vivario.org.br

Vivekananda Centre London, 6 Lea Gardens, Wembley, Middlesex HA9 7SE, UK. www.vivekananda.co.uk

Westminster Interfaith Centre, 23 Kensington Square, London W8 5HN, UK www.westminster-interfaith.org.uk

World Conference on Religion and Peace, 777 United Nations Plaza, New York 10017, USA. www.wcrp.org

World Conference on Religion and Peace-South Africa, P. O. Box 93642, Yeoville 0008, Johannesburg, South Africa; Durban University of Technology Room M2 - 18 - 2nd Floor - Block A M. L. Sultan Campus, Durban, South Africa.

WORLD CONGRESS OF FAITHS, London Inter Faith Centre, 125 Salusbury Rd, London NW6 6RG, UK. www.worldfaiths.org

WORLD COUNCIL OF CHURCHES, Interreligious Relations Team, 150 route de Ferney, P.O. Box 2100, 1211 Geneva 2, Switzerland. www.wcc-coe.org

WORLD COUNCIL OF RELIGIOUS LEADERS, Empire State Building, 350 Fifth Avenue, Suite 5403, New York, NY 10118, USA. www.millenniumpeacesummit.com

WORLD FAITHS DEVELOPMENT DIALOGUE, c/o The International Study Centre, The Precincts, Canterbury, Kent CT1 2EH, UK. www.wfdd.org.uk

WORLD FELLOWSHIP OF INTERRELIGIOUS COUNCILS, Upasana, Thodupuzha-685584, Kerala, India.

WORLD INTERFAITH CONGRESS http://interfaithcongress.org

WORLD PEACE PRAYER SOCIETY, The World Peace Sanctuary, 26 Benton Road, Wassaic, NY 12592 USA. www.worldpeace.org

WORLD ZOROASTRIAN ORGANIZATION HQ, 135 Tennison Road, South Norwood, London SE25 5NF, UK. www.w-z-o.org

YOUNG JAINS www.youngjains.org.uk

YOUTH SOCIETY FOR PEACE, Katmandu, Nepal. *UK Support group*: www.hvpuk.org.uk

BOOKS

ALEAZ, K P: *Harmony of Religions, The Relevance of Swami Vivekananda;* Punthi-Pustak, Calcutta 1993

BARNEY, G O: *Threshold 2000: Critical Issues and Spiritual Values*; Conexus Press, Grand Rapids, 2000

BEVERSLUIS, JOEL: *A Sourcebook for the Community of Religions*; The Council for a Parliament of the World's Religions, Chicago, 1993

BHARAT, SANDY: *Christ Across the Ganges: Hindu Responses to Jesus,* O-Books, UK, 2007

BHARAT, SANDY and JAEL (eds/compiled by): *Touched by Truth: A Contemporary Hindu Anthology*; Sessions, 2006

BHARAT, JAEL and SANDY: *Mapping the Cosmos, An Introduction to God;* Sessions, 2006

BLEI, KAREL: *Freedom of Religion and Belief: Europe's History;* Van Gorcum, 2002

BOWKER, JOHN: *The Oxford Dictionary of World Religions*; Oxford University Press, Oxford, 1997

BRAYBROKE, MARCUS: *Pilgrimage of Hope, One Hundred Years of Global Interfaith Dialogue;* SCM Press, London 1992

BRAYBROOKE, MARCUS: *Faith and Interfaith in a Global Age*; Conexus Press, Grand Rapids, 1998

BRAYBROOKE, MARCUS: *A Wider Vision, A History of the World Congress of Faiths*; Oneworld Publications, Oxford, 1996

BRAYBROOKE, MARCUS: *A Heart for the World*; O-Books, 2006

BRAYBROOKE, MARCUS and BAYFIELD, TONY: *Dialogue with a Difference*; SCM, 1992

BRAYBROOKE, MARCUS and MOFID, KAMRAN: *Promoting the Common Good: Bringing economics and theology together again, A theologian and an economist in dialogue*; Shepheard-Walwyn Publishers, London, 2005

BROWN, STUART, compiled by: *Meeting in Faith, Twenty Years of Christian-Muslim Conversations;* World Council of Churches, Geneva, 1989

CANTWELL-SMITH, WILFRED: *Towards A World Theology*; Orbis, 1990

COLES, ROBERT, ed: *Spiritual Innovators;* Skylights Paths Publishing, Woodstock, 2002

COWARD, HAROLD: *Hindu-Christian Dialogue, Perspectives and Encounters;* Orbis Books, New York, 1989

COWARD, HAROLD G: *Modern Indian Responses to Religious Pluralism;* State University of New York Press, 1987

COHN-SHERBOK, DAN, ed: *Interfaith Theology, A Reader;* Oneworld Publications, Oxford, 2001

CUPITT, DON: *Sea of Faith;* SCM, 2003

DALAI LAMA: *The Mystic Heart: Discovering a Universal Spirituality in the World's Religions;* New World Library, 2003

ECK, DIANA L & JAIN, DEVAKI, eds: *Speaking of Faith, Cross-cultural Perspectives on Women, Religion and Social Change;* Hazell Watson & Viney Limited, Aylesbury, 1986

ESACK, FARID: *On Being a Muslim;* Oneworld, 2002

FISHER, MARY PAT: *Living Religions;* Prentice Hall, 2002

FRY, HELEN P, compiled/ed: *Christian-Jewish Dialogue, A Reader;* University of Exeter Press, 1996

FRY, HELEN et al: *Women's Voices: New Perspectives for the Christian-Jewish Dialogue;* SCM, 2005

GRIMES, JOHN: *Problems and Perspectives in Religious Discourse, Advaita Vedanta Implications;* State University of New York Press, 1994

HARRIS, ELIZABETH J: *Theravada Buddhism and the British Encounter;* Routledge, 2006

HASSAN, PRINCE: *Islam and Global Dialogue: Religious Pluralism and the Pursuit of Peace;* Ashgate, 2005

HICK, JOHN: *God and the Universe of Faiths;* Oneworld, 1993

HICK, JOHN: *An Interpretation of Religion;* Palgrave, 2004

HICK, JOHN: *Death and Eternal Life;* Palgrave, 1985

HUSSAIN, ASAF: *Political Perspectives on the Muslim World;* Palgrave McMillan, 1984

INTER FAITH ORGANISATIONS IN THE UK: A DIRECTORY, Inter Faith Network for the UK, 2006

KLAES, NORBERT: *Conscience and Consciousness: Ethical Problems of Mahabharata;* Dharmaram College, 1985

KNITTER, PAUL: *One Earth, Many Religions: Multi-Faith Dialogue and Global Responsibility;* Orbis, 1995

KNITTER, PAUL and MUZAFFAR, CHANDRA, eds: *Subverting Greed: Religious Perspectives on the Global Economy;* Orbis, 2003

KÜNG, HANS: *Global Responsibility, In Search of a New World Ethic;* SCM, London, 1991

KÜNG, HANS: *Yes to a Global Ethic;* SMC Press, London, 1996

LAKHANI, SEETHA (LAKHANI, JAY, ed): *Hinduism for Schools*: Vivekananda Centre London, 2005

LESHER, A JEAN, ed: *Pathways to Peace: Interreligious Readings and Reflections,* Cowley, 2005

LEWIS, KAROKI: *Mehrauli: A View from the Qutb;* Harper Collins, 2002

MACOMB, SUSANNA STEFANACHI: *Joining Hands and Hearts: Interfaith, Intercultural Wedding Celebrations: A Practical Guide for Couples;* Atria Books, 2003

MARKHAM, IAN S, ed: *A World Religions Reader;* Blackwell Publisher, Oxford, 1996

MARKHAM, IAN S and OZDEMIR, IBRAHIM, eds: *Globalization, Ethics, and Islam;* Ashgate 2005

MARSHALL, VERNON: *The Large View;* Lindsey Press, 2006

MAY, JOHN D'ARCY: *Transcendence and Violence: The Encounter of Buddhist, Christian and Primal Traditions;* Continuum, 2003

MITCHELL, ADRIAN: *The Shadow Knows: Poems 2000-2004;* Bloodaxe Books, 2004

MITCHELL, DONALD: *Spirituality and Emptiness, The Dynamics of Spiritual Life in Buddhism and Christianity;* Paulist Press, New York 1991

MOFID, KAMRAN: *Globalisation for the Common Good;* Shepheard-Walwyn, 2002

MUZAFFAR, CHANDRA: *Rights, Religion and Reform: Enhancing Human Dignity Through Spiritual and Moral Transformation;* Routledge Curzon, 2002

NAMBIAPARAMBIL, ALBERT: *Pilgrims on the Seashore of Endless Worlds, Experiences in Interfaith Dialogue;* Asian Trading Cooperation, Bangalore, 2005

NASR, SEYYED HOSSEIN: *Religion and the Order of Nature;* OUP, 1996

O'NEILL, MAURA: *Women Speaking, Women Listening: Women in Interreligious Dialogue;* Orbis Books, New York, 1990

PATEL, EBOO and BRODEUR, PATRICE: *Building the Interfaith Youth Movement: Beyond Dialogue to Action;* Rowman & Littlefield Publishers Inc, 2006.

RACE, ALAN: *Interfaith Encounter: The Twin Tracks of Theology and Dialogue;* SCM, 2001

RAMBACHAN, ANANTANAND: *Five Voices, Five Faiths;* Cowley, 2005

RAO, K L SESHAGIRI: *Mahatma Gandhi and Comparative Religion;* South Asia Books, 1990

RAVINDRA, RAVI: *The Gospel of John In the Light of Indian Mysticism;* Inner Traditions Bear and Co, 2004

ROMAIN, JONATHAN: *Till Faith Us Do Part: Couples Who Fall in Love Across the Religious Divide;* Fount, 1996

RUNZO, JOSEPH, MARTIN, NANCY & SHARMA, ARVIND, eds: *Human Rights and Responsibilities in World Religions;* Oneworld, Oxford, 2003.

RYAN MAURICE: *Another Ireland: An Introduction to Ireland's Ethnic-Religious Minority Communities;* Stranmillis College, 1996

SACKS, JONATHAN: *To Heal A Fractured World: The Ethics of Responsibility;* Continuum, 2006

SACKS, JONATHAN: *The Dignity of Difference: How To Avoid A Clash of Civilisations;* Continuum, 2003

SHARMA, ARVIND and YOUNG, KATHERINE K: *Her Voice, Her Path;* Westview Press, 2004

SINGH, KARAN: *An Autobiography (1931-1967);* OUP, 1989

SIVARAKSA, SULAK and MUZAFFAR, CHANDRA: *Alternative Politics for Asia: A Buddhist-Muslim Dialogue;* Lantern Books, 2003

SMART, NINIAN: *The World's Religions;* Cambridge University Press, Australia, 1992

SMITH, HUSTON: *World's Religions, A Guide to Our Wisdom Traditions;* Harper, San Francisco, 1994

STOREY, CELIA and DAVID, eds: *Visions of an Interfaith Future;* International Interfaith Centre, 1994

SWAMI AGNIVESH: *Harvest of Hate: Gujarat Under Seige;* Rupa and Co, 2002

SWAMI SATCHIDANANDA: *Peace is Within Our Reach: Spirituality, Power and Politics - Solutions for a New Age;* Integral Yoga Publications, 1985

SWIDLER, LEONARD, and others: *Death or Dialogue, From the Age of Monologue to the Age of Dialogue;* Trinity Press International, Philadephia, 1990

SWING, WILLIAM E: *The Coming United Religions;* Conexus Press, Grand Rapids, 1998

TEASDALE, WAYNE, ed: *Awakening the Spirit, Inspiring the Soul: 30 Stories of Interspiritual Discovery in the Community of Faiths;* Skylight Paths, Woodstock, 2004

TRAER, ROBERT: *Quest for Truth: Critical Reflections on Interfaith Cooperation, Faith, Belief, and Religion;* Davies Group, Aurora 1999

TRAER, ROBERT: *Faith in Human Rights: Support in Religious Traditions for a Global Struggle;* Georgetown University Press, 1991

TRAER, ROBERT: *Faith, Belief and Religion*; Davies Group, 2003
TRAER, ROBERT: *Jerusalem Journal: Finding Hope*, 2006 www.christian-bible.com
TUCKER, EVA and JARMAN, PETER: *Patterns and Examples: Experiencing the Spirit of Other Faiths*; Sessions of York, 2005
TYNDALE, WENDY: *Visions of Development: Faith Based Initiatives*; Ashgate, 2006
UCKO, HANS: *Faces of the Other: A Contribution to Interreligious Relations and Dialogue*; World Council of Churches, 2006
WARD, KEITH: *Images of Eternity*; Oneworld, 1993
WHITE, ANDREW: *Iraq: Searching for Hope*; Continuum, 2005
WOLFF, MARGARET: *In Sweet Company: Conversations with Extraordinary Women about Living a Spiritual Life*; Jossey-Bass, San Francisco, 2004
YOGANANDA, PARAMAHANSA: *Autobiography of a Yogi*; Self-Realization Fellowship, Los Angeles, USA. Multiple reprints.
ZAEHNER, R.C: *Hindu & Muslim Mysticism;* Oneworld Publications, Oxford 1994

JOURNALS

COMMON GROUND, Council of Christians and Jews, 1st Floor, Camelford House, 89 Albert Embankment, London SE1 7TP, UK www.ccj.org.uk

CROSSCURRENTS, 475 Riverside Drive, New York, NY 10115, USA. www.crosscurrents.org

CURRENT DIALOGUE, World Council of Churches, 150 route de Ferney, PO Box 2100, 1211 Geneva 2, Switzerland. www.wcc-coe.org/wcc/what/interreligious/index-e.html

DIALOGUE & ALLIANCE, Inter Religious Federation for World Peace, 4 West 43rd Street, New York, NY 10036, USA. www.irfwp.org/library/dialogue.shtml

DHARMA WORLD, 2-7-1 Wada, Suginami-ku, Tokyo 166-8535, Japan. www.kosei-shuppan.co.jp

HAND TO HAND, HEART TO HEART, Interfaith Youth Poetry Project, 3723 Chestnut St, Philadelphia, PA 19104, USA. www.artsandspirituality.org/iypp/jpournal

HINDUISM TODAY, 107 Kahollele Road, Kapaa, Hawaii 96746-9304 USA. www.hinduismtoday.org

GLOBALIZATION FOR THE COMMON GOOD www.commongoodjournal.com

INITIATIVE: Northside, Grange-in-Borrowdale, Keswick, Cumbria CA12 5UQ, UK. www.uri.org.uk/initiative_magazine

INTERRELIGIOUS INSIGHT, 980 Verda Lane, Lake Forest, Illinois 60045, USA. www.interreligiousinsight.org

JAIN SPIRIT, Suite 3D Cowdray Office Centre, Cowdray Avenue, Colchester, Essex CO1 1QB , UK. www.jainspirit.com

JOURNAL OF ECUMENICAL STUDIES, Temple University, 1114 W. Berks Street, Ste. 511, Philadelphia, PA 19122-6090, USA. www.temple.edu

ONE WORLD PERSPECTIVES http://us.oneworld.net/section/us/perspectives

RESURGENCE, Ford House, Hartland, Bideford, Devon, EX39 6EE, UK. www.resurgence.org

SELF-REALIZATION, Self-Realization Fellowship, 3880 San Rafael Avenue, Los Angeles, CA 90065-3298, USA. www.yogananda-srf.org

VEDANTA, Ramakrishna Vedanta Centre, Blind Lane, Bourne End, Bucks SL8 5LG, UK. www.vedantauk.com

How should we end this book?

Interfaith will and should not ever end.

We hope you will find your right place in this network of well intentioned and dedicated individuals.

SANDY BHARAT AND O-BOOKS

CHRIST ACROSS THE GANGES: HINDU RESPONSES TO JESUS

In the last two centuries, some of Hinduism's greatest saints and scholars have lovingly embraced Christ and made him their own. Continuing and aggressive Christian mission in India is now making some Hindus anti-Christ as well as anti-Christian.

Find out why mission disturbs Hindus and how they have responded to their encounter with Christ and Christianity from colonial to contemporary times, in India and in the West. This is their story in their words.

Knowing and understanding others is always challenging. Make your own interfaith journey and discover what happened when Christ crossed the Ganges.

1-84694-000-1 240pp £14.99 $29.95

From Foreword by Marcus Braybrooke, President, World Congress of Faiths: There is much to learn from Sandy Bharat's important book. I hope it will encourage many Christians and Hindus to enter into a deeper dialogue with each other.

From the Foreword by HE Dr Karan Singh, Rajya Sabha India: In her well researched book Sandy Bharat has studied in depth some of the Hindu encounters with Christ. This book is part of the growing literature on the Interfaith movement, and will be of value to students both of Hinduism and Christianity.

Ramesh Kallidai, Secretary General, Hindu Forum of Britain: Christ Across the Ganges provides a fascinating account of interaction between Hindus and Christians, and offers a refreshing view of Christ seen through the eyes of some of the greatest Masters who walked the face of the earth.

Dr John May, Irish School of Ecumenics: I think this would be of the greatest interest to many people involved in interreligious relations; I know of nothing like it, which brings the story right up to date.

Marianne Rankin, Alister Hardy Society
This is a fascinating and wide-ranging overview of a subject of great importance. It is a must for anyone interested in the history of religious traditions and in the interaction between faiths.

O-BOOKS WORLD RELIGIONS / INTERFAITH

A Heart for the World: The Interfaith Alternative
Marcus Braybrooke

This book is really needed. This is the blueprint. It has to be cherished. Faith in Jesus is not about creeds or homilies. It is a willingness to imitate Christ - as the Hindu guru Gandhi did so well. A must book to buy. *Peacelinks, IFOR*

1905047436 168pp £12.99 $24.95

Bringing God Back to Earth
John Hunt

Knowledgeable in theology, philosophy, science and history. Time and again it is remarkable how he brings the important issues into relation with one another... thought provoking in almost every sentence, difficult to put down. *Faith and Freedom*

1903816815 320pp £9.99 $14.95

Trading Faith: Global Religion in an Age of Rapid Change
David Hart

Argues boldly that the metaphor of trading provides the most useful model for religious exchanges in a world of rapid change. It is the inspiring biography of an intensely spiritual man with a great sense of humour who has chosen an unusual and courageous religious path. *Dr Anna King, Lecturer in Hinduism, University of Winchester*

1905047967 260pp £10.99 $24.95

Transcending Terror: A history of our spiritual quest and the challenge of the new millennium
Ian Hackett

A return to the core values of all our faiths, putting aside partisanship and the desire to dominate is the only sure way forward, in order to "allow both our human and spiritual quests to continue as one family sharing one world." *Westminster Interfaith*

190381674 320pp £12.99 $19.95

OTHER BOOKS BY SANDY AND JAEL BHARAT

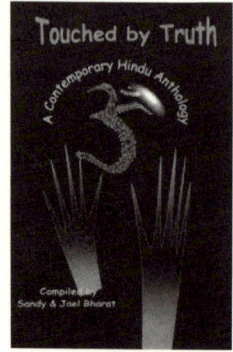

Touched by Truth: A Contemporary Hindu Anthology
Sandy and Jael Bharat (Compiled/Edited by)
Sessions of York September 2006

Here are very personal reflections on ways in which so many have found, within the Hindu umbrella, spiritual enlightenment, help on the journey and answers to questions and heart longings. Gurus, teachers and sacred books within Hinduism today still provide a rich fountain of wisdom on which to draw for those who yearn to be 'Touched by Truth.' Inspirational.
Gwyneth Little, Ed, Meeting Hindus.

1-85072-355-9 170pp £8 $12

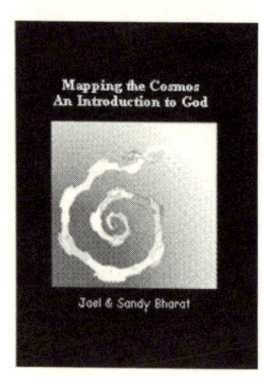

Mapping the Cosmos: An Introduction to God
Jael and Sandy Bharat
Sessions of York January 2006.

A stimulating read, providing much food for thought, both for the newcomer to the reading of spiritual literature and even for the jaded pallet of one who has read many books on spiritual life. *Vedanta*

It's inspiring, thought provoking, hope-filled and an important book for anybody concerned about the future of humanity. *Yoga Chicago.*

1-85072-341-9 48pp £4 $6

For more information: www.spiritualityfordailylife.com

O

is a symbol of the world, of oneness and unity. O Books explores the many paths of wholeness and spiritual understanding which different traditions have developed down the ages. It aims to bring this knowledge in accessible form, to a general readership, providing practical spirituality to today's seekers.

For the full list of over 200 titles covering:

ACADEMIC/THEOLOGY • ANGELS • ASTROLOGY/NUMEROLOGY • BIOGRAPHY/AUTOBIOGRAPHY • BUDDHISM/ENLIGHTENMENT • BUSINESS/LEADERSHIP/WISDOM • CELTIC/DRUID/PAGAN • CHANNELLING • CHRISTIANITY; EARLY • CHRISTIANITY; TRADITIONAL • CHRISTIANITY; PROGRESSIVE • CHRISTIANITY; DEVOTIONAL • CHILDREN'S SPIRITUALITY • CHILDREN'S BIBLE STORIES • CHILDREN'S BOARD/NOVELTY • CREATIVE SPIRITUALITY • CURRENT AFFAIRS/RELIGIOUS • ECONOMY/POLITICS/SUSTAINABILITY • ENVIRONMENT/EARTH • FICTION • GODDESS/FEMININE • HEALTH/FITNESS • HEALING/REIKI • HINDUISM/ADVAITA/VEDANTA • HISTORY/ARCHAEOLOGY • HOLISTIC SPIRITUALITY • INTERFAITH/ECUMENICAL • ISLAM/SUFISM • JUDAISM/CHRISTIANITY • MEDITATION/PRAYER • MYSTERY/PARANORMAL • MYSTICISM • MYTHS • POETRY • RELATIONSHIPS/LOVE • RELIGION/PHILOSOPHY • SCHOOL TITLES • SCIENCE/RELIGION • SELF-HELP/PSYCHOLOGY • SPIRITUAL SEARCH • WORLD RELIGIONS/SCRIPTURES • YOGA

Please visit our website,
www.O-books.net